Data Engineering Design Patterns

Scalable data engineering for efficient data systems and workflows

Amit Kulkarni

Santosh Hegde

bpb

www.bpbonline.com

First Edition 2026

Copyright © BPB Publications, India

ISBN: 978-93-65891-768

To View Complete
BPB Publications Catalogue
Scan the QR Code:

Dedicated to

My wife Aboli Aradhye, son Dhrupad, parents Varsha and Hemant Kulkarni, sister Manuja, and in-laws Amruta and Ajit Aradhye

- Amit Kulkarni

My wife, Ramya; my children, Tapasya and Tanay; and my parents, Geetha and Chandrashekar

- Santosh Hegde

About the Authors

- **Amit Kulkarni** has 14+ years of experience working in distributed systems, databases, and cloud storage systems. As a senior manager working in Couchbase India, he has gained expertise in building and managing large-scale, performant, and fault-tolerant systems. Amit also has a strong background in data protection and cloud storage solutions, having worked at industry-leading companies like Druva and NetApp. With a deep understanding of databases, cloud storage, and disaster recovery, Amit brings a wealth of knowledge to the tech community. Being an alumnus of the prestigious institute of IIT Kanpur, Amit brings in strong expertise in computer science fundamentals, required to design large-scale and high-performance data solutions.

- **Santosh Hegde** is a seasoned technology leader with 18+ years of experience specialising in distributed systems and data engineering. As the senior director of engineering at Couchbase India, he leads the core R&D team, focusing on transactional and analytical NoSQL database systems. Previously, as director of engineering at Visa, he advanced SQL technologies significantly. At IBM Software Lab, he made impactful contributions to various database projects. Santosh holds multiple patents in distributed systems and database internals, underscoring his innovative contributions to the field.

About the Reviewers

❖ **Dev Krishan** is a senior solutions architect with over 15 years of experience in the area of data science and data engineering. He is currently focused on architecting solutions in the area of GenAI, cloud-native implementations, and big data. He is also focused on the design and implementation of highly scalable real-time and batch data processing solutions. He is an expert in big data technology stack, including technologies like Spark (batch and streaming), Kafka, HBase, Hive, Flink, and Kudu. He is a certified cloud architect with cloud certifications, including Google Certified Professional Cloud Architect and Professional Data Engineer.

Dev has contributed to many high-impact data engineering projects in domains including banking and finance, healthcare and homecare, insurance, logistics, and the public sector for clients from the USA, Germany, India, the UK, and Ireland. Dev enjoys working on the design of mission-critical enterprise-grade, highly scalable systems. He is proficient in data strategy, data modelling, database management, data warehousing, and the implementation of various data storage and processing architectures.

❖ **Susmitha Nair** is an accomplished software engineer with over 19 years of experience in the technology industry, specializing in the design and deployment of scalable software systems. With expertise in Java, Python, JavaScript, and emerging fields like artificial intelligence and deep learning, she has played a key role in delivering high-impact solutions across the retail and automotive sectors. In addition to her professional work, Susmitha is an independent researcher with a strong interest in AI and data analytics. Her deep-rooted curiosity drives her to explore innovative applications of ML and AI in solving real-world problems. Known for her ability to bridge technical depth with strategic vision, she consistently leads projects that improve efficiency, enhance user experience, and embrace the latest in intelligent automation. Her work reflects a commitment to lifelong learning, innovation, and excellence in software engineering.

❖ **Tanvi** is a seasoned technology leader with a career in technological transformation since 2008. She is currently working as a senior cloud solutions consultant at Google. She leads transformative data and AI initiatives in the cloud for global enterprises, specializing in the semiconductor and security industries. With deep expertise in high-performance computing and platforms like Google Cloud and AWS, she architects complex solutions that drive significant business value. As a recognized thought leader and certified technical expert, she is dedicated to contributing to technological advancement by architecting the next generation of scalable, high-performance AI platforms.

Acknowledgements

We would like to thank our families and friends who have supported us during the writing of this book. We could not have done this without their unconditional support and their words of motivation and encouragement.

We also extend our profound thanks to leaders and colleagues at Couchbase Inc., who helped us directly or indirectly in the successful completion of the book.

We are very grateful to BPB Publications for trusting us with this book. Thank you for your guidance and support in every step of writing this book. A special thanks to the technical review team for providing valuable inputs during the technical review process, which contributed to improving this book.

Preface

This book presents a comprehensive collection of data engineering patterns, each illustrated with relevant enterprise use cases to highlight their value and simplicity. It showcases both open-source and cloud technologies, guiding readers in building data systems for on-premise and cloud environments. The book covers patterns for data ingestion, transformation, storage, and serving, while also offering insights into performance engineering for data pipelines. The first few chapters cover data ingestion and processing of different types, and help the reader gain an understanding of batch, real-time, and micro-batching data processing and ingestion patterns. This is followed by chapters on more complex data processing patterns like Lambda, ETL, and ELT. Next, we learn about data engineering patterns associated with data storage and serving. These patterns teach us how to build both transactional and analytical data stores. Following that, we learn about data lakes and modern architectures like medallion. Once we understand these fundamental data engineering patterns, we then shift focus to patterns that help us build high-performance, low-latency data systems. We cover data caching, partitioning, and replication. Finally, this book explores the chapters on horizontal data engineering patterns that apply across all types of systems, like observability, security, and orchestration. In the last few chapters, the book explains how to select the technology stack for building out the patterns learn in this book.

This book is designed for data engineers with beginner to intermediate experience in building enterprise-grade data systems. It assumes familiarity with distributed systems and key technologies like databases, Kafka, Spark, and Hadoop. ETL developers transitioning into data engineering roles will also find this book valuable for understanding essential data engineering patterns. The code snippets provided throughout the book are written in Python or Scala, so a basic understanding of either language will help readers more easily grasp the concepts presented.

Chapter 1: Understanding Data Engineering- This chapter offers an overview of the fundamental concepts, processes, and roles involved in building and managing data pipelines. It explores the lifecycle of data, from collection and transformation to storage and analysis, highlighting key technologies, tools, and best practices that enable scalable, efficient data management.

Chapter 2: Data Engineering Patterns, Terminologies, and Technical Stack- This chapter offers an in-depth exploration of data engineering patterns, explaining their importance and how they can be effectively utilised to tackle common challenges in the field. It also includes straightforward examples of these patterns, illustrating how they solve typical problems encountered in data engineering. The book outlines the various types of data engineering patterns, categorised by their role in the data lifecycle, whether related to data ingestion, transformation, storage, or serving.

Chapter 3: Batch Ingestion and Processing- This chapter explores the process of gathering and processing data at scheduled intervals, a common pattern of traditional data engineering workflows. It explains how batch ingestion is used to efficiently move data from various sources into storage systems, where it can be transformed and analysed. The section also covers key design considerations, tools, and best practices, helping readers understand when and how to implement batch ingestion pipelines.

Chapter 4: Real-time Ingestion and Processing- This chapter explores the techniques and technologies used to capture and process data as it is generated, enabling immediate insights and decision-making. It discusses the importance of real-time ingestion in scenarios such as fraud detection, recommendation engines, IoT, fleet management, etc. where timely data processing is critical. The section also covers the architecture and design of real-time ingestion pipelines using technologies like Kafka and Flink. Readers will gain an understanding of the key concepts involved in real-time ingestion, including latency, throughput, and scalability.

Chapter 5: Micro-batching- This chapter explores an approach that bridges the gap between batch processing and real-time ingestion. It covers how micro-batching enables near-real-time data processing by breaking data into small, manageable batches that are processed at frequent intervals. The section discusses the advantages of micro-batching, such as reduced latency and improved resource efficiency, along with its use cases and implementation strategies. Examples illustrate how to design a micro-batching pipeline for near-real-time processing.

Chapter 6: Lambda Architecture- This chapter explores a data processing framework that combines the goodness of both batch and real-time processing. It walks through the architecture's three key layers, such as batch, speed, and serving, and how they work together to provide accurate and low-latency data views. The chapter also covers the benefits, challenges, and common use cases of Lambda architecture, offering insights into its practical implementation. Examples help readers understand how to leverage Lambda architecture for scalable and reliable data systems.

Chapter 7: ETL and ELT- This chapter explores the process of **extract, transform, load (ETL)**, which is fundamental to data engineering pipelines. It explains how data is extracted from various sources, transformed into a target format, and loaded into target systems for analysis and storage. The chapter highlights best practices, common tools, and challenges in designing efficient ETL pipelines. This chapter also covers the **extract, load, transform (ELT)** process, a newer approach to data ingestion that leverages distributed storage and data processing capability within target data systems. Unlike ETL, ELT loads raw data into the target system first, allowing for more flexible and scalable transformations directly within the target data warehouse or data lake.

Chapter 8: Data Fundamentals- Data can take on many different shapes, sizes, and forms, originating from a wide array of sources. Each data source may produce data that varies significantly in type, structure, and volume. The selection of appropriate data storage and serving solutions depends on these characteristics, as well as the latency and performance requirements for accessing and processing the data. This chapter provides an essential foundation by introducing key terminologies and technologies that will be referenced in the subsequent chapters, equipping the reader with the necessary context to fully understand the concepts discussed.

Chapter 9: Databases and Transactional Data- This chapter explores the various use cases associated with transactional data management, exploring how modern databases address the challenges inherent in managing transactional data. It discusses how contemporary database systems, including both relational and NoSQL databases, have been designed to meet the demands of transactional workloads. In addition to providing insights into the specific data storage and serving patterns utilised by these databases, the chapter also highlights the trade-offs and design considerations that influence the choice of database systems for different transactional use cases.

Chapter 10: Data Warehouse for Data Analytics- This chapter explores the landscape of data analytics use cases and introduces the foundational concepts of data warehousing. A significant portion of data analytics relies on the advantages offered by columnar storage formats, which differ fundamentally from traditional row-wise storage formats. The chapter provides an in-depth analysis of the trade-offs between these two storage approaches, highlighting how columnar storage can optimize query performance and storage efficiency for analytical workloads. Additionally, this chapter introduces the concept of materialized views, a powerful technique frequently employed in data analytics to enhance query speed and efficiency.

Chapter 11: Data Lake and Medallion Architecture- User data typically enters data management systems in its raw, unprocessed form. Before this data can be effectively utilized by downstream data analysis applications, it must undergo a series of cleansing, processing, and storage steps. This chapter introduces the concept of a data lake—a storage architecture designed to handle raw data of various types and formats. A data lake serves as a centralized repository where diverse datasets can coexist, ready for subsequent transformation and analysis. The chapter also explores the medallion architecture, a layered data processing approach that maximizes the value extracted from raw data stored in a data lake.

Chapter 12: Data Replication and Partitioning- Data storage and serving applications are inherently vulnerable to hardware and software failures, often referred to as faults. To ensure system reliability and minimize the impact of these faults, data replication is commonly employed as a fault-tolerance strategy. This chapter provides an in-depth exploration of the various data replication patterns widely adopted in the industry. These patterns are critical for maintaining data availability and consistency, even in the face of system failures. In addition to replication, this chapter introduces the concept of data partitioning, a technique used to divide large datasets into smaller, more manageable segments. Data partitioning plays a crucial role in enhancing both the performance and scalability of data systems.

Chapter 13:Hot Versus Cold Data Storage- Data storage costs can escalate rapidly, particularly when dealing with vast volumes of data. However, not all data requires immediate, low-latency access. Infrequently accessed data, often referred to as cold data, can be stored using more cost-effective storage solutions, albeit with a trade-off in access speed. This chapter explores strategies for optimizing storage costs by distinguishing between hot data, which requires fast access, and cold data, which can tolerate higher latencies. The chapter explores various patterns for hot versus cold data separation, offering insights into how organizations can strategically allocate storage resources based on data access patterns.

Chapter 14: Data Caching and Low Latency Serving- A wide array of modern use cases demand the ability to serve data with exceptionally low latencies. These scenarios rely heavily on data caching patterns to meet the stringent performance requirements necessary for seamless user experiences and real-time processing. This chapter explores the critical role of data caching in sustaining low-latency data access across diverse, high-demand applications. We explore various real-world use cases that benefit from effective caching strategies, demonstrating how caching can significantly enhance performance by reducing the need for repeated access to slower, underlying data stores.

Chapter 15: Data Search Patterns- Modern applications increasingly deal with unstructured data formats such as text, images, videos, and audio. The need to search through these vast and diverse datasets to find relevant content has become a ubiquitous challenge across industries. This chapter provides an in-depth exploration of the techniques and technologies that enable efficient and effective search capabilities within unstructured data. We begin by examining use cases related to full-text search, which allows for the rapid retrieval of relevant textual information from large datasets. The chapter then transitions into the mathematical representation of unstructured data—such as text, audio, and video—in the form of vectors. This vectorization process is crucial for enabling advanced search techniques, such as similarity search, where content is identified based on how closely it matches a given query. Furthermore, the chapter introduces the concept of **retrieval-augmented generation (RAG)**, a cutting-edge pattern that enhances the performance of **large language models (LLMs)**.

Chapter 16: Domain Specific Patterns- This chapter offers a comprehensive overview of specialized use cases centred around time series data, edge computing, and ML. We begin by exploring use cases involving time series data, which requires unique handling and storage techniques to efficiently manage the sequential and often high-volume nature of the data. Next, the chapter explores data at the edge, where computing resources are deployed closer to the source of data generation. Edge computing is vital for reducing latency and conserving bandwidth. The chapter also addresses feature storage and serving patterns, essential for ML applications. Finally, we examine model versioning patterns, which are critical for managing the lifecycle of ML models in production.

Chapter 17: Data Security Patterns- This chapter explores the essential strategies for safeguarding data throughout its lifecycle. It explores various security patterns that ensure data confidentiality, integrity, and availability, including encryption, access control, and secure data transmission. It covers how to implement these patterns in different stages of the data pipeline, from ingestion to storage and processing, while also addressing the challenges of balancing security with performance. By understanding these patterns, readers will be equipped to build robust data systems that protect sensitive information and comply with regulatory requirements.

Chapter 18: Data Observability and Monitoring Patterns- This chapter focuses on the practices for maintaining the health, reliability, and performance of data systems. This chapter explores patterns that provide visibility into data pipelines, including end-to-end monitoring, anomaly detection, and data quality checks. It covers how to implement these patterns to proactively identify and resolve issues, track data lineage, and ensure data integrity. By mastering these observability and monitoring patterns, readers will be equipped to maintain robust data systems that operate efficiently, minimize downtime, and support informed decision-making.

Chapter 19: Idempotency and Deduplication Patterns- Distributed data operations are inherently prone to a variety of failures, such as network interruptions. These failures can lead to issues such as data corruption or data loss. To ensure the integrity and quality of data in such environments, ensuring data idempotency is crucial. In this chapter, we will explore various patterns and strategies for achieving data idempotency in distributed systems. As organizations ingest large volumes of data from diverse sources, the likelihood of duplicate data entering the system increases significantly. Duplicate data not only skews analytics and decision-making processes but also leads to inefficient use of storage resources, driving up costs unnecessarily. To address these challenges, this chapter will also cover a range of patterns and techniques for identifying and eliminating duplicate data.

Chapter 20: Data Orchestration Patterns- In this chapter, we explore the patterns that underpin data orchestration in modern data engineering. Data orchestration is the process of automating, scheduling, and managing complex data workflows, ensuring that data flows seamlessly across various systems and stages of processing. This chapter explores key orchestration patterns such as pipeline chaining, event-driven orchestration, fan-out/fan-in, and the use of **directed acyclic graphs (DAGs)**. This chapter also explains various types of schedulers and when and how to use them.

Chapter 21: Common Performance Pitfalls- This chapter in a data engineering book explores the frequent challenges and mistakes that can lead to suboptimal performance in data systems. It explores issues such as poorly designed data models, inefficient query execution, inadequate resource allocation, and improper handling of data skew. It also discusses the impact of network latency, I/O bottlenecks, and the mismanagement of large datasets. By identifying these pitfalls, the chapter provides practical guidance on how to avoid or mitigate them, ensuring that data pipelines and systems operate efficiently and effectively.

Chapter 22: Technology and Infrastructure Selection- This chapter provides a comprehensive guide to choosing the right tools, technologies, and infrastructure to build efficient and scalable data systems. This chapter covers the key factors to consider when selecting databases, processing frameworks, storage solutions, and cloud services, emphasising the importance of aligning choices with specific use cases and business requirements. It also explores trade-offs between different technologies, such as cost, performance, scalability, and ease of management. By the end of the chapter, readers will be equipped with the knowledge to make informed decisions that best fit their data engineering needs.

Chapter 23: Recap and Next Steps- This chapter provides a summary of the key data engineering patterns, use cases, and technologies covered throughout this book. It reinforces the importance of understanding and applying these data engineering patterns to design and implement reusable engineering solutions. This section serves as a quick reference guide, highlighting the key patterns that readers should take away and apply in their data engineering projects. It suggests ways to apply the concepts learned, including hands-on projects, further reading, and exploring advanced topics. This chapter also guides readers on how to stay updated on emerging trends and technologies, helping them upskill and adapt to the evolving landscape of data engineering.

Code Bundle and Coloured Images

Please follow the link to download the
Code Bundle and the *Coloured Images* of the book:

https://rebrand.ly/c079b3

The code bundle for the book is also hosted on GitHub at
https://github.com/bpbpublications/Data-Engineering-Design-Patterns.
In case there's an update to the code, it will be updated on the existing GitHub repository.

We have code bundles from our rich catalogue of books and videos available at
https://github.com/bpbpublications. Check them out!

Errata

We take immense pride in our work at BPB Publications and follow best practices to ensure the accuracy of our content to provide with an indulging reading experience to our subscribers. Our readers are our mirrors, and we use their inputs to reflect and improve upon human errors, if any, that may have occurred during the publishing processes involved. To let us maintain the quality and help us reach out to any readers who might be having difficulties due to any unforeseen errors, please write to us at: errata@bpbonline.com

Your support, suggestions and feedbacks are highly appreciated by the BPB Publications' Family.

At www.bpbonline.com, you can also read a collection of free technical articles, sign up for a range of free newsletters, and receive exclusive discounts and offers on BPB books and eBooks. You can check our social media handles below:

| *Instagram* | *Facebook* | *Linkedin* | *YouTube* |

Get in touch with us at: business@bpbonline.com for more details.

Piracy

If you come across any illegal copies of our works in any form on the internet, we would be grateful if you would provide us with the location address or website name. Please contact us at business@bpbonline.com with a link to the material.

If you are interested in becoming an author

If there is a topic that you have expertise in, and you are interested in either writing or contributing to a book, please visit www.bpbonline.com. We have worked with thousands of developers and tech professionals, just like you, to help them share their insights with the global tech community. You can make a general application, apply for a specific hot topic that we are recruiting an author for, or submit your own idea.

Reviews

Please leave a review. Once you have read and used this book, why not leave a review on the site that you purchased it from? Potential readers can then see and use your unbiased opinion to make purchase decisions. We at BPB can understand what you think about our products, and our authors can see your feedback on their book. Thank you!

For more information about BPB, please visit www.bpbonline.com.

Join our Discord space

Join our Discord workspace for latest updates, offers, tech happenings around the world, new releases, and sessions with the authors:

https://discord.bpbonline.com

Table of Contents

CHAPTER 1
Understanding Data Engineering

Introduction

In this chapter, we will review the fundamental concepts of data engineering, processes, and roles in building and managing data pipelines. It explores the data lifecycle, from collection and transformation to storage and analysis, highlighting key technologies, tools, and best practices that enable scalable, efficient data management. Additionally, it introduces the reader to the importance of data engineering in modern data-driven systems, setting the stage for a deeper exploration of patterns and techniques in subsequent chapters.

Structure

This chapter will cover the following topics:

- Data engineering's role in modern data systems
- Core concepts of data engineering
- Lifecycle of data

Objectives

By the end of this chapter, you will be able to understand why data engineering is fundamental to modern data systems and the various stages of data engineering and its associated roles. This chapter will help build a foundation to understand data engineering patterns further.

Data engineering's role in modern data systems

British mathematician Clive Humby declared that data is the new oil.

Modern data systems allow enterprises to use this new fuel to power their business. Organizations depend on their ability to collect, process, and analyze vast amounts of data to gain a competitive advantage. Data becomes critical to effective decision-making, leading to sound business decisions. Data engineering is the discipline of building and managing these complex data systems.

Data engineers play a pivotal role in creating these modern data systems by designing and implementing data pipelines that collect and curate data for further analysis. They also build data storage systems suitable for various data access patterns, which help use cases like ML and data science consume the curated data assets. As enterprises mature in their data journey, data engineering practice becomes critical to the company's success. All data-driven decisions need support from the data engineering teams to ensure decisions are taken based on trustworthy, high-quality data.

Providing such reliable data assets is the prerogative of the data engineering team. Along with ensuring the supply of high-quality data, data engineering teams also need to ensure that data is secured to avoid data breaches. Data engineering teams must also ensure compliance with data storage and usage-related regulations worldwide, like the **General Data Protection Regulation (GDPR)** and the **Health Insurance Portability and Accountability Act (HIPAA)**.

Core concepts of data engineering

Core concepts of data engineering revolve around creating, managing, and optimizing data pipelines that collect, process, and curate data for analytics and **machine learning (ML)**. Data pipelines form the conduit that holds the entire data system together and ensures uninterrupted data flow between systems. Pipelines read data from one set of data sources and move it to another while transforming and shaping it as per the target application's needs.

To understand data engineering in depth, it is essential not only to understand how to build data pipelines but also to know what various data storage and serving systems these pipelines read and write to. The data pipelines also need to be orchestrated and governed to ensure that the data policies of an organization are enforced and that the pipelines result in reliable data assets.

In the coming chapters, we will learn more about *transformation, ingestion, storage, serving, orchestration, and governance*, which form the core of data engineering.

Data processing and ingestion

Data generated on source systems needs to be processed and ingested into downstream systems for analysis or further processing. The data ingestion can be real-time or batch-based, depending on the latency acceptable for downstream business use cases. Also, the data needs to be processed or transformed to suit the target application's needs. The processing can be done before ingestion, commonly termed **extract, transform, and load** (**ETL**), or post ingestion using the ELT mechanism. Data transformation steps typically involve data cleansing, standardization, enrichment and application of business logic to prepare it for business analysis.

Modern architectures that combine real-time and batch data processing ingestion are also designed to support more complex and niche use cases. With the advent of modern architectures like *Medallion*, the line between different types of data processing and ingestion is blurring, with multiple techniques being combined into one data system. AI is also driving real-time consumption of data, disrupting traditional data pipelines, which can struggle to keep up with the demands of modern generative AI-driven applications.

Data storage and serving

Data generated in any enterprise comes in various shapes, sizes, and forms, and the selection of the appropriate data storage and serving solution is critical to the success of a data engineering initiative. The storage systems can be of different types, from data lakes and data warehouses for long-term storage and analytics to relational and NoSQL databases for transactional processing with low latency. A data lake is a data store for raw, unprocessed data, and a data warehouse is a data store for structured data that is prepared for analysis.

These storage systems have different costs and performance characteristics, and the proper storage system must be selected for a given use case to ensure the application requirements are met. Typically, serving characteristics are also directly dependent on the storage technology selection. For example, data lakes are suited for storing large amounts of data for batch processing. Still, they are not the right choice when building a low-latency transaction application for which a *relational* or *NoSQL database* is better. However, it is important to note that there are several other factors, like cost, storage efficiency, and maintainability, when choosing a data engineering stack.

Complementing the storage technologies with the right hardware infrastructure selection is also essential. SSDs provide fast random access to data and are well-suited for storage systems that need very low latency access. Large spinning disk-based solutions can be used to power very large data storage systems, which can be in petabytes and are cost-prohibitive to build on SSD. Primary memory sizing is also very important to ensure the right in-memory caching is achieved to meet the serving performance goals.

Data orchestration and governance

Data orchestration and governance are horizontal pillars of data engineering that ensure the data system adheres to an organization's operational, security, and quality requirements. Data orchestration manages pipelines that move data between source and target systems. It ensures the jobs are scheduled and run in the correct order while managing the dependencies between them. Data orchestration also covers monitoring and logging aspects of data pipelines while ensuring errors are handled and retried appropriately.

Data governance ensures the organization's data quality and security processes are applied to data pipelines and data systems. Data governance ensures data meets the quality bar set by the application, ensuring the insights derived from the data are trustworthy. It also ensures compliance and security requirements are met per various security standards like **Payment Card Industry Data Security Standard (PCI DSS)**, **Sarbanes-Oxley Act (SOX)**, GDPR, etc. Data governance also covers the ownership and lineage aspects of data. It assigns data stewards to data assets that tag the data with the proper labels and metadata. Lineage tracking ensures data users are aware of the origin of data and the modifications it has gone through during its lifecycle, ensuring confidence in the data produced by a pipeline.

Lifecycle of data

The data lifecycle deals with the journey of data from creation to disposal. Data is typically created in transactional systems that power the world's commerce. Data production systems include point-of-sale systems, e-banking or e-commerce portals, ATMs, hospital medical desks, airline reservations, sensors in industries, monitoring systems, etc. Every transaction needs to be recorded for further processing. The data processing and ingestion phase ensures the data is collected from various transactional systems, transformed, and stored in downstream systems for further use. Data is stored in a downstream system for multiple purposes like billing, deriving insights for upselling or recommendation, regulatory purposes, data sharing, building data products, etc.

Once the data has been collected, transformed, and utilized, it needs to continue its journey to the next stage in the data lifecycle, such as archiving, purging, or selective deletion etc. Once stored and processed, data must move further into archival systems for long-term storage. The use case dictates data retention for active processing, and once the data has been leveraged, it needs to be moved to archival storage for regulatory and compliance purposes. Along with business rules, regulations like GDPR can also dictate how long data assets can be stored and when they should be deleted. Every organization needs a data retention and purging strategy to ensure the data is appropriately disposed of at the end of its lifecycle. There may be exceptional cases where the data needs to be managed outside the regular retention and purge lifecycle for cases like *legal hold*. Typically, cheap cold storage like *tapes* or *Hadoop/S3 Glacier-based* storage is used for long-term data storage. Data lineage generally provides a good view of the data lifecycle from its creation to purging and the various enrichments the data underwent. Data engineering teams need to work closely with the data governance custodians to define the data lifecycle in any organization.

Conclusion

In this chapter, we covered the role of data engineering in an organization and how it is critical for its success. We also discussed the lifecycle of data from creation to purging and the various steps it goes through in this journey, like data collection, transformation, and ingestion. Moreover, we covered a brief overview of data storage, serving, orchestration, and governance, which are necessary for building any data engineering project.

In the next chapter, we will discuss data engineering patterns, their terminology, and the technical stack used to implement them.

Questions

1. Why is it essential to have a data purging strategy?
2. What are the various stages of a data lifecycle?
3. What happens when the proper infrastructure is not selected for a data engineering project?

Join our Discord space

Join our Discord workspace for latest updates, offers, tech happenings around the world, new releases, and sessions with the authors:

https://discord.bpbonline.com

CHAPTER 2

Data Engineering Patterns, Terminologies, and Technical Stack

Introduction

This chapter offers a high-level overview of common data engineering patterns, explaining their importance and how they can be effectively utilized to tackle common challenges in the field. It also includes examples of these patterns, illustrating how they solve typical problems encountered in data engineering. It introduces key terminologies in data engineering, explaining their relevance within the context of patterns. Understanding these terms is crucial, as they are consistently referenced throughout the book to explain patterns, their applications, and examples.

The book outlines the various types of data engineering patterns, categorized by their role in the data lifecycle, whether related to data ingestion, transformation, storage, or serving. Within each category, patterns are further classified based on specific use cases, such as real-time vs. batch processing or hot vs. cold storage, providing a comprehensive understanding of how these patterns can be applied in different scenarios. It also explores the diverse technologies that underpin data engineering patterns, spanning from data ingestion tools to database storage systems tailored for different use cases. It discusses the benefits and trade-offs of each technology, examining factors such as cost, management overhead, and complexity to help you make informed decisions when selecting the right tools for your data engineering needs.

Structure

This chapter covers the following topics:

- Understanding data engineering patterns
- Importance of data engineering patterns
- Examples of data engineering patterns
- Effective use patterns
- Data processing and ingestion patterns
- Data storage and processing patterns

Objectives

By the end of this chapter, we will understand data engineering patterns and discuss a few examples of data engineering patterns. We will also understand how patterns can be used to build reusable components of data pipelines. Moreover, we will understand the various data ingestion, processing, storage and serving patterns along with the technologies used.

Understanding data engineering patterns

Data engineering has reusable solutions and templates that can be applied to a varied set of problems. These reusable solutions are referred to as data engineering patterns. Like software engineering patterns, they support the building of robust data systems by leveraging the standardization and architecture resiliency achieved through many years of innovation that led to the invention of these data engineering patterns.

Importance of data engineering patterns

Data engineering patterns are key to building robust data systems because they standardize architectures that have been fine-tuned over many years by experts in the data engineering field. Every data engineering problem can be solved in multiple ways, but it is important that it is solved by leveraging the most efficient architectures and technologies for that problem solution. This is where data engineering patterns help data engineers identify the architecturally proven solutions that have been tried and tested and found to be robust and cost-effective.

Data engineering patterns also help data engineers avoid performance pitfalls often encountered when trying to build custom solutions, thus reducing TCO for the data system by reducing the hardware footprint needed for the system. They also ensure a secure data system by imbuing the security best practices within the patterns. Data engineering patterns have another distinction of helping data engineers who are not yet highly skilled in the trade build great data systems by following the problem to pattern mapping.

Examples of data engineering patterns

This section explains a couple of data engineering pattern examples to give us a good insight into what data engineering patterns are and how they can be used to solve business use cases in an enterprise.

In this section, we will cover two examples, one around recommender systems using real-time data engineering patterns and the second being the use of data caching patterns to solve the user profile look-up problem for consumer applications. Both these examples demonstrate how data engineering patterns are critical to solving business problems in a methodical and proven way.

Real-time data ingestion

Many enterprise use cases need real-time data ingestion, such as fraud detection for financial transactions, product recommendation in e-commerce, dynamic pricing for flight, cab, and taxi booking, shipment tracking in logistics, etc. The latency requirements for a real-time system can vary between sub-milliseconds and a few seconds, depending on the type of system, but batch data engineering techniques cannot provide this level of performance. It needs specialized techniques to achieve sub-millisecond latency requirements, and the real-time data engineering patterns demonstrate such techniques.

Let us take an example of an e-commerce recommendation system that uses the clickstream data from the application to understand user preferences. Time is of the essence in this use case, as the personalized recommendation to the user should be displayed while the user continues to browse the product catalogue. To achieve this, the recommendation system should have real-time clickstream information for a given customer.

However, the recommendation system typically runs on an analytics and AI platform and not on the transactional system running the e-commerce application. This would require the clickstream information to be sent to an analytics platform in real-time. This can be achieved by reading the clickstream on the transactional system, ingesting it into a messaging system like Apache Kafka, and then leveraging Kafka connectors to push the data to an analytics system. Apache Kafka provides the necessary flow control and guarantee of message delivery needed for such a system, where the source and sink systems can be online or offline for scheduled or unscheduled maintenance. The following figure explains the architecture of the recommender system using a real-time system with Apache Kafka:

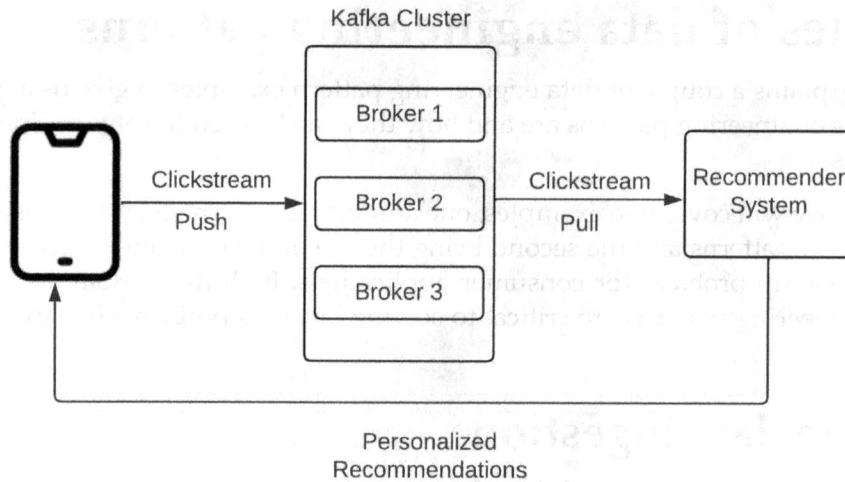

Figure 2.1: *Real-time system for recommendations*

Caching

Caching is one of the most popular data engineering patterns. Caching is a pattern where data is stored in a high-speed temporary layer to improve the speed of data retrieval. When the data retrieval speed from the persistent storage is not fast enough to serve the application's needs, a cache is typically built on top of the persistent storage system. A database providing persistence uses disk-based storage to make the data durable. The disk can be either spinning or SSD. However, these do not provide fast enough fetch times to achieve sub-millisecond latencies. Caching systems instead use primary memory like DRAM to cache the data from persistent storage.

Let us take an example of a user profile caching system for a social media platform. When users register themselves on a social media platform, their profile data is typically stored in a relational or NoSQL persistent database. However, these databases struggle to provide a sub-millisecond response time when the profile must be loaded back into the application when the user logs back in.

To achieve sub-millisecond response times for loading the user profiles, social media apps use a cache like *Redis* or *Couchbase* to cache the user profiles from the persistent data store. When the application requests the user profile, it is then served from the cache instead of fetching it from the persistent database. The following architecture figure demonstrates how a cache can work with a persistent database to provide fast response times for data fetch:

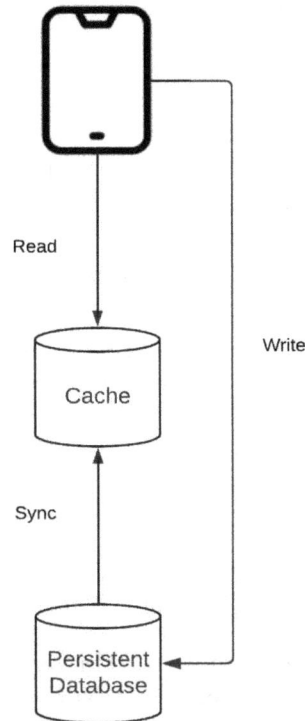

Figure 2.2: Cache write through with sync

Effective use of patterns

Data engineering patterns simplify the life of a data engineer by allowing them to use robust, reusable solutions. However, it is critical that the correct data engineering pattern is identified for a given use case or problem statement. Patterns are only as good as their fit to a given problem statement. Using the incorrect pattern for a use case can not only make the pattern ineffective but also lead to sub-optimal solutions, which can lead to cost overruns and a failed implementation.

Let us consider an example to demonstrate how the right selection of the right pattern is important to fully reap the benefits of a data engineering pattern. In social media, analytic tools perform sentiment analysis on a given post or a set of posts for various purposes like understanding brand engagement, understanding positive/negative influence, etc. This activity needs to happen continuously as new comments keep coming in on a post. At a high level, this use case looks like a good fit for real-time ingestion and analysis, but that is not the case. There are a couple of problems with doing real-time ingestion and analysis of this data.

Firstly, the comments on the post need not be analyzed and acted upon on an individual comment basis, but instead at an aggregate level over small periods of time, and secondly, it is extremely computationally intensive to analyze comments in real-time on an individual comment basis, making the solution prohibitively expensive to run. Instead, a pattern called

Micro-batching is more suited for this use case, where the comments are aggregated on a per-minute or per-hour basis and then analyzed.

It is called *micro-batching* because a set of comments is batched together for analysis, but the batch is kept small and runs at very small intervals to keep the analysis current. The cost of running a micro-batching pattern vs. a real-time pattern is vastly different, given the additional infrastructure that Kafka needs to process real-time messages. As you see, selecting the micro-batching pattern over real-time is an exercise of mapping the use case to a data engineering pattern and needs to be thought through carefully to ensure the effective use of patterns.

Data processing and ingestion patterns

Data processing and ingestion patterns can be leveraged to solve problems in building pipelines that source data from upstream transaction processing systems, transform the data, and move it to downstream analytic or ML systems. There are various patterns in the category based on the nature of the data processing needed and the latency requirement of the use case.

Batch ingestion and processing

Batch is the most used data engineering pattern. This is the simplest pattern and is also the most widely adopted in the industry. The reason for its popularity is its simplicity and low cost of implementation, both in terms of engineering effort and technical stack requirements. Also, a lot of industry use cases run analytics at periodic intervals to generate scheduled business reports, and this use case fits very well within the batch paradigm.

Batch processing involves collecting and processing large amounts of data in one iteration of the pipeline, typically at a pre-scheduled interval. A good example would be end-of-day reporting at banking institutions to the central bank regulator. Such reports would typically contain the liquidity report, daily balance sheet, financial crime reporting, derivatives and Forex reporting, and others. To generate such reports, the bank needs to aggregate the data from various sources into its analytics systems and run the report at the end of a business day. Given that the reports run on a pre-defined schedule at the end of the day, it is sufficient to collect and ingest the data into the analytics system in batches throughout the day. To achieve this, a simple job that extracts data hourly from the source system by selecting the previous hour's data, applying the necessary data transformations on it, and loading it into the target analytic database is sufficient. The job can be defined in a standard data processing framework like Apache Spark and be scheduled via a scheduler like cron or orchestrated via more complex tools like Apache Airflow.

As demonstrated in the previous paragraph, it is surprisingly simple to run a batch processing and ingestion pattern without the need for complex technologies like change data capture and messaging systems. This simplicity makes batch patterns a powerful tool in a data engineer's repertoire. While designing a solution for any use case, every data engineer needs to ask themselves if it can be solved using the batch pattern before discussing more complicated solutions.

The following technologies are commonly used to implement a batch pattern:

(More details on using these technologies with code examples will be explained in further chapters)

- MapReduce, Hive, Apache Spark, and AWS EMR for data processing
- Apache Airflow, Control-M for orchestration
- S3, HDFS for data storage

Real-time ingestion and processing

Real-time processing pattern is a pattern that has been picking up more steam of late, given the demand for instant insights into user behavior. This pattern is extremely common in e-commerce, payment systems, ride-hailing, media and entertainment, and other industries where there is a real-time user interaction with the system. The definition of real-time is use case dependent and can vary between sub-milliseconds and a few seconds.

Real-time systems need to source data from downstream systems as soon as it is generated. To achieve this, they typically use change data capture technologies to capture the event as soon as it is generated on the source. For example, if the source is a database system, the change can be captured as soon as it occurs by reading the database transaction logs for new log messages. If the source system is a messaging system like Kafka, the change can be captured by reading new messages generated. Once the data is sourced in real-time, the next important step is transformation. Real-time systems do not recommend complex transformations as they can delay data availability for analysis. Instead, real-time systems apply the bare minimum simple transformation on data. For example, in Kafka, **Single Message Transforms** (**SMT**) can provide a mechanism to inject simple transformations into the real-time pipeline.

Once data has been sourced and transformed in real time, the next step is making it available for analysis. Typically, real-time systems are combined with caching patterns to make data available at low latency for analysis. The real-time data processing pipeline can load data into low-latency databases like Redis or Couchbase to make the data query able and accessible in real time for point queries and simultaneously load into analytical databases to make data available for complex analytics. While change data capture and messaging systems underpin the source and transform the side of real-time data pipelines, caching systems typically power the store and serve the side of the pipeline. Here, you see that multiple patterns can be combined to solve a given use case.

The following technologies are commonly used to implement a real-time pattern (More details on using these technologies with code examples will be explained in further chapters):

- Apache Kafka, Apache Flink, AWS MSK, GCP Pub Sub for messaging
- Redis and Couchbase for data caching and low-latency serving
- Oracle Golden Gate, Debezium, IBM InfoSphere Data Replication for **change data capture** (**CDC**)
- Spark structured streaming for data processing

Micro-batching

Micro-batching is a pattern that provides data availability at a speed that is somewhere between a batching and a real-time pattern. This pattern is low-cost to implement, like the batching pattern, while providing data availability near real-time. Architecturally, micro-batching is very similar to the batching pattern; however, the batches are run at very low intervals, making the data available near real-time.

The following technologies are commonly used to implement a micro-batching pattern (More details on how to use these technologies with code examples will be explained in further chapters):

- Apache Hadoop, MapReduce, and Hive
- Apache Spark and Apache Airflow
- AWS EMR and S3

Note: **You will see that the technologies are the same as the batching pattern, as micro-batching is an improvement over the traditional batching pattern.**

Lambda architecture

Lambda architecture combines the benefits of batch and real-time patterns and delivers high-quality data processing while making data available in real-time. In this architecture, there are three layers, namely batch, speed, and serving. The purpose of the batch layer is to provide high-quality, curated data after complex data transformations over historical data. Given that it operates on large amounts of historical data with complex transformations and aggregations, the batch process runs slowly; however, its value lies in the complex analysis that can only be done leveraging the historical view of data. The speed layers' goal is to make data available for analysis in real-time so that action can be taken based on the data as the event occurs. It does not allow complex data transformations that can delay the data delivery. The serving layer combines the data views from both the batch and speed layers to provide a unified view of data to the user. This is one of the more complex patterns which needs to be used sparingly, only when the use case demands it. Given that it internally implements both the batch and real-time patterns to provide a unified view, it is a high-cost pattern to implement, with the need for a varied technology stack.

The technology stack for a batch layer is as follows:

- MapReduce, Hive, Apache Spark, and AWS EMR for data processing
- Apache Airflow, Control-M for orchestration
- S3, HDFS for data storage

The technology stack for a speed layer is as follows:

- Apache Kafka, Apache Flink, AWS MSK, GCP Pub Sub for messaging

- Redis and Couchbase for data caching and low-latency serving
- Oracle Golden Gate, Debezium, IBM InfoSphere Data Replication for CDC
- Spark streaming for data processing

ETL and ELT

Extract, transform, and load (ETL), as the name suggests, is a pattern that injects a data transformation phase between extracting data and loading it to the target system. The transformation step performs data cleansing, standardization, format conversion, enrichment, and many other data processing tasks. Historically, the transformation was done in proprietary tools like IBM DataStage or AbInitio, but modern architectures prefer Apache Spark to run these transformations. ETL is a preferred pattern to use when we wish to move only processed and cleansed data into the target system. The reason for only moving cleaned data to the target system can be varied, like regulatory requirements or target systems not having the capacity to store and process the raw data. ETL also fits well in the traditional data warehouse architecture, where it is recommended to use the data warehouse to only run BI queries on transformed high-quality data.

ELT is a pattern where the data is extracted and loaded into the target system first, but into staging tables. The data is then transformed and loaded from the staging tables to the main tables. This approach avoids the need for intermediate systems for transformations but transfers the computing burden of transformation to the target system itself. This approach does not work well for data warehouses, which are focused on running BI workloads. The transformation process, when run on the data warehouse, can disrupt the BI workloads if there is no clear isolation of resource usage between the transformation job and the BI workload. The ELT pattern is better suited to be run on big data architectures like Hive with HDFS, where the data is moved to HDFS in the raw format and then, using Hive, transformed and shaped into the necessary target format before being made available for analysis.

The technology stack for ETL and ELT patterns typically is like the batch pattern, as complex transformations can only be done in a batch process, as they are slow and consume a lot of compute resources.

The following technology stack is commonly used to build ETL and ELT patterns:

- MapReduce, Hive, Apache Spark, and AWS EMR for data transformation jobs
- Apache Airflow, Control-M for orchestration
- S3, HDFS for staging data storage
- Oracle Exadata, Vertica, DB2 BLU, ClickHouse for data warehousing

Data storage and processing patterns

Data storage and processing patterns deal with solutions that require varied methodologies for storing and retrieving data. Every business use case has a different requirement from storage cost, retrieval latency, throughput, scalability, reliability, and compression perspectives. These data patterns provide proven templated solutions for different combinations of these requirements. These patterns help users avoid architectural errors when building complex data engineering solutions for storage and retrieval.

Databases and transactional data

Databases are of many types, and database patterns define which type of database to use for a given use case. Relational databases store data in tables in a structured format of rows and columns. This type of database has existed for several decades now and runs most of the world's critical software infrastructure. However, relational databases are not very flexible and are expensive to scale. They are not well-suited for modern programming paradigms like web and mobile.

To overcome the challenges of using relational databases for web and mobile applications, NoSQL databases were invented. NoSQL databases store data in semi-structured and unstructured ways and provide more flexibility than fixed schemas of relational databases. NoSQL databases are of many types, such as key-value stores, document stores, wide columnar stores, etc. They are simple to scale and operate, and provide much more flexible data models that modern applications require. Many NoSQL databases are also multi-model because a single database supports multiple data storage and access patterns. For example, Couchbase supports storing data as key-value pairs and accessing the data via the store and get functions while also supporting storing JSON documents and querying them via SQL language.

The following is the technology stack for relational databases:

- MySQL and Postgres are popular open-source databases
- Oracle, DB2, SQL Server, and AWS RDS are popular enterprise relational databases

The following are the technologies for NoSQL databases:

- MongoDB and Couchbase are multi-models supporting both key-value and document data
- Cassandra is a wide-columnar database
- DynamoDB is a key-value store

Data warehouse for data analytics

Data warehouses are the analytical cousins of transactional relational databases. They are purpose-built to be able to run complex analytical queries for data analysis over large datasets. Data warehouses aggregate data from multiple transactional systems and provide the enterprise with a single view of data for analysis. The data is transformed using the ETL pattern before it reaches the data warehouse to ensure that only cleansed and trustworthy data enters it. Business intelligence tools like *Power BI* and *Tableau* source their data for reports from data warehouses.

Data warehouses typically use databases that store data in columnar format and are capable of massively parallel processing. These two capabilities are critical to ensure that user queries run efficiently and quickly over large datasets. While the data lakehouse pattern emerges, combining the performance of the data warehouse and the scalability and flexibility of a data lake, data warehouses continue to be very popular due to their simplicity and purpose-built nature.

The following are the technologies used for data warehouses:

- Oracle Exadata, DB2 BLU, and Vertica are some of the popular enterprise data warehouses on-premises
- ClickHouse is a popular open-source data warehouse
- Redshift and Snowflake are very popular cloud data warehouses

Data lake and medallion architecture

Data lakes are systems where an enterprise collects all its data for storage and processing. They provide cheap storage and processing to allow an organization to collect vast amounts of unprocessed data. Data lakes ensure that various data engineering teams in the organization have access to raw data being generated in the company for building curated data engineering projects.

Medallion architecture is a modern data pattern where the data processing system consists of 3 layers, which are bronze, silver, and gold. The bronze layer is meant to store the raw data in systems like a data lake and be a collect-all repository for the enterprise for raw, unprocessed data. The silver layer consumes data from the bronze layer and cleanses and transforms the raw data into usable data, along with additional enrichment. This layer is used for exploratory analysis of data. Finally, the gold layer consumes data from the silver layer, refines it further, specific to use cases, and prepares it for data warehouse and machine learning. For example, the gold layer builds an aggregate to be stored in the data warehouse for supporting business intelligence.

The following are the technologies for building data lakes:

- HDFS, S3 for storage
- MapReduce, Hive, and Apache Spark for data processing
- Apache Kafka for data integration

The following are the technologies for medallion architecture:

- The bronze layer can use HDFS, S3, and Hadoop for cheap storage of raw data
- Silver layer can be built on top of lake house formats like Delta Lake, Apache Iceberg, Apache Hudi with Apache Spark
- The gold layer is built with data warehouses like Vertica, Oracle Exadata, ClickHouse, and Snowflake, as well as cloud-based data management platforms like Databricks

Data replication and partitioning

Data replication and partitioning patterns are critical in ensuring the reliability and performance of large-scale systems. Data storage and serving applications are inherently vulnerable to hardware and software failures, often called faults. To ensure system reliability and minimize the impact of these faults, data replication is commonly employed as a fault-tolerance strategy. Data replication strategies can be of many types depending on the goal of replication, whether it is being done to protect against a machine failure or a data center failure or to load balance across systems, etc. Within a single system, to protect against machine failures, multiple replicas of the data can be stored on different machines; these types of systems are typically referred to as having replicas. However, if the goal is to protect against complete system failure or data center failure, the data needs to be replicated to another system using change data capture technologies.

Data partitioning plays a crucial role in enhancing both the performance and scalability of data systems. The scatter-gather pattern is one of the most common data partitioning patterns, a data processing and serving technique that leverages partitioning to efficiently distribute and aggregate data across multiple nodes.

Data partitioning is a feature of most distributed databases. It does not require any specific technology for its implementation. Data replication is also mostly a capability of the database; but however, some databases do not support this out of the box and recommend using change data capture technologies like *Oracle GoldenGate*.

Hot vs. cold storage

Data storage costs can escalate rapidly, particularly when dealing with vast volumes of data. However, not all data requires immediate, low-latency access. Infrequently accessed data, often referred to as *cold data*, can be stored using more cost-effective storage solutions, albeit with a trade-off in access speed. A simple example of this would be a data warehouse, which is powering a business intelligence application where the data can be moved to a cheaper storage, like a data lake, once the old data is no longer accessed by the BI application. Similarly, while using S3 object storage, when the application does not need frequent and fast access to data, the data can be moved to S3 Glacier storage, which provides cheaper storage than regular S3 at the cost of access speeds.

The following are the technologies commonly used for cold storage:

- S3 Glacier
- HDFS

Data caching and low-latency serving

Data caching and low-latency serving are very commonly found patterns in the industry that are used to provide a sub-millisecond response to user queries. This pattern is implemented using databases that act as a memory database over other persistent data stores or databases that can run on very fast storage technologies like *Flash/NVMe storage*.

Data caching and low-latency serving patterns explore infrastructure design in detail. Unlike other patterns, a good data caching solution is as dependent on infrastructure selection as software. Another critical aspect to understand with the caching pattern is dealing with **data greater than memory** (**DGM**) problems, as it is not always possible for large enterprise use cases to fit the data fully in memory without incurring a prohibitive infrastructure cost.

The following are the technologies used for data caching and low-latency serving:

- Redis and Couchbase are used as in-memory databases
- Aerospoke with flash storage
- Amazon ElastiCache

Data search patterns

Data search can either be a text search or a semantic search. Text search looks for phrases, words, patterns, wild cards, etc., in the data, while semantic search tries to find conceptually equivalent content that cannot be matched using text search. Text search is powered by reverse indexes, which are a map of search terms and all the records where the search term appears. However, semantic is powered by vector indexes, which are indexes on top of embeddings of data. With the advent of LLMs, semantic search has gained immense popularity due to its usage in the **retrieval-augmented generation** (**RAG**) pattern.

The following are the technologies used for search:

- Elastic, OpenSearch and Lucene are popular for performing text search
- Pinecone, Couchbase, Weaviate, and FAIS are popular for performing semantic search

Domain specific patterns

Data engineering has many domain-specific patterns, like patterns that deal with time series data, patterns for handling data at the edge, patterns for building feature stores for machine learning, and many others. These domain-specific patterns have their unique challenges; for example, the data at the edge pattern must be able to deal with a patchy internet connection, as the edge devices may not always have good internet connectivity in remote areas. The edge pattern also must deal with a very limited memory footprint on the device and thus has the need for specialized databases like *SQLite*. On a similar note, the feature store pattern has unique requirements like *ASOF join*, which allows machine learning features to be fetched for a certain amount of time. Not all databases support ASOF joins, putting the burden on the data engineer to build intelligent solutions to support these domain-specific requirements. As you see, the technologies used in these domain-specific requirements are very specific to the requirement and are niche; this chapter does not recommend generic technology choices for domain-specific patterns. Subsequent chapters, when covering some of these domain-specific patterns, will delve into their technical stack.

Miscellaneous patterns

Miscellaneous data engineering patterns cannot be categorized under any single category, like data ingestion or data storage patterns. They are on a horizontal tangent when compared to data ingestion and data storage patterns and are applicable to most data engineering systems. They encompass security, observability, and orchestration patterns that make the system ready for production use.

Data security patterns

Data security patterns are the ones that provide strategies for safeguarding data throughout its lifecycle. Data security patterns ensure data confidentiality, integrity, and availability, including encryption, access control, and secure data transmission. Common data security patterns are those for authentication and authorization. Authentication can be done with multiple patterns, like Password-based authentication, but due to enhanced security, more often than not, modern systems use more complex patterns like multi-factor authentication, where, along with username and password, typically another form of identification using OTP or biometric-based authentication is used.

While authentication patterns help identify the identity of the user, authorization patterns help control the activities the user can perform on the system. The most common authorization pattern is the **role-based access control (RBAC)**, which defines the activities a user is allowed to do on the system based on the role they are assigned and the permissions associated with the role.

Data encryption is another key aspect of data security, and data encryption patterns ensure the data is always protected, whether it is in transit or at rest. **Transport Layer Security (TLS)** is the most popular pattern for ensuring data security for data in motion. TLS uses a combination of symmetric and asymmetric cryptography to securely transmit data.

Data at rest is encrypted using encryption algorithm types, where AES and RSA are the most popular symmetric and asymmetric encryption algorithms, respectively. These data at rest encryption patterns ensure that even if the data is inadvertently accessed by threat actors, they cannot leverage that data for malicious activities. All modern data storage systems like object stores, databases, and data lakes implement some or the other form of data encryption at rest.

Data observability and monitoring patterns

Data observability and monitoring become extremely critical to running a production data system reliably while meeting all the governance, security, and reliability requirements. These patterns provide visibility into data pipelines, including end-to-end monitoring, anomaly detection, and data quality checks. These patterns help to proactively identify and resolve issues, track data lineage, and ensure data integrity. Observability and monitoring patterns help maintain robust data systems that operate efficiently, minimize downtime, and support informed decision-making.

Data observability patterns focus on data quality, governance, lineage, and access, while data monitoring patterns focus on reliability, performance, efficiency, and cost.

The following technologies are commonly used in data observability:

- Data catalogs like Collibra, Alation, and Apache Atlas
- Data quality tools like IBM DataStage, Oracle EDQ, Talend

The following technologies are commonly used in data monitoring:

- Metrics collection and monitoring with Datadog, Splunk, and Prometheus
- Monitoring and dashboarding with Grafana
- Alerting and notifications using tools like PagerDuty and Slack

Idempotency and deduplication patterns

Idempotency and deduplication patterns are important because distributed data operations are inherently prone to a variety of failures, including network interruptions, hardware malfunctions, and software bugs. These failures can lead to issues such as data corruption or data loss. To ensure the integrity and quality of data in such environments, implementing data idempotency is crucial. **Exactly once semantics (EOS)** with messaging systems like Kafka can be used to achieve idempotency for data movement. Checkpointing is a common technique to achieve idempotency by tracking the completion of operations in a separate checkpoint log. Data loading operations commonly achieve idempotency for large data movement jobs by partitioning the jobs by range, which ensures reprocessing requires processing only certain date ranges.

As organizations ingest large volumes of data from diverse sources, the likelihood of duplicate data entering the system increases significantly. Duplicate data not only skews analytics and decision-making processes but also leads to inefficient use of storage resources, driving up costs unnecessarily. To address these challenges, it is important to use patterns for identifying and eliminating duplicate data. *A checksum is a method to identify duplicate data by generating a unique checksum for each piece of data using checksum algorithms like SHA-256 or MD5.* Data processing pipelines can then verify the checksum of the data being processed with existing checksums to identify potential duplicate data content. Eliminating duplicate data not only saves storage and processing costs but also improves the performance of data systems by not repeatedly processing the same data content.

The technologies for achieving idempotency are as follows:

- EOS can be achieved using messaging systems like Kafka or AWS SQS
- Data processing systems like Apache Kafka support checkpointing

- Databases like MongoDB, Couchbase, and Postgres support Upsert, Merge statements, and primary keys, which can be used to ensure duplicate data does not get inserted

The technologies for achieving data deduplication are as follows:

- SHA-256/SHA-512 functions in Apache Spark
- MD5/SHA-256 functions in Postgres, Oracle, and other popular databases

Data orchestration patterns

Data orchestration is the process of automating, scheduling, and managing complex data workflows, ensuring that data flows seamlessly across various systems and processing stages. Data orchestration patterns work in conjunction with all other data patterns described in this book to build an end-to-end data pipeline. We can think of them as glue for stitching various patterns together to solve a use case and a framework to run the solution in production.

The technologies used to implement data orchestration are as follows:

- Apache Airflow for job scheduling and orchestration
- Apache NiFi for building data pipelines
- Terraform and Ansible to manage infrastructure orchestration

Conclusion

By the end of this chapter, we covered common data engineering patterns, the technologies used to implement those patterns and discussed the usage of common terminologies across the chapter. We also understood how different patterns can be combined to design a cohesive solution. This chapter covered various data ingestion and processing as well as storage and serving patterns, in brief, to set the stage for future chapters that cover each of these patterns in detail.

In the next chapter, we will discuss in detail batch ingestion and processing, along with industry use cases. We will also see a few code examples of how batch patterns can be implemented.

Questions

1. Why are data engineering patterns important?
2. How can data engineering patterns be combined to build a data system?
3. Why are real-time systems expensive to build compared to batch-based systems?
4. How can you secure your data using data engineering patterns?
5. Why is it important to understand infrastructure selection for caching patterns?

CHAPTER 3
Batch Ingestion and Processing

Introduction

In this chapter, we will understand the details of the batch pattern and make the reader familiar with how to build a solution using a batch pattern. It will cover the use cases that batch patterns can help solve. We will also discuss how to design a batch system using open-source technologies and demonstrate a sample application along with the code snippets. Additionally, we will also cover real-world examples of batch patterns in use.

Structure

This chapter covers the following topics:

- Use cases for batch systems
- Designing a batch system
- Technologies for batch systems
- Real-world examples

Objectives

By the end of this chapter, you will have a deep understanding of the batch pattern. You will also be able to design and build your data pipelines using the batch pattern and write code to implement the design. You will know the technical stack to use and how to stitch the various components to build an end-to-end pipeline. Finally, you will also understand the real-world use cases where this pattern can be used, with examples from the banking and retail industries.

Use cases for batch systems

Batch patterns can be used in varied cases, from building ETL pipelines to data backup strategies. The following are some of the use cases where batch patterns would be a great fit.

ETL pipelines for a data warehouse

Data warehouses are systems that enterprises use to deliver on their most critical analytical reporting needs. They run all the scheduled enterprise reports on a daily, weekly, and monthly basis. The data in the data warehouse is sourced from varied systems within an organization. The process of moving the data from these varied sources after transformation into the data warehouse is called **extract, transform, and load** (ETL).

The transactional source systems in enterprises continuously generate data every second, every minute, throughout the year. However, the reporting does not always need to be in real time, as most of the use cases are reports that have an SLA in days, but not in milliseconds or seconds. As a result, it is not always required to move the data from the source systems to the data warehouse in real time. You can see that the data movement needs for most data warehouses are batch in nature, where the data needs to be available for querying before the scheduled report starts. The ETL jobs can be scheduled at periodic intervals, batch the set of rows generated over a period of time on the source system, followed by transforming and loading them into the data warehouse.

The same can be achieved via the real-time data engineering pattern. However, the cost of implementing a real-time system is significantly higher than running the batch pattern for ETL in the data warehouse. A real-time system would need a change data capture technology that can capture changes on the transactional source system instantly and move them via a message bus like Kafka to the data warehouse. Also, given that the transformations in ETL are typically complex, they are difficult to achieve in real-time, and performing complex transformations in real-time requires large infrastructure investments in computing.

Let us look at the design of an ETL system for a data warehouse in the following figure:

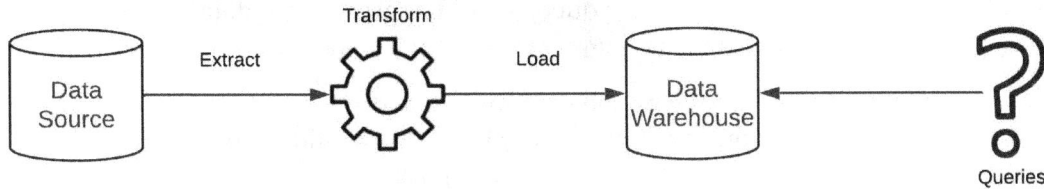

Figure 3.1: *Architecture of ETL for data warehouse*

Data archival pipelines

Data archival is the process of copying data into cold, cheap storage for the long term. This is typically achieved by running extract and copy jobs from active systems to cheap archival storage. Archival activity is done at periodic intervals; by that nature, it is suited for a batch pattern where a certain amount of data is batched together for archiving.

One of the most common uses of archiving data is rolling over the oldest data from the data warehouse when it is no longer needed frequently for business intelligence. This can be easily done by exporting the oldest date partition of data into a cold object storage like S3 Glacier using the native export tools of the database.

For example, if we had to archive a table's data at the end of every month from Snowflake to S3 Glacier storage, it would be as follows:

- Create a stage for an S3 bucket:
  ```
  CREATE   STAGE   my_s3_stage   URL='s3://unload/files/'   STORAGE_INTEGRA-
  TION = s3_int
  ```

- Create a task to run on the last day of the month to copy the table data to S3:
  ```
  CREATE        TASK        monthly_task        SCHEDULE        =        'US-
  ING CRON 0 0 31 * *'  AS COPY INTO @my_s3_stage/t1 FROM (SELECT * FROM t1)
  ```

The aforementioned task batches all the table records once a month and copies them over to S3.

Building precomputed aggregates for BI

Business intelligence workloads typically analyze data over a period of time and commonly explore aggregated data. However, when the data has to be analyzed over long periods of time, the amount of data that may need to be aggregated may be very large. Doing such aggregations for every query can be computationally expensive. To overcome this problem, many analytical systems create precomputed aggregates, which can be used to serve the queries instead of computing the aggregate every time.

Let us understand this with an example. A common BI question may be to find the sales from each city and by product category.

To answer such a question, the following query would aggregate the data:

```
SELECT CITY, PRODUCT, SUM(SALES) FROM SALES_TABLE GROUP BY CITY, PRODUCT
```

This query would, however, aggregate the data by city and product and sum the sales every time, resulting in wasted computing. A better way to do this would be to create a precomputed aggregate.

The following is an example of how to create this in Oracle:

```
CREATE MATERIALIZED VIEW sales_materialized_view ON DEMAND
AS SELECT CITY, PRODUCT, SUM(SALES) FROM SALES_TABLE GROUP BY CITY, PRODUCT
```

The table **SALES_TABLE** can be continuously updated; however, the materialized view can be refreshed every day at the end of the day by batching all the updates for the day. Updating the materialized view for every change in the main table is computationally inefficient.

In Oracle, the materialized views can be updated using the statement as follows:

```
EXEC DBMS_MVIEW.refresh('SALES_MATERIALIZED_VIEW');
```

Training ML models

Model training is a memory-intensive activity, and as a result, when the training data is very large, it is not possible to fit all of the training data in memory. To overcome this challenge, model training APIs provide the ability to train in batches. After processing each batch of training data, the model weights are updated until all the training data is consumed. Algorithms like **stochastic gradient descent (SGD)** are used to calculate the precision loss and update the weights as the batches are processed. Training frameworks like PyTorch allow developers to specify the batch size in their data loaders.

Designing batch processing and ingestion system

In this section, let us develop a batch processing and ingestion system that reads from a transactional MySQL database, processes the data using Apache Spark in batches, and then loads the data into a ClickHouse database.

The spark job is scheduled via a cron job to run once every day, as shown in the following figure:

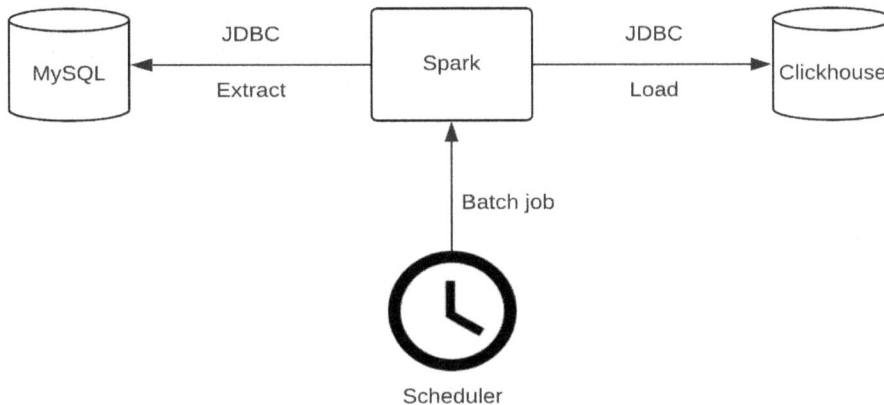

Figure 3.2: Batch data ingestion

The system contains a MySQL table called **sales_table**, which contains the sales data for the month. The table has a **transaction_date** column, which contains the transaction date stored in the table. The Spark program reads one day's data at a time in batches, processes it, and loads it into a target ClickHouse database table for analysis.

This program needs JDBC to drive for both MySQL and ClickHouse, which can be downloaded from their respective software download pages.

It also needs Spark to be installed on the system, which is done using the following command:

```
brew install apache-spark
```

Before creating the MySQL table, MySQL needs to be installed, and the service started. The steps for this are beyond the scope of this book and can be found in the MySQL documentation.

Similarly, ClickHouse must be installed or provisioned on the cloud before creating the database and tables. The details are as follows:

1. Create a MySQL database first, as follows:
   ```
   CREATE DATABASE sales_db;
   ```

2. Connect to the **sales_db** database and create the MySQL table that stores the transactional sales data for a month, as shown:
   ```
   USE sales_db;
   CREATE TABLE sales_table (
       transaction_id INT AUTO_INCREMENT PRIMARY KEY,
       transaction_amount DECIMAL(10, 2) NOT NULL,
       product_id INT NOT NULL,
       location_id INT NOT NULL,
       transaction_date DATE NOT NULL
   );
   ```

Load sample data into MySQL as follows:

```
LOAD DATA INFILE '/tmp/sales_table_january_2024.csv' INTO TABLE sales_
table FIELDS TERMINATED BY ',' ENCLOSED BY '"' LINES TERMINAT-
ED BY '\n' IGNORE 1 LINES (transaction_id, transaction_amount, product_
id, location_id, transaction_date);
```

3. Create a database on ClickHouse, as follows:

```
CREATE DATABASE sales_db;
```

Connect to the database **sales_db** and create a table in ClickHouse for analytics as follows:

```
USE sales_db;
CREATE TABLE sales_table (
    transaction_id UInt32,
    transaction_amount Decimal(10, 2),
    product_id UInt32,
    location_id UInt32,
    transaction_date Date
)
ENGINE = MergeTree()
ORDER BY transaction_id;
```

4. Spark job to move data daily as follows:

```
from pyspark.sql import SparkSession
# Create a SparkSession
spark = SparkSession.builder \
    .appName("MySQL to Clickhouse") \
    .getOrCreate()
# Setup the MySQL JDBC connection properties
mysql_url = "jdbc:mysql://localhost:3306/sales_db"
mysql_properties = {
    "user": "root",
    "password": "MyPassword",
    "driver": "com.mysql.cj.jdbc.Driver"
}
# Query to batch query the day's data in MySQL
query = "(SELECT transaction_id, transaction_amount, product_id, loca-
tion_id, transaction_date FROM sales_table where dayofmonth(transaction_
date)=dayofMONTH(CURDATE()) limit 5) AS tmp"
# Read from MySQL daily data table into DataFrame
mysql_df = spark.read.jdbc(url=mysql_url, table=query, properties=mysql_
```

```
    properties)
    # Setup ClickHouse JDBC connection properties
    clickhouse_url   =   "jdbc:clickhouse://yywbylab29.ap-south-1.aws.click-
    house.cloud:8443/default"
    clickhouse_properties = {
        "user": "default",
        "password": "MyPassword",
        "ssl": "true",
        "driver": "com.clickhouse.jdbc.ClickHouseDriver"
    }
    # Write daily data from MySQL to Clickhouse in a batch
    mysql_df.write \
        .mode("append") \
        .jdbc(url=clickhouse_url, table="sales_table", properties=clickhouse_
    properties)
    # Stop the SparkSession
    spark.stop()
```

5. Run the Spark job using cron as follows:

```
    crontab -e
    0 22 * * * spark-submit --jars "/tmp/jdbc_dir/mysql-connector-j-9.0.0.
    jar,/tmp/jdbc_dir/clickhouse-jdbc-0.7.0.jar" spark_program.py
```

Technologies for batch systems

Batch processing systems commonly work with large amounts of data at a time, given they collect data for the batch duration and then operate on it at once. As a result, most technologies commonly used for batch processing are the ones that can operate on large-scale data without performance bottlenecks and can scale out as more data is batched horizontally. Historically, Hadoop MapReduce was a common way of processing batch data as MapReduce jobs could consume and process large amounts of data reliably without job failures. The MapReduces jobs using HDFS storage technology for temporary and persistent data.

While building modern systems, data engineers realized MapReduce is not very efficient with its resource use and switched to Apache Spark for executing batch processing jobs. Spark, with its ability to restart jobs from failure points, is a much more performant and reliable execution framework for batch-processing jobs. On the storage front, object storage is gaining popularity over HDFS as the default storage system for batch processing.

Batch jobs need to be scheduled and orchestrated based on the batching frequency. Apache Airflow has emerged as a strong technology choice due to its versatility in working with various systems and its ability to model workflows such as **directed acyclic graphs** (**DAG**).

For simple use cases that do not require complex job orchestration, the Linux Cron scheduler proves itself to be a handy tool for scheduling batch jobs.

Real-world examples

Let us look at a couple of real-world examples of batch patterns in the banking and retail media networks domain. These examples help you understand how to apply the patterns discussed in this chapter to domain-specific solutions. They also help bridge the gap between the theory and application of a pattern for an industry use case.

Batch processing in banking

The banking industry is governed by very strong regulations, given the sensitive nature of its financial transactions. All banks need to send end-of-the-day reports to the banking regulator to ensure compliance with these regulations. This end-of-the-day reporting needs to contain various data points associated with the transactions conducted throughout the day, like cash flow statements, exposure to markets and currency positions, suspected fraud reports, forex transaction reports, etc.

Banking systems are complex and integrate multiple technology systems. Generating the above-mentioned reporting information is a complex exercise needing data integration from multiple systems before the end-of-the-day report can be generated. This requires a batching system that integrates data from various systems throughout the day to a central analytic system to run the end-of-the-day reports promptly. An end-of-the-day report may need integration from the bank's payment system, fraud detection system, core banking technologies, and forex systems.

The following architecture (*Figure 3.3*) showcases how various components of a banking system are integrated using a batching pattern for end-of-day reporting:

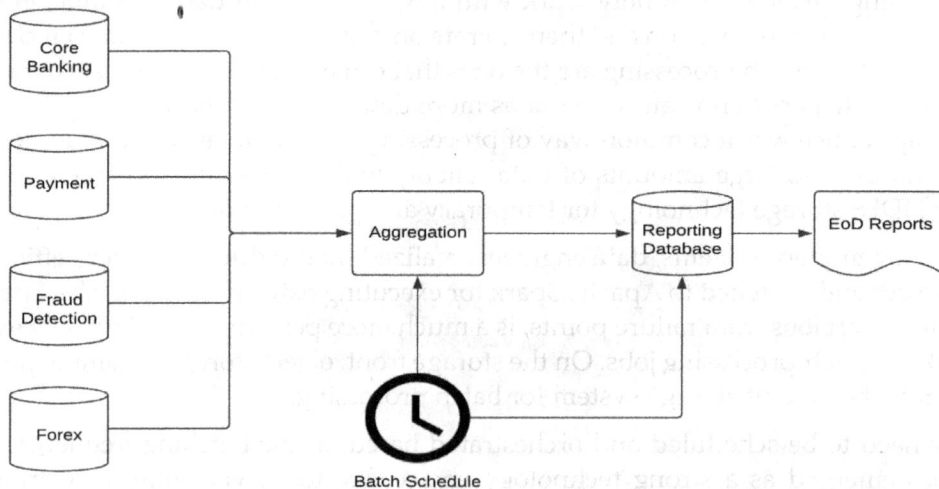

Figure 3.3: Batch system for end-of-day reporting

Batch processing in retail media networks

Retail media networks (RMN) are powerful advertising platforms that retailers own and run on their digital assets, such as apps or websites. Brands can advertise on these RMNs to target customers at the point of purchase, thereby increasing the chance of a sale.

Now, let us understand how batch processing is used in RMNs. Advertisers publish their ads on RMNs, which are then published to consumers when they use the retail app associated with the RMN. The platform tracks user behavior on the retail app, such as page views, cart events, ad engagement, conversion rate, etc. These details need to be shared back with the advertisers so that they can run better-targeted campaigns and improve ad conversion rates.

However, advertisers do not need individual user interactions but instead aggregated information over a noticeable period. RMNs typically batch user interactions over the whole day and aggregate them before sending them to advertisers at the end, indicating the efficiency of their campaigns.

Let us look at an architecture that collects and integrates user behavior for analysis using a batch pattern, as shown in the following figure:

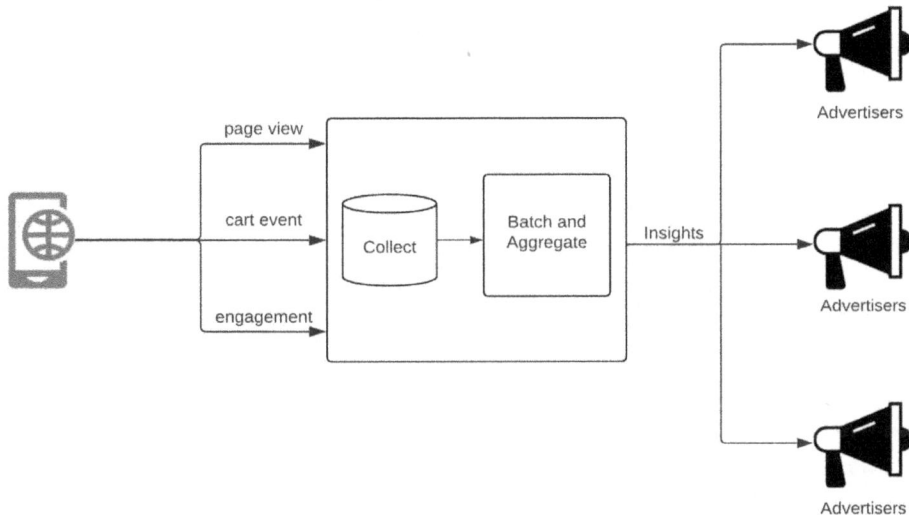

Figure 3.4: Batch pattern in RMN

Conclusion

By the end of this chapter, we covered a few common use cases for batch systems, followed by designing a batch system for periodically moving data from a transactional system like MySQL to an analytic system like ClickHouse. We also understood how the design pattern is implemented in code using Apache Spark and JDBC technologies. Moreover, we discussed a few real-life examples of batching in the banking and retail media domains, where we understood the high-level batching architecture of these examples. Additionally, we reviewed the technologies commonly used in batching systems and their application.

In the next chapter, we will understand what real-time systems are and their design. We will also review use cases and real-life examples of real-time systems in various domains.

Questions

1. Why are modern data systems moving from MapReduce to Apache Spark for batch data processing?

2. What technologies can be used for scheduling batch jobs?

3. Why is Apache Kafka not commonly used for implementing batch design patterns?

4. What are some of the real-life use cases of batch systems in travel technology?

Join our Discord space

Join our Discord workspace for latest updates, offers, tech happenings around the world, new releases, and sessions with the authors:

https://discord.bpbonline.com

CHAPTER 4
Real-time Ingestion and Processing

Introduction

This chapter examines the details of the real-time pattern and familiarizes the reader with how to build a solution using it. It covers the use cases that real-time patterns can help solve. This chapter also discusses how to design a real system using open-source technologies and demonstrates a sample application along with code snippets. Additionally, we will cover real-world examples of real-time patterns in use.

Structure

This chapter covers the following topics:

- Use cases for real-time systems
- Designing a real-time system
- Technologies for real-time systems
- Real-world examples

Objectives

By the end of this chapter, you will have a deep understanding of the real-time pattern. You will also be able to design and build your data pipelines using the real-time pattern and write code to implement the design. You will know the technical stack to use and how to stitch the various components to build an end-to-end pipeline. Finally, you will understand real-world cases where this pattern can be used, with examples from the payments and e-commerce industry.

Use cases for real-time systems

Real-time patterns can be used for varied use cases, from building data pipelines for real-time analytics to ML scoring. Real-time systems differ from batch systems in that they handle data continuously as it arrives, enabling low-latency processing and immediate insights or actions, while batch systems process large volumes of data at scheduled intervals with higher latency, making them more suitable for historical analysis and reporting. The following are some of the use cases where real-time patterns would be a great fit.

Pipelines for real-time analytics

Real-time analytics systems source data from upstream transactional systems as it occurs and allow the data to be analyzed as soon as it is generated. These types of systems are critical for use cases where action needs to be taken as soon as the event occurs, rather than waiting for the events to be batched. They are critical in fraud detection, logistics, inventory management, and many other domains.

For example, in fraud detection, it is very important to stop the fraud while it is happening, and for this, the data to detect fraud needs to be available in real-time. There is no room for data delay using technologies like batching.

Real-time systems are much harder to build than batch-based systems, typically. They need technologies that can support message passing in real-time while maintaining delivery guarantees. Apache Kafka has proven itself to be a high-performance, reliable messaging system for building real-time data pipelines. Kafka also has a rich ecosystem built around it with connectors for the most popular data sources and sinks.

Let us consider a real-time analytics system that analyses clickstream information from a web application or mobile application. Clickstream is a trail of user navigation on a website or a mobile application. It contains the pages viewed, buttons clicked, sign-ups done, ads viewed, etc., during a user's interaction on a website.

Clickstream data can be analyzed in real time to identify user behavior on the website or the mobile application. The analysis can further be used to roll out recommendations or offers to users while they are still on the website to achieve immediate targeted advertising. This can lead to higher conversion rates as the *user's recommendation or offer is given to them* while they are actively shopping.

As you see, one of the key challenges in this system is that the clickstream data should be available for analysis as it is being generated to identify the right recommendations and offers to the customer, and once generated, the recommendations and offers need to be sent back to the application in real-time so that it can be displayed to the user. Apache Kafka allows this dual-channel communication using different topics.

Let us look at the following architecture (*Figure 4.1*) of a system that processes clickstream information using Kafka:

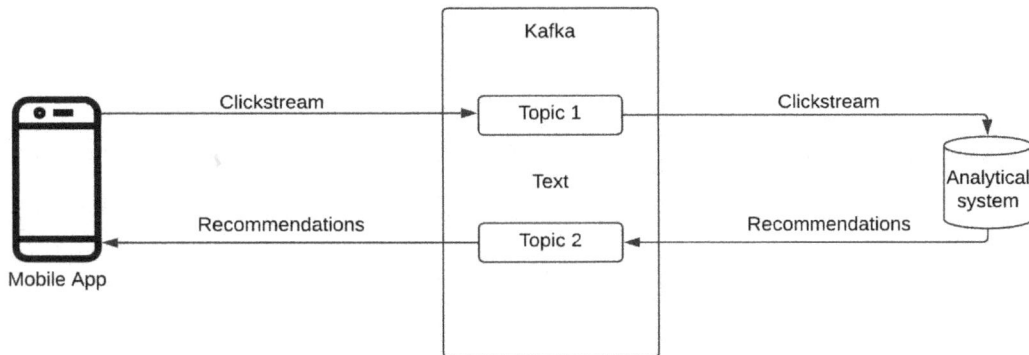

Figure 4.1: *Clickstream analysis with Kafka*

Change data capture for high availability

Databases for mission-critical applications need to be always up without downtime, even during natural disasters, which can possibly disrupt data centers where the application is running. To achieve this type of high availability, the data needs to be propagated from the primary database to the secondary database in real-time. The secondary database runs in a different data center, which is geographically located in a different region.

The database change propagation from the primary database to the secondary database can be achieved in multiple ways. Some databases, like Couchbase, provide this capability natively within the database by providing a real-time change stream from the primary database to the secondary database. However, even when such a capability is not available out of the box in the database, it can be implemented using database change logs and a reliable message transfer framework like Apache Kafka.

Let us now look at how Apache Kafka can be used to build a real-time secondary database from the primary database using **change data capture** technology. Almost all databases produce something called **transaction logs**. These are log files that contain the changes that occur in a database in a predefined manner. These log messages can be read and processed to propagate the database changes to a secondary database. Apache Kafka supports connectors for databases that can read from these transaction logs and push them as messages to Kafka. The messages can then be consumed by **sink connectors**, which convert the messages to the appropriate insert, update, or delete statements on the target database side. Once the insert, update, or delete statement is applied to the target secondary database, it becomes in sync with the primary database. Depending on the requirement, the secondary database can be in the same region as the primary or in a secondary region to support just high availability or disaster recovery.

Let us now look at the following design of a system that builds high availability for databases by creating a secondary database using change log capture technology:

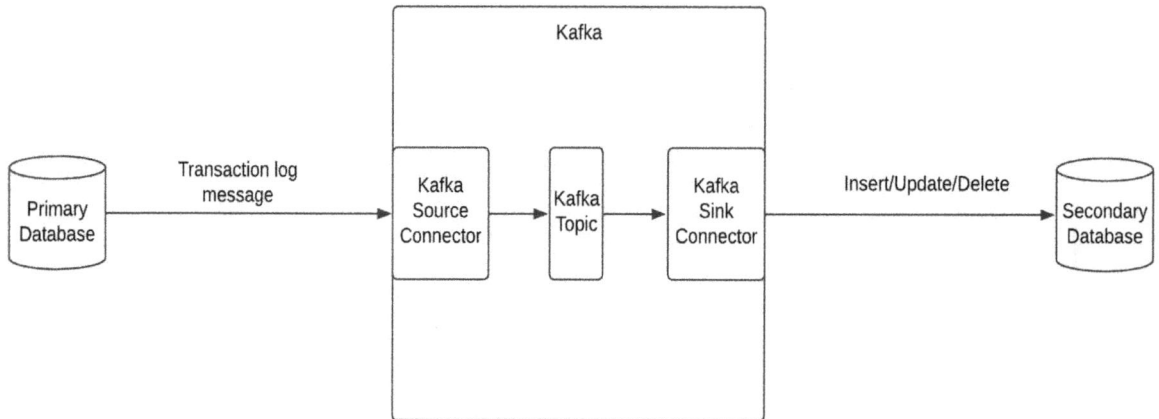

Figure 4.2: *High availability using change log capture*

Real-time ML scoring

Real-time ML scoring involves generating a prediction score with very low latency to ensure action can be taken based on the score to prevent a problem from happening. Real-time ML scoring is commonly used across many industries now for its ability to prevent problems from happening in the first place instead of doing an after-the-fact detection, which can lead to huge savings for an organization. Some of the areas in which ML scoring is commonly used are detecting machine failures in factories before they happen, identifying fraudulent transactions in payments and banking, predicting inventory stockouts before they happen, identifying cybersecurity attacks before they cause widespread damage, etc.

Let us look at how real-time ML scoring is used to prevent or mitigate cybersecurity attacks. Every system behavior can be measured using certain parameters, and these parameters are in an acceptable range when the system is operating normally. These parameters are typically called telemetry data. However, typically, during a cybersecurity attack, many of these parameters start varying and do not fall in the normal range of values. An ML model that is trained on this telemetry data as its features can predict attacks when their values are continuously fed to the model for scoring. For example, the system may have a pattern of network activity and memory usage over a period of time. The model can be trained on the data collected for these parameters over a long period of time, and then current values can be fed to the model for scoring an anomaly.

Building a real-time anomaly detection framework like this is a two-step process. First, the data has to be collected for ML model training. The telemetry information has to be collected from all the source systems using SAR metrics, operating system logs, network logs, etc. This information is fed via a streaming platform like Apache Kafka into an offline feature store. Features are then extracted from this raw data using feature engineering, and the features are used to train the ML model.

Let us now look at the architecture of a system that does model training on telemetry data as shown in the following figure:

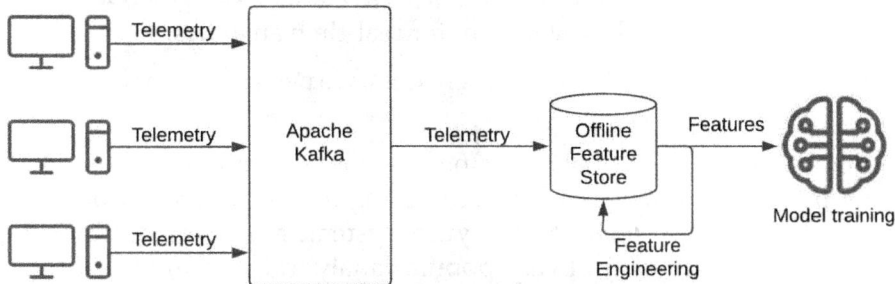

Figure 4.3: Model training on telemetry data

In the second step, the trained model is deployed on an inference server for scoring purposes. The telemetry data is then sent to the ML model for scoring at a low interval. The features for scoring are extracted from an online feature store to ensure low-latency access. Finally, based on the score generated, the system triggers alerts and actions for potential cybersecurity attacks.

The following is the architecture of a system that does online inferencing based on incoming telemetry data:

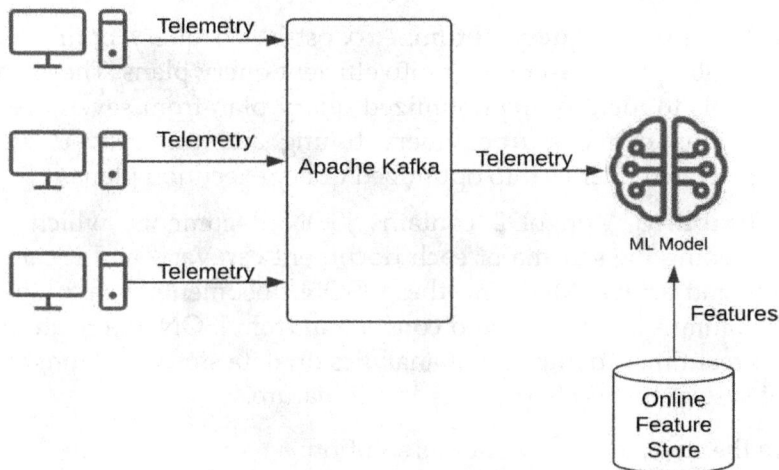

Figure 4.4: Online inferencing on telemetry data

Designing a real-time system

In this section, let us design a real-time analytics system that ingests data from a NoSQL document-based transactional system into an analytical system and then runs real-time dashboards from the analytical system. Doing real-time analytics on a NoSQL document-based system poses additional challenges compared to real-time analytics on relational data. These challenges are compounded by the schema-less nature of the document data model. To build real-time systems for document data models, we need specialized technology that can run analytics on document data. In this example, we will use MongoDB as the transactional system and Couchbase as an analytical system for real-time analytics.

To achieve real-time analytics on JSON document data, we need a system that has the capability to do the following:

- **Columnar storage**: This capability is needed for the fast retrieval of only the selected column data in the queries instead of fetching all the columns. Columnar storage is the preferred storage type for all analytical systems as it significantly reduces the I/O requirement on the system. Every popular analytical system in the market, starting from Oracle Exadata to AWS Redshift to Snowflake, is columnar storage based.

- **Massive Parallel Processing (MPP)**: MPP allows the system to execute a single query in parallel on multiple servers, reducing the time taken by the query to execute, thus making the analysis real-time. MPP allows leveraging scale-out compute to accelerate query processing and provides near-linear scalability in the absence of other bottlenecks like I/O.

- **SSD-based cache storage**: SSD-based cache storage provides fast data access, further reducing the time taken by the query to execute. SSDs are an order of magnitude faster than spinning disk-based storage systems and can provide low latency and high throughput I/O access.

- **Intelligent cost-based query optimizer**: Cost-based query optimizers intelligently convert the sub-optimal user query into efficient query plans. They leverage complex costing models to identify the optimized query plan from several candidates. They remove the human factor from query tuning and can convert even suboptimal machine-generated queries into optimized query execution plans.

- **Schema flexibility**: MongoDB contains JSON documents, which have a flexible schema, meaning the schema of each document can vary, and it can contain nested documents and arrays. Modeling these JSON documents as a relational table with rows and columns is complex, and conversion from JSON to a relational table cannot be done in real-time. To implement analytics on data stored in MongoDB, we need an analytical system that is also schema-less in nature.

The following are the steps to implement this solution:

1. Create an Apache Kafka cluster and topic in the cluster to hold the data being moved from MongoDB to Couchbase.

2. Enable replica set on MongoDB to allow change data capture from MongoDB to Kafka.

3. Deploy a MongoDB Source Kafka Connector to transfer data from MongoDB to Kafka topic.

4. Create a Kafka link in the Couchbase cluster by providing details of the Kafka cluster and topic.

5. Connect the Kafka link to start the data transfer from MongoDB to Couchbase.

Let us look at the architecture of a data system that performs real-time data analysis of JSON leveraging Couchbase and Apache Kafka, as shown in the following figure:

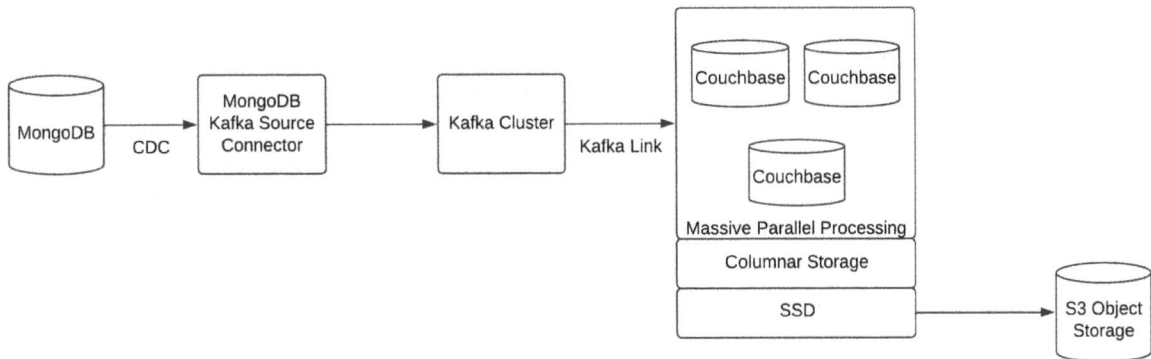

Figure 4.5: *Real-time JSON analysis with Couchbase*

Technologies for real-time systems

As you have seen in this chapter, real-time systems have two key characteristics. They are able to process data in real-time, a stream of data instead of batches, and they are able to provide very low-latency access to this data for processing. Achieving these requires two key technology stacks: streaming, data storage and serving.

To achieve a very high throughput streaming with very low latency, message delivery technologies like Apache Kafka, Apache Flink, and Spark structured streaming are very popular. Among these, Apache Kafka is the most popular streaming technology due to its wide availability of connectors for every type of source and sync system. Apache Kafka provides at least one message delivery semantics, thereby simplifying application development for real-time systems to a great extent.

Table 4.1 describes the use cases that are best fit for Apache Kafka, Apache Flink and Apache Spark Structured streaming.

Real-time systems typically use databases for data storage and serving, which can provide very high throughput and low-latency access. Databases like *Redis, Couchbase, and Aerospike* are very popular with real-time systems because they provide very fast access to data for processing. If the real-time system is processing small amounts of data that can be fully stored in primary memory, then a database like Redis, which is an in-memory cache, is preferred.

However, for larger use cases where the data needs to be served fast from primary memory but also needs to be persisted to secondary storage due to its large size database like Couchbase, which is a persistent data store with an integrated cache, is preferred. Refer to the following table:

Technology	Kafka	Flink	Spark Structured Streaming
Workload type and use case	<ul><li>Latency in low ms</li><li>Event collection</li><li>Messaging</li><li>Data integration</li></ul>	<ul><li>Latency in low to mid ms</li><li>Event processing</li><li>Real-time event analytics</li></ul>	<ul><li>Latency in high ms to seconds</li><li>Near real-time data pipeline</li><li>ETL in real time</li></ul>

Table 4.1: Use cases

Real-world examples

The following section discusses some real-world examples in credit card payment fraud detection and the gaming industry. These examples showcase how real-time patterns help these data systems take action at the point of the event instead of delaying it for later processing. This ability to act at the time of the event is paramount for both of these systems to work as designed. These examples also show how real-time patterns are embedded in systems we interact with in our daily lives.

Payment fraud detection

In any digital payment system, preventing fraud is extremely important to protect the consumer from monetary loss. The fraud must be detected and prevented at the time it occurs and not acted on it on an after-the-fact basis. Real-time systems play a critical role in payment fraud detection and prevention, as the transaction needs to be evaluated in real-time while it is happening, without consumers experiencing any delays in their payment transaction.

Fraud detection is typically done by an ML model, which scores the incoming transaction with a risk score. A transaction with a high fraud score is either blocked or a workflow to confirm with the customer is initiated, and transactions with a low fraud score are allowed to be completed.

To achieve this fraud scoring in real-time, the system must achieve the following workflow. Once the user initiates a transaction, it is processed by the payment gateway. The gateway sends the transaction details to an ML platform, which does the scoring via a messaging bus like Kafka. In the ML platform, first, the feature attributes associated with the transaction are extracted from an online feature store. An **online feature store** is a data store that contains all the ML features necessary for the scoring model and has a very low latency serving capability, because of which the features are immediately made available for scoring. Tools like *Tecton* and *Feast* can be used as online feature stores. The features can be the home location of the user, average transaction amount from the user, frequency of transactions by the user, etc. Using these features, the ML model scores the transaction with a fraud score.

The following architecture demonstrates the components of this fraud detection system:

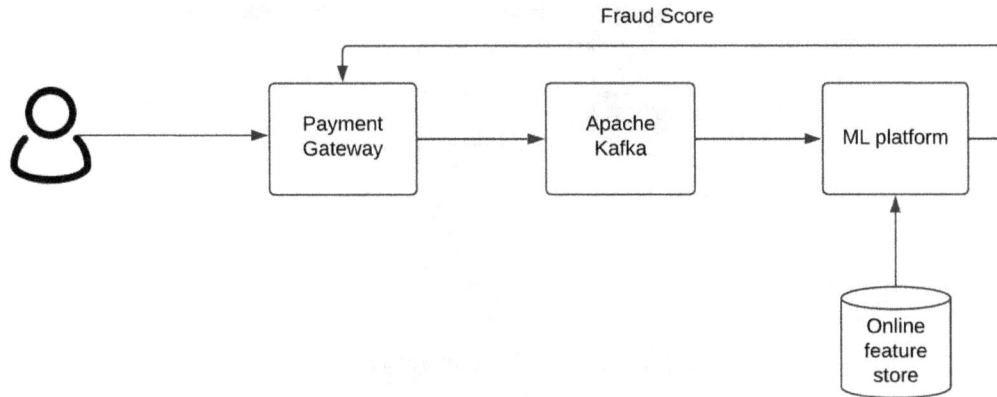

Figure 4.6: Fraud detection in real-time

Gaming

Real-time systems are extensively used in the gaming industry to solve multiple use cases. A rich, interactive experience without delays is the cornerstone of any good gaming experience, like *PUBG* and *Fortnite*. To achieve this, the gaming industry is heavily reliant on real-time systems.

Let us consider the following examples of real-time system uses in gaming:

- In multiplayer games, it is very important to quickly synchronize activities from all the different players to ensure an interactive gaming experience. The activities done by one gamer, like the selection of a weapon or shooting, need to be visible to other users in real-time. Any lag in reflecting the activity to other gamers in the game ruins the experience and will lead to the game not being successful. To achieve this real-time experience in gaming, games use databases like Couchbase for very low-latency data serving.

- A lot of games nowadays use personalization to tailor the gaming experience to individuals' expertise, tastes, behavior, and purchases. To achieve this personalization in real time, gaming systems need to be able to collect and analyze the gamer's preferences and behavior in real time. Gaming systems use Apache Flink and Kafka for real-time data streaming and databases like Redis and Couchbase for data storage and serving.

The following architecture demonstrates how real-time gaming systems are built using Apache Kafka and caches like Couchbase or Redis:

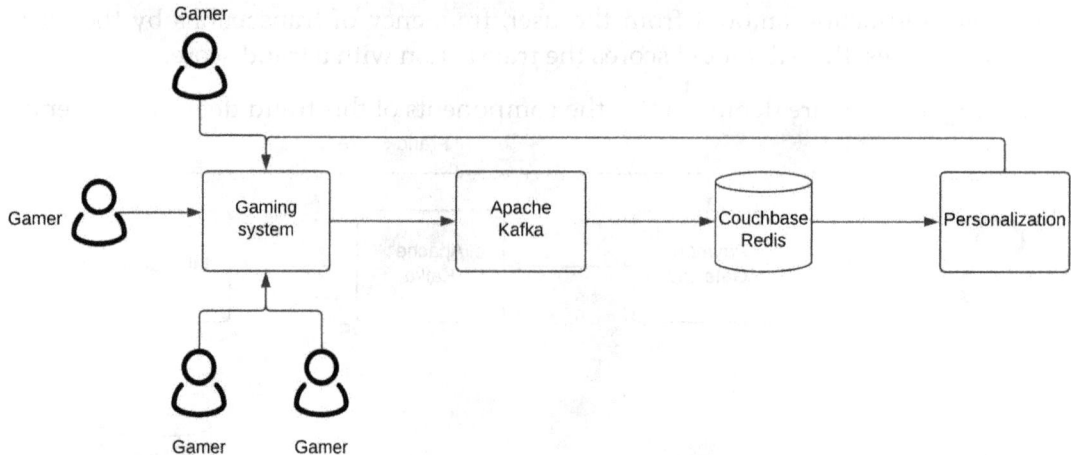

Figure 4.7: Real-time gaming system

Conclusion

In this chapter, we covered a few common use cases for real-time systems, followed by designing a real-time system for moving data from a NoSQL transactional system in MongoDB to an analytic NoSQL system like Couchbase Columnar. We saw how the design pattern is implemented using Apache Kafka and discussed a few examples of real-time systems in the banking and retail media domains, where we understood the high-level batching architecture of these examples. We also review the technologies commonly used in real-time systems and their application.

In the next chapter, we will understand the batching design pattern. We will also review use cases and real-life examples of systems using micro-batching in various domains.

Questions

1. Why is Apache Kafka a popular technology in implementing real-time systems?

2. What are the key capabilities of an analytics system for real-time analytics?

3. Why should batch systems be preferred over implementing real-time systems if there is no critical business need for real-time analysis?

4. Is Hadoop a preferred technology of choice for real-time systems? Provide supporting data points for your answer.

CHAPTER 5
Micro-batching

Introduction

This chapter looks into the details of the micro-batching design pattern and makes the reader familiar with how to build a solution using a micro-batching pattern. It will cover the use cases that micro-batching patterns can help solve. This chapter will also delve into designing a system using micro-batching on open-source technologies and demonstrate a sample application along with the code snippets. We will also cover real-world examples of micro-batching patterns in use.

Structure

The chapter covers the following topics:

- Use cases for micro-batching
- Designing micro-batching system
- Technologies for micro-batching systems
- Real-world examples

Objectives

By the end of this chapter, you will have a deep understanding of the micro-batching pattern. You will also be able to design and build your data pipelines using the micro-batching pattern and write code to implement the design. You will know the technical stack to use and how to stitch the various components to build an end-to-end pipeline. Finally, you will also understand the real-world use cases where this pattern can be used with examples from logistics and smart factories.

Use cases for micro-batching

Micro-batching design patterns can be used for varied use cases, like building data systems for data ingestion into a data lake and data analysis in near real-time. These use cases demonstrate how micro-batching data patterns can implement solutions at a low cost when compared to real-time systems while still providing near real-time data availability. The following are some of the use cases where a micro-batching design pattern would be a great fit.

Data ingestion into data lake

As you have seen in the previous two chapters, batch-based and real-time systems have their own challenges and do not fit all use cases from latency, throughput, and cost perspectives. Batch-based systems are simpler and cheaper to implement. However, they cannot provide low-latency data processing when the use case demands it. However, on the other hand, real-time systems are able to process data with very low latency but can be complex and expensive to implement. This is where micro-batching as a data pattern can help bridge the gap between batch-based and real-time systems by providing benefits for both these types of systems while avoiding some of the challenges they bring in. Micro-batching can help build a near-real-time system with a significantly simpler and cheaper architecture when compared to real-time systems.

Before we discuss the use of micro-batching to build a data ingestion pipeline into a data lake, let us first understand the small file problem in big data systems. With the advent of using S3 or HDFS and Apache Spark as a common technology to build a data lake, we have a problem pattern called the small file problem. When data is stored and processed as very small files in the data lake, both storage systems, like HDFS/S3, and processing engines like Spark struggle to perform optimally. This is due to the overhead involved in the processing of a large number of small files from the perspective of memory usage, reduced parallelism due to concurrency, storage inefficiency, and increased I/O cost. However, when the incoming data is processed in real-time, the data gets written to the data lake instantaneously, creating a large number of small files, leading to the small file problem. Batch-based systems typically solve this by combining data over the entire day or the hour and processing data in very large batches. However, that leads to data delay as it waits to batch the data for the entire day or hour.

If the data lake is backed by HDFS, small files cause issues on the name node by exhausting its memory due to the metadata storage consumed by each file. Also, small files lead to inefficient storage as each block of data is 128 or 256 MB, and if the file is smaller than the block size, the remaining space is wasted. This leads to a lot of fragmentation, which cannot be reclaimed. However, if S3 is used as the storage for the data lake, it does not experience wasted space, as there is no block size concept in S3. However, the S3 cost includes the number of GET/PUT calls on the files. So, when the data has to be read for analysis, small files can lead to a large number of GET/PUT calls, leading to very high processing costs. As a best practice, S3 recommends not using very small files to avoid this problem. In the following, example there is a high-level cost saving for processing a billion records in micro-batches of ten thousand instead of processing one record at a time. AWS charges approximately $0.005 for every 1000 GET/PUT requests.

$$Cost\ without\ batching = \$0.005\ x\ 1B\ /\ 1000 = \$5000$$

$$Cost\ with\ batching\ of\ 10000\ records = \$0.005\ x\ 1B\ /\ (1000 * 10000) = \$0.5$$

Let us look at the architecture (*Figure 5.1*) showing a real-time system ingesting data from a transactional database to the data lake:

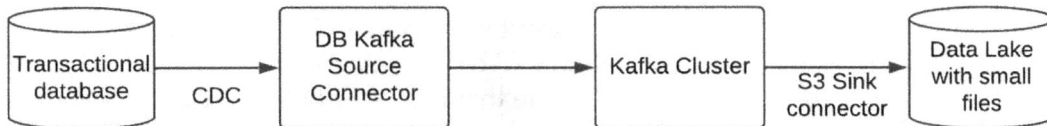

Figure 5.1: Real-time ingestion

Micro-batching provides a middle ground to solve this problem. By using the batching architecture for data processing but reducing the batch size to a very small window, micro-batching provides near real-time processing of data but avoids generating small files. This ensures that there is no data delay, and it is available for processing very near to when it is produced as well. By avoiding small files, the data is now suitable for efficient analysis without the overhead of processing a large number of small files. As you see, a micro-batching data pattern solved both the problem of the cost of real-time systems and the data delay of batch-based systems in a single solution.

Let us look at the architecture of a micro-batch ingestion of data from a transactional database to a data lake, as shown in the following figure:

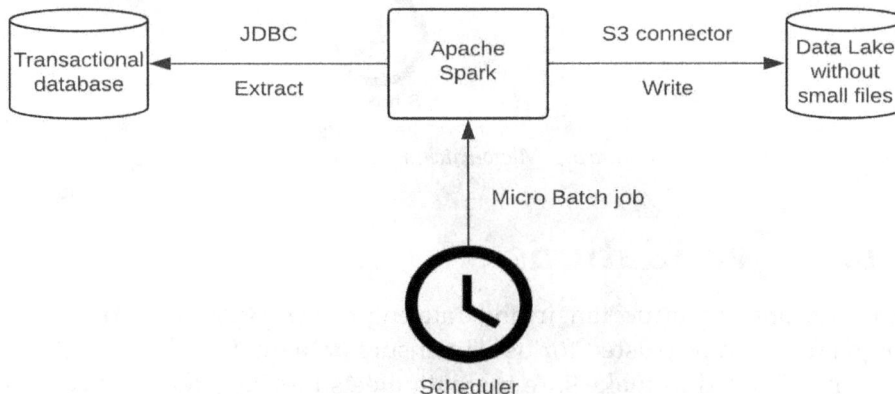

Figure 5.2: Micro-batch ingestion

Near real-time data analysis

Near real-time data analysis is a type of analysis where the data needs to be available for analysis within a couple of seconds of the event occurring. This is different from batch-based analysis, where the data delay could be in minutes or hours, and also different from real-time systems, where the acceptable data delay is in milliseconds. An example use case for a near-real-time system is making the financial transaction data available to the bank's contact center analyst. When a banking customer does a financial transaction, if the transaction does not complete successfully for some reason, the customer can call the contact center to understand the reasons. Typically, the time between a customer performing a transaction and the point where they call the contact center has a few seconds of delay, as this is a manual task by the customer. This problem can be solved using a micro-batching system, which batches the transaction data every couple of seconds and ingests it into the analytic systems, which are accessible to the contact center analyst.

The financial transaction data is typically executed on a mainframe system or a traditional RDBMS like Oracle. This transaction data has to be extracted every couple of seconds and loaded into an analytical system. The technique that can be applied here is the same as that was done for batch-based systems where data is extracted from the source system based on timestamp. It does not need technology that can record and transmit the change as soon as it happens, like change data capture or streaming technology like Kafka, as the data does not have to be captured right at the time of occurrence.

The following architecture figure shows how to use micro-batching for moving data to analytical systems:

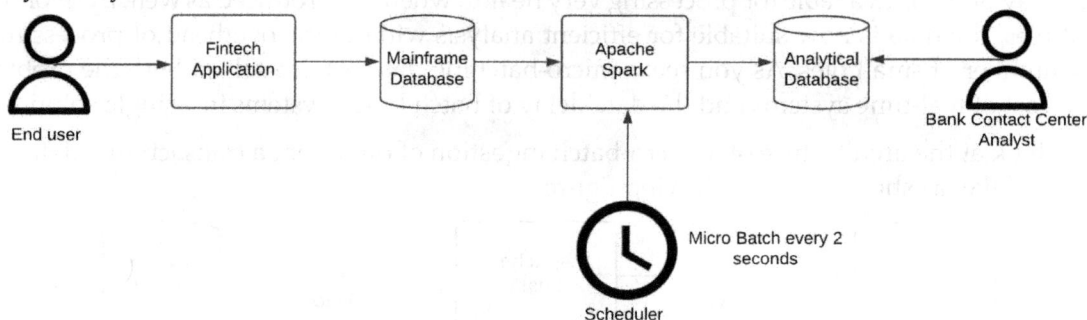

Figure 5.3: Micro-batching for analytics

Data quality validations

Data quality checks are very important in any data engineering system to ensure the quality of the data is high and it can be trusted for use. To ensure data quality, rules are defined against which the data is validated to make sure the data meets the expected quality, and alerts are raised if there is a deviation in data quality. However, performing a data quality check is a computationally expensive operation as the rules can be complex, and validation can be tricky. Doing such data validations in real-time leads to an extremely complex system with a very high computing cost. However, the data quality checks in many scenarios cannot be left until the end of day batch jobs as well because the data may need to be consumed throughout the data, and using bad data for making business decisions can lead to loss of business. An intermediate solution to this problem is leveraging micro-batching to run data quality checks. Depending on the freshness of the data required for business analysis, the data quality checks can be run at small batch intervals.

For example, let us consider a system that records new customers of a financial institution. When a new customer is onboarded, their address is recorded in the financial institution's books. However, addresses can often be non-standard and may need to be checked and standardized. The city names can often be misspelled and need to be corrected to the standard name the institution uses. This is important to be done before the address of the customer propagates through the many auxiliary systems of the institution. As a result, the data validation check cannot be delayed until the end of the day batch job. However, validating addressed need fuzzy computations, which can be expensive to execute and cannot be done in real-time easily. A micro-batch job that runs every few minutes can perform data validation checks for all the new customers onboarded in the last few minutes while ensuring any inconsistencies are found and fixed before the data flows to downstream systems.

The following architecture shows how a customer onboarding application can benefit from using the micro-batching pattern:

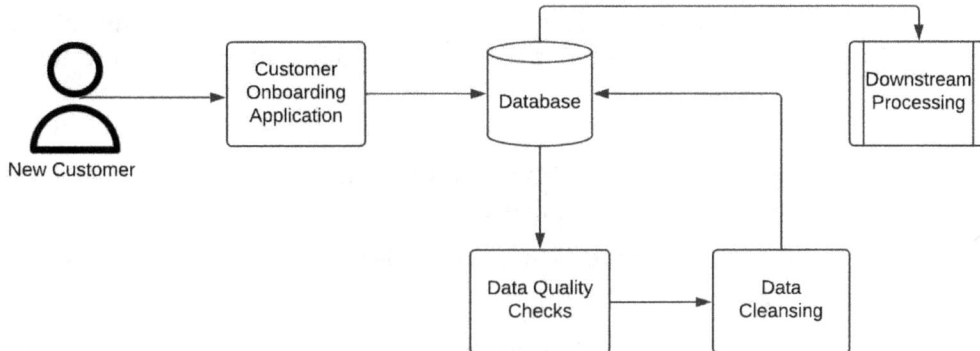

Figure 5.4: *Customer onboarding leveraging micro-batching*

Designing micro-batching system

In this section, let us develop a micro-batch processing system that does the following:

- Reads from a transactional MySQL database
- Processes the data using Apache Spark in micro-batches
- Loads the data into a ClickHouse database

The spark job is scheduled via a cron job to run every tw seconds, as shown below. This example is similar to the one we used to help understand batch-based systems. However, the critical difference is that instead of running end-of-day jobs, we now demonstrate how to run micro-batching jobs every 5 seconds.

Let us look at the following figure showcasing a simple ETL job using micro-batching, as shown:

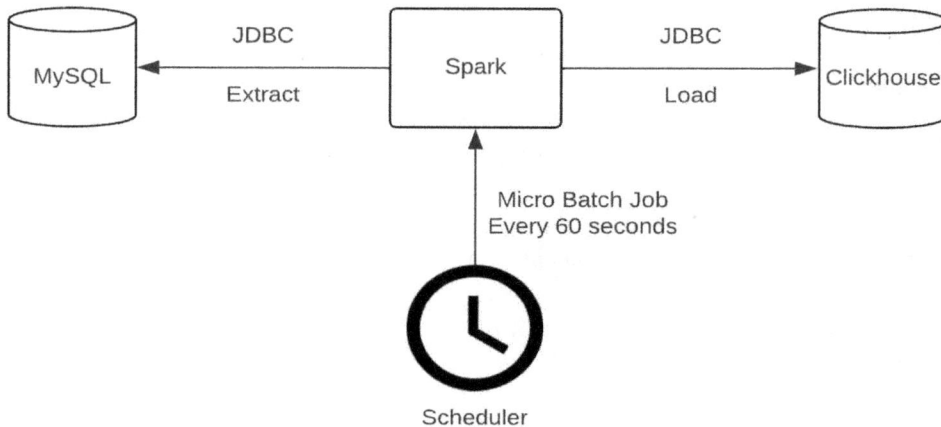

Figure 5.5: ETL with micro-batching

The system contains a MySQL table called **sales_table**, which contains the sales data for the month. The table has a **transaction_ts** column, which contains the timestamp of the transaction, including the date stored in the table. The Spark program reads one day's data at a time in batches, processes it, and loads it into a target ClickHouse database table for analysis.

This program needs JDBC drives for both MySQL and ClickHouse, which can be downloaded from their respective software download pages.

It also needs Spark to be installed on the system, which is done using the following command:

```
brew install apache-spark
```

Before creating the MySQL table, MySQL needs to be installed, and the service started.

Steps for this are beyond the scope of this book and can be found in the documentation of MySQL. Similarly, ClickHouse needs to be installed or provisioned on the cloud before creating the database and tables, as follows:

1. Create a MySQL database first:
   ```
   CREATE DATABASE sales_db;
   ```
2. Connecting to the **sales_db** database and creating the MySQL table that stores the transactional sales data for a month:
   ```
   USE sales_db;
   CREATE TABLE sales_table (
   ```

```
    transaction_id INT AUTO_INCREMENT PRIMARY KEY,
    transaction_amount DECIMAL(10, 2) NOT NULL,
    product_id INT NOT NULL,
    location_id INT NOT NULL,
    transaction_ts TIMESTAMP NOT NULL
);
```

3. Load sample data into MySQL:

```
LOAD DATA INFILE '/tmp/sales_table_january_2024.csv' INTO TABLE sales_
table FIELDS TERMINATED BY ',' ENCLOSED BY '"' LINES TERMINAT-
ED BY '\n' IGNORE 1 LINES (transaction_id, transaction_amount, product_
id, location_id, transaction_ts);
```

4. Create a database on ClickHouse:

```
CREATE DATABASE sales_db;
```

5. Connect to the database **sales_db** and create a table in ClickHouse for analytics:

```
USE sales_db;
CREATE TABLE sales_table (
    transaction_id UInt32,
    transaction_amount Decimal(10, 2),
    product_id UInt32,
    location_id UInt32,
    transaction_ts Timestamp
)
ENGINE = MergeTree()
ORDER BY transaction_id;
```

6. Spark job to move data on a daily basis:

```
from pyspark.sql import SparkSession
# Create a SparkSession
spark = SparkSession.builder \
    .appName("MySQL to Clickhouse") \
    .getOrCreate()
# Setup the MySQL JDBC connection properties
mysql_url = "jdbc:mysql://localhost:3306/sales_db"
mysql_properties = {
    "user": "root",
    "password": "MyPassword",
    "driver": "com.mysql.cj.jdbc.Driver"
}
```

```
# Query to batch query the day's data in MySQL
query = "(SELECT transaction_id, transaction_amount, product_id, loca-
tion_id, transaction_ts FROM sales_table where  transaction_ts> DATE_SUB-
(CURRENT_TIMESTAMP, INTERVAL 10 SECOND)
# Read from MySQL daily data table into DataFrame
mysql_df = spark.read.jdbc(url=mysql_url, table=query, properties=mysql_
properties)
# Setup ClickHouse JDBC connection properties
clickhouse_url   =   "jdbc:clickhouse://yywbylab29.ap-south-1.aws.click-
house.cloud:8443/default"
clickhouse_properties = {
    "user": "default",
    "password": "MyPassword",
    "ssl": "true",
    "driver": "com.clickhouse.jdbc.ClickHouseDriver"
}
# Write daily data from MySQL to Clickhouse in a batch
mysql_df.write \
    .mode("append") \
    .jdbc(url=clickhouse_url, table="sales_table", properties=clickhouse_
properties)
# Stop the SparkSession
spark.stop()
```

7. Run Spark job using cron:

```
crontab -e
* * * * * spark-submit --jars "/tmp/jdbc_dir/mysql-connector-j-9.0.0.
jar,/tmp/jdbc_dir/clickhouse-jdbc-0.7.0.jar" spark_program.py
```

Technologies for micro-batching systems

Technologies for micro-batching and batching do not vary a lot. What varies is the frequency at which batching occurs. Batch processing systems commonly work with large amounts of data at a time, given that they collect data for the batch duration and then operate on it at once. However, in the case of micro-batching systems, they do not need to process a lot of data at once. As a result, most technologies commonly used for batch processing can be used for micro-batching, but at a smaller scale. Historically, Hadoop MapReduce was a very common way of doing batch data processing, as MapReduce jobs could consume and process large amounts of data reliably without job failures. The MapReduce jobs used HDFS as storage technology for both temporary and persistent data. However, MapReduce may not be suitable for running micro-batching jobs as they have very high startup and execution times. The startup time itself can be higher than the batch window, in some cases, potentially delaying the batches.

The following is a technology selection guide between MapReduce and Spark jobs for micro-batching:

Technology	MapReduce	Spark
Startup latency	Medium to high	Low
Restartability	No	Yes
Job complexity	High	Low to medium
Performance	Low to medium	High
Data size	Medium to high	Low to medium

Table 5.1: *Technology selection guide*

Instead, Apache Spark is an excellent technology for micro-batch jobs. Spark, with its ability to restart jobs from failure points, is a much more performant and reliable execution framework for batch-processing jobs.

On the storage front, object storage is gaining popularity over HDFS as the default storage system for batch processing. Given the low-latency access provided by S3, it is ideal to be used as the stage storage area for micro-batching jobs. The data can be accumulated in S3 storage for a given batch and accessed quickly at the end of the batch window for processing.

Apache Airflow can also be used for micro-batching job schedules and is a strong technology choice for its versatility in working with various systems and its ability to model workflows as **directed acyclic graphs (DAG)**. For simple micro-batch jobs, which do. not require complex job orchestration, Linux Cron scheduler proves itself to be a handy tool to schedule micro-batch jobs. Enterprise schedulers like Control-M can also be used to schedule micro-batching jobs apart from the open-source schedulers.

Micro-batching is also a very commonly used data pattern in the cloud. Due to the ability to run serverless Lambda functions in the cloud, micro-batching jobs can be started and stopped at a very low compute cost on the cloud. The elastic compute nature of the cloud is a match made in heaven for micro-batching. The data can be accumulated for the batch on cheap object storage on the cloud, and on-demand compute can be used to run the micro-batching job. This combination can deliver near real-time data processing at a fraction of the cost needed to run Kafka-like real-time systems.

Real-world examples

This section will discuss some real-world examples of micro-batching in logistics and IoT domains. It will demonstrate how micro-batching can be used to build cost-efficient solutions when compared to real-time data patterns in these domains.

Vehicle tracking in logistics

In today's time, tracking the location of vehicles has become a very common use case in industries such as logistics and transportation. Every ride-sharing application provides active location tracking to view the current location of the taxi. In logistics, perishable and high-value goods are tracked through their journey to the destination to ensure safe and on-time delivery of the goods. This type of vehicle tracking is possible due to the GPS data sent by the device in the vehicle.

As the vehicle moves, the GPS location changes continuously, and if this location change is sent continuously to the server and processed to display on the map in the ride-sharing application or logistics application, the bandwidth and computing power requirement is very high. To optimize resource usage, it is much more efficient if the GPS signal is sent only at periodic intervals that are small enough for the user to see the vehicle moving and get its location instead of live streaming every small GPS location change of the vehicle. This way, the data bandwidth and the computing needed to track the vehicle are significantly reduced. The interval at which data is sent can be low enough to show the vehicle moving and its current location, which is the end goal of both live location sharing in ride-sharing apps and goods tracking in logistics. Both these use cases do not need the exact GPS location of the vehicle on a second basis.

As you can see, this use can be solved using both a real-time system and a micro-batching system. The real-time system is significantly expensive to build from both cost and resource points of view when compared to the micro-batching system, though both solve the business use case of vehicle tracking. In the real-time way of solving this problem, every single GPS location change is streamed right away and processed immediately, but in the case of micro-batching, the GPS signal changes are batched for a few seconds and then sent for processing. The few seconds of delay due to micro-batching do not alter the usability of the maps application while reducing the cost significantly.

The following figure demonstrates the use of micro-batching for real-time location tracking use case:

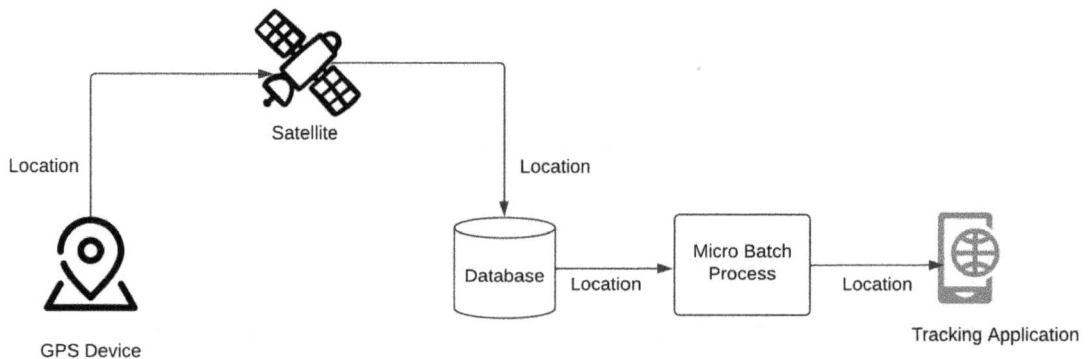

Figure 5.6: *Micro-batching in logistics*

IoT

Micro-batching is a good fit for industrial IoT use cases as well. Modern industries consist of hundreds or thousands of sensors that monitor and track every piece of equipment on the floor for premature failure. These sensors continuously send data, which is analyzed and used to identify anomalies that can lead to the detection of systems that are potential candidates for failure. These potential candidates are then examined by the maintenance staff on the floor and replaced or repaired if found to be faulty. By doing this, industries can ensure minimal downtime due to machinery breakdown and make sure the factory is continuously operational. It also helps the operational staff plan the maintenance schedules better, leading to improved operational expenses for the company.

In a typical industrial setup, the factory has an IoT gateway that receives the data from all the sensors continuously. The data is typically in MQTT format. The gateway then sends the data to the cloud servers, where the data is collected, stored, and processed for the long term. Machine learning algorithms analyze this data on the cloud and identify potential failures. The algorithms have been trained on historical data that was tagged with failure information. As you can see, the system can be built in ways where the data is continuously streamed from the sensor to the gateway to the cloud in real-time and processed for each sensor metric as it arrives. Alternatively, the data can also be collected for a day and analyzed at the end of the day in a batch fashion. However, neither of these is suitable or the most optimal way of solving this problem. To achieve a real-time solution to this problem, we need expensive Kafka Clusters and connectors for MQTT to process the data in real-time. However, the maintenance crew typically does not operate in real-time, so there is very little value gained by deploying this solution. However, batching the data for a day could also lead to failures not being detected soon enough for the maintenance crew to act on.

A great middle-ground solution to this problem is using micro-batching, where the data is collected for a few seconds or minutes and then processed. This ensures the maintenance crew gets the alerts soon enough for them to take up the repair or replacement activity, as well as keep the cost low by avoiding Kafka or equivalent messaging systems needed for real-time processing.

Another advantage of using micro-batching here is the more efficient use of ML models. Most ML models are better at batch scoring rather than scoring one request at a time. By leveraging micro-batching, the cost of ML scoring also comes down for predicting machine failure.

The following figure demonstrates the use of micro-batching to process sensor data in factories in a cost-efficient way:

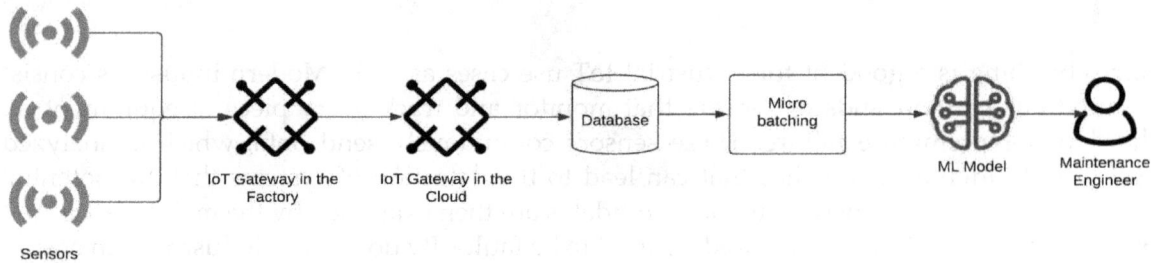

Figure 5.7*: Micro-batching in IoT application*

Conclusion

In this chapter, we covered common use cases for micro-batching-based systems, followed by designing a micro-batching system for moving data from MySQL to ClickHouse in near real-time without incurring the cost overhead of building real-time systems. We also saw how the design pattern is implemented using various technologies that are common to batch-based systems. We also learned about a few examples of micro-batching systems in logistics and IoT domains, where we understood the high-level micro-batching architecture of these examples and saw how micro-batching could simplify solutions in these domains.

In the next chapter, we will understand what Lambda architecture is. We also review use cases and industry examples of systems using Lambda architecture in various domains.

Questions

1. How is micro-batching different from traditional batching systems?

2. Why is it cheaper and simpler to implement micro-batching systems when compared to real-time systems?

3. Design and implement a micro-batching system to read data from S3 and load it into a database every five seconds.

4. Design a micro-batching system and a real-time system to solve loading data into S3 from an application, and then compare their cost of goods.

CHAPTER 6
Lambda Architecture

Introduction

This chapter looks into the details of the Lambda architecture data engineering pattern and makes the reader familiar with how to build a solution using a Lambda pattern. It will cover the use cases that Lambda patterns can help solve. This chapter will also delve into designing a system using Lambda on open source and cloud technologies and demonstrate a sample application along with the code snippets. We will also cover real-world examples of the Lambda pattern in use.

Structure

The chapter covers the following topics:

- Use cases for Lambda architecture pattern
- Designing system with a Lambda pattern
- Technologies for building systems with Lambda architecture
- Real-world example

Objectives

By the end of this chapter, you will be able to develop a deep understanding of the Lambda architecture pattern. You can also design and build your data pipelines using the Lambda architecture pattern and write code to implement the design. You will know the technical stack to use and how to stitch the various components to build an end-to-end pipeline with Lambda architecture. Finally, you will also understand the real-world use cases where this pattern can be used with examples from the Fintech domain.

Use cases for Lambda architecture pattern

Lambda architecture is a complex data engineering pattern that needs to be used sparingly and with caution. It is a pattern that can combine the benefits of a real-time and batch-based system, but that comes with a high implementation cost. It is suitable for domains where the return on investment of building a system that can do both real-time and batch processing can be justified. It is a multi-layer framework consisting of speed, batch, and serving layers.

Machine learning model creation and scoring

Lambda architecture can be used to create a system that can help build ML models while also providing a scoring system with real-time data. The key things needed to create ML models are clean, defined historical data, along with a training framework. This historical data can be provided from a batch layer in the Lambda framework, while the speed layer can provide real-time scoring based on the model created in the batch layer. The serving layer will combine real-time scoring along with any batch scoring needed to provide valuable insights for making business decisions. Let us look in detail at how such a system can be built.

Let us first look at the batch layer of this Lambda system. To collect data for a batch-based machine learning model training, data needs to be first collected from the transactional source system into a data lake. This can be done by periodically offloading data from the transactional system into a cheap storage sub-system like S3 or HDFS. Once the data is in the data lake, it is processed by a batch Spark job, which can cleanse the data and extract the features from the raw data. Features are nothing but valuable fields of interest in the right form in the dataset, which are used as input to the ML model training. As you can see, the batch layer in a Lambda-based system need not be a single batch job. It can be a series of batch jobs like data extraction from the source, cleansing it, and extracting features.

Once the features are ready, the next step is to train the ML model using a training framework like TensorFlow or PyTorch. Again, this is a batch process where a set of feature values is extracted at a given point in a batch and fed for model training. The model is incrementally built with this batch training, and finally, a versioned model is ready for use. This whole process of extraction of raw data from source, cleansing, feature extraction, and finally training can be repeated periodically in batches to generate different versions of the model as the data evolves. This process makes sure the model represents the changing nature of the data it is trained on. The following figure represents how data is extracted from the source system using a batch extraction job to the data lake, cleansed and features extracted using Spark and finally trained on an ML model training framework:

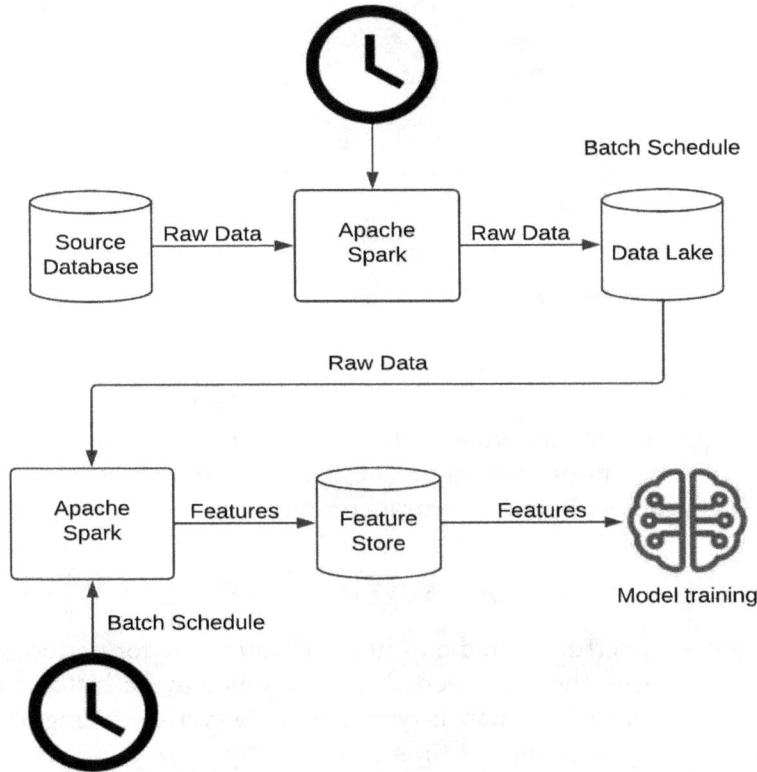

Figure 6.1: Batch extraction for feature engineering

Now, let us look at the speed layer of the Lambda architecture, which does the real-time scoring using the ML model created in the batch layer. Before we perform the scoring, the data generated in the transactional system needs to be processed in real-time and features extracted from it for use in scoring. To extract the data in real time from the transactional system, typically, change data capture technologies are used in conjunction with messaging technology like Kafka Connect and Kafka. The features are extracted using **Single Message Transforms (SMT)** and sent to the ML model for scoring. SMT is the functionality in Kafka that can help users apply business logic transformation to every message that arrives in Kafka. As seen in the batch layer, newer versions of the ML can be created as the data evolves, and the speed layer has to leverage the latest version of the model generated in the batch layer for scoring. The following figure presents how the speed layer gets continuous data for scoring from source systems:

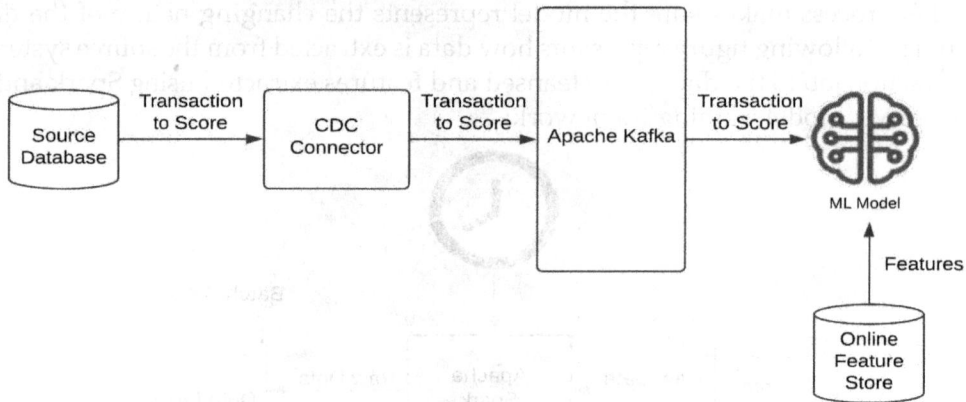

Figure 6.2: Real-time inferencing

The serving layer in the Lambda architecture combines the data from the batch layer and the speed layer and provides a single view of data to make business decisions. In this case, the batch layer will provide the accurate, well-formed historical view of data, and the speed layer will provide the real-time scored value of data. Combining these two, the serving layer provides users with the ability to make accurate predictions.

Real-time data analysis with historical bias

Data analysis becomes powerful when the right data is available for performing the analysis. Depending on the use cases, the data needed for analysis may be historical or current. We have seen that for historical analysis, data is typically made available using batch systems, and current data is made available using real-time systems. However, these need not be mutually exclusive. There can be use cases where having both curated historical data and real-time data can really enhance the ability to do analysis. A simple example of such a use case is data made available to contact center analysts at a bank. When a bank customer calls the contact center, for example, about a failed debit transaction, it is an opportunity for the bank to turn the negative experience into a positive one. At this point, having real-time data about the failed transaction will certainly help the contact center executive to address the customer's immediate concern. Having historical information about the customer's banking transactions may allow them to offer customized banking solutions like deposits and insurance.

Now, let us look at how to build the speed, batch, and serving layers for this system. Let us first look at what is needed to build the speed layer. On the target analytics system, we need two different tables that correspondingly store the real-time and batch data. Let us call them the speed table and batch table. The batch table is loaded every day once, and the speed table is continuously updated as the source transactional system gets the needed data.

As you have seen in the real-time data engineering pattern chapter, moving data from a transactional system to a real-time analytics system typically uses change data capture technology on the source database system. Every change occurring on the transactional system is written to the change log, and source Kafka connectors read this change log and write Kafka messages to a Kafka topic. The sink database connector for the analytics system then reads the Kafka message, converts it to a corresponding insert, update, or delete statement, and executes it on the target speed table.

The following figure demonstrates how source data is continuously moved to the speed table using the change data capture technology:

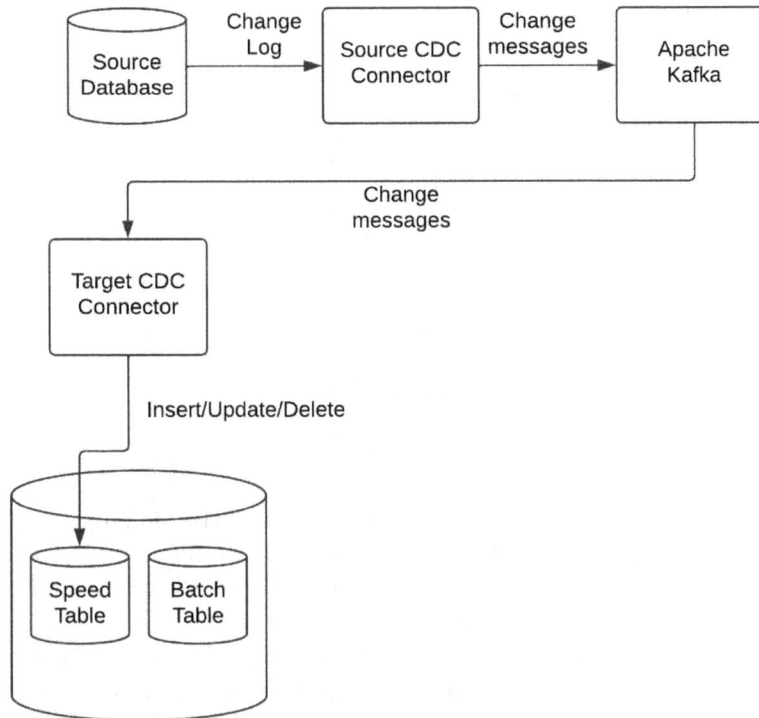

Figure 6.3: Speed layer using CDC

The batch table can be derived from the speed table at the end of the day. Typically, the batch table data is a lot more curated after processing and is not a direct copy of the speed table at the end of the day. At the end of every day, the speed table can be read by a Spark job, data curated and then inserted into the batch table. Following this, the speed table can be truncated to be made empty. This ensures duplicate data does not show up in the serving layer when the batch and the speed tables are combined. The following figure shows how the speed layer can be used as a source of data for the batch layer at the end of the day:

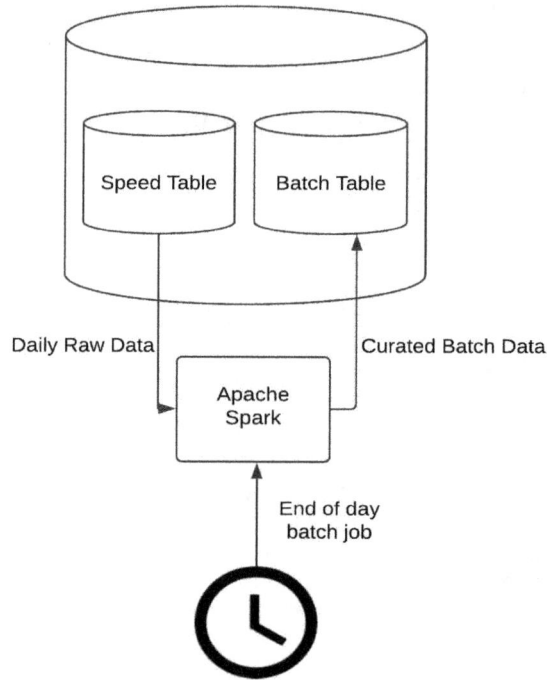

Figure 6.4: *Batch layer ingestion from speed layer*

Now, let us get to defining the serving layer for this system. The serving layer has to combine data from both speed and batch layers and make it available for analysis, and it can be built in two ways. The serving layer can either be logical or physical in the sense that it can either combine data from the existing tables using a view or create new tables and copy data from the batch and speed tables. The serving layer is made logical when the latency of serving is not very critical, as the data is combined on query time using a view and executed against the underlying batch and speed tables. However, if the serving latency needs to be very low, the data is combined and, if necessary, pre-aggregated into a serving table to ensure that at query time we do not need to process it again.

The following figure shows the physical serving layer built over the batch and speed layers:

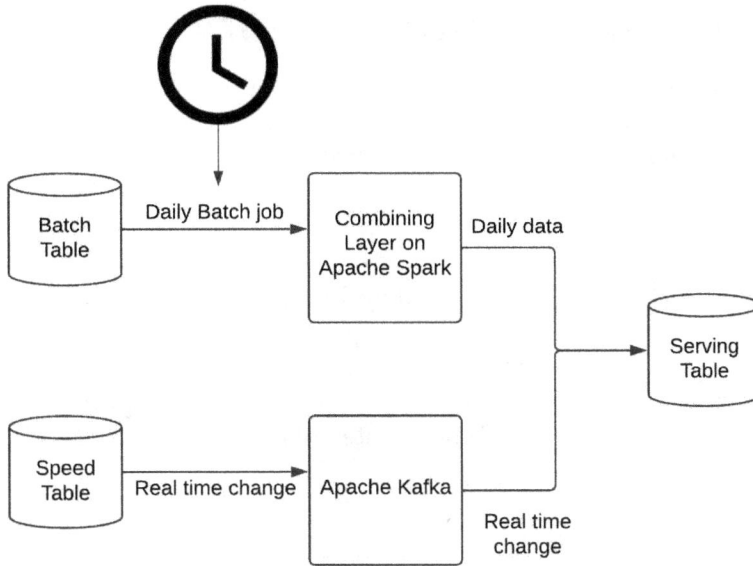

Figure 6.5: Physical data serving layer

The following figure shows the logical serving layer built over the batch and speed layers:

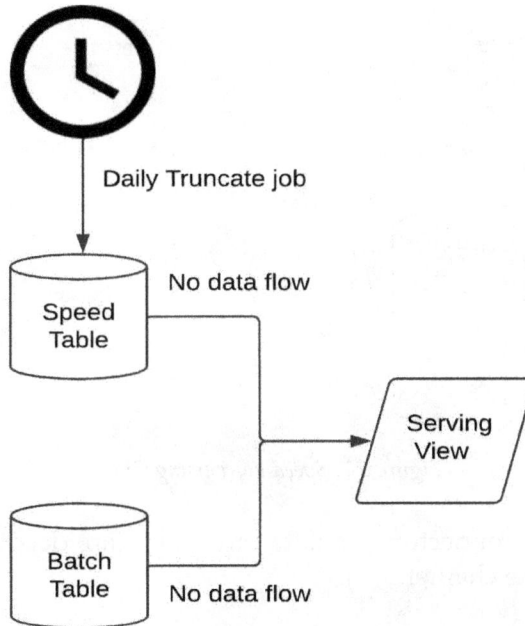

Figure 6.6: Logical data serving layer

Designing system with a Lambda pattern

In this section, let us design and build a Lambda system that can help do data analysis by combining historical data with real-time data. Let us use MySQL as the source system and ClickHouse as the target system for this demonstration.

Speed layer

The speed layer will be built by extracting data in real-time from MySQL using the source Kafka connector, which reads the change data capture logs. The data is then pushed to Kafka topics, which are then read by the ClickHouse sink connector. The sink connector then converts the Kafka messages to insert, update, and delete operations and populates the speed table in ClickHouse. The following figure demonstrates real-time data loading using Kafka from MySQL to ClickHouse:

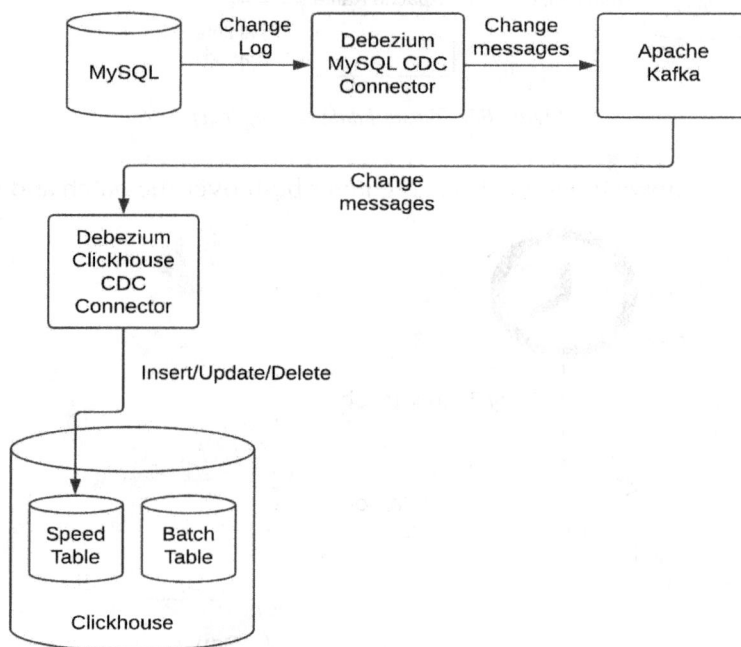

Figure 6.7: *Speed layer using CDC*

The steps to set up Kafka connectors for data movement are described in the section *Setup instructions* at the end of the chapter.

Batch layer

The batch layer will be built by extracting data on a daily basis from the MySQL table and processing it in an Apache Spark job to curate the data and ingest it into the batch table in

ClickHouse. Apache Spark uses JDBC connectors for MySQL and ClickHouse to extract and ingest data, respectively. Cron can be used to schedule the daily data movement batch job.

The following figure demonstrates the batch layer job moving data from MySQL to ClickHouse:

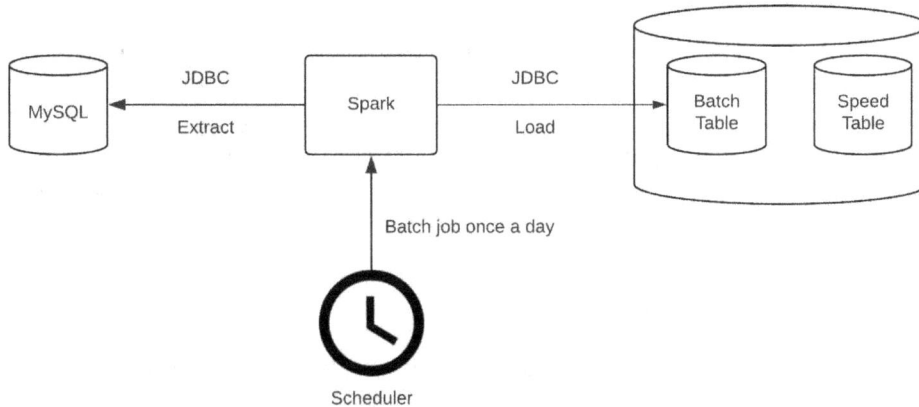

Figure 6.8: Batch layer with ETL

The system contains a MySQL table called **sales_table,** which contains the sales data for the month. The table has a **transaction_ts** column, which contains the timestamp of the transaction stored in the table. The Spark program reads one day's data at a time in batches, processes it, and loads it into a target ClickHouse database table for analysis.

This program needs JDBC drives for both MySQL and ClickHouse, which can be downloaded from their respective software download pages.

It also needs Spark to be installed on the system, which is done using the following command:

```
brew install apache-spark
```

Before creating the MySQL table, MySQL needs to be installed, and the service started. Steps for this are beyond the scope of this book and can be found in the documentation of MySQL. Similarly, ClickHouse needs to be installed or provisioned on the cloud before creating the database and tables.

The following steps and their code demonstrates how to move data from MySQL to ClickHouse for the batch layer:

1. Create a MySQL database first:
   ```
   CREATE DATABASE sales_db;
   ```

2. Connecting to the **sales_db** database and creating the MySQL table that stores the transactional sales data for a month:
   ```
   USE sales_db;
   CREATE TABLE sales_table (
       transaction_id INT AUTO_INCREMENT PRIMARY KEY,
   ```

```
        transaction_amount DECIMAL(10, 2) NOT NULL,
        product_id INT NOT NULL,
        location_id INT NOT NULL,
        transaction_ts TIMESTAMP NOT NULL
);
```

3. Load sample data into MySQL:

```
LOAD DATA INFILE '/tmp/sales_table_january_2024.csv' INTO TABLE sales_
table FIELDS TERMINATED BY ',' ENCLOSED BY '"' LINES TERMINAT-
ED BY '\n' IGNORE 1 LINES (transaction_id, transaction_amount, product_
id, location_id, transaction_ts);
```

4. Create a database on ClickHouse:

```
CREATE DATABASE sales_db;
```

5. Connect to the database **sales_db** and create a table in ClickHouse for analytics:

```
USE sales_db;
CREATE TABLE sales_table (
        transaction_id UInt32,
        transaction_amount Decimal(10, 2),
        product_id UInt32,
        location_id UInt32,
        transaction_ts Timestamp
)
ENGINE = MergeTree()
ORDER BY transaction_id;
```

6. Spark job to move data on a daily basis:

```
from pyspark.sql import SparkSession
# Create a SparkSession
spark = SparkSession.builder \
        .appName("MySQL to Clickhouse") \
        .getOrCreate()
# Setup the MySQL JDBC connection properties
mysql_url = "jdbc:mysql://localhost:3306/sales_db"
mysql_properties = {
        "user": "root",
        "password": "MyPassword",
        "driver": "com.mysql.cj.jdbc.Driver"
}
# Query to batch query the day's data in MySQL
```

```
query = "(SELECT transaction_id, transaction_amount, product_id, loca-
tion_id, transaction_date FROM sales_table where  transaction_ts> DATE_
SUB(CURRENT_TIMESTAMP, INTERVAL 10 SECOND)
# Read from MySQL daily data table into DataFrame
mysql_df = spark.read.jdbc(url=mysql_url, table=query, properties=mysql_
properties)
# Setup ClickHouse JDBC connection properties
clickhouse_url = "jdbc:clickhouse://url:port/default"
clickhouse_properties = {
    "user": "default",
    "password": "MyPassword",
    "ssl": "true",
    "driver": "com.clickhouse.jdbc.ClickHouseDriver"
}
# Write daily data from MySQL to Clickhouse in a batch
mysql_df.write \
    .mode("append") \
    .jdbc(url=clickhouse_url, table="sales_table", properties=clickhouse_
properties)
# Stop the SparkSession
spark.stop()
```

7. Run Spark job using cron:

```
crontab -e
0 22 * * * spark-submit --jars "/tmp/jdbc_dir/mysql-connector-j-9.0.0.
jar,/tmp/jdbc_dir/clickhouse-jdbc-0.7.0.jar" spark_program.py
```

Serving layer

The serving layer can be done by just creating a view between the speed and the batch tables in ClickHouse. The view can do a union of the two tables and present it as a single entity. If latency is of concern, the two tables can be loaded into a single table to avoid the union operation in the view. Eventually, the decision to develop the serving layer as a logical view or a materialized view will be dependent on the latency acceptable to the application. Any low latency use case such as real time fraud detection or recommendation systems will need a materialized view whereas traditional batch based BI or offline loyalty applications can be developed as a logical view.

Create a serving view in ClickHouse:

```
create view serving_view as select * from batch_table union select * from speed_
table
```

Technologies for Lambda systems

Technologies for Lambda systems are a combination of systems used for batch and real-time systems. As Lambda architectures leverage both batch and speed layers, the technologies needed are also very diverse. The serving layer also uses different technologies depending on whether it is a logical or physical serving layer.

Technologies for the batch layer work with large amounts of data at a time, given that they collect data for the batch duration and then operate on it at once. As a result, most technologies commonly used for batch processing are the ones that can operate on large-scale data without performance bottlenecks and have the capability to horizontally scale out as more data is batched. Historically, Hadoop MapReduce was a very common way of doing batch data processing, as MapReduce jobs could consume and process large amounts of data reliably without job failures. The MapReduces jobs using HDFS as storage technology for both temporary and persistent data. While building modern systems, data engineers realized MapReduce is not very efficient with its use of resources and switching to Apache Spark for executing batch processing jobs. Spark with its ability to restart jobs from failure points is a much more performant and reliable execution framework for batch processing jobs. On the storage front object storage is gaining popularity over HDFS as the default storage system for batch processing.

Batch jobs need to be scheduled and orchestrated based on the batching frequency. Apache Airflow has emerged as a strong technology choice for its versatility to work with various systems and also its ability to model workflows as **directed acyclic graphs (DAG)**. For simple use cases which do not require complex job orchestration Linux Cron scheduler proves itself to be a handy tool to schedule batch jobs.

The speed layer needs to achieve a very high throughput streaming with very low latency for message delivery and hence technologies like Apache Kafka, Apache Flink, and Spark streaming are very popular. Among these, Apache Kafka is the most popular streaming technology due to its wide availability of connectors for every type of source and sync system. Apache Kafka provides at least one message delivery semantics, thereby simplifying application development for real-time systems to a great extent.

The speed layer may also need databases that can provide very high throughput and low latency access. Databases like Redis, Couchbase, and Aerospike are very popular with real-time systems because they provide very fast access to data for processing. If the real-time system is processing small amounts of data that can be fully stored in primary memory, then a database like Redis which is an in-memory cache is preferred. However, for larger use cases where the data needs to be served fast from primary memory but also needs to be persisted to secondary storage due to its large size database like Couchbase which is a persistent data store with an integrated cache is preferred.

The serving layer can either be physical or logical. If the serving layer is logic, it usually does not need any additional technology, and it is created as a view over the existing speed and batch tables. However, if the serving layer is physical, the data from the speed and batch layers needs to be combined. To do this, we typically need both Apache Spark and Kafka to combine both speed and batch tables.

The following figure shows a word cloud of data layers in Lambda architecture and the technologies that are suited for each layer:

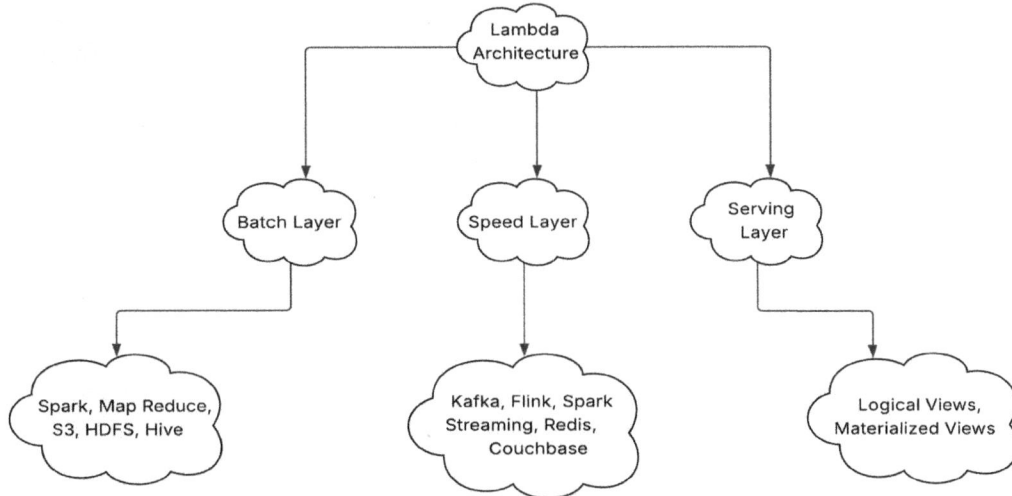

Figure 6.9: Data layers in Lambda architecture and its suitable technologies

Real-world examples

The following section will discuss a real-world example leveraging Lambda architecture in Fintech domain. The solution leverages the speed and batch layers of the Lambda architecture to provide a current and historical view of customer transaction data to bank support analysts. The unique architecture enables support functions as well as cross-selling possibilities via the same system.

Fintech

Lambda pattern can be used in Fintech to build sophisticated customer support systems that can support loyalty and marketing plays as well. One such example is the customer transaction visibility system that is used by the bank's contact center support staff to provide timely support to customers. Given the support system provides the bank staff an opportunity to connect with the bank's customers, it can be leveraged to provide a positive experience by offering customized banking solutions to the customer, leveraging their historical transaction information. Lambda architecture is a perfect solution for this problem by leveraging the speed layer to provide real-time transaction information to the contact center staff while using the batch layer to provide a historical view of customers' transactions.

Let us first look at how the speed layer can be built for such a customer support system. Typically banking transactions are executed on mainframe-based systems for their reliability and uptime. Data needs to be extracted in real-time from these mainframe-based systems into a secondary system like Oracle or DB2 LUW for the bank contact center staff to query it. This can be done with either Kafka and Kafka CDC connectors for the mainframe or by leveraging tools provided by IBM for extracting data from the mainframe, like IBM Change Data Capture. IBM CDC is commercial off the shelf software from IBM that can extract data from various data sources including DB2 on mainframe. Once the data is extracted by reading the change logs on the mainframe system, it is ingested into Oracle or DB2 LUW database using Insert, Update, Delete statements.

The following figure demonstrates the speed layer architecture:

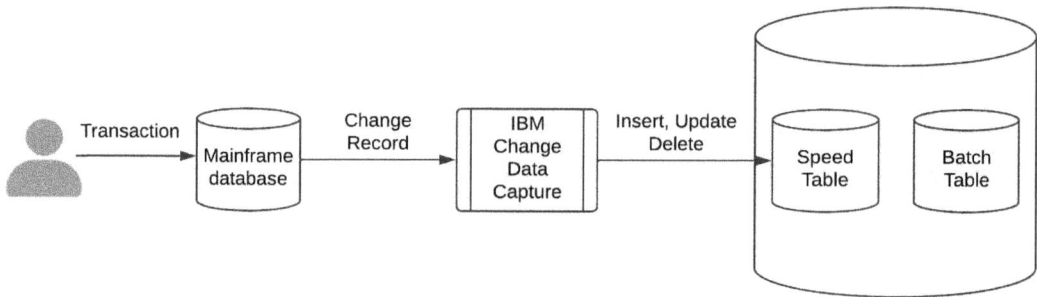

Figure 6.10: *Speed layer for mainframe offload*

Next, the batch layer for this system can be built by extracting daily data from the real-time speed layer and ingesting it into the batch table before truncating the speed layer table. You may note here we are not extracting data from the mainframe system again to create the batch layer, but instead using the speed layer for an incremental population of the batch layer. This type of incremental population is called the forward population of the table. The only time the mainframe system will be used for loading the batch layer is for something called back population which can be done using tools like IBM InfoSphere DataStage. Back population is the process of loading historical data into a table.

The reason we do not use the mainframe system during forward population is that the mainframe cost is typically based on **millions of instructions per second (MIPS)** and every time data is read from the mainframe MIPS cost increases. Thus, using the real-time speed layer as a source for the batch table reduces the cost of the overall system. MIPS cost can be a significant cost in the overall system, and reducing it by leveraging the following architecture can lead to impactful cost savings for the overall project.

The following figure shows the architecture of the batch layer:

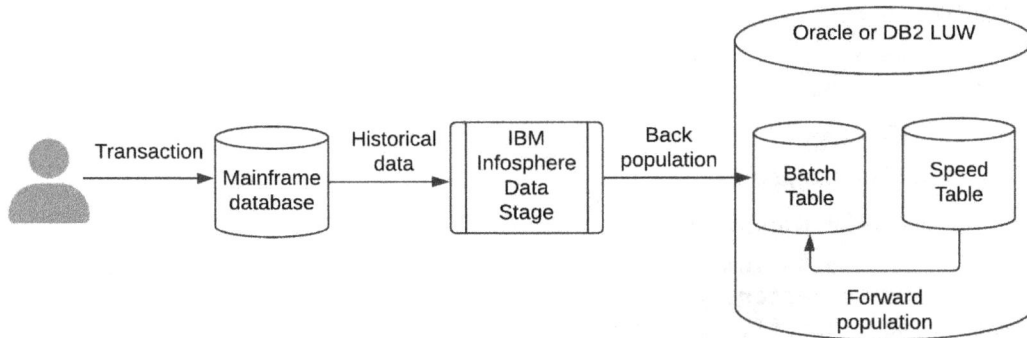

Figure 6.11: Batch layer for mainframe offload

Finally, the serving layer can be a simple view over the speed and batch tables in Oracle or DB2 LUW, which the contact support staff can access to view both the historical data and real-time transaction data together.

Kafka setup instructions

The instructions to set up the Kafka source and sink connectors for MySQL and ClickHouse, respectively. Follow these steps:

1. Download and install Kafka cluster:

```
wget https://dlcdn.apache.org/kafka/3.9.0/kafka_2.12-3.9.0.tgz
tar -xvf kafka_2.12-3.9.0.tgz
mv kafka_2.12-3.9.0 /opt/kafka
cd /opt/kafka
```

2. Start Zookeeper and Kafka Broker:

```
/opt/kafka/bin/zookeeper-server-start.sh        /opt/kafka/config/zookeeper.
properties
/opt/kafka/bin/kafka-server-start.sh /opt/kafka/config/server.properties
```

3. Create Kafka topic:

```
/opt/kafka/bin/kafka-topics.sh \
--create -topic <topic> \
--bootstrap-server <broker-node-list> \
--replication-factor <num-replicas>
--partitions <partition-count> \
```

4. Download the MySQL Kafka connector and configure:

```
wget            https://repo1.maven.org/maven2/io/debezium/debezium-connec-
tor-mysql/ 3.0.6.Final/debezium-connector-mysql-3.0.6.Final.jar
```

```
mkdir -p /opt/kafka/plugins/mysql

tar  -xvzf  debezium-connector-mysql-3.0.6.Final.jar    -C  /opt/kafka/
plugins/mysql
```

5. Start Kafka connect:

```
/opt/kafka/bin/connect-standalone.sh connector.properties
```

6. Create MySQL Kafka connector config file:

```
{ "name": "debezium-mysql-connector", "config": { "connector.class": "io.
debezium.connector.mysql.MySqlConnector", "tasks.max": "1", "database.
hostname": "host", "database.port": "port", "database.user": "debezium",
"database.password": "password", "database.server.id": "1", "database.
server.name": "mysql_server", "database.include.list": "database-name",
"table.include.list": "table-name", "database.history.kafka.bootstrap.
servers": "ip:port", "database.history.kafka.topic": "topic-name", "in-
clude.schema.changes": "true", "snapshot.mode": "initial" } }
```

7. Deploy MySQL source connector:

```
curl -X POST -H "Content-Type: application/json" \ --data @<mysql-config-
file> \ http://ip:port/connectors
```

8. Create ClickHouse Kafka connector config file:

```
{ "name": "clickhouse-sink-connector", "config": { "connector.class": "com.
altinity.clickhouse.sink.connector.ClickHouseSinkConnector",     "tasks.
max": "1", "topics": "<kafka_topic_name>", "clickhouse.url": "http://
host:port", "clickhouse.database": "database-name", "clickhouse.user-
name": "username", "clickhouse.password": "password", "clickhouse.table.
name": "clickhouse-table", "key.converter": "org.apache.kafka.connect.
storage.StringConverter", "value.converter": "org.apache.kafka.connect.
json.JsonConverter", "value.converter.schemas.enable": "false", "batch.
size": "1000", "insert.mode": "insert" } }
```

9. Deploy ClickHouse Kafka sink connector:

```
curl  -X  POST  -H  "Content-Type:  application/json"  \  --data  @<click-
house-config-file> \ http://ip:port/connectors
```

Conclusion

In this chapter, we covered common use cases for Lambda architecture-based systems followed by designing a Lambda architecture for combining historical data from the batch layer with the real-time data from the speed layer to perform data analysis. We also saw how the Lambda system is implemented using various technologies that combine technologies from batch-based systems and real-time systems together. We also learned about a few examples of Lambda-based systems, batching systems in Fintech, where we understood the architecture of these examples and saw how Lambda architecture can help build unique solutions in this domain.

In the next chapter, we will look at ETL and ELT design patterns, which are the most fundamental data engineering patterns. We also review use cases and industry examples of systems using ELT and ETL in various domains.

Questions

1. How can a batch layer be built using a speed layer in many Lambda systems?

2. Design and implement a Lambda architecture-based system for payment fraud detection.

3. What are the two different types of serving layers, and how do they differ?

4. Why are Lambda architecture systems expensive to implement?

Join our Discord space

Join our Discord workspace for latest updates, offers, tech happenings around the world, new releases, and sessions with the authors:

https://discord.bpbonline.com

CHAPTER 7
ETL and ELT

Introduction

This chapter examines the operation of the **extract, transform, and load** (ETL) and **extract, load, and transform** (ELT) data patterns. It makes the user familiar with the use cases that ETL and ELT data engineering patterns can help solve. This chapter will also explore the design of a system utilizing both ETL and ELT patterns on open-source and cloud technologies and demonstrate a sample application along with code snippets. We will also cover some examples of ETL and ETL patterns in use.

Structure

This chapter will cover the following topics:

- Use cases for ETL and ELT patterns
- Designing ETL and ELT system
- Technologies for ETL and ELT systems
- Real-world examples

Objectives

By the end of this chapter, readers will gain an in-depth understanding of ETL and ELT data engineering patterns. You will also be able to design and build data pipelines using the ETL and ELT patterns and write code to implement the design. You will know the technical stack to use for creating pipelines that do ETL or ELT. Finally, you will also understand the real-world use cases where this pattern can be used with examples from the banking domain.

Use cases for ETL and ELT patterns

ETL is probably the second most common data engineering pattern after the batch pattern. Nearly all the legacy data warehousing systems were built leveraging this data engineering pattern, where the data from the source transactional system is extracted, transformed, and loaded into the data warehouse. More modern data warehouses also leverage the ELT pattern, and the power of the database itself can be used for the transformation of data after the initial ingestion. Real-time systems, in particular, leverage the ELT pattern as there is little possibility of transforming data in real-time.

ETL in data warehousing

Data warehouses have existed since the late 1980s with the advent of databases that could handle large amounts of data. The data warehouses do not store their data from applications, but instead, they source data from upstream transactional databases. To source this data from upstream transactional systems, there needs to be an extract process that fetches the necessary data from the transactional systems. This extract process needs to account for one-time and continuous data movement from source systems to the data warehouse. This forms the extract part of the ETL pattern.

Once the data is extracted from the source system, it is rarely loaded into the data warehouse as is. The data needs to be enriched in various forms before it is ready for consumption in the data warehouse. This enrichment process forms the transform process of the ETL pattern. For example, the data needs to be denormalized and modeled into a Snowflake or star schema before it reaches the data warehouse. A star schema is a data model where a centralized fact table is connected to multiple dimension tables, whereas the Snowflake data model is a variation of the star schema that has dimension tables further normalized into sub-tables. It also needs to go through a data cleansing process, which standardizes the data for reporting purposes. Data cleansing may include address sanitizations, removal of private information, improving data quality, etc.

The data transformation process is followed by loading the data into the data warehouses. Data loading can include both bulk loading for the back population and trickle feeding of new changes for the forward population. Depending on whether data loading is for the back population or the forward population, different loading technologies are used.

Note: ETL is a higher-level pattern. It can internally use other base patterns like batching and micro-batching patterns.

For example, ETL almost always uses batch or micro-batch patterns because the transformation of data is a computationally intensive process that cannot be done on the fly. It is more efficient to batch a set of records and then transform them together. Similarly, data loading in ETL is also almost always done using batch or micro-batch patterns.

The following figure shows data loading from a transactional database to a data warehouse using transformation in Apache Spark:

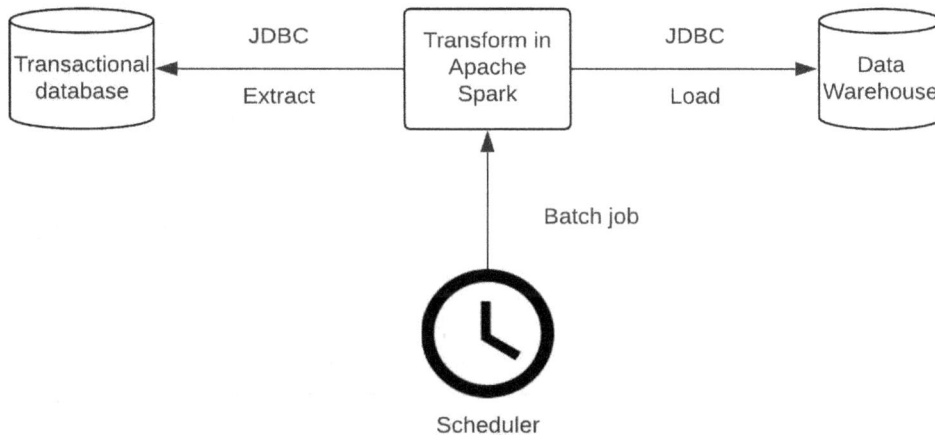

Figure 7.1: ETL with Apache Spark

ELT in clickstream analysis

Analysis of clickstream data from mobile applications and websites is critical in understanding consumer behavior. This information is used to identify user search and buying patterns, which is then fed into recommendation engines to generate appropriate ad and promotion plans for the customer. On any reasonably successful mobile application or website, the clickstream information generated is massive, and it is real-time. This data needs to be captured right away for processing.

The raw clickstream information needs to be processed and stored before it can be useful. For example, it is important to know the fall-off rates from a particular webpage in a website and to do that, the clickstream information from many users over time needs to be aggregated. However, doing this in real-time is challenging, and aggregating before storing the data will slow down the data ingestion of the clickstream data. This problem can be solved by using the ELT pattern, where the data is ingested as it arrives in the database. The transformation or aggregation is done post-loading the data into the database. Modern MPP database engines are very efficient at doing such transformations within the database.

The raw clickstream information can be extracted from the application and loaded into the data warehouse using technologies like Apache Kafka and Kafka Connect. The stream of data is ingested as is without any transformation to make sure the ingestion rate catches up with the data generation rate. Also, performing any real-time transformation on Kafka is very computationally expensive, though **Single Message Transforms** (**SMT**) allow lightweight transformations on the fly. SMTs are suitable for simple data conversions on single messages like case conversions, casting to different data types or rounding up data. It is not suitable for complex transformations like aggregations or computationally intensive activities like data cleansing.

The following figure shows the ELT pattern with the transformation happening within the data warehouse after data loading:

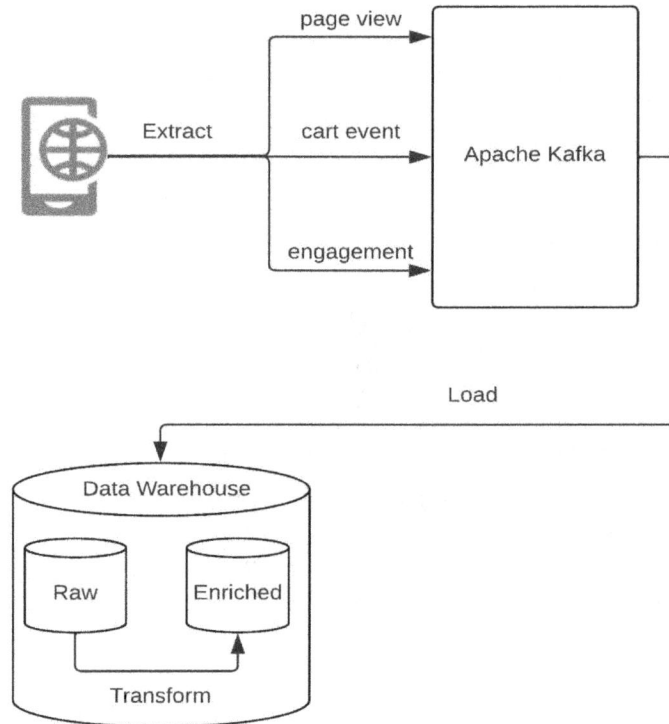

Figure 7.2: ELT pattern

Designing ETL and ELT system

In this section, let us design and build a system using Lambda architecture with ETL and ELT patterns. The ETL pattern will support the back population of data, while the ELT pattern will be used for the forward population process. This system can help do data analysis by combining historical data with real-time data. Let us use MySQL as the source system and ClickHouse as the target system for this demonstration. Apache Spark will be used for the transformation step in this ETL process.

The following is a high-level comparison of the back and forward population of data:

Data loading use case	Back population	Forward population
Ingestion type	Batch	Batch and real-time
Data characteristic	Past data	Current and future data
Common use case	Migration or for data correction	New data ingestion

Table 7.1: Comparison of back and forward population of data

Forward population using ELT

The forward population of the speed layer table will be built by extracting data in real-time from MySQL using the source Kafka connector that reads change data capture logs. Forward population involves bringing the new data that is being generated into the system. The data generated is then pushed to Kafka topics, which are then read by the ClickHouse sink connector. The data is pushed as is, and no transformation is applied to keep the data ingestion into Kafka in real-time.

The ClickHouse sink connector then converts the Kafka messages to insert, update and delete operations and populates the speed table in ClickHouse. There is no data transformation applied in this stage as well because we need the consumption from Kafka to keep up with the data generation.

The following figure demonstrates real-time data loading using Kafka from MySQL to ClickHouse without any transformation, showcasing the ELT pattern:

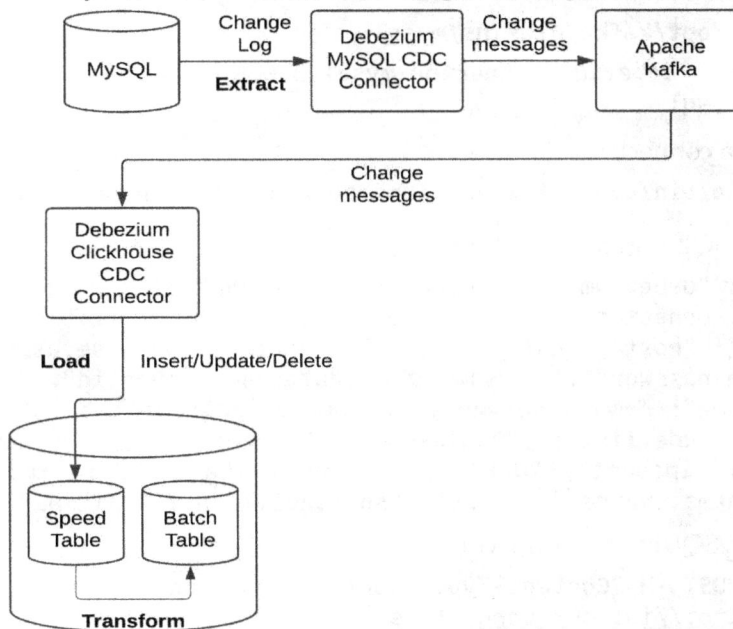

Figure 7.3: Forward data population

The following instructions provide the steps needed to set up the forward population of data from MySQL to ClickHouse using Apache Kafka:

1. Download and install the Kafka cluster:

```
wget https://dlcdn.apache.org/kafka/3.9.0/kafka_2.12-3.9.0.tgz
tar -xvf kafka_2.12-3.9.0.tgz
mv kafka_2.12-3.9.0 /opt/kafka
cd /opt/kafka
```

2. Start Zookeeper and Kafka broker:

```
/opt/kafka/bin/zookeeper-server-start.sh       /opt/kafka/config/zookeeper.
properties
/opt/kafka/bin/kafka-server-start.sh /opt/kafka/config/server.properties
```

3. Create Kafka topic:

```
/opt/kafka/bin/kafka-topics.sh \
--create -topic <topic> \
--bootstrap-server <broker-node-list> \
--replication-factor <num-replicas>
--partitions <partition-count> \
```

4. Download MySQL Kafka connector and configure:

```
wget          https://repo1.maven.org/maven2/io/debezium/debezium-connec-
tor-mysql/ 3.0.6.Final/debezium-connector-mysql-3.0.6.Final.jar
mkdir -p /opt/kafka/plugins/mysql
tar  -xvzf  debezium-connector-mysql-3.0.6.Final.jar    -C  /opt/kafka/
plugins/mysql
```

5. Start Kafka connect:

```
/opt/kafka/bin/connect-standalone.sh connector.properties
```

6. Create MySQL Kafka connector config file:

```
{ "name": "debezium-mysql-connector", "config": { "connector.class": "io.
debezium.connector.mysql.MySqlConnector", "tasks.max": "1", "database.
hostname": "host", "database.port": "port", "database.user": "debezium",
"database.password": "password", "database.server.id": "1", "database.
server.name": "mysql_server", "database.include.list": "database-name",
"table.include.list":  "table-name",  "database.history.kafka.bootstrap.
servers": "ip:port", "database.history.kafka.topic": "topic-name", "in-
clude.schema.changes": "true", "snapshot.mode": "initial" } }
```

7. Deploy MySQL source connector:

```
curl -X POST -H "Content-Type: application/json" \ --data @<mysql-config-
file> \ http://ip:port/connectors
```

8. Create ClickHouse Kafka connector config file:

```
{ "name": "clickhouse-sink-connector", "config": { "connector.class": "com.
altinity.clickhouse.sink.connector.ClickHouseSinkConnector",      "tasks.
max": "1", "topics": "<kafka_topic_name>", "clickhouse.url": "http://
host:port", "clickhouse.database": "database-name", "clickhouse.user-
name": "username", "clickhouse.password": "password", "clickhouse.table.
name": "clickhouse-table", "key.converter": "org.apache.kafka.connect.
storage.StringConverter", "value.converter": "org.apache.kafka.connect.
json.JsonConverter", "value.converter.schemas.enable": "false", "batch.
size": "1000", "insert.mode": "insert" } }
```

9. Deploy ClickHouse Kafka sink connector:

```
curl -X POST -H "Content-Type: application/json" \ --data @<click-
house-config-file> \ http://ip:port/connectors
```

Backward population using ETL

The backwards population of data in the batch layer will be built by extracting data on a daily basis from the MySQL table and transforming it into an Apache Spark job to curate the data and ingest it into the batch table in ClickHouse. Back population is the process of loading the historical data into the system. Apache Spark uses JDBC connectors for MySQL and ClickHouse to extract and ingest data, respectively. Cron can be used to schedule the daily data movement batch job.

The following figure demonstrates the batch layer job moving data from MySQL to ClickHouse:

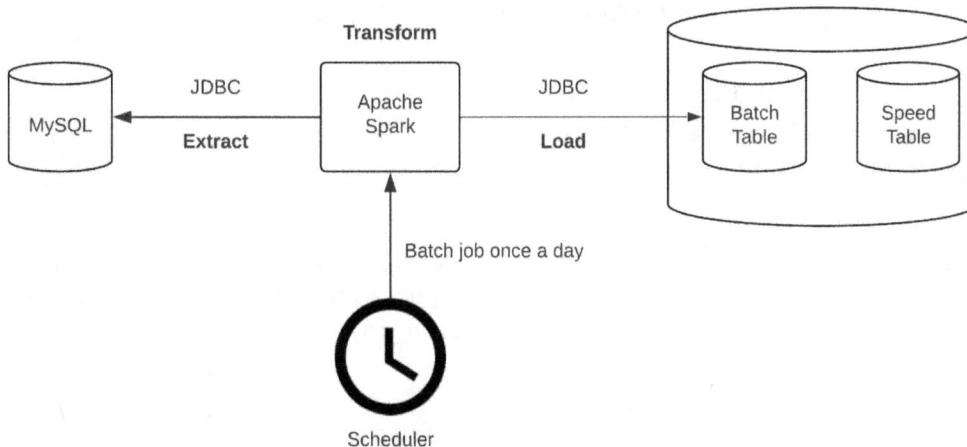

Figure 7.4: Batch layer job moving data from MySQL to ClickHouse

The system contains a MySQL table called **sales_table**, which contains the sales data for the month. The table has a **transaction_date** column, which contains the date of the transaction stored in the table. The Spark program reads one day's data at a time in batches, processes it, and loads it into a target ClickHouse database table for analysis.

This program needs JDBC drives for both MySQL and ClickHouse, which can be downloaded from their respective software download pages. It also needs Spark to be installed on the system, which is done using the following command. In the ETL steps, we use JDBC to extract data from MySQL, then transform the data in Spark using a simple rounding transformation, and finally load the data back into ClickHouse using JDBC. Data warehouses typically support bulk loading capabilities for loading large amounts of data during the ETL process, but to keep the example simple, we are using JDBC as the technology for loading data.

```
brew install apache-spark
```

Before creating the MySQL table, MySQL needs to be installed, and the service started. Steps for this are beyond the scope of this book and can be found in the documentation of MySQL. Similarly, ClickHouse needs to be installed or provisioned on the cloud before creating the database and tables.

The steps to do so are as follows:

1. Create a MySQL database first:

   ```
   CREATE DATABASE sales_db;
   ```

2. Connecting to the **sales_db** database and creating the MySQL table that stores the transactional sales data for a month:

   ```
   USE sales_db;
   CREATE TABLE sales_table (
       transaction_id INT AUTO_INCREMENT PRIMARY KEY,
       transaction_amount DECIMAL(10, 2) NOT NULL,
       product_id INT NOT NULL,
       location_id INT NOT NULL,
       transaction_date DATE NOT NULL
   );
   ```

3. Load sample data into MySQL:

   ```
   LOAD DATA INFILE '/tmp/sales_table_january_2024.csv' INTO TABLE sales_table FIELDS TERMINATED BY ',' ENCLOSED BY '"' LINES TERMINATED BY '\n' IGNORE 1 LINES (transaction_id, transaction_amount, product_id, location_id, transaction_date);
   ```

4. Create a database on ClickHouse:

   ```
   CREATE DATABASE sales_db;
   ```

5. Connect to the database **sales_db** and create a table in ClickHouse for analytics:

   ```
   USE sales_db;
   CREATE TABLE sales_table (
       transaction_id UInt32,
       transaction_amount Decimal(10, 2),
   ```

```
    product_id UInt32,
    location_id UInt32,
    transaction_ts Timestamp
)
ENGINE = MergeTree()
ORDER BY transaction_id;
```

6. Spark job to move data daily by applying a simple transformation of getting the absolute value of the transaction amount before loading it into the data warehouse:

```
from pyspark.sql import SparkSession
# Create a SparkSession
spark = SparkSession.builder \
    .appName("MySQL to Clickhouse") \
    .getOrCreate()
# Setup the MySQL JDBC connection properties
mysql_url = "jdbc:mysql://localhost:3306/sales_db"
mysql_properties = {
    "user": "root",
    "password": "MyPassword",
    "driver": "com.mysql.cj.jdbc.Driver"
}
# Query to batch query the day's data in MySQL
query = "(SELECT transaction_id, abs(transaction_amount), product_id, lo-
cation_id, transaction_date FROM sales_table where DAYOFMONTH(transac-
tion_date)=DAYOFMONTH(CURDATE()) limit 5) AS tmp"
# Read from MySQL daily data table into DataFrame
mysql_df = spark.read.jdbc(url=mysql_url, table=query, properties=mysql_
properties)
# Setup ClickHouse JDBC connection properties
clickhouse_url = "jdbc:clickhouse://url:port/default"
clickhouse_properties = {
    "user": "default",
    "password": "MyPassword",
    "ssl": "true",
    "driver": "com.clickhouse.jdbc.ClickHouseDriver"
}
# Write daily data from MySQL to Clickhouse in a batch
mysql_df.write \
```

```
    .mode("append") \
    .jdbc(url=clickhouse_url, table="sales_table", properties=clickhouse_
properties)
# Stop the SparkSession
spark.stop()
```

7. Run Spark job using cron:

```
crontab -e
0 22 * * * spark-submit --jars "/tmp/jdbc_dir/mysql-connector-j-9.0.0.
jar,/tmp/jdbc_dir/clickhouse-jdbc-0.7.0.jar" spark_program.py
```

Technologies for ETL and ELT systems

Technologies for ETL and ELT systems are like the ones used for batch, micro-batch, and real-time systems. The reason for this is that ETL and ELT systems underneath leverage batch, micro-batch, or real-time data patterns.

ETL systems are typically built using the batch or micro-batch pattern. The reason for this is that it is rarely possible to do more than simple transformations in real-time. Since ETL uses batch or micro-batch patterns, it should be able to deal with large amounts of data that were batched together. Historically, Hadoop MapReduce was a very common way of doing batch data processing, as MapReduce jobs could consume and process large amounts of data reliably without job failures. The MapReduces jobs using HDFS as storage technology for both temporary and persistent data. While building modern systems, data engineers realized MapReduce is not very efficient with its use of resources and switching to Apache Spark for executing batch processing jobs. Spark, with its ability to restart jobs from failure points, is a much more performant and reliable execution framework for batch-processing jobs. On the storage front, object storage is gaining popularity over HDFS as the default storage system for batch processing.

Also, ETL jobs need to be scheduled and orchestrated based on the batching frequency. Apache Airflow has emerged as a strong technology choice for its versatility to work with various systems and also its ability to model workflows as **directed acyclic graphs** (**DAG**). Since ETL jobs can have a dependency on one another, DAG is a great way to represent them. For simple use cases that do not require complex job orchestration, the Linux Cron scheduler proves itself to be a handy tool for scheduling batch jobs.

There are several legacy commercial off-the-shelf ETL products available, like IBM DataStage, Informatica, etc., while new entrants have come up in this space, namely *Fivetran*, *Hevo Data*, and *Airbyte*. These ETL tools are more popularly used when data has to be extracted not only from databases but also from our sources, like business software such as ERP and CRM systems, due to their rich connector ecosystem. These tools typically combine all capabilities needed from an ETL process and do not require separate data extraction, orchestration, or loading tools.

The following table lists a high-level comparison of Fivetran, Airbyte and Informatica:

Dimension	Informatica	Fivetran	Airbyte
Cost	High	Medium	Medium to Low
Open-source	No	No	Yes
Deployment model	SaaS, hosted on cloud, on-prem	SaaS	SaaS, hosted on cloud, on-prem
Use case	ETL, ELT, governance, master data management	ETL	ETL and data integration

Table 7.2: Comparison of Fivetran, Airbyte and Informatica

The ELT pattern mostly leverages a mixture of real-time and batch patterns. For extracting and loading the data into the database, it typically uses the real-time pattern to ingest the data as it is generated, but uses the batch pattern to transform the data after it is loaded. As a result of the real-time extract and load, ELT systems need low-latency message delivery, and hence, technologies like Apache Kafka, Apache Flink, and Spark streaming are very popular. Among these, Apache Kafka is the most popular streaming technology due to its wide availability of connectors for every type of source and sync system. Apache Kafka provides at least one message delivery semantics, thereby simplifying application development for real-time systems to a great extent. However, due to the limitations of the transformations that can be done with the SMT, the transformation steps have to be delayed to post-data loading.

Real-world examples

The following section will provide a real-world example from the banking industry.

Let us discuss the details in the following section.

Banking

ETL process is commonly used by banks to build their reporting systems. Banks have multiple lines of business, like credit, forex, commercial banking, retail banking, insurance, etc., and these lines of business have their own data stored in their respective data marts. The enterprise data warehouse consumes data from these data marts and collates it to provide things like *Customer 360*, which is a single view of the customer. To achieve this, the data from the individual line of business data marts needs to be transformed and combined with data from other data sources.

One of the challenges of combining data from these various lines of business data marts into a single enterprise data warehouse is the variation in the data models and formats at the individual data marts. Some data marts may be relational, while others may be document models. The data may also be in flat files in CSV, parquet, and other file formats. Combining all this into a single data warehouse is challenging. This is where the ETL process comes in handy, extracting data from these various data sources and using a transformation framework to standardize the data into a single data model and format, and then loading this transformed data into the data warehouse.

Let us look at an example architecture where data from multiple data sources is extracted, merged, transformed, and loaded into a database warehouse. The data from various lines of business data marts, object storage, flat files, etc., is extracted and transformed using Apache Spark, followed by loading it into the data warehouse.

The following figure shows how data from multiple LoB data marts is transformed to generate the reportable data in the data warehouse:

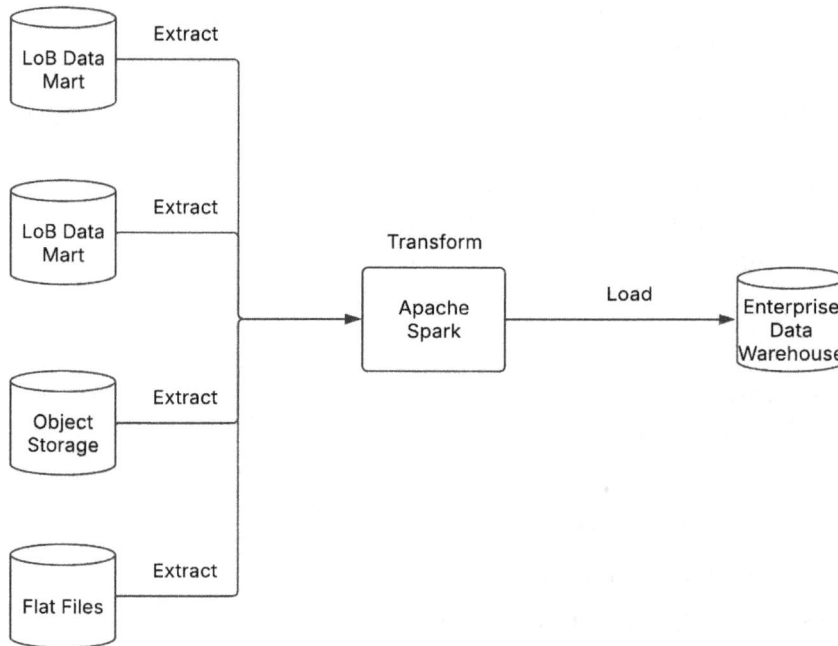

Figure 7.5: ETL in banking

However, banks also use ELT processes where applicable. One of the cases where transformation before loading is not possible is fraud detection. For real-time fraud detection, the data must be immediately available for scoring as the transaction is occurring. The delay injected by the transformation step is not acceptable, as this can delay the transaction or, worse, let the fraud happen. Hence, the data is loaded into the database in real-time and made available for scoring.

The data may need to be transformed later for doing feature engineering on the real-time transaction data upon which it is extracted and feature-engineered. Extracting features can be a complex operation that is not possible to achieve in single message transforms in a real-time system. Feature engineering typically also needs data from other data sources, such as look-up tables and other feature tables. This combination of current transaction data and external data is difficult to achieve in a single message transformation as well.

The following figure demonstrates how the real-time pattern is used to do the EL part of the ELT process, and the data is then transformed for feature engineering:

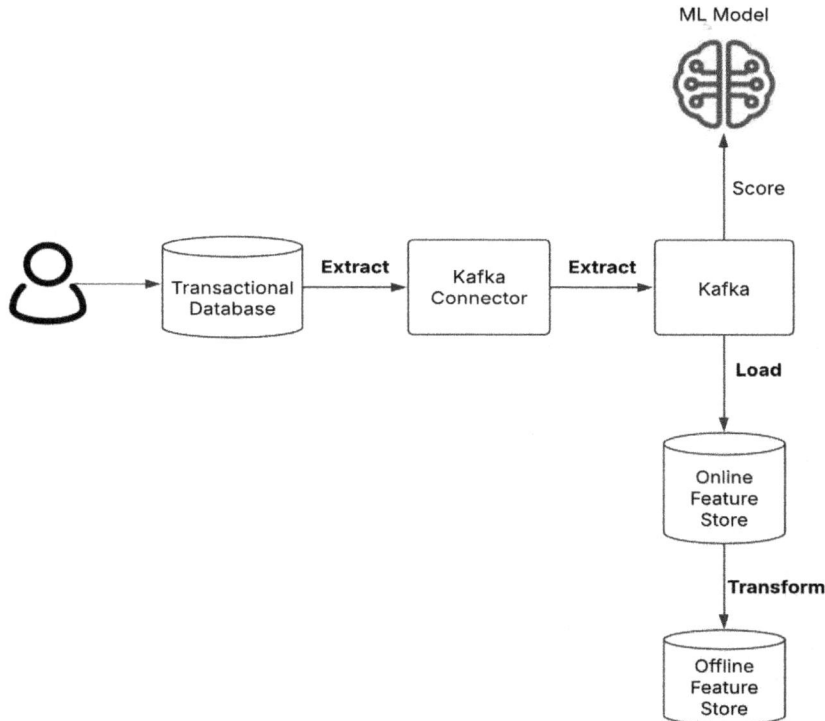

Figure 7.6: Real-time pattern for ELT

Conclusion

In this chapter, we covered common use cases for both ETL and ELT data patterns-based systems, followed by designing a system that uses ETL for the batch layer and ELT for the speed layer in a Lambda system. We saw how the ETL and ELT patterns are implemented using various technologies that are commonly used in batch and real-time systems. We also learned about an industry example in banking, which used both ETL and ELT processes to provide a 360 customer view of data and support fraud detection.

In the next chapter, we will look at the fundamentals of data before looking into data storage and serving patterns.

Questions

1. What critical factors decide if we need to use an ETL pattern or an ELT pattern?
2. Why are many modern systems leaning towards the ELT data pattern?

3. Design and implement an ETL system that cleanses customer addresses before loading the data into the data warehouse.

4. Explain how you can leverage both ETL and ELT data patterns for building a retail recommendation system.

Join our Discord space

Join our Discord workspace for latest updates, offers, tech happenings around the world, new releases, and sessions with the authors:

https://discord.bpbonline.com

CHAPTER 8
Data Fundamentals

Introduction

In this chapter, the readers will understand the various data types and mechanisms used by data engineers to represent and organize that data. We will discuss this further using an e-commerce application as an example to understand the fundamentals of the data. The readers will also be introduced to the concept of data modeling and the structuredness of the data.

Structure

The following topics will be covered in this chapter:

- E-commerce application example
- Structured data and tabular data representation
- Semi-structured data and JSON data format
- Unstructured data and binary data format
- Transactional and analytical data

Objectives

By the end of this chapter, we will be able to understand how to map the domain-specific data concepts to appropriate data types, define the structure of the data, and represent our data in the specific format required for your application. We will also gain the conceptual understanding of transactional and analytical data.

E-commerce application example

Let us consider the example of an e-commerce application where one seller wants to display their products on their website, and multiple users will perform actions like registering, logging in, purchasing, returning, asking for help, etc. In modern-day applications, each action requires various steps, which require intricate interaction between the user interface and the backend application server.

For example, while registering as a new user, the application user interface will need to check if the user-provided email address is already registered. Also, the underlying data systems will generate a unique identifier, which various subsystems will use to identify the user uniquely. The *user profile* will be generated and stored in the backend database. The data engineer needs to identify and design underlying data systems that will functionally work, perform, and scale to ensure the best user experience. Here, we have identified the user profile as one of the entities during the use case analysis.

Let us consider the second example of the user action of purchasing a product, which is a more extensive multistep process.

The following is a minimal list of steps required for purchasing products:

1. Search for the product using the search box and get the listing.
2. Select products and corresponding quantities for the purchase.
3. Add items to the shopping cart and check the inventory.
4. Accept the address for delivery and validate delivery logistics.
5. Process payment, handle payment failure, and finalize the order.
6. Ship the product.

Each step requires retrieving the data stored in the data store and storing the outcome of the steps in the underlying data store for further processing by subsequent steps.

For example, *step 1* requires retrieving the product catalog for the search query. *Step 3* checks if the user-specified quantity is available in the *product inventory* and adds items to the shopping cart. Here, the *shopping cart* is the outcome of *step 3*, which is consumed by *step 5* for the purpose of order finalization. In this use case analysis, we have identified more entities like *product inventory* and *shopping cart*.

Overview of data modeling

If we focus on the above examples, we have identified a set of *data objects,* such as user profiles, product catalog, product inventory, and shopping carts. Data objects represent logical units of data that will be created, stored, modified, and accessed by one or more data processors. The data objects can be transferred from one data processor to another. The process of identifying and defining data objects is called **data modeling**.

After the data objects are identified, the next logical step is to define them and where they will be associated with their properties. For example, the user profile should consist of information such as username (or ID), email address, phone number, postal address, etc. Similarly, the product catalog should consist of product ID, product name, brand name, price, etc.

Table 8.1 shows properties of the products in the product catalog, and their corresponding data types:

Property name	Data type
Identifier (id)	String
Name	String
Brand	String
Price	Integer

Table 8.1: Properties of the products in the product catalog and their data types

Let us look at the following example definition of a product catalog:

```
class Product (
      var id: String,
      var name: String,
      var brand: String,
      var price: Int
)
```

In this example, each product in the catalog has four properties. The first three (i.e., id, name, and brand) are represented as string data types, while the fourth property (i.e., price) is represented as a number (an integer). Assigning the right data type to the right properties is important as it allows users to perform specific operations on those properties. For example, as price is a number, a percentage discount can be applied to the price at the time of checkout.

Data modeling is dependent on the user application requirement, as well as the underlying data storage technology. At a high level, data modeling includes the following tasks:

- Identify and define data objects.
- Identify the relationship among the data objects.
- Define storage and retrieval mechanisms for the data objects.

We will discuss these data modeling tasks in this chapter and the subsequent chapters.

Structured data and tabular data representation

Tabular representation of the structured data and the ability to retrieve it using **Structured Query Language** (**SQL**) dates back to the 1970s. This ability is at the core of **relational database management systems** (**RDBMS**). One of the most popular RDBMS software is MySQL, which is free to use and open source. MySQL allows users to create tables, views, and indexes to store and access structured data.

Let us take the example of a product catalog to see how the product catalog can be represented in a MySQL table as follows:

```
CREATE TABLE product (
    Id VARCHAR(64),
    Name VARCHAR(255),
    Brand VARCHAR(128),
    Price INT
)
```

Here, **VARCHAR(*)** represents the *string* data type.

To visualize the data stored in the **product** table created, see *Table 8.2*.

This visualization emphasizes two concepts. Firstly, the data type of all entries in any column is the same. Secondly, each product in the catalog has appropriate values assigned to all columns in the table. These two concepts provide the required structure for the data. If your data exhibits these qualities, then you can treat your data as *structured* and choose to use traditional RDBMS to store and retrieve your data, as shown in the following table:

Id	Name	Brand	Price
"Id-0001"	"Smartphone A 1.1"	"Brand X"	239
"Id-0002"	"Smartphone B 3.2"	"Brand Y"	459
"Id-0003"	"Smartphone C 8.0"	"Brand Z"	999

Table 8.2: Product catalog

We will discuss this in detail in *Chapter 9, Databases and Transactional Data.*

Semi-structured data and JSON data format

Towards the start of the 21st century, the technology industry started seeing a paradigm shift. The internet became much more accessible, and a bunch of innovative web-based applications started flooding the internet. Social media attracted more users to start not just consuming the internet on a daily basis but also generating data on a regular basis. Social media posts and product reviews became more prevalent.

While end users saw this paradigm shift, large enterprises started implementing more frequent innovations in their businesses, requiring underlying data models to change more frequently.

The limitation of structured data is that it enforces structure, making it difficult to adapt to the ever-changing nature of requirements. That is when semi-structured data representation started getting popular.

Let us continue with the example of a product catalog. In modern times, users like to see detailed product information before buying. However, the product details vary as the product type changes. For example, smartphone details include display size, phone memory, processor, etc. On the other hand, details of a refrigerator include capacity, number of doors, defrost system, etc. For an e-commerce website, it is expected to sell 100s of types of products. Also, the introduction of any new kind of product should be simple. So, strict schema enforcement by structured data systems becomes counter-productive, and semi-structured data models tend to become more quickly adaptable.

JSON data format

One of the most popular data formats for semi-structured data is **JavaScript Object Notation (JSON)**. It is a human-readable, open standard file format used to store and transfer data, and most modern applications use it.

Let us continue the previous example of a product catalog, where we want to store product details in the product catalog, as shown in the following:

```
Product 1 - Smartphone
{
        "Id": "Id-0001",
        "Name": "Smartphone A 1.1",
        "Brand": "Brand X",
        "Price": 239,
        "Details": {
                "Size": 5.4,
                "Memory": "256 GB",
                "Processor": "Proc-A"
        }
}
Product 2 - Refrigerator
{
        "Id": "Id-0105",
        "Name": "Refrigerator M",
        "Brand": "Brand K",
        "Price": 1025,
        "Details": {
```

```
        "Capacity": 210,
        "doors": 2,
        "defrost": "auto"
    }
}
```

In the preceding example, smartphones and refrigerators are represented in JSON data format. Here, the JSON, and hence JSON-based semi-structured data systems, allow users to store and access the smartphone's size and the refrigerator's capacity without enforcing any schema.

Structured vs. semi-structured data model

As we saw above, JSON data format exposes the schema flexibility needed by modern applications which can undergo fast changes. Now, let us see how the structured data model has rigid schema enforcement. Continuing with our example of a product catalog, let us assume that when the product catalog was initially designed, the e-commerce website sold only smartphones. So, the properties and data types of the products were very specific to the smartphones, as shown in *Table 8.3*:

Property name	Data type
Identifier (id)	String
Name	String
Brand	String
Price	Integer
Size	Floating point number
Memory	String
Processor	String

Table 8.3: Product catalog schema for smartphones

In this example, the corresponding SQL table that represents the product catalog, has seven columns, as depicted by the following **CREATE TABLE** command.

```
CREATE TABLE product (
    Id VARCHAR(64),
    Name VARCHAR(255),
    Brand VARCHAR(128),
    Price INT,
    Size FLOAT,
    Memory VARCHAR(32),
    Processor VARCHAR(64)
)
```

Now, let us assume that the e-commerce website needs to add *refrigerators* to its catalog. Unlike smartphones, refrigerators have properties like capacity, number of doors, defrost mode etc. So, the same product table will now have extra properties for refrigerators. These extra properties need to be added to the table, without changing any of the smartphone properties. To do this, an **ALTER TABLE** command needs to be executed to add new columns to the table. The command would look as follows:

```
ALTER TABLE Product
ADD COLUMN Capacity INT,
ADD COLUMN Doors INT,
ADD COLUMN Defrost VARCHAR(32);
```

While using JSON for a semi-structured data model, such **ALTER TABLE** command is not required, as JSON does not enforce any structured schemas. Apart from that, there are other limitations of schema rigidity of the SQL-based structured data model, as explained in the following:

1. Due to the presence of different types of products in the product table, not all column values will be valid for all product types. For example, defrost mode, and the number of doors columns values in the table will be invalid for a smartphone. This leads to non-optimal use of storage space. On the other hand, the JSON data model does not require extra columns to be created, avoiding extra storage space usage.

2. **ALTER TABLE** commands are typically expensive to execute, especially if used with default values for new columns, as existing rows need to be updated. Also, if the default values are specified, the user application may experience downtime if the table needs to be rebuilt. On the other hand, the JSON data model exposed by NoSQL databases does not require any **ALTER TABLE** command to be run due to schema flexibility.

Choosing a data model that fits well with your data engineering requirements is very important. Structured data models are more robust and less error-prone because they enforce schemas, while semi-structured data models are easily adaptable.

A different set of underlying software storage and retrieval systems is used for efficient use of semi-structured data compared to structured data. Once the data engineering system is designed based on the data model, moving from one to the other is costly and time-consuming. Hence, it is necessary to choose *the right data model* very early in designing large data systems.

Unstructured data and binary data format

We live in a world where everybody with a smartphone is a photographer and a videographer. Daily, a large amount of unstructured data is generated in texts, images, or videos. There are a large number of modern-day use cases that require this unstructured data to be stored cost-effectively and retrieved efficiently on demand. The unstructured data is typically larger in size and stored in a data lake (usually backed by a blob store) instead of a database or a data warehouse. Texts, images and videos are encoded into a binary data format before they are stored in the data lake.

Modern-day applications use AI/ML to extract intelligence from unstructured data. For example, product reviews posted on an e-commerce website (in text format) can be processed for sentiment analysis. The output of sentiment analysis can then be aggregated to identify products that get net negative reviews and can be discontinued from the website. Similarly, if users want to search for products by uploading *similar images*, then data engineers can use vector databases and image search pipelines to deploy the solution. We will learn the data engineering patterns used to solve such business use cases in *Chapter 16, Domain Specific Patterns*.

Transactional and analytical data

The data generated by (or required for) day-to-day business operations is called *transactional data*. The transactional data is typically stored in transactional databases, and the corresponding user applications are called **online transaction processing** (**OLTP**) applications. Continuing with our e-commerce website example, all day-to-day activity like user registration, order confirmation, recording failed payments, etc., requires access to the transactional data. Transactional data must be stored and retrieved at very low latencies, so transactional databases are used for such data. For an e-commerce website, the quality and speed of transactional data access dictate the user experience while interacting with the website.

On the other hand, analytical data is curated and filtered to be used for specific use cases, such as analytics, business intelligence, strategic decision-making, etc. Let us reconsider the example of discontinuing products with net negative reviews.

To implement a solution for this problem, the data engineers and business analysts collaborate to do the following:

- Identify the subset of information required to identify net negative reviews. For example, here, the product details are not needed. Only the product ID and product reviews are required.

- Create an ETL pipeline and store the filtered and curated data in the analytics storage.

- Perform sentiment analysis and store the output of sentiment analysis.

- Run an analytics query to get a list of products with net negative feedback.

The above example shows the difference between transactional and analytical data. User applications performing data analytics are called OLAP applications. In *Chapter 2, Data Engineering Patterns, Terminologies, and Technical Stack,* and *Chapter 3, Batch Ingestion and Processing,* we will discuss concepts and data engineering patterns related to OLTP and OLAP applications.

Table 8.4 provides a summary of differences between transactional and analytical data systems. Detailed differences are explained in *Chapter 10, Data Warehouse and Data Analytics*.

OLTP system	OLAP system
The data is typically generated by the day-to-day user-facing business applications	The data is typically ingested from the OLPT systems for further analysis
The data is typically stored in transactional databases	The data is typically stored in the data warehouses
Typical consumers are the end users	Typical consumers are the data analysts
Very low latencies are mandatory as it impacts end user experience	Higher latencies are acceptable as it can avoid hardware and software platform costs

Table 8.4: Product catalog schema for smartphones

Conclusion

In this chapter, we established the data engineering foundation by introducing the data modeling concept. With the help of examples, we understood structured, semi-structured, and unstructured data and how to model these types of data to achieve the required business outcome. We also introduced concepts of transactional and analytical data.

In the next chapter, we will discuss relational and NoSQL databases, transactional data semantics, and the design patterns commonly used by OLTP applications.

Exercises

1. What are the different basic and advanced data types that can be defined and used at the time of data modeling?

2. What are the overheads of moving from structured data to semi-structured data?

3. What are alternative representations to the JSON data format for representing semi-structured data?

Join our Discord space

Join our Discord workspace for latest updates, offers, tech happenings around the world, new releases, and sessions with the authors:

https://discord.bpbonline.com

CHAPTER 9

Databases and Transactional Data

Introduction

This chapter introduces relational and distributed NoSQL databases. We then explore use cases and design patterns for using views, secondary indexes, etc. We also introduce the concepts of ACID transactions in the context of traditional RDBMS and modern distributed NoSQL databases.

Structure

The chapter covers the following topics:

- Understanding relational databases
- Introduction to distributed databases
- Database views
- Primary and secondary indexes
- ACID transactions in traditional RDBMS
- Transactions in distributed databases

Objectives

By the end of this chapter, we will cover the various design patterns used by the applications using RDBMS and NoSQL databases. The reader will be able to understand the benefits and costs of creating views and indexes. We will also discuss the importance of database transactions and how to make use of them to ensure data quality.

Understanding relational databases

As discussed in the previous chapter, we use relational databases to store structured data in the database and represent it in the form of tables. Relational database software comes with an abundance of features that help users solve problems related to the following:

- Data consistency with the help of ACID transactions
- Defining various data objects and relationships between them
- Ability to create views and indexes to access the data faster
- Ability to write and execute complex queries using SQL to perform data filtering, data aggregation, etc.

With the help of modern-day business use cases, we will discuss the aforementioned database features.

Introduction to distributed databases

The CEO of Domino's Pizza has famously said *Domino's is a technology company that delivers pizza*. This statement implies that modern-day businesses rely heavily on their underlying technology for their day-to-day operations. This also means that a failure of the underlying database system means a loss of revenue for the businesses. If the underlying database system is running on a single computer, failure of that single computer can lead to loss of availability. To avoid such scenarios, modern-day businesses use distributed databases, which use more than one computer in the backend. If one computer fails, another can serve the business requests.

Some examples of distributed databases are MongoDB, Couchbase Server, Redis, Amazon Aurora DB, etc. In the following chapters, we will discuss data engineering patterns related to high **availability**, **fault tolerance**, and **load balancing** using distributed databases.

Database views

Database view is a logical representation of (typically) a subset of data residing in the database tables. This logical representation allows users to access the subset of data required for specific use cases while filtering out unnecessary details from the database table. The ability to filter the data using views is useful for two purposes:

- To focus on a specific subset of the data, for example, to generate specific reports.
- Use **role-based access control (RBAC)** to provide limited access to data.

Let us continue with the example of an e-commerce website from the previous chapters.

Suppose the e-commerce website ships the goods across multiple states in the US, and each state has its own distribution center. In this case, the product inventory table will have three fields: product ID, distribution center ID, and available quantity, as shown:

```
CREATE TABLE inventory (
    ProductId VARCHAR(64),
    DistCenterId VARCHAR(64),
    Quantity INT
);
```

Now, the operations manager of each distribution center needs to generate a weekly inventory report to check which inventory is running low and send the dispatch orders up the supply chain.

To generate such a report, the following database query can be executed:

```
SELECT ProductId, Quantity
FROM inventory
WHERE DistCenterId = "NY";
```

To execute such a query on the database, the operations manager of the New York distribution center needs full read access to the **inventory** table:

```
GRANT SELECT ON inventory
TO 'opmgr_ny';
```

In this case, the operations manager of the New York distribution center can access the inventory information for other distribution centers as well. However, suppose the data security teams want to limit the data access to the operations managers based on their distribution centers. In that case, the database admin can create a view specifically for the NY distribution center using the **WHERE** clause:

```
CREATE VIEW inventory_ny
SELECT  ProductId, Quantity
FROM inventory
WHERE DistCenterId = "NY";
```

Here, **SELECT** access can be granted to the operations manager only for the view **inventory_ny**; hence, the operations manager cannot access the inventory from other distribution centers.

The following command can be used to grant access to the New York inventory to the operations manager of the New York distribution center:

```
GRANT SELECT ON inventory_ny
TO 'opmgr_ny'\
```

Finally, to generate a report using the view **inventory_ny**, the operations manager will run the following SQL command, and the **WHERE** clause is not needed at the time of running the **SELECT** query, as the data filter is already specified at the time of view creation:

```
SELECT ProductId, Quantity
FROM inventory_ny;
```

In a typical traditional RDBMS, views do not store the actual data by default. View definitions are stored as metadata that refers to the original tables. That is why when the original data in the table is updated, views will also return the updated data.

Data access can be further optimized with the help of materialized views, where the data belonging to the view is stored on persistent storage, separate from the actual table data. In the next chapter, we will discuss materialized views and how to choose between views and materialized views.

> Note: **View creation can include more complex logic, such as joins across multiple tables, aggregate queries, etc. This enables database admins to write complex logic only once at the time of view creation, while application developer queries can be simpler.**

Primary and secondary indexes

Database indexes are the primary tools to get fast performance for your **SELECT** queries. Indexes make use of the data structures (like B+ trees, skip lists, etc.), which provide the ability to perform fast lookup and range scans for the data without iterating over the entire data. The indexes consume resources like RAM, disk space, disk bandwidth, and CPU to be kept updated and persisted. However, the query performance increases dramatically to **O(log n)** from **O(n)** when executed with the help of indexes.

Primary indexes

Let us continue with the product catalog example, where the user wants to perform a database lookup by providing product ID as input and getting product details like name, branch, and price as output. Here, we will reuse the same product table definition used in the previous chapter as follows:

```
CREATE TABLE product (
    Id VARCHAR(64),
    Name VARCHAR(255),
    Brand VARCHAR(128),
    Price INT
);
```

In the aforementioned example, we do not see any field that is tagged as a primary key, but we intend **Id** to be the primary key for the table. So, to define a primary key, we can modify the above and create a table statement for the following statement:

```
CREATE TABLE product (
    Id VARCHAR(64) PRIMARY KEY,
    Name VARCHAR(255),
    Brand VARCHAR(128),
    Price INT
);
```

Note: **The primary key is a field in the database that has a unique value across all rows in that table.**

MySQL database internally enforces a **NOT NULL** clause, if not explicitly mentioned, and creates a primary index based on the **Id** field, which is a primary key. The database can use this primary index to serve queries that retrieve product details for an input product ID. An example query can be as follows:

```
SELECT Name, Brand, Price
FROM product
WHERE Id="Id-1021";
```

Due to the presence of the primary index, the query can quickly look up product details related to product **Id-1021**.

Note: **You can create a multi-field primary key to ensure uniqueness across these multiple fields.**

Secondary indexes

Secondary indexes are those created on the tables' non-primary key fields. Like primary indexes, secondary indexes are also used to speed up lookups and range scans when the input parameters are based on secondary keys. Secondary keys are other properties of the data objects (like name, brand, price, etc.), which may not be unique across other entries in the table.

Let us consider a use case where the user wants to get the list of smartphones sorted in increasing order of their price. For this example, we will consider the product table, which also has a *type* field for each of the products, and for smartphones, the type is smartphone. So, the product catalog here will look like:

```
CREATE TABLE product (
    Id VARCHAR(64) PRIMARY KEY,
    Name VARCHAR(255),
    Brand VARCHAR(128),
    Price INT,
    Type VARCHAR(32)
);
```

Now, to display the list of smartphones sorted in an increasing order of the price, we will create a secondary index.

Let us assume that the smartphone listing needs to display the product name and product brand as well. So, one way to create a secondary index for this type of query is as follows:

```
CREATE INDEX type_price_index
ON product(Type, Price);
```

Now, the **SELECT** query that will use this index is:

```
SELECT Price, Name, Brand
FROM product
WHERE Type = "smartphone"
ORDER BY Price ASC;
```

This index can serve many more types of queries. For example, if the user wants to provide a price range, the user can write the following query:

```
SELECT Price, Name, Brand
FROM product
WHERE Type = "smartphone" AND Price > 100 AND Price < 400
ORDER BY Price ASC;
```

In both aforementioned queries, the **WHERE** clause ensures that the query execution needs to iterate over a subset of data that has a type of *smartphone*. In the index **type_price_index**, all the entries for a specific type are stored adjacent to each other so that the query execution starts with finding the first smartphone in the product catalog and iterates through the adjacent entries to find all smartphones. Once an entry of any type other than a smartphone is encountered, the iteration stops, as there are no remaining products that match the specified parameters. In the second query, query execution needs to iterate over an even smaller subset of data, as there is a filter on price as well.

Note: **In this example query, ORDER BY Price ASC is not really required, as the index is sorted in an ascending order of values of keys. For example, the type_price_index already has all smartphones sorted in ascending order of their prices.**

Note: Secondary indexes created on multiple fields are called composite indexes. Composite indexes allow users to specify filters on multiple fields and yield good performance for the given set of filters.

Importance of index key order in secondary indexes

Analyze the above-mentioned example of the secondary index. You can see that the secondary index allows you to drastically reduce the number of database entries you need to iterate through to get the required data. The query performance is directly proportional to the number of entries a query needs to iterate over, and the user experience is directly dependent on query performance. In the case of a database table having billions of entries, a wrongly created index can lead to performance orders of magnitude worse than what one can get with the right index.

Let us take an example of a bad index and see why it performs way worse than a good index. For this example, let us assume a new field exists in our product catalog called **rating**, and it represents the average rating (rounded to the nearest integer value) given to this product by the buyers.

Now, let us continue our example of smartphones, where the user wants to get the listing of smartphones in an ascending order of rating and only wants to get the smartphones that have a rating of 4 or higher (in the rating system of 1 to 5). There are two filters for this query, so the index should include both fields.

For this example, we need to introduce the **Rating** field to the table, as follows:

```
CREATE TABLE product (
    Id VARCHAR(64) PRIMARY KEY,
    Name VARCHAR(255),
    Brand VARCHAR(128),
    Price INT,
    Type VARCHAR(32),
    Rating INT
);
```

The corresponding SQL query is as follows:

```
SELECT Id, Rating
FROM product
WHERE Type = "smartphone" AND Rating >= 4
ORDER BY Price ASC;
```

Now, let us consider the product catalog is large, say 10 million different products, out of which only 1000 are smartphones, while the remaining 9.999 million products are not smartphones. Let us also assume that the ratings are evenly distributed from 1 to 5 for all the products. This means that out of 10 million, only 400 products satisfy this query criteria.

Here, we have the two following options to create an index. The first option is to use **Rating** as the first field, followed by **Type**, and the second option is to use **Type** as the first field, followed by **Rating**:

- **Index option 1**:

  ```
  CREATE INDEX rating_type_index
  ON product(Rating, Type);
  ```

- **Index option 2**:

  ```
  CREATE INDEX type_rating_index
  ON product(Type, Rating);
  ```

Let us say we created index option 1 (i.e., **rating_type_index**). As the query says **Rating >= 4**, the query execution engine needs to iterate over all the products with a **Rating** greater than or equal to 4 and filter out the products by type. So, query execution needs to iterate through 4 million index entries to get the desired 400 entries. This non-optimal behavior can be visualized in *Figure 9.1*:

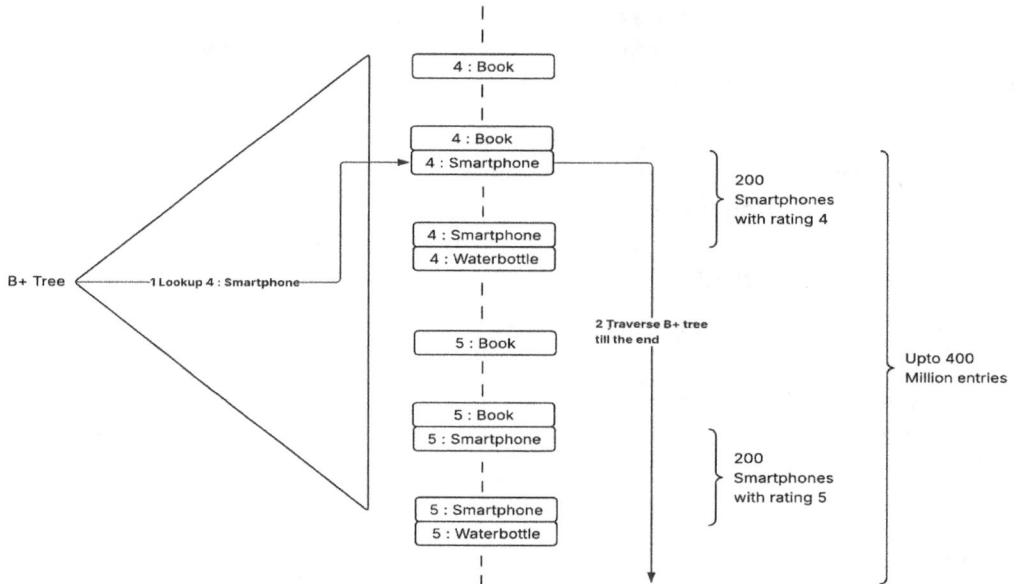

Figure 9.1: A non-optimal secondary index

This behavior can be improved by creating index option 2 (`type_rating_index`) instead of option 1. With `type_rating_index`, query execution directly jumps to the part of the index with `Type = "Smartphone"` and `Rating >= 4`. This way, query execution needs to iterate through only 400 qualifying entries, and iteration will stop once the product type for the next entry is different than the *Smartphone*. This optimal behavior can be visualized with the help of *Figure 9.2*:

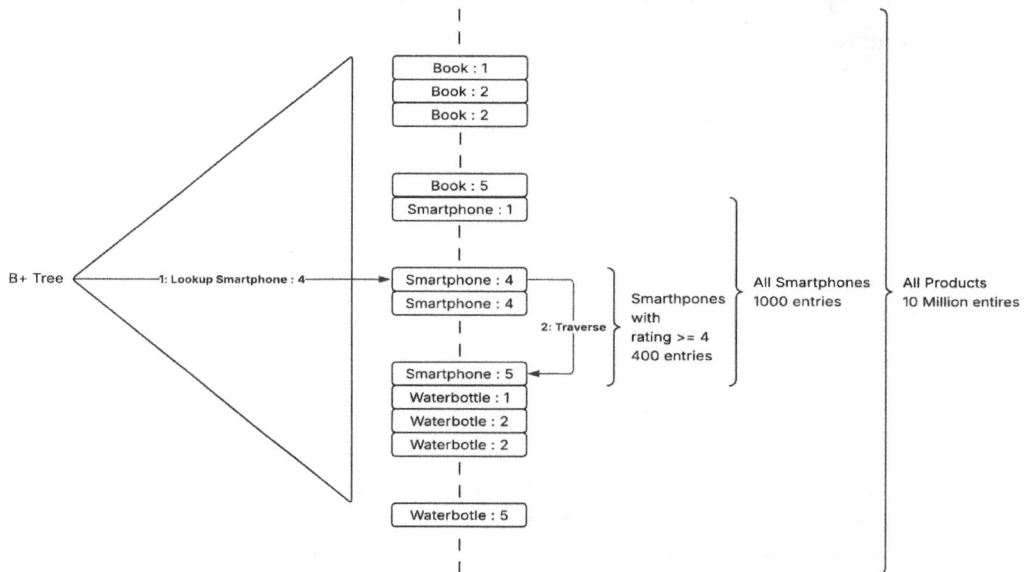

Figure 9.2: An optimal secondary index

Note: **The query execution engine performs better with the quality operator (=) than with inequality operators (like >= in this example).**

ACID transactions in traditional RDBMS

Support for transactional semantics is the first level of failure safety net provided by the relational databases. The basic properties of transactions are:

- Atomicity
- Consistency
- Isolation
- Durability

Here, we will understand the basic definitions of the ACID properties of transactions by looking at the example of the user finalizing the order at the time of checkout. The e-commerce website needs to perform the following steps when finalizing the order:

1. Check if the *Inventory* has enough quantity. If not, do not finalize the order.
2. Add an entry in the *Orders* table for this order.
3. Reduce the quantity from the *Inventory*.
4. Cross-check the quantity in the *Inventory* table. If the final quantity is equal to the initial quantity minus the order quantity, then finalize the order. Otherwise, do not finalize the order.

For this example, we will consider the following schemas for the *Inventory* and *Orders* tables. To simplify the example, we will assume that one order can contain only one type of product with varying quantities:

```
CREATE TABLE inventory (
    ProductId VARCHAR(64),
    Quantity INT
);
CREATE TABLE orders (
    Id VARCHAR(64),
    ProductId VARCHAR(64),
    Quantity INT
);
```

Given the aforementioned table schemas for inventory and orders tables, the following code (implemented as a stored procedure, i.e., *Procedure 9.1*) represents the aforementioned order finalization steps:

```
DELIMITER //
CREATE PROCEDURE finalizeOrder(
    IN OrderId VARCHAR(64),
```

```
      IN OrderProductId VARCHAR(64),
      IN OrderQuantity INT
)
BEGIN
  DECLARE qty INT;
  DECLARE final INT;
  DECLARE newQty INT;

  -- Start the transaction.
  START TRANSACTION;

  -- Fetch current quantity from the inventory.
  SELECT Quantity INTO qty FROM inventory WHERE ProductId = OrderProductId;
  IF qty < OrderQuantity THEN
    -- Don't finalize the order.

    ROLLBACK;

  ELSE
    -- Store the order details to the orders table.
    INSERT INTO orders (Id, ProductId, Quantity)
    VALUES (OrderId, OrderProductId, OrderQuantity);
    -- Decrement the quantity in the inventory
    SET newQty = qty - OrderQuantity;
    UPDATE inventory
    SET Quantity = newQty
    WHERE ProductId = OrderProductId;

    -- Validate the quantity from inventory before finalizing the order.
    SELECT Quantity INTO final FROM inventory WHERE ProductId = OrderProductId;
    IF final = newQty THEN
      -- The quantities match. Safe to finalize the order using COMMIT.
      COMMIT;
    ELSE
      -- The quantities don't match. Rollback the transaction.
      ROLLBACK;
    END IF;
  END IF;
END
```

Procedure 9.1: Order finalization

Now, let us understand the ACID properties of the database transactions in the context of the aforementioned example as follows:

- **Atomicity**: It means the transaction is executed as a single operation, even if it has multiple steps. It can either fail or succeed without leaving any side effects. In our example, there are two steps that update or modify the database. The first is to insert order details in the orders table, and the second is to update the inventory table. If the database software crashes after performing the first step, the database software will rollback the updates made by that step to ensure atomicity.

- **Consistency**: It means the data remains correct after the transaction is done (either succeeds or fails). The total quantity of the product in the database should always match the actual quantity. If order finalization succeeds, then the quantity in the inventory should be decremented by the order quantity. On the other hand, if order finalization fails, then the quantity in the inventory should not be decremented.

- **Isolation**: It means the ability of the database system to treat each transaction as an isolated event in the system. Even if there are other transactions running in the system, they should not show any side effects on each other. In our example, we can see that if some other transaction updates the inventory quantity, then the transaction fails (and can be retried).

- **Durability**: This means that once the transaction is successful, it will continue to be successful. Any system event, like a database software crash, database computer restart, etc., should not lead to loss of data or information about the finalized order. Once the software recovers from the failure event, order details will be available to serve the user.

These ACID properties of the database transactions were defined decades ago, and they still hold up to their promise. However, these definitions were based on a database system of the older times, where the software was running on a single computer. In modern-day distributed databases, the meanings of these properties have changed for good.

Let us discuss the concept of transactions in distributed databases.

Transactions in distributed databases

As discussed previously, distributed databases run on more than one computer to ensure fault tolerance as well as load balancing. To ensure fault tolerance, multiple copies of the same data are stored across multiple computers (each computer is known as a *node*, as per distributed system terminology). Each node has its own processing capacity (i.e., CPU), its own memory (i.e., RAM), and its own secondary storage (i.e., disk). So, each node can store and serve the data owned by it.

In this chapter, we will focus only on the properties of transactions in the distributed databases. However, in *Chapter 1, Understanding Data Engineering*, we will discuss the data engineering patterns used for data replication and partitioning.

Now, because the data is partitioned and replicated across multiple nodes, the underlying meaning behind the traditional ACID properties changes. For example, in a traditional RDBMS, a transaction is said to be durable if the data generated by the transaction is stored on the disk. In the event of a disk failure, it is termed a data loss event, which traditional RDBMS cannot handle. However, with distributed databases, the data generated by the transaction will be replicated and stored across multiple nodes. The transaction is termed as durable only when data generated by the transaction is stored on a *pre-defined* minimum number of nodes, say *n* (and not just on one node). This avoids data loss even in the event of simultaneous failure of *n-1* database nodes.

Various distributed databases work with varying definitions of ACID properties in the context of distributed transactions. So, there is no single meaning for these properties across all databases. The meanings can vary as per the database implementation. In this chapter, we will focus on two frequently used patterns in modern-day distributed databases.

Note: **In theory, distributed databases can enforce the traditional meaning of ACID properties, but this will lead to performance overheads. So, many distributed databases implement a variant of ACID properties that fit well in the context of distributed transactions.**

The modern distributed databases attempt to find the right trade-off among the three important aspects of the distributed systems, viz., the performance, the availability, and the data partitioning. This trade-off is well known in the industry as the *CAP theorem*. The CAP theorem dictates that any distributed system can guarantee only two of the three aspects (i.e., the performance, the availability, and the data partitioning). Therefore, the most distributed databases implement a relaxed version of consistency while ensuring the ability to perform data partitioning and availability.

Durability in MongoDB

Modern-day applications demand write-heavy workloads to be performed on the underlying databases. This type of write-heavy workload can lead to slow data ingestion as the disk bandwidth can become a bottleneck. To avoid this, NoSQL databases like MongoDB, Couchbase Server, etc., dilute the durability requirements and return success to the user application even if the data is not stored on the disk. In this case, data will be written only to the in-memory data structures. While the database service is running, all the incoming read requests can be served using in-memory data, but durability is not guaranteed. If the database service crashes or restarts before the data is written to the disk, data will be lost.

The database system will persist the data to the disk at a regular interval, but for distributed databases, this is not enough. In a multi-node MongoDB cluster, the data needs to be replicated across multiple nodes to make it durable, in the true sense of the word.

MongoDB provides two parameters to the user: the first is called *write concern*, and the second is called *journaling flag*. Let us understand how you can trade off durability, performance, and availability with each other by using these two flags.

Let us take an example of the order finalization workflow. In the final step, once the payment is processed successfully, the user's order details need to be stored in the database. These order details will be consumed by the order dispatch department for delivery. For this example, we will consider a MongoDB cluster of 3 nodes, where one node hosts the primary replica set, and the other two host secondary replica sets (P-S-S in short).

Note: **The replica sets in MongoDB are copies of the data stored on different nodes to provide high availability via replication.**

Write to majority with journaling enabled

The default configuration of MongoDB allows users a reasonably good durability guarantee with the help of writing to the *majority*. For the P-S-S configuration, the write majority is achieved when the data is written to the primary and at least one of the secondaries.

The update request for order details goes to the primary replica set when the user order is finalized. The in-memory data structures are updated on the primary replica set, and the order details are forwarded to both the secondary replica sets. The acknowledgment for the order finalization is not sent to the user until the data is stored *on the disk* on the primary and on one of the secondaries.

After the data write acknowledgment goes to the user, if the primary replica set fails, the data will not be lost, as it can be read from one of the secondaries.

Write to all replica sets

With default behavior, we have seen how MongoDB ensures durability in case of one node failure. But what if two nodes fail? If the primary replica set fails, along with the secondary replica set that had stored the order details, then the data can get lost, as we cannot know if the data had successfully persisted to the other secondary replica set.

To handle such scenarios of multi-node failure, users can decide to write to all replica sets. In our example, this can be achieved by setting the value of the *write concern* to three. If the write concern is set to three, the user application will not get an acknowledgment for the write operation until the order details have persisted to the disk on all three replica sets.

However, this creates another challenge. What if one of the replica sets fails at the time of order finalization? Then, with write concern as three, the order finalization will fail if there is at least one failed node. Therefore, extra care must be taken while deciding the appropriate value for write concern.

Eventual consistency in DynamoDB

DynamoDB is one of the most popular distributed NoSQL databases, which is a part of **Amazon Web Services (AWS)**. Given the distributed nature of the database, DynamoDB has implemented a different variation of consistency called *eventual consistency*. Eventual consistency does not adhere to the standards of consistency in the traditional sense, but user applications can work with it while getting better performance.

To understand the difference between consistency in traditional RDBMS vs eventual consistency in DynamoDB, let us take an example as shown in *Table 9.1*:

Operation	Traditional RDBMS	DynamoDB
Store value = 10	Write operation successful	Write operation successful
Read value	Returns value 10	Returns value 10
Update value = 20	Write operation successful	Write operation successful
Read value immediately after update operation	Returns value 20	May return value 10 or 20
Read value after some time	Returns value 20	Returns value 20

Table 9.1: *Understanding eventual consistency in DynamoDB*

Let us say the user wants to *update* the quantity in the inventory after the order has been finalized. In traditional RDBMS (without using transactions), if an update operation succeeds, then all the following *read* operation is guaranteed to return the value of the last write operation.

However, DynamoDB (without using transactions) does not guarantee to read the value of the last write operation. Due to the distributed nature of DynamoDB, the write/update operation is said to be successful when it is replicated to *a majority* of nodes in the cluster. To ensure the write operation's availability and performance, DynamoDB does not wait until the write is replicated to all nodes. Due to this, if the subsequent *read* is served by the node that has not yet received the last update, that node can return the older value.

Note: The exact time required for the database to be eventually consistent is not known. So, the user applications need to work around this with the help of strongly consistent reads.

By default, read operations in DynamoDB are eventually consistent, and users can set the `ConsistentRead` parameter to `true` for `GetItem, Query,` and `Scan` APIs of DynamoDB to perform strongly consistent reads. However, performing strongly consistent reads has two overheads. First, they are slower than eventually consistent reads, and second, they cost twice as much in dollars.

Note: The eventual consistency applies only to the update operations in DynamoDB.

After a successful *initial write* operation, a read operation always returns a consistent result because of read-committed isolation. Read-committed isolation guarantees that the committed value can be read from the database, even if it is not a strongly consistent read.

Conclusion

By the end of this chapter, we discussed the benefits of database views, for example, reducing the complexity of writing SQL queries and granting access only to the filtered data. After understanding the views, we were introduced to the primary and secondary indexes and how database indexes can yield better performance. We also covered why having the right order of secondary index keys is essential to getting good performance. Additionally, we discussed the ACID properties of database transactions and how to use the transactions in traditional RDBMS (MySQL) to guarantee the quality of the data.

Moreover, with the help of a couple of examples, we understood how the conceptual meanings of the ACID properties of the transactions change in the context of the two most famous distributed NoSQL databases, DynamoDB and MongoDB. Here, we observed that the terminology and concepts used in the APIs for ACID properties in MongoDB differ dramatically from those of DynamoDB. This fact suggests that there *is not* one single conceptual meaning for the ACID properties in the world of distributed databases. However, many databases choose to dilute the meaning of consistency to gain better performance and availability.

In the next chapter, we will introduce the concepts of data analysis and business intelligence. We will understand the use of data warehouses in solving data analytics problems. We will also dive deeper into the features provided by the data warehouse, like materialized views, columnar storage format, start and Snowflake schemas, etc.

Questions

1. What are the names of the popular distributed relational databases?

2. Write a view definition to get the names of the products with zero quantity in the inventory. (Hint: View definition will require a join on product catalog and product inventory tables)

3. What are the other overheads of using distributed databases besides financial or cost overheads?

4. One way to increase the write throughput of your MongoDB is to disable journaling during write operations. What is the side effect of disabling the journaling?

5. What is the difference between serializable atomicity and read-committed atomicity used in DynamoDB?

6. DynamoDB supports distributed transactions. How much does GetItem cost when called from inside of a transaction boundary?

7. In MongoDB, if the data is written using write concern majority and after that, the data is read using majority read concern, it always returns the latest data from the database. Is this true?

Join our Discord space

Join our Discord workspace for latest updates, offers, tech happenings around the world, new releases, and sessions with the authors:

https://discord.bpbonline.com

CHAPTER 10
Data Warehouse and Data Analytics

Introduction

In today's competitive landscape, understanding customer behavior is paramount. This chapter explores how businesses transform raw e-commerce data into powerful insights using data analytics and warehousing. Here, we extend the e-commerce website example from previous chapters. We will discuss a couple of **business intelligence** (**BI**) use cases and see how those use cases can be solved using data analytics. We also introduce the concept of the data warehouse and describe its usefulness in designing solutions for data analytics.

We will perform a deep dive to understand the performance and cost benefits provided by the columnar storage format used by various data warehouse software. We will also learn the design pattern for using materialized views to reduce the latency of plotting graphs on the BI dashboards. Lastly, we will understand the star and Snowflake schema used to store the data in the data warehouse.

Structure

This chapter covers the following topics

- Data analytics and business intelligence
- Data warehouse
- Features of data warehouse

Objectives

By the end of this chapter, you will understand common data analytics and business intelligence use cases and how these use cases differ from day-to-day operational use cases. You will also learn about data warehousing software and how it is better suited to solve data analytics problems than traditional databases. You will also understand how materialized views generate pre-defined types of reports (like weekly or monthly sales reports) quickly.

Finally, you will learn the trade-offs between the choice of row-oriented storage format and columnar storage format, and the concepts of star and Snowflake schemas.

Data analytics and business intelligence

In the last chapter, we looked at the design patterns used for day-to-day business operations. Those patterns made use of various types of databases and database features to handle the business operations. However, apart from operational needs, businesses also need to optimize and grow by strategizing for future business needs. This step of identifying and defining future strategy is called business intelligence.

Let us continue with our example of an e-commerce website, where the business owners want to decide on a future strategy. To define future strategy, one needs to find bottlenecks and problems with the existing business and fix those problems. One also needs to identify what is working well for the business and decide how to double down on it.

Let us take a couple of examples to understand the role of business intelligence better:

- Find the top five best-selling products for a specific calendar month of last year, and optimize inventory to accommodate the sales needs for this year
- Identify top badly reviewed (or returned) products and decide if they need to be discontinued
- Identify regions having the largest turnaround time for shipping orders and trigger an initiative to find and fix the bottlenecks (if any)
- Use real-time predictive analysis techniques to identify the top product recommendations for the specific user

Data analytics helps in finding answers to such business questions. In this chapter, we will make use of the above examples to explain the core concepts of data analytics.

Let us start with the example of monthly sales reports, where the top five best-selling products of a specific calendar month. Top-selling items for different months can change due to external factors like seasons (summer, winter, etc.), holidays, etc. For example, during summer, flip flops and sunglasses could be the top-selling items, while in the month of December, sweaters and Christmas decorations could be at the top of the charts. Now, e-commerce businesses need to estimate potential demand in the coming months and ensure they stock up the products well in advance to fulfill the demand in the *near future*.

As you read through the above use case, you will gather that we are looking at historical data. The question is: *Where do you keep the historical data?* One can always keep the historical data in the operational database, but that can bloat up the operational database very much and will start impacting the performance of operational queries.

For example, a typical e-commerce application may want to hold only recently fulfilled (in the last three months) order details in the operational database, while older data can be moved out of the operational database. This historical data is typically moved from the operational database to a *data warehouse.*

Data warehouse

The definition of a data warehouse is *a centralized repository used to store and analyze the historical business data, typically sourced from one or more transactional data systems.* The most commonly used data warehouse software is Amazon Redshift, Google BigQuery, Snowflake, Apache Hive, Apache Druid, ClickHouse, etc.

Now, let us continue with our example to understand the benefits of using a data warehouse and how it is different than a transactional database. To get the top five best-selling items, we need to transfer order data from the transactional database to the data warehouse. As learned in the previous chapters, users can define and set up data ingestion pipelines to transfer the order data from transactional databases. We have learned about setting up such pipelines in the previous chapters in detail. Let us do a quick recap of that.

At the time of setting up the pipeline, the user must:

- Identify the source table in the transactional database; the data will be ingested from this table
- Create a corresponding table on the destination data warehouse
- Create a connection between the source and destination table
- Decide on ingestion mechanism (batch vs. real-time, full vs. incremental, etc.)

Figure 10.1 helps in visualizing the logical connection between the source and the destination tables:

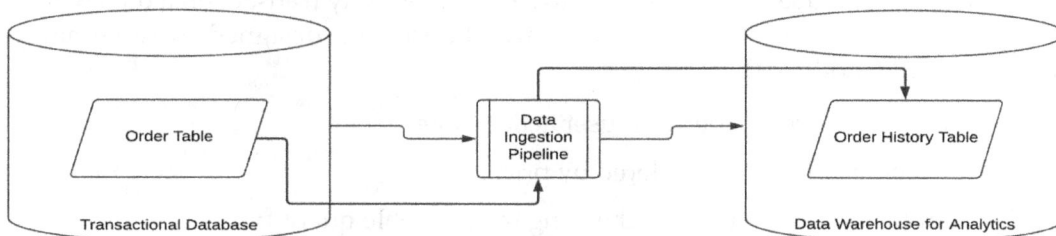

Figure 10.1: *Connecting Order Table in Transactional Database to the Order History Table in the data warehouse*

So, in our example, we will create a table in the data warehouse to store all historical orders. One possible schema for this table is as follows:

```
CREATE TABLE order_history(
    Id VARCHAR(32),
    ProductId VARCHAR(32),
    Quantity INT,
    OrderTime TIMESTAMP
);
```

To get the list of the top five best-selling products each month for the last year, we can write the following SQL query:

```
-- Here the select query below is the parameterized query.

-- :input_month is the input parameter specified by the user.

SELECT ProductId, SUM(Quantity) AS totalQuantity
FROM order_history
WHERE EXTRACT(YEAR FROM OrderTime) = EXTRACT(YEAR FROM CURRENT_DATE) - 1
AND EXTRACT(MONTH FROM OrderTime) = :input_month
GROUP BY ProductId
ORDER BY totalQuantity DESC
LIMIT 5;
```

Now, if you focus on the syntax of **CREATE TABLE** and the **SELECT** queries, we can observe that the syntax looks very similar to the SQL syntax exposed by the databases. Along with that, we can also see that the data warehouse is designed to efficiently store and serve the data (same as the databases). What are the key differences between databases and data warehouses?

Differences between database and data warehouse

Let us look into the key differences between a database and a data warehouse with the help of example use cases. These use cases, in turn, will help us understand a set of design patterns used for data analytics use cases.

Types of data workload

As discussed earlier, databases are designed to serve day-to-day transactional data workloads (OLTP workloads). On the other hand, data warehouses are designed to serve analytical workloads (OLAP workloads).

The databases are optimized to perform user actions like:

- Get a list of television sets ordered by price.
- Confirm the order of a user by checking the available quantity.
- Store the order details for three to six months to allow the processing of return requests.

The data warehouses are optimized to answer user queries like:

- Get the list of the top five best-selling products per month.

- Get the list of the most returned products over the last year.

- Get the list of products which has the lowest average rating.

Databases are typically used for serving point lookups and range scans on a small set of data, while data warehouses are typically used for serving aggregate queries on complex joins across multiple tables over large amounts of data.

Databases are optimized for both read and write workloads, while the data warehouses are optimized for read workloads.

Data serving latency

As discussed in the previous chapter, the data serving latencies of the underlying databases directly impact the overall user experience. Users are likely to move on, without making a purchase on an e-commerce website, if operations like *add to cart, order finalization,* etc., do not succeed quickly, as slow operations lead to a bad user experience and, hence, loss of revenue. So, typical database systems are expected to serve the queries at sub-millisecond to single-digit-millisecond latencies.

However, the same is not true for data warehouses. The user of a data warehouse is a data analyst whose job is to make strategic decisions for the business. In many cases, the queries being served for analytical purposes look at a much larger size of data and can observe latencies up to a few seconds. However, these are acceptable latencies as they do not have any business impact.

Recent data vs. historical data

For a popular e-commerce website, the historical data of successfully fulfilled orders can be large. Storing large amounts of data in the operational database has overheads, as the hardware resources required for efficient operation by the operational database are directly dependent on the amount of data being stored in it. So, the larger the data stored, the more hardware resources will be required, which will raise the cost. Also, not all historical data is relevant for day-to-day business. For example, an order successfully fulfilled more than a year ago does not need to be held in the operational database. The e-commerce website can always enforce a no more than one-month return policy, making one-year-old data unnecessary. Such old data can be moved to the secondary storage and can be served on demand. In *Chapter 13, Hot Versus Cold Data Storage,* we will understand data patterns related to secondary storage and archival use cases.

On the other hand, historical data is required for running analytical use cases like identifying purchase patterns across months and years. So, the data warehouses are optimized to efficiently store and serve the historical data.

Raw data vs. filtered and processed data

The data is stored in the databases in its raw form. Let us continue with our example of order details. Until now, we have focused on the minimal details of the order, which are necessary to understand specific use cases. However, the order details can contain a lot of information like shipping address, billing address, shipping instructions, payment method, delivery method, delivery partner details, invoice number, etc. All this information is required to be stored in its raw form in the **Order** table in the operational database so that it can be retrieved and displayed whenever required.

However, a data warehouse may not require all the properties of the data in the raw form. For example:

- Data analysis may not require a billing address, so there is no need to store billing addresses in the data warehouse.

- Shipping instructions may not be important for any business intelligence use cases, so we can avoid storing them in the data warehouse.

- Data analytics may focus on details like `zip` code and city from the shipping address, but it may not require details from address lines. So, only the required data can be extracted and stored in the data warehouse.

Data storage format

The format used to store the data differs based on the workload and the data serving use cases. Let us take an example of displaying product details on the UI, where the user would like to view all the details, specifications, etc., about the product before deciding to purchase it. That is why all the product details are typically stored together, i.e., the entire row of the table, or the entire JSON document holding the product information, will be stored in a single storage object in the database storage. This type of data store is called a **row-oriented data store**.

On the other hand, one analytics query requires performing aggregate operations on specific columns. For example, calculating the total quantity sold requires finding the sum of the quantities across all orders of the month. For executing this type of aggregation query, it is beneficial to store all the quantities (across all orders) grouped together in memory. This type of data store is called a **columnar data store**.

Typical operational databases prefer to use row-oriented data storage, while data warehouses prefer to use columnar data storage. We will look further into the trade-offs between row-oriented and columnar data stores later in this chapter.

Database vs. data warehouse

Until now, we have learned a bunch of differences between operational databases and analytical data warehouses. These differences range from the use cases and workload types to data storage formats and performance expectations.

The following table summarizes these differences:

Database	Data warehouse
Used for day-to-day business operations	Used for long-term decision-making and strategizing for the business
Used for running **online transaction processing (OLTP)** workloads	Used for running **online analytical processing (OLAP)** workloads
Stores data required for day-to-day business operations in a raw format	Stores historical, analytical, filtered, and processed data
Optimized for read as well as write workloads	Optimized primarily for read workloads
Optimized for point lookups and small range scans	Optimized for aggregate scans over a large amount of data, join across tables, etc.
Commonly uses row-oriented storage format	Commonly uses columnar storage format
Optimized for very low serving latencies, less than a few milliseconds	Optimized for low latencies, less than a few seconds

Table 10.1: Summary of the differences between the database and the data warehouse

Features of data warehouse

Now that we understand the key differences between a database and a data warehouse, let us explore important features of data warehouses, which are used for data storage design patterns by OLAP applications. These features are very specific to data warehouses and are not common in the world of databases.

Materializes views

In the previous chapter, we learned about *database views* and how they can be used to limit access to the data. A database view is just a piece of metadata that represents a logical table. The data filtering conditions specified in a database view get evaluated at the query runtime. Now, let us take an example of analytical queries to identify badly reviewed items to understand the use cases for the materialized views.

To identify the list of badly reviewed items, we must look at product reviews. Let us assume that each record of product reviews will have the following fields:

- **Product ID**: The ID of the product being reviewed
- **Product type**: For example, smartphones, food products, packaged drinks, stationary, etc.
- **Order ID**: The ID of the order for which the review was submitted
- **Other order details**: Shipping location, dispatch location, etc.
- **Rating**: Out of 1 to 5, where 1 is the lowest rating and 5 is the highest rating

To hold this information in the table in the data warehouse, we will create the table as follows:

```
CREATE TABLE product_ratings(
    ProductId VARCHAR(32),
    ProductType VARCHAR(32),
    ShipLocation VARCHAR(32),
    DispatchLocation VARCHAR(32),
    OrderId VARCHAR(32),
    Rating int
);
```

Now, to get the top five products with the lowest ratings, we have to run the following query:

```
SELECT ProductId, AVG(Rating) AS avgrating
FROM products_ratings
GROUP BY ProductId
ORDER BY avgrating ASC
LIMIT 5;
```

Now, this query execution needs to perform two resource-intensive operations. These two operations are as follows:

- Iterate over all the entries in the **product_ratings** table

- Calculate the average rating for each product and perform a group by operation on **ProductId**

However, for a large e-commerce business, there will be multiple data analysts helping with the business analytics. These analytics will focus on their own subset of data to make business decisions. For example, a data analyst looking at food product sales and ratings may not want to look at the sales and ratings for consumer electronics products.

So, when a food products data analyst runs the following query to get the top 5 worst-rated *food* products:

```
-- Query to get top 5 worst rated food products
SELECT ProductId, AVG(Rating) AS avgrating
FROM products_ratings
WHERE ProductType = "Food"
GROUP BY ProductId
ORDER BY avgrating ASC
LIMIT 5;
```

Now, given that the food products are fast-moving and sold very frequently, analysts may need to run the analytics query more frequently. This means that the same or similar (resource-consuming) work will be repeated multiple times, leading to slow response as well as high hardware costs. To avoid this, we can create a materialized view.

A **materialized view** is a subset of data that is precomputed and prefiltered to avoid repeated processing during query execution.

Let us take an example of a materialized view, which will reduce the filtering overhead while executing the above-mentioned **SELECT** command. The command to create the materialized view is as follows:

```
CREATE MATERIALIZED VIEW food_ratings AS
SELECT * FROM product_ratings WHERE ProductType = "Food";
```

Now, the query engine will identify that the materialized view **food_ratings** can be used to execute the above-mentioned query. If the total reviews of food product ratings represent only 10% of the total ratings across all products, then with the help of the materialized view **food_ratings**, we will need to iterate over only 10% of the data. Hence, the query execution time and resource requirements will be reduced drastically. It also means the filtered data needs to be stored on the disk twice, once in the actual data table and the second time in the materialized view. Also, it is costly to keep the materialized views up to date. So, creating a materialized view is always a tradeoff.

For fast-moving food products, it can be useful to create a materialized view, as the query will be run frequently. For consumer electronics, the queries will run only once a week or so. For such cases, it is less costly to run a query that will iterate over the entire ratings table than bearing the cost of storing the materialized view on the persistent storage.

Refreshing materialised views

By definition, a materialized view holds a copy of the pre-computed, filtered form of the original data. The original data can undergo changes, updates, etc. In such a case, the materialized view gets out of date. Working with the older data can give stale results, which may lead to sub-optimal business decisions by the data analysts.

To avoid getting stale results, the materialized views need to be kept updated, which is a costly operation and has the following overheads:

- The cost and overhead to read the original data from the tables to recompute the views.
- The cost to perform re-computation to generate the latest view.
- The cost and overhead of writing the view data to the persistent storage.

Considering these costs and overheads, a typical data warehouse allows users to:

- Manually refresh the materialized view OR
- Configure an automatic refresh interval

If a business needs analysts to examine *hourly* sales data, it is useful to set the refresh interval to a few minutes. On the other hand, if the analyst wants to examine *daily* sales data, the refresh interval can be kept to a few hours.

Automatic refresh can be disabled for generating quarterly sales reports, and manual refresh can be used at the time of generating the report.

Database views vs. materialized views

In this chapter, we learned the concept of materialized views, use cases that can benefit from using them, and the overheads of creating and maintaining them. Now, let us look at the summary of how materialized views are as compared with the database views in *Table 10.2*:

Database view	Materialized view in a data warehouse
Does not hold a pre-computed, filtered copy of the original data.	Does hold a pre-computed, filtered copy of the original data.
Only the view metadata is stored on the disk.	View metadata, as well as a pre-computed, filtered copy of the original data, are stored on the disk.
Does not help with reducing query execution overheads.	Helps in reducing query execution overheads.
Does not require extra disk storage space.	Requires extra disk storage space.
Always up to date. No need for explicit refresh.	Needs to be refreshed to be kept up to date.
To make use of the views, a typical SQL query will specify the name of the view in the FROM clause.	To make use of materialized views, a typical SQL query will specify the name of the table in the FROM clause, and the query engine will decide to use the materialized view whenever useful.

Table 10.2: Comparison between database views and materialized views in a data warehouse

Note: **Modern-day operational databases like Oracle, allow users to create materialized views.**

Columnar storage format

Now, let us say that the data analyst wants to identify the pattern of orders returned by the users. For that, the analyst will ask the following types of questions:

- How many of the total returns were by a specific user?
- How many of the total returns are from a specific region?
- How many of the total returns were for a specific product or a specific product type?

Now, these queries represent an exploratory part of the data analysis where the analyst is trying to find a pattern. So, the analyst will run a bunch of queries by varying and tuning the parameters until a real pattern emerges.

In exploratory analysis cases, a large amount of data is accessed, which leads to high costs. To reduce these costs, data engineers need to choose the right storage format; in this case, it is the columnar storage format.

To understand the benefit of the columnar storage format, let us take an example of a table of returned orders. This table will contain the **OrderId**, **ProductId**, **Region**, **UserId**, and **ProductType** for the order that has been returned.

The code is as follows:

```
CREATE TABLE returns(
    OrderId VARCHAR(32) PRIMARY KEY,
    ProductId VARCHAR(32),
    Region VARCHAR(32),
    UserId VARCHAR(32),
    ProductType VARCHAR(32)
);
```

Now, let us look at the example queries that will be run to identify the patterns, if any. The following query can be used to get the total number of returned orders:

```
SELECT COUNT(*)
FROM returns;
```

Now, to get the total number of returns for a particular product type, the analyst can write the following query:

```
SELECT COUNT(*)
FROM returns
WHERE ProductType = "Food";
```

To get the total number of returns in a specific region, the analyst can write the following query:

```
SELECT COUNT(*)
FROM returns
WHERE Region = "NY";
```

Here, we can observe that these queries need to access only one column of the table, but they will iterate over a large subset of the data. To optimize such data access, we can use a columnar storage format. Now, let us understand the row-oriented storage format and columnar storage format with an example.

Example of row-oriented and columnar storage formats

Here, we will consider the same **returns** table, and the dataset in our example is represented in *Table 10.3*. In this example, we can see that food-type products are being returned a lot of times and from multiple regions. However, the amount of data that needs to be read from the disk to get the count of food items returned depends on the storage format.

On the disk, the data is stored in logical units called disk pages. All disk pages are fixed in size. The query performance and the cost to run the query eventually boil down to the total number of disk pages being read from the disk, as shown in the following table:

OrderId	ProductId	Region	UserId	ProductType
"Order-11"	"Product-52"	"NY"	"User-408"	"Food"
"Order-21"	"Product-986"	"CA"	"User-408"	"Stationary"
"Order-33"	"Product-53"	"NY"	"User-85"	"Food"
"Order-914"	"Product-199"	"FL"	"User-31"	"Smartphone"
"Order-1007"	"Product-54"	"FL"	"User-9076"	"Food"
"Order-734"	"Product-64"	"TX"	"User-96"	"Cosmetics"

Table 10.3: Example table to understand the difference in row-oriented and columnar storages

For our example, we will consider the disk page size as 256 bytes. Each row has five values in it, which are attributes represented by five columns. Each value is of type **VARCHAR(32)**, which is 32 bytes in size. So, each record will take 160 bytes.

Table 10.4 represents how the data will be stored in the row-oriented data format across multiple pages:

Page 1	"Order-11"	"Product-52"	"NY"	"User-408"
	"Food"	"Order-21"	"Product-986"	"CA"
Page 2	"User-408"	"Stationary"	"Order-33"	"Product-53"
	"NY"	"User-85"	"Food"	"Order-914"
Page 3	"Product-199"	"FL"	"User-31"	"Smartphone"
	"Order-1007"	"Product-54"	"FL"	"User-9076"
Page 4	"Food"	"Order-734"	"Product-64"	"TX"
	"User-96"	"Cosmetics"		

Table 10.4: Row-oriented storage representation of tabular data from Table 10.3

Here, we can see that, to get the number of returns of product type **"Food"**, we need to iterate over and read all the pages. The cost is four times the cost of reading one page from the disk. On the other hand, with columnar implementation, we only need to read a subset of data pages to get the count of returns of product type **"Food"**. The storage representation for a columnar store is shown in *Table 10.5*:

Page 1	"Order-11"	"Order-21"	"Order-33"	"Order-914"
	"Order-1007"	"Order-734"		

Page 2	"Product-52"	"Product-986"	"Product-53"	"Product-199"
	"Product-54"	"Product-64"		
Page 3	"NY"	"CA"	"NY"	"FL"
	"FL"	"TX"		
Page 4	"User-408"	"User-408"	"User-85"	"User-31"
	"User-9076"	"User-96"		
Page 5	"Food"	"Stationary"	"Food"	"Smartphone"
	"Food"	"Cosmetics"		

Table 10.5: Columnar storage representation of tabular data from Table 10.3

As per *Table 10.5,* we can see that all the entries for product type belong to *Page 5*. So, the columnar store needs to read only one page (as compared to 4 in a row-oriented store) to identify the count of all returned food products.

Note: As there are only a limited number of columns, it is very trivial for the columnar storage engine to store the starting page numbers for each column in the table metadata.

The following are the benefits and limitations of columnar storage formats:

- **Benefits:** Apart from the performance and cost benefits mentioned above, columnar storage formats also benefit from achieving high compression ratios, as similar types of data are stored close to each other.

- **Limitations**: The primary limitation of using columnar storage is the overhead in reconstructing the original records. As the values for various fields of a single record are stored far from each other, reconstruction becomes a costly task.

Star schema and Snowflake schema

As the data warehouse stores historical data, the storage costs and running queries can be high, with large data sizes. One of the trade-offs data engineers can make is using specific schemas while storing the data in the data warehouse. Here, we will understand the two popularly used schemas, viz., *star schemas* and *Snowflake schemas*.

Let us continue with our example of order history. In practice, there will be a bunch of details in each order. In this example, we will consider the following information, as mentioned in the **CREATE TABLE** statement, which will be stored in the order table, as shown in the following code:

```
CREATE TABLE orders(
    OrderId VARCHAR(32) PRIMARY KEY,
    ProductId VARCHAR(32),
    ProductType VARCHAR(32),
```

```
    ProductSize int,
    ProductColor VARCHAR(32),
    Quantity int,
    UserId VARCHAR(32),
    ShippingName VARCHAR(32),
    ShippingAddress VARCHAR(256),
    BillingName VARCHAR(32),
    BillingAddress VARCHAR(256),
    ShippingInstructions VARCHAR(256)
);
```

A transactional application is likely to store all these details in a single row of a table during order finalization, as it keeps the application program logic simple. However, there is a lot of duplication of data, specifically across records in the table. The duplication of data leads to higher storage costs. So, at the time of storing the data in the data warehouse, data engineers may choose to normalize this data, as shown in the following figure:

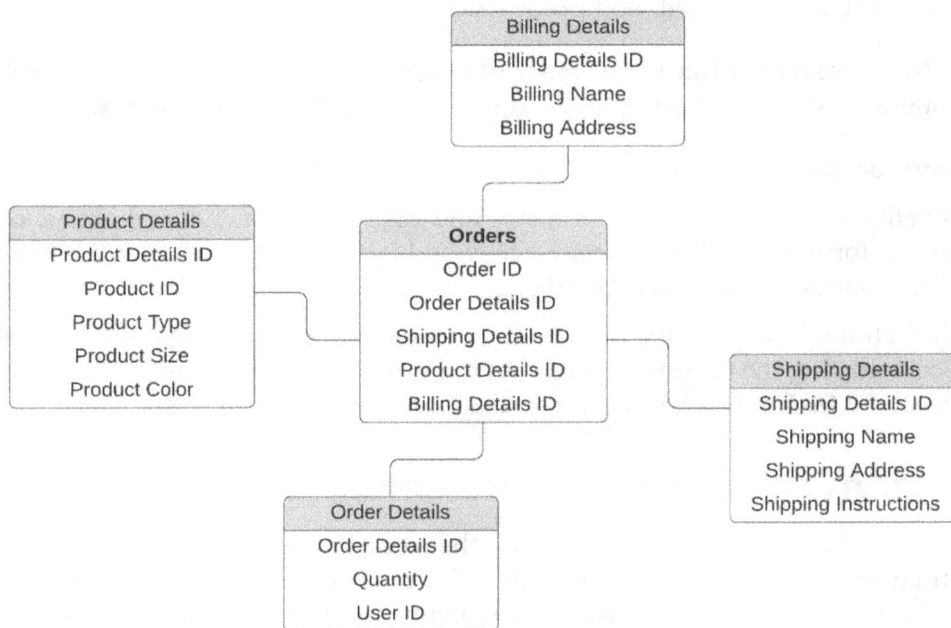

Figure 10.2: *Star schema for order history*

Figure 10.2 shows the visual representation of the data objects stored after the normalization. Here, we have created the following set of tables to store a specific subset of information:

- Order Details
- Product Details
- Billing Details
- Shipping Details

Looking at the visualization, we can observe that a single *fact table* is divided into multiple *dimensional tables*, forming a star-like structure. So, this type of schema is called a star schema.

With the star schema, we can see that some further normalization is possible. For example, if the data analyst wants to find patterns related to a particular ZIP code or a particular city, then a further normalization of the data is required. This leads to the requirement for *sub-dimensional tables*. These sub-dimensional tables are linked to the dimensional tables and not to the fact tables, creating a Snowflake-like visualization, as shown in *Figure 10.3*:

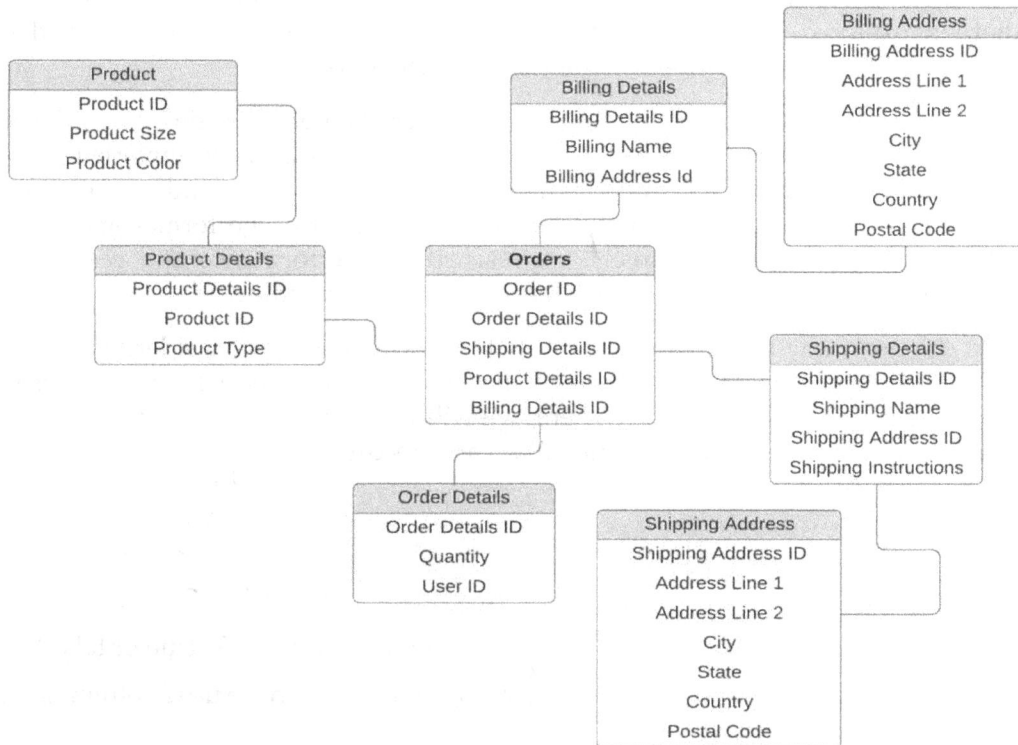

Figure 10.3: Snowflake schema for order history

Here, we can see that the Shipping Address table is a sub-dimensional table directly related to the Shipping Details table, which is a dimensional table. The same is true for the Billing Address and Product tables. A dimensional table can have any number of sub-dimensional tables.

Choice between star and Snowflake schemas

A bunch of data duplication gets avoided just by moving from only the fact table to a star schema. Furthermore, using Snowflake schemas, all the duplication can be avoided. This helps in reducing the storage cost. However, having dimensional and sub-dimensional tables requires a query engine to perform join operations at the query runtime. Join operations are costly and require holding a large amount of data in memory while the query is running.

So, the data engineers need to find the right trade-off while designing the star or Snowflake schema.

Conclusion

In this chapter, we started by discussing various business intelligence and data analysis use cases and established a clear requirement for the data warehouse. We then identified key differences between the database and the data warehouse with the help of various examples. After that, we explored three important data warehouse features, viz., materialized views, columnar storage format, and star Snowflake storage schemas.

We looked in-depth into understanding the differences between database views and materialized views. We also identified trade-offs of creating and using materialized views. We also looked at the cost impact of refreshing materialized views. We studied the differences between the row-oriented storage format and the columnar storage format and the trade-offs of choosing between them. Finally, we learned the performance and cost impact of normalization, and the trade-offs in using star vs. snowflake schemas.

In the next chapter, we will learn about the data lake architecture by considering the use case scenarios of a travel aggregator website. We will also discuss data enrichment use cases with the help of the medallion architecture. There, we will understand the benefits of storing the pre-processed data in each layer of the medallion architecture.

Questions

1. What are the popular open-source data warehouse software?

2. Materialized views have more storage cost than database views; true or false?

3. What is the benefit of using a columnar storage format? Can we use a columnar storage format for NoSQL data?

4. What are the drawbacks of using a Snowflake schema instead of a star schema?

Join our Discord space

Join our Discord workspace for latest updates, offers, tech happenings around the world, new releases, and sessions with the authors:

https://discord.bpbonline.com

CHAPTER 11
Data Lake and Medallion Architecture

Introduction

In this chapter, we will move away from the previously used example of an e-commerce website and introduce another popular industry of travel aggregators. Travel aggregators provide various types of services like flight bookings, hotel bookings, train bookings, bus bookings, etc. For day-to-day business, these services run independently of each other, while from a data analytics perspective, the data generated by these services needs to be analyzed together to find patterns and make strategic business decisions.

The formats and schemas for the data generated by multiple applications can be different. So, for storing such data with varying formats, data engineers make use of a popular data storage pattern called data lake. In this chapter, we will understand the concepts of a data lake with the help of an example. We will also learn the benefits of using data lakes.

The data generated by the user applications is raw. It requires further processing to make it more usable for business-specific use cases. The data, when entered for the first time in the data lake, is raw. Data engineers can make use of medallion architecture to filter, process, and enrich the data. In the data lake storage pattern, the data, which is processed, filtered, and enriched, is stored back in the data lake itself. With the help of examples, we will learn how to perform data filtering, processing, and enrichment.

Structure

This chapter covers the following topics:

- Travel aggregator example
- Data lake architecture
- Organizing data in data lake
- Use of extract-load-transform pattern
- Medallion architecture
- Benefits of medallion architecture

Objectives

By the end of this chapter, you will understand the data lake storage pattern with the help of examples. You will understand how to choose between the data warehouse and the data lake, and what the trade-offs of the choice are. With the help of an example, you will also learn how the data can be organized in the data lake.

You will also learn about medallion architecture, which is used to iteratively improve your data. We will also learn the benefits of using medallion architecture towards the end of the chapter.

Travel aggregator example

Travel aggregator websites provide features like flight booking, hotel booking, bus travel, train travel, cab booking, etc. To provide users with a seamless booking experience, travel aggregators need to:

- Gather the flight, hotel, bus, and train data from corresponding independent external services
- Interface with these external services for booking finalization
- Implement payment settlement workflows
- Manage booking confirmations, invoices, payment receipts, etc.
- Interface with third-party vendors for cancellations and payment settlements after cancellations
- Analyze user actions, booking patterns, and click streams to make future booking recommendations

The transactional part of the website will use a backend database to perform the following functions:

- Store the information about flights, hotels, buses, trains, cabs, etc.
- Allow users to search for these services
- Allow users to book these services and finalize the booking after the payment is done
- Provide a facility to cancel the bookings and settle the payment

The data generated by these transactional workflows can be transferred to a data warehouse or a data lake for further data analysis. In the previous chapter, we learned about a data warehouse. In this chapter, we will learn about a data lake and how it is different from a data warehouse.

A *data lake* is a data object repository, typically backed by a blob storage engine, used to store structured, semi-structured, or unstructured data, and it can scale for vast amounts of data.

Data lakes are largely popular due to the flexibility they offer. For example, the data lake architecture allows users to store rows and column values of the data objects stored in a relational database along with user application-generated JSON or CSV data and unstructured data like text files, images, audio, and video files, etc. In reality, all these different types of data will be stored together in a backend blob storage engine like AWS S3 or Azure Blob Store. Thanks to the schema-less design, all these different types of objects can be stored in a single S3 bucket or a single Azure Blob Store container to form a data lake. The data stored in the data lake is typically in a raw form.

To understand the data lake architecture in detail, let us look at the points of comparison between the data warehouse and the data lake.

Differences between data warehouse and data lake

The following table depicts the differences between the data warehouse and the data lake from the perspective of the purpose of use, cost, performance, etc.:

Data warehouse	Data lake
The primary purpose of the data warehouse is to store structured data across one or more tables.	The primary purpose of the data lake is to store structured, semi-structured, and unstructured data.
Data warehouse uses a schema-on-write pattern as the schema is enforced at the time of data ingestion.	Data lake users use a schema-on-read pattern, as the schema enforcement can be done at the time of reading the data. Until then, the data is treated as schema-less and stored in the form of blobs of data objects.
Query execution is optimized for performance.	Query execution is not optimized for performance.

Likely to use **extract, transform, and load** (**ETL**) workflows.	Likely to use **extract, load, and transform** (**ELT**) workflows.
The cost is higher due to the out-of-the-box availability of performance optimizations.	As there are not many performance optimizations, the cost is lower.
Primarily used for data analysis use cases.	Primarily used for data analytics, as well as data science and machine learning use cases.
Used by data analysts and business decision makers.	Used by data scientists and machine learning engineers, along with analysts and decision makers.

Table 11.1: Differences between the data warehouse and the data lake

Data lake architecture

To understand the data lake better, let us take an example use case where the travel aggregator wants to upsell hotel bookings or cab bookings, in case the user has booked a flight or train to a particular destination city.

Now, let us make the following assumption about the design choices made at the time of the evolution of the travel aggregator website:

- When the travel aggregator website started, it only had a flight booking workflow.
- Flight booking details are stored in a relational database, like MySQL.
- Once enough revenue started coming in from flight bookings, the business expanded into other services, like train, cab, and hotel bookings.
- The business decision was to build the capabilities in-house for train and hotel booking.
- For cab booking, the business decision was to integrate with a third-party cab aggregator.
- Given the past experiences with the limitations of traditional relational databases, in-house architects decided to use a distributed NoSQL database, like Couchbase, for storing the train and hotel bookings.
- The third-party cab booking service returns the successful booking response in plaintext form, and it does not use any known formats like JSON or XML. So, the travel aggregator will dump the plaintext response as a binary document in the cab bookings table, with some metadata like booking ID and user ID.

Now, looking at all these assumptions mentioned above, we can see that the booking data is stored in different databases (or data stores), and is stored with different data formats. For further data analysis, we need to consume this data from different transactional data sources and store it in a single storage backend, which forms a data lake. *Figure 11.1* shows the high-level block diagram for data lake architecture.

In *Figure 11.1*, we can see that the data lake architecture has the following:

- **Data storage layer**: Backed by blob storage engine.

- **Data transformation layer**: This can transform data coming from various sources (and having different data types) to a blob data format. This transformed data will be used for various business-specific use cases.

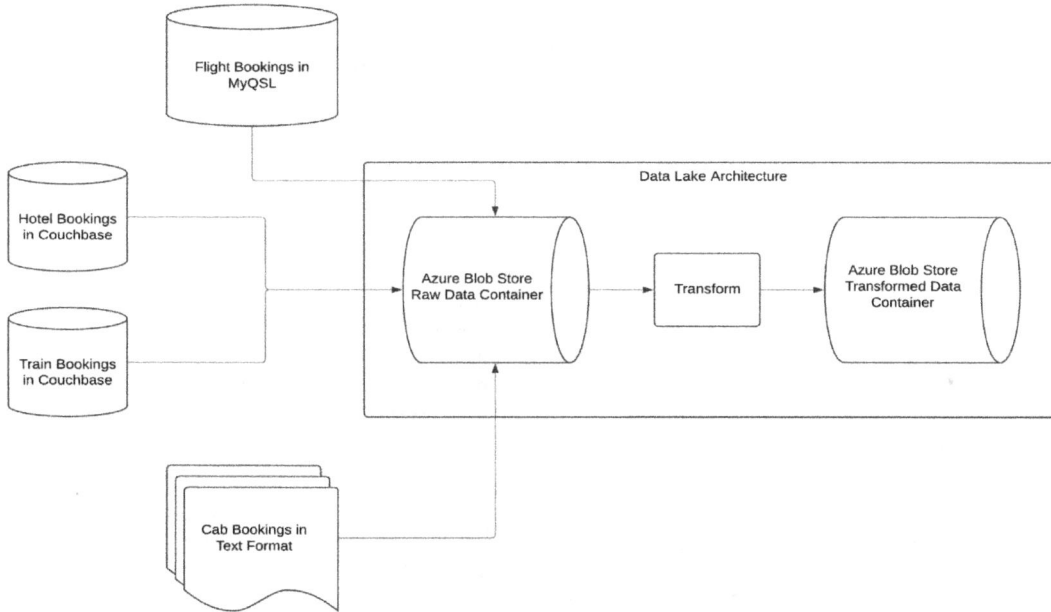

Figure 11.1: *Introduction to the data lake architecture*

Now, let us see how we can organize the data in an Azure Blob Store container.

Organizing data in data lake

As mentioned earlier, a data lake is backed by data object/blob stores. A typical object store will expose very simple APIs to store and retrieve the data, based on key-value storage semantics. User programs can make use of either blob metadata or manipulate the key names to logically divide various types of data. Using blob metadata is typically a costly operation if the user application needs to traverse a larger subset of data. So, key name manipulation is a more commonly used method for data organization.

To understand how key-name manipulation works, we first need to understand the basic APIs exposed by blob storage. The basic key-value APIs exposed by the Azure Blob Storage are as follows:

- Put (key, value)
- value = Get(key)
- List[keys] = List Blobs(key-prefix)

The first two APIs, i.e., Get and Put, are self-explanatory. However, the third API to get the list of blobs, for a specified key prefix, allows users to treat object storage as a file system in a logical sense. This ability to emulate the directory listing helps users to easily visualize the logical organization of the data. Let us continue our example where the data is coming from multiple sources to understand this further.

If we were to organize the booking details in a file system-like layout, we would have created a directory structure as shown in *Figure 11.2*:

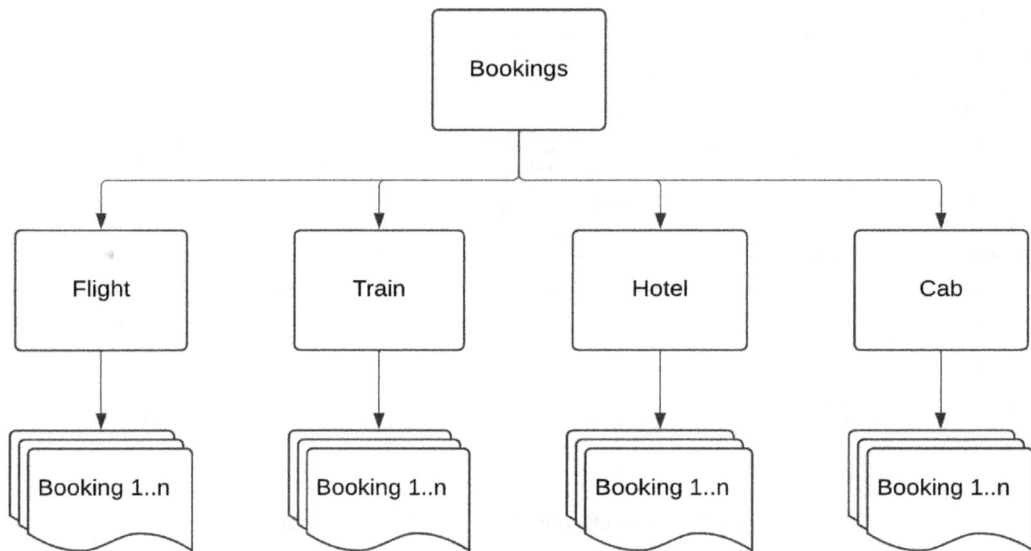

Figure 11.2: Directory structure for bookings using directories and files

In *Figure 11.2*, we can see that the user has decided to put all booking information under a single top-level directory called **Bookings**. Under that directory, there are sub-directories based on booking type (i.e., *Flight, Train, Hotel,* or *Cab*). Under these sub-directories, data related to an individual booking is stored in separate files. For simplicity, we can assume the names of the files are Booking1, Booking2, and Booking3, where the number in the file name represents the booking identifier. As the files are stored independently, there is no enforcement of the file format. The file system also provides the ability to get the list of bookings under any folder, which is useful for searching for a booking with a specific ID without opening the actual data files.

Using Azure Blob Storage (or any other blob storage service), this file system behavior can be simulated using Get, Put, and List Blobs APIs. The user can construct the blob store keys–like the file paths–while storing the data in the blob store. For example, the blob store path

Bookings/Flight/Booking101 represents the booking details for a flight booking with ID 101. Similarly, the blob store path **Bookings/Hotel/Booking302** points to a file containing hotel booking details for booking ID 302.

The following is an example PySpark code to transform the flight booking data from a MySQL table to individual JSON documents per booking, stored in the Azure Blob Store. Here, Azure Blob Store will be used as a data lake.

In this example, we can see that the aforementioned directory structure is being simulated by manipulating the key prefixes:

```
from pyspark.sql import SparkSession
from pyspark.sql.functions import to_json, struct, col
from azure.storage.blob import BlobServiceClient

spark = SparkSession.builder \
    .appName("Store flight bookings to data lake") \
    .config("spark.jars", "/path/to/mysql-connector-java.jar") \
    .getOrCreate()

# MySQL connection parameters.

mysql_db_url = "jdbc:mysql://<db-host>:<db-port>/<database-name>"
mysql_db_properties = {
    "user": "<db-username>",
    "password": "<db-password>",
    "driver": "com.mysql.cj.jdbc.Driver"
}
mysql_table_name = "<mysql-table-name>"

# Azure blob store connection parameters

azure_blob_container_name = "<your-container-name>
azure_account_url = "https://<storage-account-name>.blob.core.windows.net"

# A function to read from MySQL table

def read_mysql_table():
    return spark.read.format("jdbc") \
    .option("url", mysql_db_url) \
    .option("dbtable", mysql_table_name) \
    .option("user", mysql_db_properties["user"]) \
    .option("password", mysql_db_properties["password"]) \
    .option("driver", mysql_db_properties["driver"]) \
    .load()

def convert_to_individual_json_docs(df):
    json_df = df.withColumn("document",
        to_json( struct([col(c) for c in df.columns]))
    )
    return json_df

def write_individual_json_docs_to_blob(json_df):
```

```
    json_df.rdd.foreach(lambda row: write_to_blob(row['document']))
def write_to_blob(json_data):
    blob_service_client = BlobServiceClient(azure_account_url,
        credential=<azure_credential>)

    container_client = blob_service_client \
        .get_container_client(container=azure_blob_container_name)
    # filename simulates the directory structure mentioned in Figure 11.2
    filename = "Bookings/Flight/" + json_data["bookingId"] + ".json"
    blob_client = container_client.upload_blob(name=filename, data=json_data)
# Read from MySQL, Convert to JSON and Write to Azure blob store.
mysql_df = read_mysql_table()
json_df = convert_to_individual_json_docs(mysql_df)
write_individual_json_docs_to_blob(json_df)
```

Use of extract-load-transform pattern

Referring to *Figure 11.1,* we can see that at the ingestion time, data gets loaded into the raw data container. Only key names are manipulated before storing the data in the raw data container. However, to perform activities like business intelligence, it is optimal to transform, filter, and sanitize the data. The transformed data can further be stored back in the data lake, either in a different container or in the same container with a different prefix (logical directory).

To continue with our example, we need to upsell hotel bookings or cab bookings to the customers based on train and flight bookings. To achieve this, the data analytics software needs to perform the following steps.

We can assume that the following steps are performed daily:

1. Find the list of train and flight bookings done on the last day.

2. For each of the bookings in the list, perform the following steps:

     a. Check if the booking is canceled; if canceled, then move to the next booking.

     b. If the booking is not canceled, then extract the user ID, user email, and travel date from the booking details.

     c. Check if the same user id has any hotel or cab bookings on the day of travel.

     d. If either of them does not exist, send a promotional email to the user to offer discounts on the corresponding missing bookings.

     e. Mark the promotion email that sent the flag to avoid multiple emails.

If the user program looks at the raw data, it needs to perform the following:

*   Traverse the entire list of train and flight bookings as the bookings are stored based on booking id, and not based on booking date. The booking date needs to be extracted from the value field.

- Traverse the entire list of cab and hotel bookings to check if the hotel and cab booking is not done for the travel date by the same user.

If 1000 train and flight bookings are done on an average day, then on an average day, the two operations mentioned above will be performed by the user program 1000 times. Performing traversal for the entire list of bookings and extracting information from the value has performance overheads as well as a high cost in dollars. To optimize this, the data can be transformed, filtered, and stored in an optimal form.

For this use case, the optimal form is where:

- Train and flight bookings are ordered based on the booking date as a key prefix.
- Cab and hotel booking are based on user ID, travel date, and city as a key prefix.

As the keys for train and flight bookings are ordered based on the booking date as a key prefix, we can list and read only the bookings made on a specific day. This avoids a lot of time, as well as Azure Blob Storage and read costs.

Also, when we are searching for the cab and hotel bookings made by a specific user for a specific travel day and specific city, based on the improved key prefixes, it will be a quick search, saving a lot of time and Azure Blob Store read cost.

Note: **For a typical cloud provider, the cost of the read operation is dependent on the number of bytes read from the service and the number of read requests made.**

The following code snippet is an example of the PySpark program to read the booking data from Couchbase (an open source, distributed, NoSQL database) and store the booking details for train and hotel bookings in the data lake using Azure Blob Store. Here, the train bookings will be stored with the booking date as a key prefix, while the hotel bookings will be stored with a user ID, travel date, and city as key prefixes.

In this example, we will assume hotel and train bookings are stored in a single Couchbase bucket. In reality, there can be a separate bucket used for train bookings, and a separate bucket can be used for hotel bookings:

```
from pyspark.sql import SparkSession
from azure.storage.blob import BlobServiceClient

# Couchbase config parameters
cb_cluster = "couchbases://YourCouchbaseClusterHostname"
cb_username = "username"
cb_password = "password.123"

# Connect to Coucubase Server using SparkSession
spark = SparkSession.builder \
    .appName("Couchbase Spark Connector Example") \
    .config("spark.couchbase.connectionString", cb_cluster) \
    .config("spark.couchbase.username", cb_username) \
    .config("spark.couchbase.password", cb_password) \
```

```
    .getOrCreate()
# Azure blob store connection parameters
azure_blob_container_name = "<your-container-name>"
azure_account_url = "https://<storage-account-name>.blob.core.windows.net"
# Create a dataframe by connecting to the Couchbase Server.
df = spark.read.format("couchbase.query") \
    .option("bucket", "bookings") \
    .load()
# Function to write the data to Azure blob store
def write_to_blob(row):
    row_json = row.asDict(recursive=True)
    json_data = json.dumps(row_json, indent=4)
        blob_service_client = BlobServiceClient(azure_account_url,
        credential=<azure_credential>)
        container_client = blob_service_client \
        .get_container_client(container= azure_blob_container_name)
        filename = "Bookings/Hotels/" + \
        row_json["bookingDate"] + "/" + row_json["bookingId"] + ".json"

    blob_client = container_client.upload_blob(name=filename, data=json_data)
# Store the data in the azure blob store
df.foreach(write_to_blob)
```

Until now, we have learned how one can use a data lake design pattern to store the data of different types in a schema-less manner to exploit the benefits of differences in data formats. We also learned how data transformation, performed after data loading, can help in designing a performant and cost-effective user application.

A rightly performed transformation on raw data can lead to reducing the number of computations and costs. One of the most popular data transformation and storage patterns used by user applications is the medallion architecture.

Medallion architecture

In medallion architecture, data is represented in three different forms based on data quality. The medallion architecture uses three layers to represent the data. The data passes through each layer where its quality is improved progressively. With the help of the use case for upselling cab and hotel bookings, we will understand how the users can implement the medallion architecture.

Previously in this chapter, we have seen that the source data can be available in different formats and can belong to different types of databases. The raw data will be stored under the bookings prefix as it arrives from the corresponding data source. This raw data, when it arrives, is stored as is in the data lake. This is the first layer of the medallion architecture, also called the **bronze layer**.

Transforming data from bronze layer

After the data is ingested into the bronze layer, the user can perform transformations on that data. These transformations are dictated by various data analysis use cases. Let us understand more about these transformations with the help of the following examples:

- Not all booking data may be required for data analysis. For example, if there is no plan to perform any data analysis based on payment details, the payment details from the data can be filtered. This type of data transformation is called **data filtering**.

- As seen previously, we can reorganize the data using different keys to avoid costly and time-consuming operations. This type of data transformation is called **data reorganizing**.

- In case of bookings getting canceled, the analysts can choose to keep the data related to canceled bookings to analyze cancellation patterns. However, if there is no workflow to analyze the canceled bookings, we can choose to skip canceled data bookings from entering the next layer. This type of data transformation is called **data cleansing**.

- As you know, the destination city for flight booking and the destination city for train booking can be named differently. This can happen as there are multiple airports and multiple train stations in a single big city. Also, the airports and train stations are not referred to by the actual city names, but by their corresponding codes. In such cases, the data engineer needs to map all such airport and train station codes to a single city name. This type of data transformation is called **data enrichment**.

Once all such transformations are performed, the transformed data represents the enterprise view. This layer in the medallion architecture is called the **silver layer**.

The following PySpark program reads the raw data from a bronze layer of medallion architecture, performs data enrichment by mapping train station names and airport names to the corresponding city names, and stores it in the silver layer of medallion architecture:

```
from pyspark.sql import SparkSession
from azure.storage.blob import BlobServiceClient

# Azure blob store connection parameters
azure_blob_src_container_name = "<your-source-container-name>"
azure_blob_dst_container_name = "<your-destination-container-name>"
azure_account_url = "https://<storage-account-name>.blob.core.windows.net"

# Connect to Coucubase Server
spark = SparkSession.builder \
    .appName("Azure Spark Connector") \
    .config(azure_account_url, <azure_account_credential>) \
    .getOrCreate()

# Create a dataframe by connecting to the Azure blob store
read_src = azure_blob_src_container_name
read_url = "wasbs://read_src@blob_storage_account.blob.core.windows.net"
```

```
df = spark.read.json("read_url/bronze/*.json")
# Write the processed json data to the azure blob store.
def write_to_blob(filename, json_data):
    blob_service_client = BlobServiceClient(azure_account_url,
        credential=<azure_credential>)
    container_client = blob_service_client \
        .get_container_client(container= azure_blob_container_name)

    blob_client = container_client.upload_blob(name=filename, data=json_data)
# Function to process the each json object from bronze layer, process it,
# and write it to silver layer.
def process_and_write_data(row):
    row_json = row.asDict(recursive=True)
    # In this example, the json object paths for raw data in bronze layer
    # and the json object paths for enriched data in silver layer remains
    # the same, except the name of the layer bronze/silver.
    in_filename = row_json["id"]
    out_filename = in_filename.replace("bronze", "silver", 1)
    if row_json["bookingType"] == "Flight":
        city = get_city_from_airport(row_json["destination"])
        row_json["destination"] = city
    elif row_json["bookingType"] == "Train":
        city = get_city_from_station(row_json["destination"])
        row_json["destination"] = city
    json_data = json.dumps(row_json, indent=4)
    write_to_blob(out_filename, json_data)
# Process and store the data in the azure blob store
df.foreach(process_and_write_data)
```

In the aforementioned example code, we can see that the functions **get_city_from_airport** and **get_city_from_station** can be implemented as simple Python dictionaries that map airport code or train station code to the corresponding city. Given the simplicity, the implementation of these functions is skipped from the example.

Transforming data from silver layer

Once the enterprise view of the data is formed in the silver layer of the medallion architecture, the data will be transformed to make it consumption-ready for data analysis or decision-making. To understand this further, let us continue with our example of identifying flight/train bookings that do not have corresponding cab/hotel bookings in the destination city.

As the primary purpose of the business is to upsell cab and hotel bookings, the data analyst will look at the answers to the following questions and work with marketing and sales teams to decide on an upsell strategy:

- *How many users are booking flight/train tickets with our platform but not hotels or cabs?*
- *Is there any pattern in age, gender, city/country of residence of the person who is booking the flight/train but not the cab/hotel?*
- *Is there any pattern in the city/country of travel for which people are booking flights/trains but not cabs/hotels?*
- *Has there been any recent change in the booking pattern? For example, were there any negative reviews in the recent past?*

The business strategy requires answers to the various questions of the above type. Business analysts will design dashboards that provide such answers. The data being represented on such dashboards can either be calculated using an enterprise view of the data (i.e., silver layer), or data engineers can perform one more level of transformation on the data in the silver layer to get consumption-ready data, also known as the **gold layer**.

The gold layer of the medallion architecture will typically store the data, like:

- List of users who have booked a flight/train but not a cab/hotel in the last month.
- Top 10 list of cities, for which users are not booking cabs/hotels.
- Top 10 list of cities that have received a bunch of negative reviews for the cab bookings or the cab ride experience.

Now, let us look at the example PySpark code:

- Traverse through the list of flight bookings
- Find the bookings that do not have any hotel booking for the travel date and destination city
- Store the list of such bookings in the gold layer of medallion architecture

For this example, we will assume the following key format steps for the silver layer:

1. For flight and train booking, the key format is as follows:
   `Silver/Flights/<bookingDate>/<BookingId>.json`

2. For hotel booking, the key format is as follows:
   `Silver/Hotels/<userId>/<travelDate>/<city>/<BookingId>.json`

The code will look as follows:

```
from pyspark.sql import SparkSession
from azure.storage.blob import BlobServiceClient

from datetime import date

# Azure blob store connection parameters
azure_blob_src_container_name = "<your-source-container-name>"
azure_blob_dst_container_name = "<your-destination-container-name>"
azure_account_url = "https://<storage-account-name>.blob.core.windows.net"
```

```python
# Connect to Coucubase Server
spark = SparkSession.builder \
    .appName("Azure Spark Connector") \
    .config(azure_account_url, <azure_account_credential>) \
    .getOrCreate()

# Create a dataframe by connecting to the Azure blob store for flights
booking_date = str(date.today())
read_src = azure_blob_src_container_name
read_url = "wasbs://read_src@blob_storage_account.blob.core.windows.net"
flight_df = spark.read.json("read_url/Silver/Flights/"+ booking_date + "/*.
json")

# Create a dataframe by connecting to the Azure blob store for hotels
# For specific user id, travel date and city
def get_hotels_dataframe(userId, travelDate, city):
    prefix = "read_url/Silver/Hotels/" + userId + str(travelDate) + city
    hotels_df = spark.read.json(prefix + "/*.json")
    return hotels_df

# Write the processed json data to the azure blob store.
def write_to_blob(filename, json_data):
    blob_service_client = BlobServiceClient(azure_account_url,
        credential=<azure_credential>)
    container_client = blob_service_client \
    .get_container_client(container= azure_blob_container_name)
    blob_client = container_client.upload_blob(name=filename, data=json_
data)

# Function to process the each json object from bronze layer, process it,
# and write it to silver layer.

def process_and_write_data(row):
    row_json = row.asDict(recursive=True)
    # Please note that row_json["city"] is already enriched as per processing
    # done during transformation from bronze to silver layer.
    hotels_df = get_hotels_dataframe(row_json["userId"],
        row_json["travelDate"], row_json["city"])
    # Check if the user has already booked hotel for given date, city. If yes,
    # then there is no need to store this booking information in gold layer.
    # The gold layer only represents the user ids, for whom business analysts
    # want to send promotional email for upsell.
    if hotels_df.count() == 0:
        gold_json_data = {}
        gold_json_data["userId"] = row_json["userId"]
        gold_json_data["travelDate"] = row_json["travelDate"]
        gold_json_data["city"] = row_json["city"]
            out_filename = "read_url/Gold/<PromotionId>/<userId>.json"
        json_data = json.dumps(gold_json_data, indent=4)
        write_to_blob(out_filename, json_data)
```

```
# Process and store the data in the azure blob store
df.foreach(process_and_write_data)
```

Putting it all together

We understood the concepts of bronze, silver, and gold layers of the medallion architecture. As seen in the code snippets, cloud blob storage services like AWS S3, Azure Blob Store, etc., provide simple and elegant APIs to store and retrieve blobs of data, and the flexibility of the data lake architecture can be exploited using these, as shown the following figure:

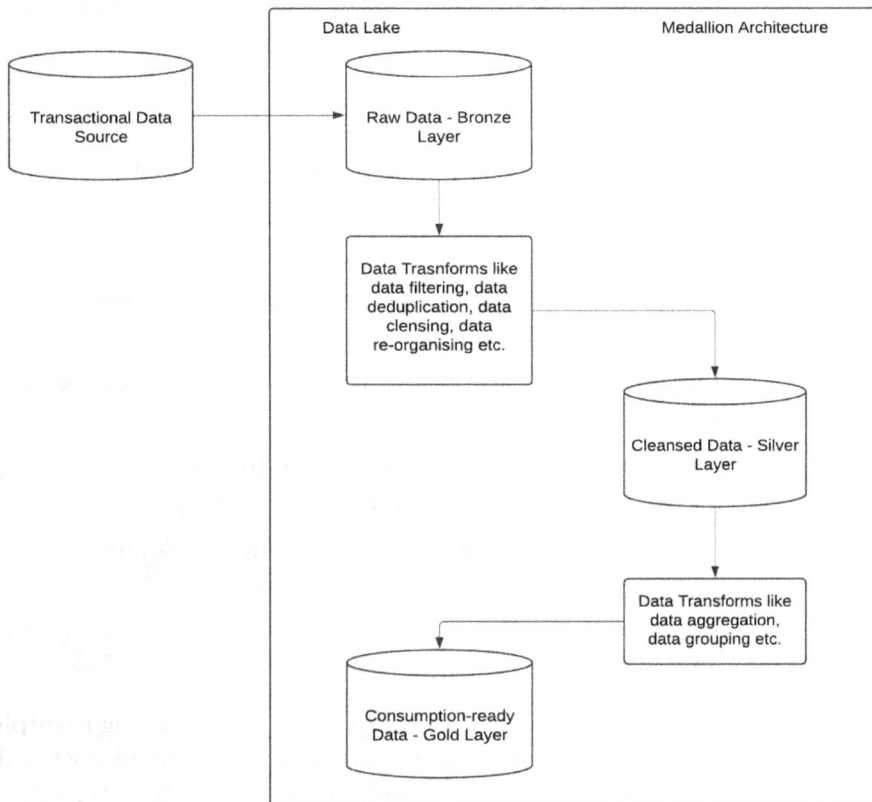

Figure 11.3: Medallion architecture

Figure 11.3 is the visual representation of the data using medallion architecture. In this figure, we can see:

- The bronze layer receives the raw data from the transactional database system.

- Various transformations, like data filtering, enrichment, deduplication, etc., can be performed on the raw data to achieve an enterprise view of the data in the silver layer.

- The data in the silver layer is cleansed and enriched as per the requirements of data analysts.

- The data from the silver layer is then processed further to make it consumption-ready for business intelligence activities.
- This consumption-ready data forms the gold layer of the medallion architecture.

Benefits of medallion architecture

There are two primary benefits of using medallion architecture:

- Separation of concerns
- Reusability of data pipelines

Separation of concerns

Each layer in the medallion architecture has its own purpose. The data in the respective layers can be stored, managed, and cleaned up separately.

For example:

- The bronze layer focuses on the data ingestion aspects. This layer is not concerned with data enrichment processes.
- The silver layer focuses on the basic transformations of the data, like data filtering, cleansing, deduplication, etc.
- The gold layer aims at transforming data from the silver layer to generate a consumption-ready view of the data and storing it efficiently.

The implementation in any of these layers does not impact the implementation in the other layers.

Reusability of data pipeline

As we have seen until now, data pipelines can be complex, time-consuming to implement, and costly to execute and manage. Medallion architecture provides a useful abstraction at each layer so that parts of the data pipeline can be reused. For example, data transformations like filtering, cleansing, and deduplication for bronze to silver transformation are typically generic and can be useful to all data analysts and business strategists, as follows:

Data Pipeline Reuse in Medallion Architecture

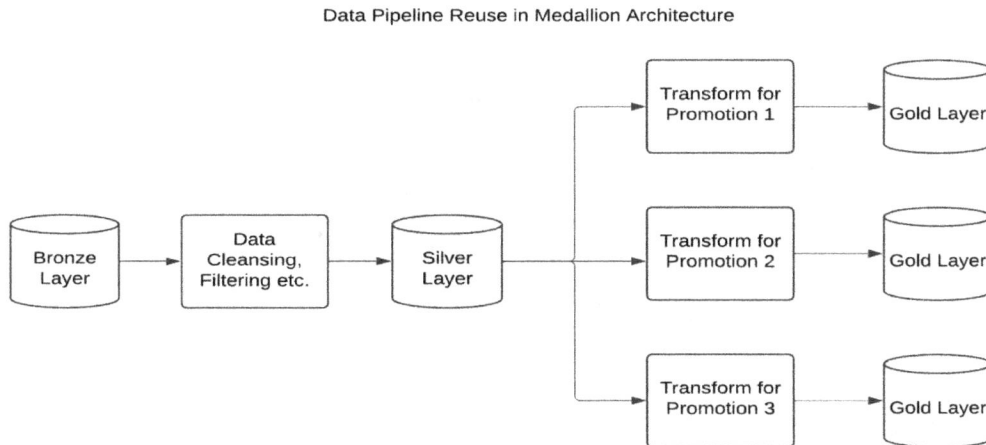

Figure 11.4: *Data pipeline reuse in medallion architecture*

Figure 11.4 shows how multiple promotions can reuse the parts of the data pipeline with the help of the medallion architecture. Here, three different marketing promotions are being executed simultaneously. Each of them will require different types of consumption-ready data in the gold layer. For example, one promotional initiative may need location-based data, while the other may need age-wise demographic booking data. In either case, the same cleansing, deduplication, and transformation can be applied from the bronze to the silver layer. This avoids the cost of transforming and storing data separately across multiple marketing campaigns.

The silver-to-gold transformation can be implemented, executed, and managed separately, as the gold layer data will almost always be specific to only one marketing campaign.

Importance of bronze layer in medallion architecture

The bronze layer provides two specific benefits to the users when using medallion architecture.

Those benefits are as follows:

- **Focus on data ingestion**: Where other layers are free to focus on business-centric data representation and pipeline optimizations.

- **Ability to store the raw data in its original form**: When there is a new business initiative, it may require data engineers to look at a subset of the data specific to that business initiative. The silver layer of the medallion architecture may not have all the required data, as data engineers may have filtered the unwanted data. Without the availability of raw data in the bronze layer, data engineers will need to implement a new (or modify an existing) data ingestion pipeline to get the required data. With the bronze layer holding all the required raw data, data engineers can focus on business-specific data processing requirements. This will save time and cost for implementing a new data ingestion pipeline or modifying the existing one.

Conclusion

In this chapter, we learned the flexibility of the data lake architecture with ever-evolving user needs and application design patterns. We compared data lake architecture with the data warehouse to understand trade-offs while making the design choice between the two.

With the help of an example, we learned how object storage could be used as a backend for data lakes using simple APIs like Get, Put, and List. We also learned the benefits of data modeling (using key prefixes) to improve performance and reduce cloud service costs. We also learned how object storage APIs can simulate file system-like behavior using Get, Put, and List APIs.

Then, we studied medallion architecture, where the data undergoes incremental improvements across multiple layers of the medallion architecture. Each layer of medallion architecture allows users to represent a version of data that is significant to that layer's purpose. We learned the purpose of each layer of medallion architecture with the help of an example of upselling the hotel and cab bookings for users who have already booked train or flight tickets to a particular destination.

In the next chapter, we will discuss the design patterns for data replication and data partitioning.

Questions

1. How can you define blob store key prefixes to organize booking data based only on the city in a directory structure?

2. What code changes are required to the code in this chapter if we were to use the AWS S3 service instead of the Azure Blob Store?

3. Without using SQL, write a PySpark program to identify the top ten most traveled destinations in a previous calendar year, and store that information in the gold layer of medallion architecture.

Join our Discord space

Join our Discord workspace for latest updates, offers, tech happenings around the world, new releases, and sessions with the authors:

https://discord.bpbonline.com

CHAPTER 12
Data Replication and Partitioning

Introduction

In *Chapter 9, Databases and Transactional Data*, we discussed the importance of distributed databases and their role in ensuring business continuity, even in case of partial system failures. We also looked at how traditional database concepts like consistency and durability differ in meaning when the concepts are looked at from the lens of distributed systems. Data replication is the primary mechanism used to achieve fault tolerance in distributed systems. In this chapter, we will explore the conceptual understanding of data replication, different types of partial system failures, and various flavors of data replication, used to solve these failures.

The use of multiple compute and storage resources not only allows us to extract fault tolerance but also allows us to achieve load balancing in the system. Such load balancing is aimed either at running multiple data serving requests in parallel or dividing a single request into multiple sub-requests and processing them in parallel. In both cases, load balancing leads to faster response times by using multiple hardware resources. Dividing a single request into multiple sub-requests and processing them in parallel is typically achieved by dividing the data into multiple subsets, which is called data partitioning. In this chapter, we will learn about various data partitioning techniques and the specific use cases that will benefit from using these data partitioning techniques.

Structure

This chapter covers the following topics:

- Fault and fault tolerance
- Basics of data replication
- Types of data replication
- Configuring more than one replica
- Reading data from the replicas
- Cross datacenter replication
- Data partitioning
- Other popular partitioning schemes
- Scatter and gather operations

Objectives

By the end of this chapter, the readers will master the basic concepts of data replication. The readers will be able to map various fault-inducing scenarios that can impact the availability of their application and will be able to apply the right set of data replication mechanisms to fight against them.

Similarly, the readers will master the basic concepts of data partitioning. The readers will also understand various partitioning schemes and how to achieve the best benefit from these partitioning schemes. The readers will also understand the trade-offs between various partitioning methods.

Faults and fault tolerance

In today's day and age, everyone is always connected to the internet. You can bet on finding your hashtag on Twitter's trending list if your web service is unavailable to serve user requests. Such service unavailability can lead to loss of business and bad publicity. As the business is backed by various types of hardware and software, any of these hardware or software components can fail at any time.

A large-scale user application runs on the hardware, which is backed by a typical data center architecture. The data center has the following types of hardware used for storing the data and ensuring data availability:

- Data storage nodes with individual disks
- Datacenter racks holding storage nodes
- Network switches required to access data storage nodes

- Main power supply
- Power backup like UPS, etc.

A typical datacenter architecture can be seen in *Figure 12.1*:

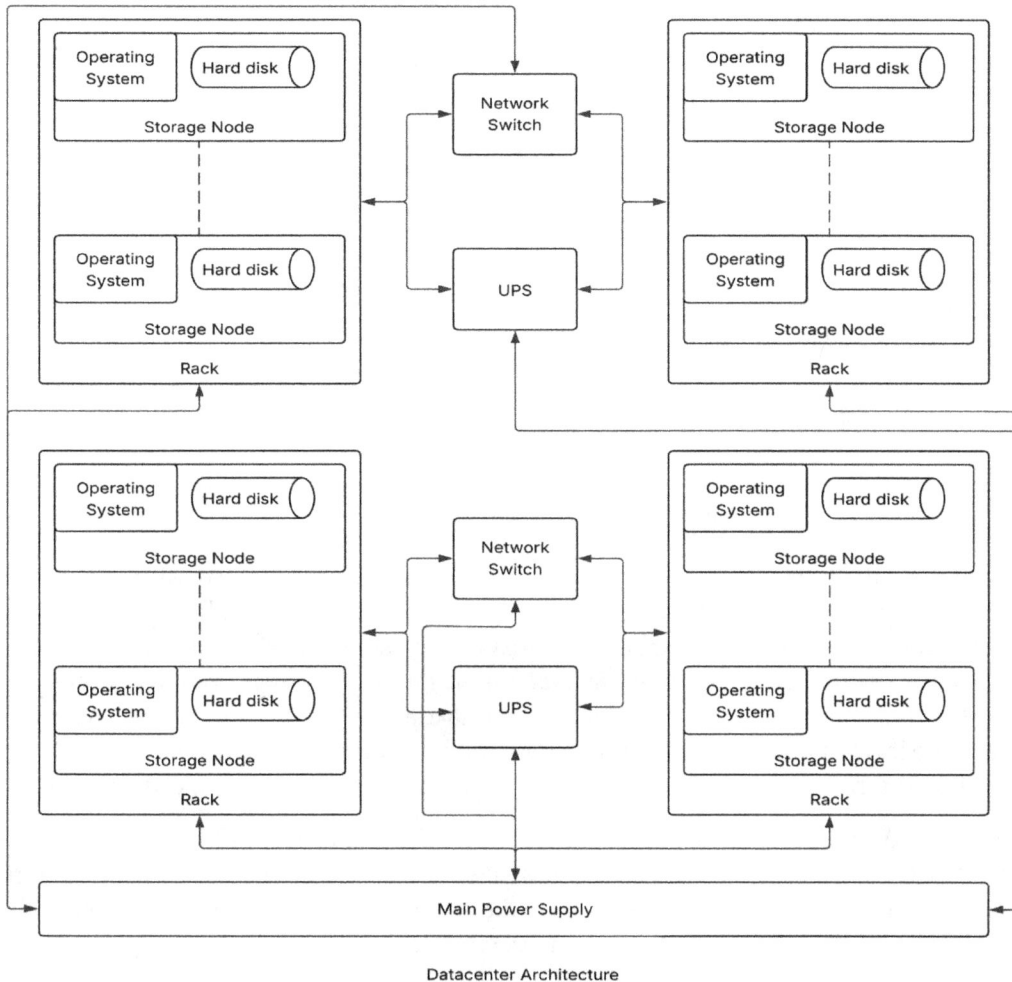

Datacenter Architecture

Figure 12.1: *Datacenter architecture*

As the datacenter has the above-mentioned type of hardware, there is a probability that any of these components can fail. Also, there is a set of software running on various data storage nodes, network switches, etc. Such software can exhibit faulty behavior. The following is a non-exhaustive list of various types of faults that can happen in a data center:

- Data storage software (database or data warehouse) can cause errors or faults.
- The operating system running on the data storage node can crash.
- The hardware (such as CPU or memory) used by the data storage nodes can fail.

- The storage disks on a data storage node can get corrupted.

- An entire datacenter rack can lose its power supply.

- The network switch used to connect to the rack can fail.

- Entire data centers can experience power outages.

- A catastrophic event like a flood, earthquake, etc., can cause the loss of an entire data center.

Even though the above-mentioned faults vary in their severity from a minor glitch to a natural disaster, their effect is a loss of business due to the unavailability of the data.

Large-scale businesses need to account for all such events, be prepared for the worst, and yet ensure business continuity. Businesses like travel aggregators and e-commerce websites require access to their data to ensure business continuity. Such data availability is ensured with the help of various data replication techniques.

Basics of data replication

Data replication is the process of creating and managing a copy of the data, which can be used to serve the data when the original data is not available.

Let us continue with our travel aggregator example. Each time a user performs actions like booking a ticket, canceling a booking, writing a review, etc., some transactional data gets written to the backend database. The backend database ensures the durability of the data being written to it. However, as learned in *Chapter 9, Databases and Transactional Data*, the durability means different things for different databases. For a traditional relational database, durability means the transaction is written to the local disk. On the other hand, for a modern distributed database, durability means the transaction is written to the local disk of the primary data store, as well as one or more replicas.

In modern-day database systems, not only distributed databases like MongoDB, Couchbase, etc., but also traditional relational databases like MySQL, PostgreSQL, etc., support data replication out of the box. Although features like failure detection, automatic switch-over to replica, ease of use, etc., are implementation-specific.

Table 12.1 shows the summary of differences between durability in traditional RDBMS and the modern distributed databases:

Traditional RDBMS	Distributed databases
Write operation is durable only when it is persisted on the local disk of a single database node	Write operation is durable only when it is persisted on the local disk of a minimum of pre-determined number of nodes
The durability is limited by the disk bandwidth of the database node	The durability is limited by the disk bandwidth of the database node, as well as the network bandwidth

If one node fails, the write operation will be lost	If one node fails, the write operation will not be lost
Write operations are typically faster than distributed databases	Write operation is typically slower than the traditional single-node RDBMS

Table 12.1: Durability in traditional RDBMS vs. distributed databases

One of the most important decisions taken by the data engineers is to decide the number of replicas for the application data. If you choose to keep only one replica, then a simultaneous failure of two different data storage nodes can lead to data loss. Although this is a rare scenario, many users choose to configure more than two replicas for their data.

Many times, users will choose to host the replicas on the storage nodes:

- Across different data center racks
- Connected via a different network switch
- Attached to different power supply sources
- Residing across different availability zones

This ensures high availability of the data and avoidance of data loss across various types of faults mentioned above.

Figure 12.2 shows how the basic replication works:

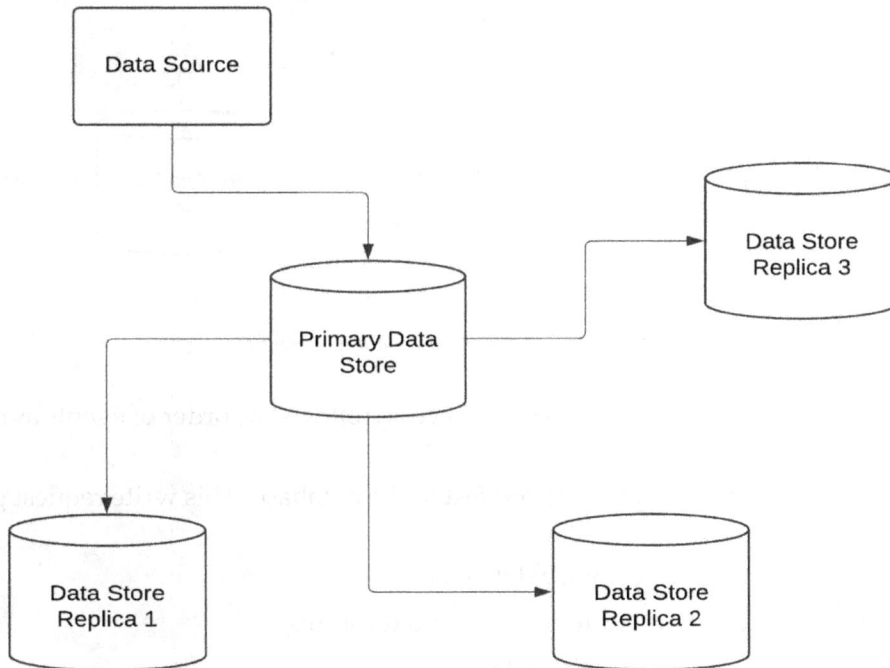

Figure 12.2: Basics of data replication

As there can be different use cases for ensuring high availability of the data, different types of data replication techniques are used. In the preceding topics in this chapter, we will understand various types of data replication techniques, the use cases that can be solved using these techniques, and the trade-offs that one should consider before choosing these replication techniques.

Types of data replication

For a travel aggregator, booking records, booking cancellations, payment details, etc., represent business-critical data. Access to such data cannot be denied at any cost. The failure of one or two storage nodes can lead to business loss if the data engineers do not configure the data replication properly. So, to ensure that the data is replicated promptly, a synchronous data replication technique is used. Synchronous data replication means that the data is written to the primary data store and the replica data store before the user operation is deemed successful. The user's transaction fails if data is not written successfully to either the primary or the replicas. Typically, the business-critical data gets replicated synchronously.

Figure 12.2 shows how synchronous replication works:

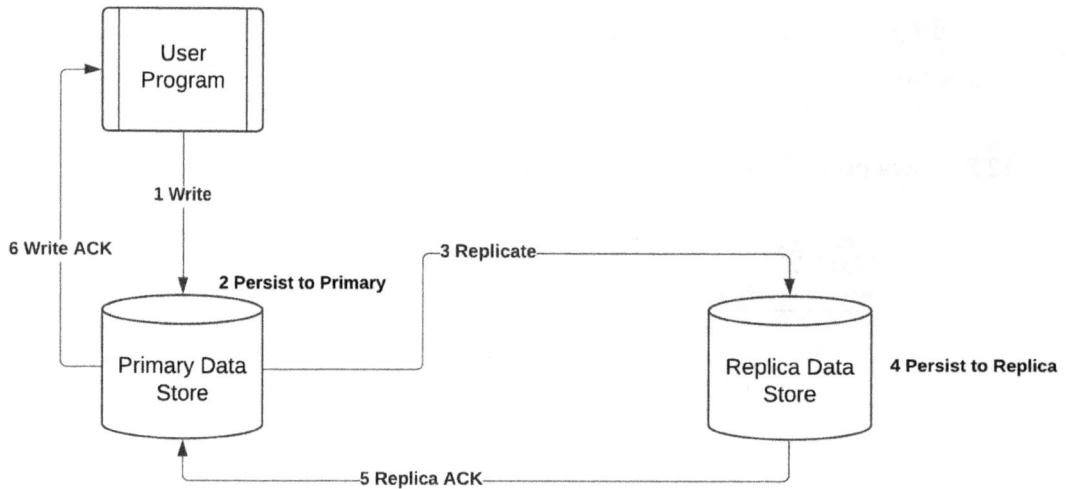

Figure 12.3: *Synchronous data replication*

As shown in *Figure 12.3*, synchronous data replication follows the order of events as mentioned in the following:

1. The user program issues a write request to the database. This write request goes to the primary data store.

2. The data persists in the primary data store.

3. The copy of the data is sent to the replica data stores.

4. The data persists on the replica data stores.

5. Replica store sends an acknowledgment to the primary data store, confirming that the data has persisted.

6. The user application gets a successful response to the write request.

In this case, if any type of failure occurs between steps one and six, the user's write request will be treated as failed. The failure happening on either the primary or the replica store will result in the failure of the user operation. Also, because the data is being persisted twice, the total latency of the write operation will be high. In the case of synchronous replication, data loss is very rare as it requires both primary and replica data stores to fail simultaneously.

To trade off the high latencies, you can choose to configure semi-synchronous replication. User-generated data, like user reviews, ratings, etc., are not equally business critical as user booking records. For such data, semi-synchronous replication is a good choice, as the loss of data in such cases will not directly lead to loss of business.

Figure 12.4 shows how semi-synchronous replication works:

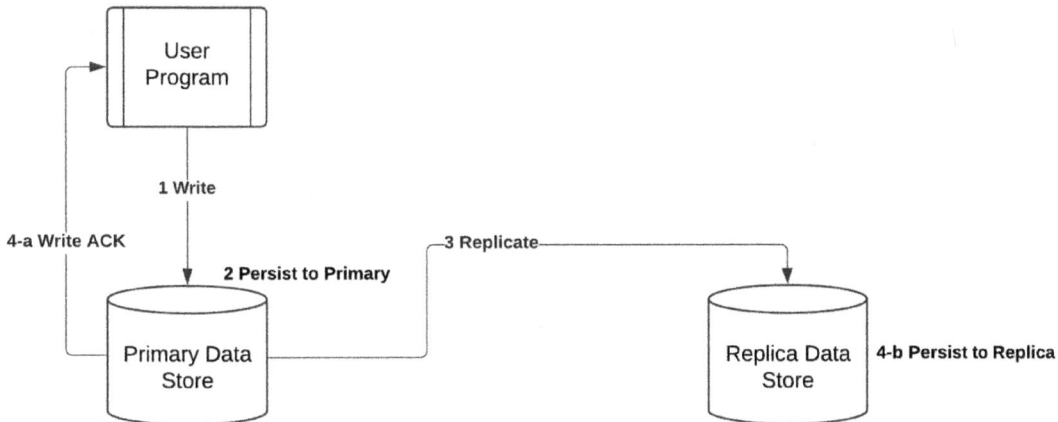

Figure 12.4: *Semi-synchronous data replication*

As shown in *Figure 12.4*, semi-synchronous data replication follows the order of the events as mentioned in the following:

- The user program issues a write to the database. This write request goes to the primary data store.
- The data gets persisted on the primary data store.
- The copy of the data is sent to the replica data stores.

  The following operations are triggered concurrently:

  o User application gets a successful response to the write request.

  o The data gets persisted on the replica data stores.

In the case of semi-synchronous replication, the user program does not wait until the data is persisted on the replica stores but rather waits until the data replication is triggered. This exposes a reasonably small window for failure to result in data loss. In other words, there are two situations that can cause data loss in semi-synchronous data replication:

- Simultaneous failure of both primary and replica data stores.
- Primary data stores fail after persisting the data on primary, after returning the success of the write operation to the user program, but before persisting the data on replica data stores.

In this case, the chances of data loss are proportional to the replication time lag. Modern-day databases, when equipped with high-performance hardware, can keep the replication time lag below one second.

A second time lag is good for most of the data that has a direct impact on business or critical user experience. However, some use cases do not require such a low replication time lag. For example, the user uploads the profile picture. Data engineers can decide to store the binary data of user profile pictures in the database. If the primary data store fails, recovering profile pictures is the last thing data engineers need to worry about. Even if the profile pictures get lost, it may not lead to any direct or indirect business impact or any impact on user experience. For such non-critical data, we can choose asynchronous data replication. *Figure 12.5* shows how asynchronous data replication works:

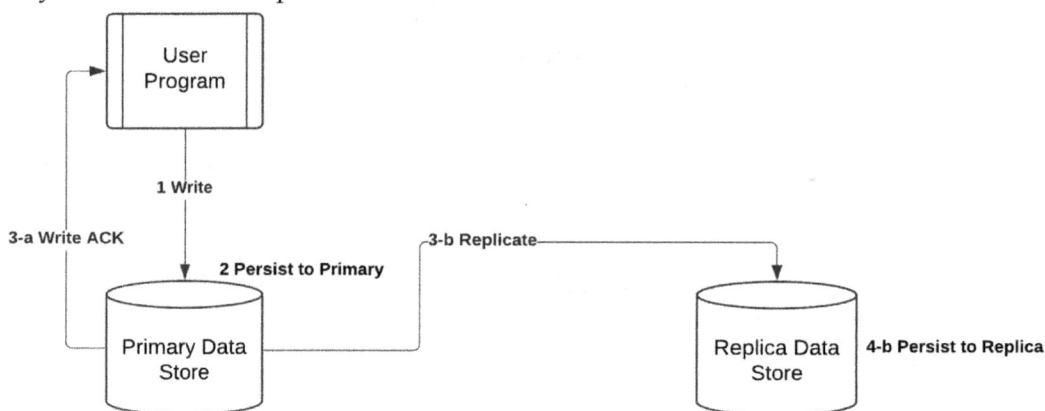

Figure 12.5: Asynchronous data replication

As shown in *Figure 12.5*, semi-synchronous data replication follows the order of the events as mentioned in the following:

- The user program issues a write to the database. This write request goes to the primary data store.
- The data gets persisted on the primary data store.

  The following operations are triggered concurrently:

o The copy of the data is sent to the replica data stores.

o User application gets a successful response to the write request.

• The data gets persisted on the replica data stores.

Note: The user application may get a successful response for the write request even before the data replication is triggered. It is because of this that the data loss time window for asynchronous data replication is higher than for semi-synchronous data replication.

Now, let us summarize the use cases for different types of replications:

• **Synchronous replication**: User data, basic movie data, etc.

• **Semi-synchronous replication**: Movie reviews, ratings, etc.

• **Asynchronous replication**: Profile pictures, movie posters, etc.

Configuring more than one replica

In the above examples, we looked at the replication techniques by considering only one replica. However, data engineers may choose to create more replicas to improve data availability. As the number of replicas increases, the overhead of data replication increases. This can lead to very slow write operations, especially when using synchronous or semi-synchronous replication. *Figure 12.6* shows the data replication overheads when we configure five replicas:

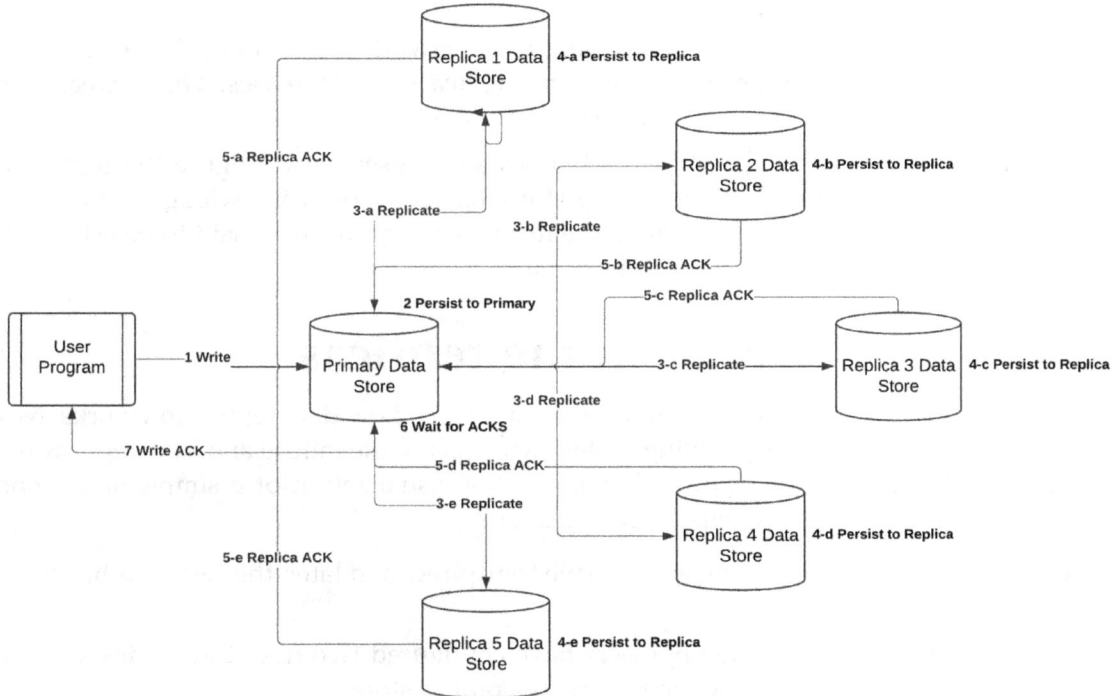

***Figure 12.6**: Five-way synchronous data replication*

As shown in *Figure 12.6*, five-way synchronous data replication follows the order of the events as mentioned in the following:

1. User program issues a write to the database. This write request goes to the primary data store.

2. The data gets persisted on the primary data store.

3. The copy of the data is sent to *all five* replica data stores *concurrently*.

4. The data gets persisted on the replica data stores. Each replica can experience a delay in getting the request and persisting it based on the latency of the underlying hardware and workload.

5. Once individual replica stores are done with data persistence, replica stores send an acknowledgment to the primary data store, confirming that the data has persisted.

6. While the fourth and fifth pointers are being executed on the replica stores, the primary store is waiting for all five replica acknowledgments.

7. Once all the acknowledgments are received, the user application gets a successful response to the write request.

As we can see, there are two primary problems with having more replicas:

*   This is because of the higher number of replicas. The overheads of replication, replica persistence, and acknowledgment are high. Even if one replica is slow, the entire write request needs to wait.

*   As there can be multiple moving parts (like network disruptions, disk errors, etc.), the probability of failure of at least one replica write increases. This increases the probability of failure of the write operation altogether.

To mitigate these problems, underlying databases allow users to configure the replication in such a way that the write becomes successful after receiving acknowledgment from the **majority** of replica stores. In our example, the majority (or **quorum**) is said to be achieved if the acknowledgment is received from **three or more** replica nodes.

Reading the data from the replicas

Until now, we have discussed various failure scenarios and how data replication works. Now, we will understand how the underlying system will react to the failure and how replicas help in ensuring data availability. *Figure 12.7* helps in the visualization of a simple single-node failure and how the replica can help in serving data.

As seen in *Figure 12.7*, the following events have transpired, and later, the system is backed up with the help of a replica:

*   At the time of setup, data engineers have configured two datastore nodes. One is a primary data store, and the second one is a replica store.

*   All the user programs will perform read as well as write operations to the primary store.

- When the data is written to the primary store, the data will be synchronously replicated to the replica store.

- The user program will get success for a write operation only when data has been successfully persisted to the replica store.

- Any data read operation will be served by the primary store.

- A failure event occurs.

- The replica store gets promoted to the primary.

- All the user programs will switch over to the new primary, and both read and write requests will be served by the new primary store.

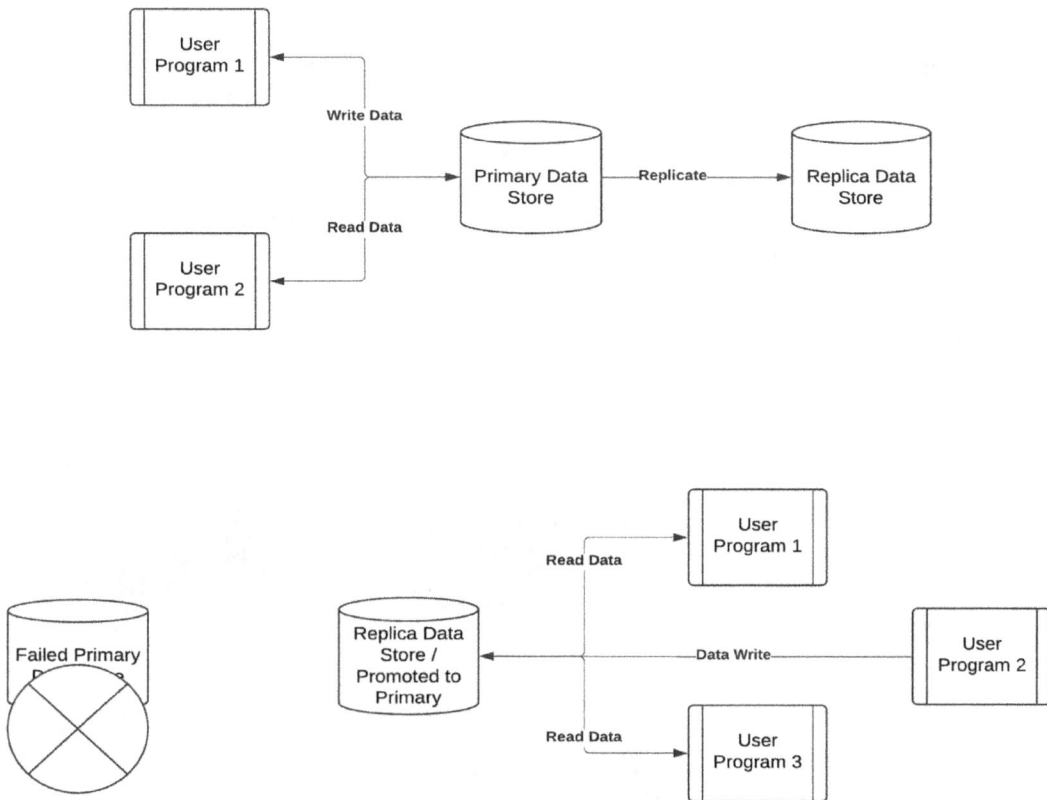

Figure 12.7: *A single-node failure and a replica are used for serving the data*

In practice, the way in which the aforementioned bulleted points seven and eight are executed depends on the underlying implementation of the database. Many modern-day databases provide features like auto-failover, automatic replica read, etc., to automate (otherwise manually taken) steps in the failure scenario:

- The **auto-failover** feature ensures automatic detection of the failure of the primary store and automatic promotion of the replica store to the primary.

- The **automatic replica** read feature ensures the data serving will be attempted using the replica store if data serving from the primary store fails or times out.

Cross datacenter replication

There are typically two broad categories of failure events.

- Hardware or software failure within a data center. For example, a disk gets corrupted, one storage node goes down, one network switch or rack fails, etc.

- A catastrophic event like a power grid failure, earthquake, flood, etc., can lead to the entire data center becoming inaccessible.

To handle failures within the data center (category 1), the replicas will be hosted in the same data center but on different nodes or racks, etc. The replication within the data center is very fast and reliable, and hence, synchronous replication can be implemented.

On the other hand, in case of catastrophic failures (category 2), the entire data center can go down. Catastrophic events typically impact a much larger geographical area, and all data centers in a single city or region can be impacted. To handle such scenarios, data engineers can configure **cross datacenter replication** (**XDCR**). *Figure 12.8* shows a visualization for XDCR:

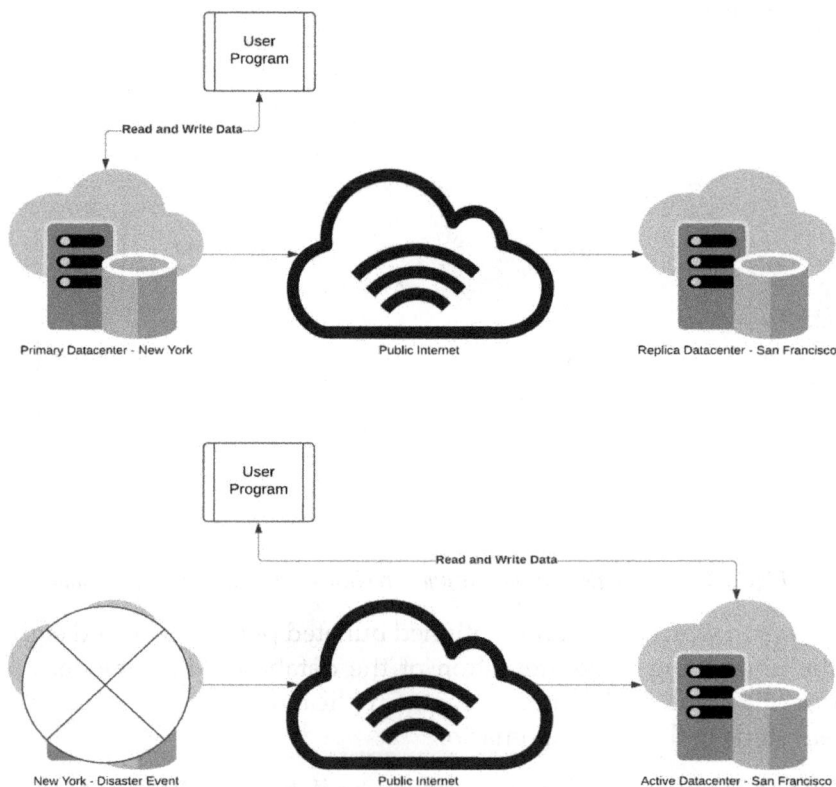

Figure 12.8: Cross data center replication

In *Figure 12.8*, we can see that:

- There are two datacenters used to host and serve the business data. The primary datacenter is in New York, and the replica datacenter is in San Francisco.
- The user program communicates with the primary datacenter in New York.
- The data from the primary datacenter is replicated to the replica datacenter in San Francisco.
- The data replication typically happens over the public internet. Therefore, the speed of replication is typically slow.

  In the worst case, replication delay can be in minutes. Due to this, XCDR is typically asynchronous replication.
- In case of a disaster event, the entire datacenter in New York becomes inaccessible. In such cases, datacenter in San Francisco is promoted to be active.

  The user program now communicates with the San Francisco datacenter, reading and writing the data.

As we can see, with the afore-mentioned XDCR architecture, the replication delay can be in minutes. In the worst case, it can take tens of minutes. Such a delay can cause a large amount of data loss in case of a disaster event. For example, if the replication delay is 20 minutes, then 20 minutes' worth of business data may get lost. To avoid such data loss (even in case of a disaster event), you can configure bi-directional XDCR.

Note: **The high replication lag across geographical regions makes highly critical OLTP application writes (for example, banking), as it can cause delays in user experience.**

Bi-directional XDCR and conflict resolution

Bi-directional XDCR architecture allows user applications to read and write the data to primary data stores as well as replica data stores without a prerequisite of a failure event. *Figure 12.9* shows how bi-directional XDCR works:

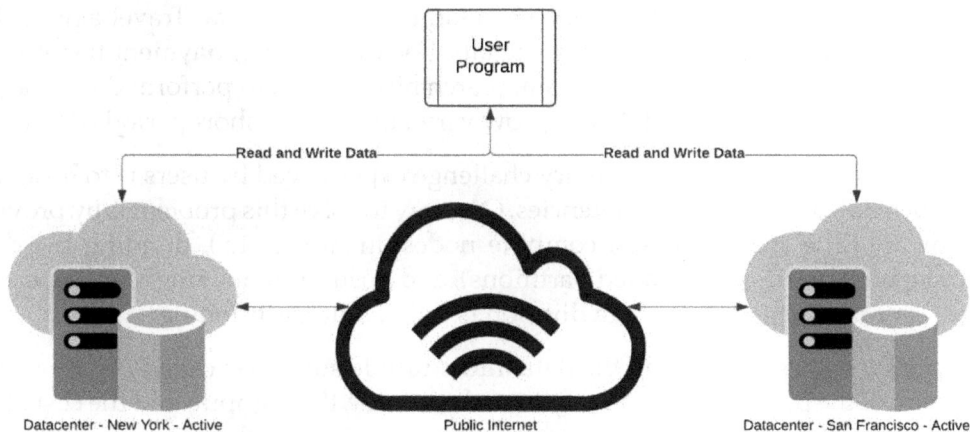

Figure 12.9: Bi-directional XDCR

In *Figure 12.9*, we can see that:

- The user has configured two datacenters (New York and San Francisco) to mitigate against a disaster event.

- Each of the data centers works as an active data store and can allow user programs to read and write the data simultaneously.

- The data replication happens from New York to San Francisco, and vice versa.

- In case of a disaster event, if one datacenter becomes inaccessible, the other data center can continue to serve the requests.

- The user applications can choose to send each write request to both the datacenters. With that, the data loss window gets reduced drastically.

With bi-directional replication, there is a possibility of experiencing write conflicts. For example, if user application one makes an update to a specific record and user application two makes another update to the same record, then these two user operations can potentially race with each other. Within a datacenter, such races are serialized by the database software. But if the two operations are directed towards two different datacenters, then the underlying database software cannot seamlessly serialize the updates. This leads to conflict.

There are various conflict resolution mechanisms, which, when configured, help users resolve conflicts. Some popular conflict resolutions are:

- Last write wins
- Use of version vectors
- Use of **conflict-free replicated datatypes** (**CRDT**)
- Manual conflict resolution

Data partitioning

A travel aggregator website needs to manage a large amount of data. Travel aggregators not only need to store data related to booking details, booking history, payment history, etc., but also need to store data like user click stream, search history, etc., to perform data analysis and generate business insights. Such data can grow very large over a short period of time.

With the growing size of data, the primary challenge experienced by users is to host, manage, and serve such data with acceptable latencies. One way to solve this problem is by provisioning more hardware (like storage nodes, compute nodes, memory, etc.), dividing the data into smaller independent sub-parts (called partitions), and hosting/managing/serving each of the sub-parts separately. This type of data division is called data partitioning.

There are various ways of dividing the data into multiple sub-parts called partition schemes, and the choice of the partition scheme can drive the latency, throughput, and the cost of serving the data. That is why choosing the right partition scheme is critical.

In this chapter, we will learn the two most popular partition schemes typically used by data engineers.

These partitioning schemes are:

- Hash partitioning
- Range partitioning

Hash partitioning

Hash partitioning is widely used to achieve equivalent load distribution across the partitions. This is achieved by applying a hash function to the partition key to find the partition number. Let us take an example of a bookings table. For this example, we will assume that the primary key of the booking table is bookingId, which is an integer starting from zero and assigned using autoincrement.

The choice of the hash function used for hash partitioning depends on the data type of the partition key. For integers, the modulo operation is a good hash function, as it will divide the data evenly across all partitions (especially when there are any gaps in the number ranges).

Let us take an example where there are 90 booking records, that is, the corresponding bookingIds are range from 0 to 89. Now, with the *modulo 4* operation on bookingId, we will get a data distribution across partitions as follows:

- Partition 0 will hold 23 records with bookingIds 0, 4, 8 … 88
- Partition 1 will hold 23 records with bookingIds 1, 5, 9 … 89
- Partition 2 will hold 22 records with bookingIds 2, 6, 10 … 86
- Partition 3 will hold 22 records with bookingIds 3, 7, 11 … 87

At the time of storing the data, the partition number is calculated using the hash function, and the records will be stored in that specific partition. While reading the data, the same hash function will be used to calculate the partition number, and the read request will be redirected to the corresponding partition. Ignoring irrelevant partitions during a read request is called **partition elimination**.

Although the hash partitioning scheme is better suited for lookup operations (that is, lookup of a single record) based on partition keys, they are not very optimal for range scans using secondary keys.

Range partitioning

The range partitioning scheme is useful to execute scans on secondary keys (or the ranges of secondary keys). For example, a data analyst wants to get the hotel bookings made at the cost price between $201 and $250. If we use bookingId based hash partitioning for such a query, the underlying system needs to traverse all records from all partitions, filter out the records that do not fit the cost price criteria, and then return the matching results. So, hash partitioning turns out to be a costly operation with extra overhead. To speed up the execution of such a query, range partitioning can be used.

With range partitioning, the user will divide the data between ranges of values of a secondary key. In our example, the secondary key is the booking cost price. Let us take an example where we divide the data into five partitions:

- **Partition 1**: Where the cost price is less than $101
- **Partition 2**: Where the cost price is less than $201 and greater than or equal to $101
- **Partition 3**: Where the cost price is less than $301 and greater than or equal to $201
- **Partition 4**: Where the cost price is less than $401 and greater than or equal to $301
- **Partition 5**: Where the cost price is greater than or equal to $401

At the time of storing the data, the right partition number is calculated by checking the booking cost price, and the records will be stored in that specific partition. While reading the data, a subset of partition numbers is calculated, and the data is searched only from that subset of partitions. In our example, we want to get a list of hotel bookings with a cost price between $201 and $250. So, we only search for the records in partition 3. Hence, range partitioning can also benefit from **partition elimination**.

As the cost price of the booking will not be evenly distributed among all possible cost prices across all bookings, the range partitioning scheme typically does not yield an even (or equivalent) data distribution. The data distribution can be skewed, and it can lead to variance in query performance and cost.

Table 12.2 shows the summary of partitioning schemes and the types of queries that will benefit from the corresponding partitioning schemes:

Partitioning scheme	Benefitting query type
Hash partitioning	Lookup queries (e.g., get user details provided a specific user id)
Range partitioning	Range queries (get all products with price between 100 and 200)
Time-based partitioning	Time range queries (get all recent transactions)

Table 12.2: Partitioning schemes and corresponding query types which benefit from them

Other popular partitioning schemes

Some other popular partitioning schemes are:

- **Time-based partitioning**: Where the data is divided into multiple partitions based on some time field in the record. For example, if most of the user queries are time window-based, like getting all bookings done in the last ten days, getting all cancellations done in the last month, etc., then time-based partitioning helps in good-quality partition elimination.

- **Round robin partitioning**: Where the data is divided evenly across all partitions. As the logic for choosing the partition does not depend on any range or lookup keys, round-robin partitioning cannot be used for partition elimination.

- **Vertical partitioning**: Where the data is divided by columns or the fields that are queried together. This partition schema exhibits similar benefits to that of the columnar storage format learned in *Chapter 10, Data Warehouse and Data Analytics*.

Scatter and gather operations

Users can choose only one of the above-mentioned data partitioning schemes. However, user queries can be complex and can require performing filtering, grouping, aggregations, limit enforcement, etc., across more than one field of the data. Let us take an example where a user wants to get *any ten cities for which the hotel booking cost has exceeded $300*. Let us assume that the partitioning scheme used here is bookingId based hash partitioning. As query execution does not need to perform any lookup based on bookingId, it needs to traverse all the partitions to find the expected results. We also assume that the query execution on each partition is performed separately by a separate storage node. Here, query execution will perform the following steps to get the expected results:

1. Query execution will send the same query to each storage node to perform the same operation on each partition independently. This operation is called a **scatter operation**.

2. On each storage node, all records belonging to its corresponding partition will be read. While performing query execution, a set of zero cities is maintained in memory, which has at least one booking where the cost price exceeds $300.

3. Once such a set of ten cities is identified on each node, the node will return the result to the query execution.

4. Query execution will collect the results from all storage nodes. Based on the number of partitions and the actual booking details, query execution may receive more than 10 city names in the results. Query execution will select only ten city names from the list and return them to the end user. This operation of collecting results from multiple partitions and post-processing them is called a **gather operation**.

Figure 12.10 shows the visualization for the scatter-gather operation, as explained in the four-step process of serving the data:

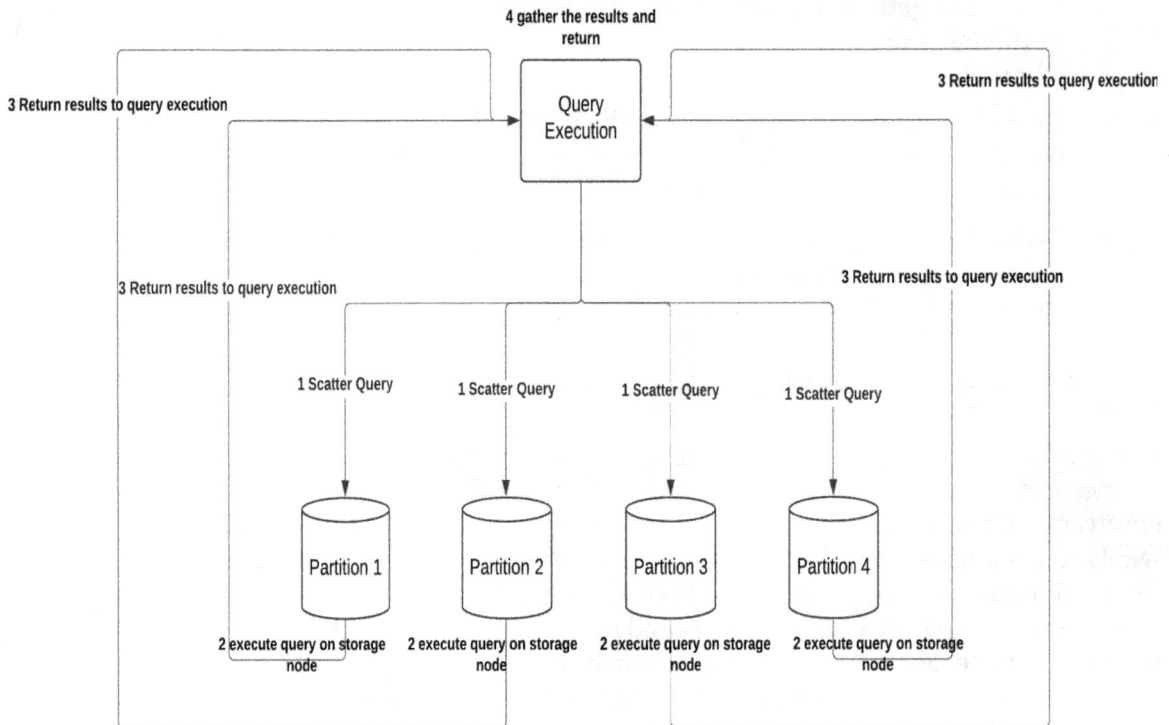

Figure 12.10: *Scatter and gather*

Conclusion

By the end of this chapter, we learned the basics of software and hardware faults and failures. To avoid business impact from such failures, we need data replication, where a copy of the data will be stored on separate hardware. We then learned about synchronous, semi-synchronous, and asynchronous replication and the benefits and limitations of each type of replication.

We also learned about how data availability can be ensured in a disaster event with the help of XDCR. We also learned the benefits of bi-directional XDCR and which mechanisms can be used to resolve the conflicts arising due to bi-directional XDCR.

We then learned the concept of data partitioning and how it is useful to divide the work across multiple storage as well as compute units. We learned various types of partition schemes and how these schemes enable users to get the benefit of partition elimination. We finally learned how the scatter-gather data serving pattern is used for serving the data residing across multiple partitions.

In the next chapter, we will discuss the mechanisms to separate hot, warm, and cold data. We will learn the design patterns to store hot data for low-latency serving. We will also study the design patterns used to store cold data to reduce the cost of data storage.

Questions

1. What are the different types of hardware and software faults that can lead to data unavailability?

2. Which of the following replication mechanisms can lead to data loss?

   a. Synchronous replication

   b. Semi-synchronous replication

   c. Asynchronous replication

3. Which replication mechanism will lead to a faster write response?

   a. Synchronous replication

   b. Semi-synchronous replication

   c. Asynchronous replication

4. With an example, explain how partition elimination can work with time-based partitioning.

Join our Discord space

Join our Discord workspace for latest updates, offers, tech happenings around the world, new releases, and sessions with the authors:

https://discord.bpbonline.com

CHAPTER 13

Hot Versus Cold Data Storage

Introduction

In the last decade, the amount of data generated by individual users, corporations, and businesses has grown very high. This fact has posed a data management challenge for very large data. The businesses that generate huge amounts of data need to identify solutions to manage the data that is being generated. Businesses also need to identify access patterns for the data and distinguish between the frequently accessed data and the less frequently accessed data. Once such data separation is done, the businesses need to design solutions to store the data such that the solution optimizes the data access and storage costs.

Solutions to optimize data access and storage costs need to trade off these two aspects. The trade-off depends on data access frequency and data recency.

Data access frequency can determine the overall user experience. For example, high latency in accessing more frequently accessed data can lead to a bad user experience for many users.

Also, there is a high likelihood that *recently added data* will be accessed in the near future. This is specifically true for the data used for time-based data analysis.

So, these kinds of data access patterns are used to determine the solutions that optimize the data access and storage costs.

In this chapter, we will learn mechanisms to identify data access layers like *hot data, warm data,* and *cold data*. We will also understand ways to differentiate between hot and cold data. In this chapter, we will introduce data storage and serving patterns for hot data with the help of *data caching*.

Chapter 14, Data Caching and Low Latency Serving, will provide a detailed discussion on data caching and low-latency serving. In this chapter, we will explore the data storage, archival, and serving patterns for *cold data*.

Structure

This chapter covers the following topics:

- Identifying hot, warm, and cold data
- Introduction to data caching
- Data archival
- Defining data lifecycle using AWS S3

Objectives

By the end of this chapter, the readers will understand the requirement for hot-cold separation of the data. The readers will understand design patterns and tools that can be used to perform hot and cold data separation. There is a trade-off between access frequency, access cost, and access latency of the data. This chapter will help the readers understand this trade-off.

This chapter introduces the concept of data archival and use cases solved using data engineering patterns for data archival.

Identifying hot, warm, and cold data

Let us continue with the travel aggregator example to learn the process of differentiating between hot, warm, and cold data. As discussed earlier, the data access pattern can be determined by data recency as well as data access frequency. Understanding data access frequency and data recency plays a crucial role in identifying hot, warm, and cold data. It, in turn, determines the performance of the travel aggregator application and the cost incurred in running this application.

Now, let us start with the data access frequency.

Data access frequency

Let us take an example of a user planning to book a hotel. For the hotel booking workflow, the user will perform the following steps:

1. Search for hotels based on destination city.
2. Sort the results based on user ratings or price.

3. Click on a few hotels to get detailed information about the hotels, like what facilities the hotel has, what the address of the hotel is, read the user reviews of the hotel, check out the user-uploaded pictures of the hotel, etc.

4. Identify the right room and select the other booking details.

5. Make the payment and finalize the booking.

Here, *step 3* requires accessing detailed information about the hotels, such as reviews, photos, amenities, facilities, etc. There can be hundreds of reviews and hundreds of photos for any hotel. Getting such data from cloud data storage (like Amazon S3) takes time as well as costs money. Every time the data is retrieved from Amazon S3, a specific dollar amount is charged. Even if the same data is accessed again, the same amount will be charged. Furthermore, data residing in Amazon S3 resides in a user-specified region. Retrieving data from different regions will incur more latency as well as more cost in dollars.

To provide a smooth user experience while browsing through hotel reviews and photos, we can cache that data using in-memory caching solutions like *Memcached* or *Redis*. So, in our example, such frequently accessed reviews and photos are being treated as *hot data*. The reviews and photos of infrequently accessed hotels are treated as *warm* or *cold data*.

Data recency

To understand the impact of data recency in identifying data access patterns, let us take an example of a booking history. Over multiple years, for the travel aggregator website, a very large number of bookings have been made. It may be required for businesses to hold on to all the booking data, invoices, etc., for a few years until they can be completely deleted from the storage systems. Even after a few years, the business can decide to archive the data if the likelihood of data access is minuscule.

So, in this example, we can see that:

- The booking data is treated as *hot data from the booking date until the checkout date*, as it can be accessed at any time.

- After the successful checkout, the booking data can be treated as *warm data* for the next couple of months, as it will be accessed, but not frequently.

- After those couple of months have passed, the booking data can be treated as *cold data*, as the likelihood of it being accessed is very low.

Visualizing hot, warm, and cold data segregation

Now, as we have defined hot, warm, and cold data for a couple of use cases, let us put all three types of data together to visualize how the overall data is segregated into these three types. As modern-day applications are hosted in the cloud, we will consider hot, warm, and cold data segregation using cloud storage services.

Looking at *Figure 13.1*, we can see the visual representation of the hot, warm, and cold data segregation:

- **Hot data**: It is typically stored in a cache. The cache is maintained in the local storage of the nodes used to serve the data. The size of the cache is typically very small compared to the size of the cloud storage used for storing the warm data. The local storage on data serving nodes is typically used as an ephemeral cache; that is, when the node goes down, all the hot data stored on that node can get lost. That is why the node's local storage is not used as a persistent data store. When a new node is brought up, it will initialize its own cache, which will be populated based on the application design policy. More on cache population in *Chapter 14, Data Caching and Low Latency Serving*.

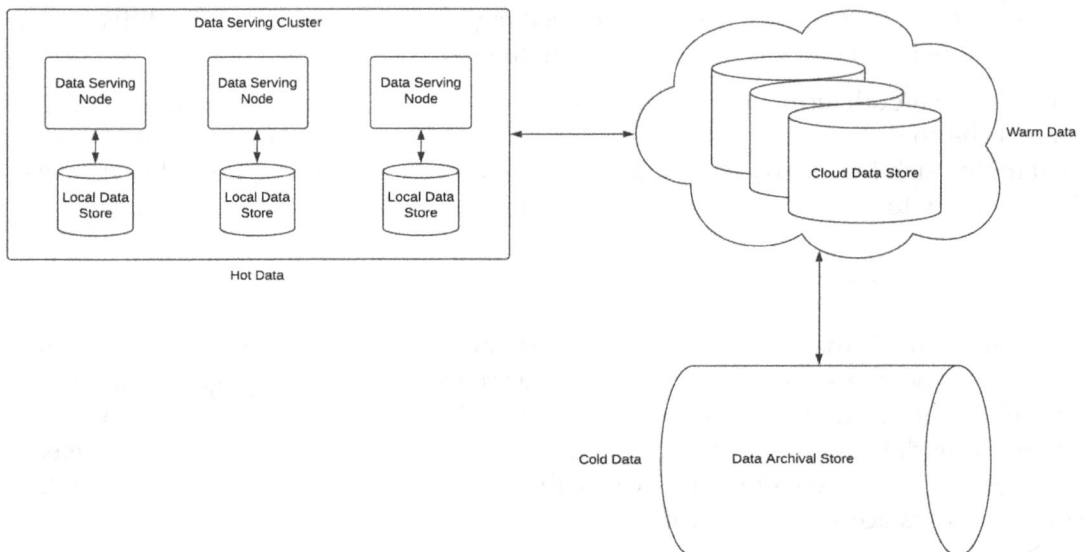

Figure 13.1: Hot, warm, and cold data segregation

- **Warm data**: It is typically stored in cloud data storage systems like Amazon S3. The user application uses this storage as persistent storage, as it internally provides high availability. The data stored in S3 is treated as warm data, as it is not located very close to the data serving nodes, but it is easily accessible in sub-second latencies if the S3 bucket is hosted in the same region as that of the data serving nodes. Every time the data is fetched from the S3 bucket, the user gets charged a dollar amount. This adds to the cost of serving the data. If the same data is cached in memory or in node-local storage for the data serving nodes, the cost of serving the data will be much less.

- **Cold data**: It is typically stored in the data archival stores. When the warm data is no longer needed for any routine business activity (either transaction or analytical), then such data is typically moved to archival storage. The storage cost of data stored in the archival storage is much less than the storage cost of the data stored in general-purpose cloud storage (like S3). However, the data access latency for archival storage can be higher. For example, Amazon S3 supports various storage classes for the data objects stored in Amazon S3. Two of the popular storage classes used by data engineers are:

  o **S3 infrequent access**, which has a storage cost of almost half of the storage cost of standard S3, but the data access latencies are higher.

  o **S3 Glacier**, which has a storage cost of almost one-third of the storage cost of S3 Infrequent access. However, the data access latencies can be even higher. Also, the expected data access frequency is much lower.

Introduction to data caching

Data caching is a technique for keeping the data closer to the data serving nodes. The closer the data, the longer it takes to access and serve it.

Let us continue with our example of hotel bookings, as shown in the following figure:

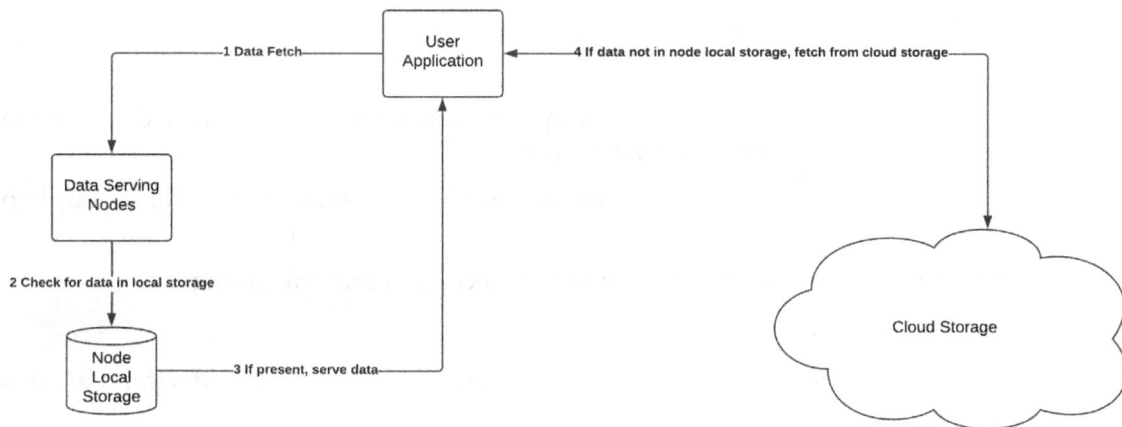

Figure 13.2: Data caching

As we discussed earlier, based on data access frequency, the reviews and photos of the most frequently viewed hotels can be cached in the local data store of the data serving nodes. So, as shown in *Figure 13.2*, when the user application needs to access the data, it will perform the following steps:

1. For a given data object, check if the data object is present in the node's local cache.

2. If available, then serve the data from the node's local cache.

3. If the data object is not available in the node's local cache, then fetch the data object from cloud storage.

4. Based on the data caching policy, cache the fetched data in the cache for future reuse.

The following are some of the popular data caching principles:

• The cached data is typically a subset of the data stored in persistent cloud storage.

- When the data is written, updated, or deleted in the first step, the operation is applied to the persistent storage. Then, the operation is reflected in the cache. This way, the contents of the cache are not modified directly from the user program, ensuring the eventual consistency of the cache.

- The contents of the cache can be thrown away and rebuilt every time an existing node goes down or a new node is brought up.

We will discuss data caching patterns and learn the cache eviction policies in *Chapter 14, Data Caching and Low Latency Serving*.

Data archival

Data archival is the process of moving unnecessary business data from warm data storage like AWS S3 to archival storage. The archived data is very rarely accessed, if at all, and it can be removed from the archival storage when it is ready for purging. There are specific reasons for storing and accessing archived data.

Some of these reasons are as follows:

- Data compliance policies, which require businesses to hold personal data, health-related data, or financial data for a few years.

- Future data audits, which require businesses to hold financial data for a couple of years.

- To protect the data from attackers by storing a copy in archival storage.

- Reduce the cost of storage.

Let us take an example of a hypothetical legal data compliance policy to understand archival requirements.

For a travel aggregator business, it may be required to store all the travel and hotel bookings for at least eight years for legal purposes. Data that is more than a couple of years old may not be required for day-to-day business needs or business analytics. However, litigation involving a particular traveler can require collecting such data to trace the footsteps of the person in question. So, we need to design a data archival system to ensure the legal compliance of the data.

In this case, we can see that:

- The data that is no longer needed for day-to-day business operations or business analytics can be only a couple of years old. Say two to three years. However, it is required to be stored for legal purposes for at least eight years. Let us call this archival data.

- The archival data will not be accessed unless there is litigation against a person related to that data.

- In most cases, only a small subset will be accessed.

- The latency of such data access does not need to be in seconds or even minutes. In some cases, acceptable latency can be in a few hours.

- Such archival data need not be stored in warm data storage systems like AWS S3, as S3-like storage systems are costly and are optimized for low latencies.

- This type of data access pattern for the archived data is called **write once read many times (WORM)**.

To understand various alternatives to optimize the cost of data storage and trade it off with data access latencies. Let us consider the data lifecycle feature provided by the Amazon AWS S3 service.

Defining data lifecycle using AWS S3

AWS S3 service provides multiple object storage classes. Each of these storage classes has a different cost for data access, different costs for data storage, and different latency for data retrieval. For our use case, we will study three storage classes:

- Standard
- Infrequent access
- Glacier

Note: **Amazon S3 ensures that the eventual data consistency by persisting the data to the disks, for any of the storage classes.**

To understand how to decide and define the storage classes, let us continue with the cab booking example.

For cab booking, let us assume the following requirements:

- Cab booking service allows booking to be made up to 60 days prior to the travel date.

- Once the cab booking is made, an invoice will be generated for it. The invoices will be stored in the S3 bucket.

- Downloading an invoice is a very rare activity. Users are likely to download the invoice a maximum of a couple of times within 30 days after the travel date. After that, the invoices are rarely accessed.

- The compliance requires the business to keep the invoice for at least three years after the booking date for auditing purposes.

- The auditor may ask for the invoice during this three-year period, after which the invoice will not be needed.

By looking at these requirements, we can define the following policies:

- When the invoices are generated, we do not need to store them using the standard S3 storage class. On the other hand, they can be stored using S3 infrequent access. With S3 infrequent access, the storage cost will be less than the standard storage class. Higher access costs will be traded off for lower storage costs due to the rarity of the access.

- After 90 days of invoice generation, the invoices can be transitioned to Glacier storage, as they will be very rarely used. With the S3 glacier, the storage cost will be further decreased. Further higher access costs will be traded off by further lower storage costs, as the access may not be required at all.

The aforementioned policies will translate to the following choices at the time of application design:

- When the invoice is being stored in S3, set the default storage class as S3 infrequent access.

- Set a lifecycle policy on the S3 bucket to transition data to the Glacier storage class.

The following code depicts how the user can set the storage class to infrequent access at the time of storing the S3 object:

```
import boto3
client = boto3.client('s3')

response = client.put_object(
    Body='<S3 Object Content>',
    Bucket='travel',
    Key='invoices/invoiceId',
    StorageClass='STANDARD_IA'
)
```

The following code depicts how you can set up the S3 lifecycle config for the S3 bucket to transition invoices from the infrequent access storage class to the Glacier storage class, using Python boto **software development kit (SDK)**:

```
import boto3
client = boto3.client('s3')

# Define filter allows to apply the lifecycle only for invoices.

filters = {
    'Prefix': 'invoices/',
},
# Define object transitions

transitions = {
    [
        {
            'Days': 90,
            'StorageClass': ' GLACIER',
        },
    ],
}
```

```
# Define lifecycle config
lifecycle_config={
    'Rules': [
        {
            'ID': 'string',
            'Prefix': 'string',
            'Status': 'Enabled',
            'Transitions': transitions,
            'Filter': filters,
        },
    ]
}
# Set lifecycle config on the bucket.
response = client.put_bucket_lifecycle_configuration(
    Bucket='bucket_name',
    ChecksumAlgorithm='CRC32',
    lifecycle_config,
)
```

Accessing archived data

Any S3 objects stored using the S3 standard or S3 infrequent access class can be accessed using the **get_object application program interface (API)** exposed by the boto SDK.

However, if the object has already transitioned to the Glacier object class, it must be restored to the Amazon S3 bucket.

So, accessing such data becomes a two-step process:

1. Restore the S3 object from Glacier to S3. This may take a few hours.
2. Check that the restore is complete. Once it is, access the object from S3 using boto SKD's **get_object** API.

The following code can be used to perform the aforementioned two-step process:

```
import boto3
import time
client = boto3.client('s3')
response = client.restore_object(
    Bucket=bucket_name,
    Key=object_key,
    RestoreRequest={
        'Days': 7,
        'GlacierJobParameters': {'Tier': 'Standard'}
    }
)
```

```
# This function is implemented as an infinite loop. A timeout (like 24 hours?)
# can be implemented in production quality implementations.
while Ture:
    response = client.head_object(
        Bucket=bucket_name,
        Key=object_key
    )
    restore_status = response['Restore']
    if 'ongoing-request="false"' in restore_status:
        # The object has been restored successfully. Get the object
        response = client.get_object(Bucket=bucket_name, Key=object_key)
        break
    # Sleep for 10 minutes are check again.
    time.sleep(10 * 60)
```

Amazon S3 restores provide different tiers based on different use cases. The following are the three restore tiers:

- **Expedited**: The data is restored in 1 to 5 minutes. Used for urgent restore requests.

- **Standard**: The data is restored in 3 to 5 hours. Used for regular restore requests.

- **Bulk**: The data is restored in 5 to 12 hours. Used for bulk restore requests.

Comparing storage classes

Let us summarize the comparison between storage classes in the following table:

Storage class	Relative cost of storage	Relative cost of data access
Standard	The highest	The lowest
Infrequent access	Less than standard	More than standard
Glacier	Less than infrequent access	More than infrequent access

Table 13.1: Cost comparison between various S3 storage classes

Conclusion

In this chapter, we learned how to differentiate between hot, warm, and cold data based on the access frequency and the recency of the data. We also looked at how the data storage cost and the data access cost can be traded off based on the data access frequency.

We did an introduction to data caching, where hot data will be stored very close to the data compute units to reduce the latency and cost of the hot data access. In this chapter, we also discuss the data archival use case and learn how data archival can be achieved with the help of AWS S3 storage classes and S3 lifecycle configuration. We also investigated the method to restore the archived data using the boto3 Python SDK. Note that the S3 lifecycle for different data objects can be changed dynamically. This allows users to tune it at any time in the future.

In the next chapter, we will explore the data engineering patterns for data caching.

Questions

1. Why is it necessary to do hot-cold data separation?
2. How does the data caching reduce the data access cost?
3. When the data is restored from the Glacier storage class, for how many days will it remain in the corresponding S3 bucket?
4. Can you use a single S3 lifecycle configuration to perform multiple storage class transitions for the data in S3?

Join our Discord space

Join our Discord workspace for latest updates, offers, tech happenings around the world, new releases, and sessions with the authors:

https://discord.bpbonline.com

CHAPTER 14
Data Caching and Low Latency Serving

Introduction

Modern-day large-scale web applications have very strict latency requirements. Higher latencies can lead to a bad user experience. Many web applications spend a large amount of time and money on optimizing specific latency requirements, like the user should be able to log in in less than 2 seconds, the home page should be loaded in less than 2 seconds, all other pages should load in less than 5 seconds, etc.

To ensure such low latencies, the most commonly used design pattern is *data caching*.

In the last chapter, we investigated the high-level use case of data caching. The cached data is typically stored very close to the compute used for serving the data. The cost of storing the data close to the compute can be high. So, not all the data is cached. We will deep dive into various ways to identify the *hot data* that needs to be cached to solve specific use cases.

Keeping multiple copies of data in different places gives rise to a data consistency problem. The delay in propagating the changes in the data across multiple copies can lead to *stale data*. In this chapter, we will look into design patterns used to avoid returning stale data.

In the last few years, mobile devices have significantly penetrated the end-user market, leading to most web services providing a mobile app as an equally important, if not more important, tool to keep customers engaged. As users carry mobile phones everywhere they go, the ease of use of the web service via mobile has seeped into people's lifestyles. However, mobile phones typically use a less reliable and slower internet connection. This can result in high latencies when using the mobile app. To solve this problem, data engineers can choose to cache the data on the mobile device itself and skip the use of a slow and less reliable internet connection for low-latency tasks.

In this chapter, we will move away from our travel aggregator use case and begin exploring a new use case, an *online movie database*.

Structure

This chapter covers the following topics:

- Online movie database
- Populating cache
- Using local Memcached for caching
- Quality of data caching and cache eviction policies
- Cache staleness, invalidation, and expiry
- Caching of pre-processed data
- Data prefetching
- Caching on laptops and mobile devices

Objectives

By the end of this chapter, you will understand various data caching use cases. You will learn about caching on the server side, which is useful for serving data faster compared to retrieving it from persistent cloud storage, such as AWS S3. You will also learn the use case and solutions for identifying stale data and how to invalidate it.

You will also understand the use cases for pre-processing the data and how to benefit from caching the pre-processed data to reduce latencies. Then, you will learn about the data prefetching use-cases and solutions used to achieve lower latencies.

Finally, you will also understand the use cases for caching data on user devices, such as laptops and mobile devices, to reduce data latencies significantly.

Online movie database

Let us discuss a hypothetical online movie database system. At a high level, let us assume that the online move database provides the following features and workflows. Some of these workflows will enable us to discuss a few use cases and the data engineering patterns used to address them.

The features or workflows provided by the online move database are:

- Maintain a database of movies, TV series, short films, and other media.
- Allow users to search for movies, TV series, etc., on the website.
- Allow users to register on the website to use features like:
  - Create a movie watchlist
  - Review the movies
  - Rate the movies
  - Get movie recommendations
- Maintain the curated home page for the users.
- Store the user's movie preferences and recommend the right set of movies to watch.
- Show trailers of the new movies, based on the user's preferences.

To better understand caching use cases, we will start with the use cases of user login and then continue with those related to loading the user's home page.

User login is the first thing users do on any website. Slowness in the user login experience can lead to a decline in the user's interest in the web service, which in turn may result in users leaving the website. To avoid this, it is crucial for any website to offer a very fast login process. One of the steps performed during user login is user password authentication.

User authentication service

Many large-scale web applications implement a user authentication service, which is responsible for password-based user authentication. To validate passwords, the service needs to validate the encrypted password received via the user request against the encrypted password stored in the authentication database.

A modern-day internet-scale application implements data serving using an auto-scaling-enabled stateless service. For our discussion, we assume that this service is responsible for user login and loading the home page. During the loading of the home page, the service needs to load the home page-specific data. For an online movie database, a typical home page will display three different sections described as follows:

- The *What's New* section will display posters (and links) to the newly released movies.
- The personalized recommendations section will display the posters (and links) to the movies recommended for the logged-in user.
- The *Visit Again* section will display posters (and links) to movies that have already been watched, but you may want to revisit.

Each of these sections will only hold a fixed number of movie posters. Let us assume that we are displaying only 10 movie posters in each of these sections, in our use case. So, once the user logs in, the webpage containing 30 movie posters needs to be loaded.

Loading a large number of movie posters (which is graphical content, i.e., images) can be costly in terms of load time as well as the cost of data access and transfer. To reduce the time taken to load the data and the cost of accessing frequently accessed data, a data caching design pattern can be used. In our example, we will cache:

- The user authentication information.
- The user's home page data, i.e., movie posters, is to be displayed on the home page.

The stateless service implementation helps users implement a read-only cache. If the service does not modify the cached data directly, it can keep the read-only cache. If there are multiple instances of the same stateless service running at the same time, they can maintain their own instances of the read-only cache without worrying about the consistency across read-only instances.

Now that we have identified the data that needs to be cached, we will investigate how to populate the cache.

Populating the cache

Before we understand how to populate the cache, let us first understand the online movie database application architecture.

Figure 14.1 illustrates the typical architecture of an online movie database application:

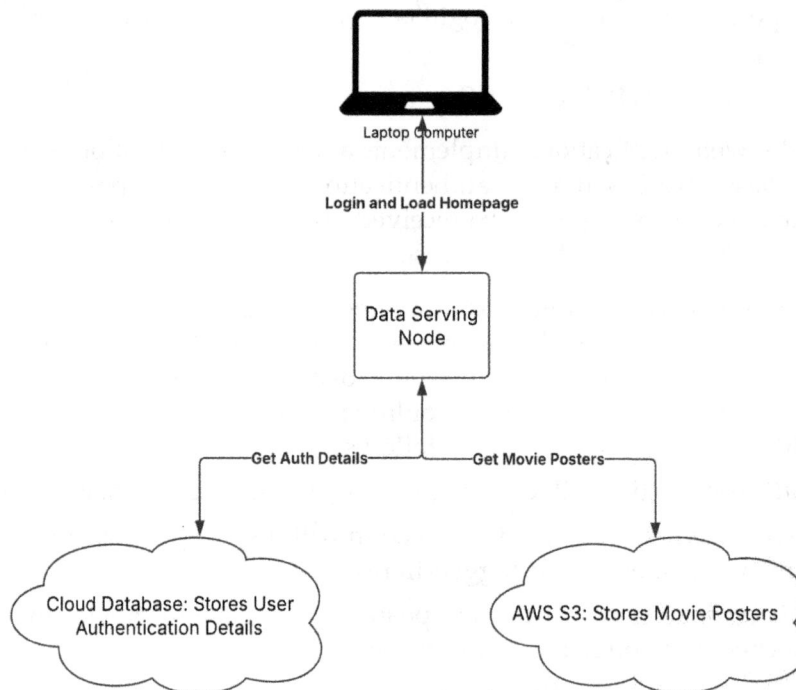

Figure 14.1: *Movie database application architecture*

In the aforementioned figure, we can see that:

- The user interface is running in the web browser, hosted on the user's laptop.
- The web browser is connected to the data serving node, which is responsible for processing various user requests.
- The data serving node communicates with the user authentication database, which is stored in the cloud. To perform and validate user authentication, the data serving node must retrieve data from the authentication database, which has high latency and associated costs.
- The movie posters are stored in the AWS S3. Obtaining movie posters from S3 incurs high latency and data access costs.

The cost of accessing authentication details and movie posters will keep growing based on the frequency of data access. To reduce such cost, caching can be implemented, where authentication details and movie posters can be cached on the data serving node itself.

Using local Memcached for caching

One popular software used for caching is Memcached, which is free to use and open-source. As the name suggests, Memcached holds the cached data in memory, leading to fast data access. You can spawn a Memcached instance locally on the data serving node. This Memcached instance will be used for caching. Memcached exposes an interface like a key-value store, so users can store/retrieve/delete any binary/structured/unstructured data based on a unique key.

The following code is a PySpark program to load the Memcached cache with user authentication details from the MySQL server:

```
from pyspark.sql import SparkSession
from pymemcache.client.base import Client

# Initialize Spark session
spark = SparkSession.builder \
    .appName("MySQLToMemcached") \
    .config("spark.jars", "/path/to/mysql-connector-java.jar") \
    .getOrCreate()

# MySQL Database connection properties
jdbc_url = "jdbc:mysql://your-mysql-host:3306/your_database"
db_table = "your_table"
db_properties = {
    "user": "your_username",
    "password": "your_password",
    "driver": "com.mysql.cj.jdbc.Driver"
}
# Read data from MySQL
```

```
df = spark.read.format("jdbc").options(
    url=jdbc_url,
    dbtable=db_table,
    **db_properties
).load()
# Initialize Memcached client
memcached_client = Client(('localhost', <memcached_port>))

def cache_to_memcached(row):
    key = f"user:{row.id}"
    value = row.password
    memcached_client.set(key, value)

# Apply caching function to each row
df.foreach(cache_to_memcached)
```

Reading from the cache

Once the data is cached in the local Memcached, the cost of frequent access to the cached data will be minimal. However, there is no guarantee that the requested object is always present in the cache, even if it was previously loaded into the cache. This occurs as caching solutions like Memcached implement a mechanism to evict data from the cache, making room for new incoming data. More on cache eviction later.

So, for reading the data, the user program needs to:

- Check if the object is present in the cache (i.e., local Memcached)
- If the object is present in the cache, return it from the cache
- If the object is not present in the cache, then get it from AWS S3 and return it

The following Python code illustrates the aforementioned behavior:

```
import boto3
from pymemcache.client.base import Client

memcached_client = Client(('localhost', <memcached_port>))

S3_BUCKET = "your-bucket-name"

def get_object(key):
    # Check if object exists in Memcached
    cached_data = memcached_client.get(key)

    if cached_data:
        return cached_data

    # Fetch object from S3
    s3_client = boto3.client('s3')
```

```
s3_response = s3_client.get_object(Bucket=S3_BUCKET, Key=key)
data = s3_response['Body'].read()
return data
```

Figure 14.2 depicts the workflow of reading data from the cache:

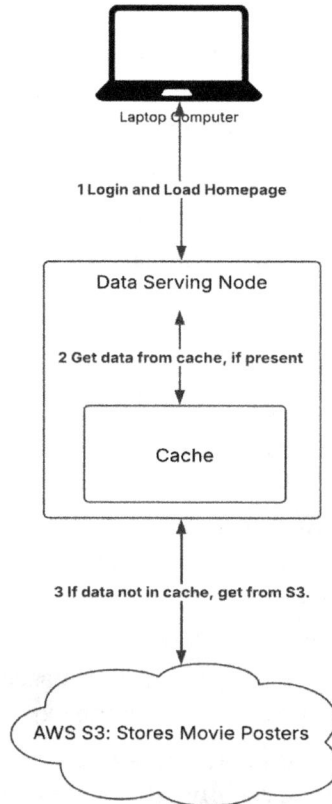

Figure 14.2: *Reading data from the cache*

An object cache is typically implemented either as an in-memory cache or as a persistent on-disk cache. Such a cache has an upper limit on the amount of data that can be cached. Memcached is an in-memory cache, and the amount of data that can be stored in Memcached is limited by the amount of RAM available on the machine. When the cache memory is full, and more data needs to be cached, some data needs to be removed (or evicted) from the cache. The methodology to identify data to be evicted is called as **cache eviction policy**.

Quality of data caching and cache eviction policies

Cache eviction policies play a key role in defining the quality of data caching. The purpose of implementing the data cache is to maximize the possibility of finding the data in the cache during reading of the data. If, during the read operation, the data is found in the cache, it is treated as a *cache hit*. On the other hand, if during the read operation, the data is not found in cache, and has to be read from AWS S3, then it is treated as a *cache miss*. The ratio of cache hits to total cache read operations is called the **cache hit ratio**. The higher the cache hit ratio, the better the cache quality.

To ensure better cache quality, it is necessary to ensure that the correct set of data objects is stored in the cache and that the remaining unwanted data objects are removed to make room for new ones. Therefore, the cache eviction policy plays a crucial role in determining cache quality.

The following is a list of popular cache eviction policies:

- **First in first out (FIFO)**: As per FIFO eviction policy, once the cache is full, the oldest data object residing in the cache (as dictated by the data insertion time in the cache), gets evicted first.

- **Evict least recently used (LRU) objects**: As per LRU policy, each cached data object will have a last accessed timestamp. Every time a data object is accessed, its last accessed timestamp will be updated. During eviction, the data object with the oldest last accessed timestamp will be evicted.

- **Evict the least frequently used (LFU) objects**: As per LFU policy, each cached data object will have a access counter associated with it. Each time a data object is accessed, its access counter is incremented. During eviction, the data object with least value of access counter will be evicted.

- **Expiration-based eviction**: As per expiration-based eviction, each data object will have expiration time. During eviction, only the expired data objects will be evicted.

As data caching improves the overall data access latency, it has significant cost associated with it. To achieve maximum gains from the caching, the user needs to understand the application's data access pattern and implement cache eviction policy that suits the aforementioned access pattern.

Memcached implements an LRU cache eviction policy, which ensures that the least recently used objects get evicted from the cache. This policy is based on the philosophy that an object once accessed is likely to be accessed in the near future. For example, with the release of a newly popular movie, more users will attempt to access it. So, data related to that movie will be held in the data cache.

Cache staleness, invalidation, and expiry

As time passes, the data objects held in the data cache can become stale. In our example of the user home page, we have a *What's New* section. Every week, a new set of movies is released, and the contents in the *What's New* section become irrelevant after a week. The movie posters stored in the data cache for the movies released last week are no longer needed in the cache.

In some cases, data stored in AWS S3 gets deleted or modified. If the copy of that data is stored in the cache, then it is treated as *stale data*. Stale data needs to be invalidated and removed from the cache. Let us understand design patterns to invalidate and remove the stale data from the cache.

Cache invalidation or cleanup

Continuing with our example of the *What's New* section, the cached data is likely to become stale every week. Therefore, we can implement a weekly task that invalidates the cached data. In our example, we are caching the movie posters. The posters for the previous week are no longer needed in the cache, so the weekly task can explicitly delete the cached movie posters for the previous week.

Memcached is a key-value store that allows users to store keys and corresponding values. The typical format of the key is a string, while the value can be an array of bytes. The user can decide to store complex objects in Memcached by converting them to an array of bytes. The process of converting complex objects into an array of bytes is known as **data serialization**. In our example, we assume the movie poster is available to us in the form of an array of bytes, so no explicit serialization will be performed.

Unlike AWS S3, Memcached does not support the List API, which could have been useful to get the list of keys (for a specific prefix). So, it is the user's responsibility to know (or store) the keys of the cached data so that the cached data can be accessed and cleaned easily.

The following Python code snippet illustrates how to delete a list of data objects, given the corresponding keys:

```python
from pymemcache.client.base import Client
memcached_client = Client(('localhost', <memcached_port>))
def cleanup_cached_objects(cleanup_keys):
    for key in cleanup_keys:
        result = memcached_client.delete(key)
```

Cache expiry

Explicitly writing the code to cache cleanup and executing it at regular intervals is a cumbersome process. To avoid this overhead, Memcached allows users to specify the expiry of the objects that are being cached.

In our example, we can set the object expiry time to seven days, so that the cached movie posters for the *What's New* section will get automatically deleted from the Memcached after seven days. The following code snippet depicts how to set the expiry for the data objects at the time of storing them:

```
from pymemcache.client.base import Client
memcached_client = Client(('localhost', <memcached_port>))
memcached_client.set(key, value, expire=7*24*60*60)
```

Note: **Although setting expiry for cached objects alleviates the cache cleanup process, for specific use cases, there is a benefit to providing the ability to manually clean up the cache.**

For example, if due to some user error, the cache gets corrupted. Depending upon the user application's data access pattern, automatic cleanup of the corrupt cache can take time. In such cases, a backdoor to perform manual cache cleanup will be helpful.

Caching of pre-processed data

Identifying personalized recommendations for every user is a complex and resource-intensive process. Therefore, the data engineering workflow performs pre-processing to identify personalized recommendations for each user. Once such recommendations are generated, they will be stored in AWS S3 for future access. The typical frequency of recalculating personalized recommendations is a week or a month.

Every time the user loads the home page, the personalized recommendations need to be loaded from AWS S3. In this example, the pre-loaded personalized recommendations are the cached data.

Furthermore, such pre-computed personalized data can be loaded into the data cache, hosted on the data serving nodes through the data engineering pattern called prefetching. Now, let us understand prefetching.

Data prefetching

We have already looked at the use case of loading the user password information in the data cache. Given that the user password information is smaller in size, it can be loaded into the data cache when the data serving application gets loaded. Most likely, it may fit in the cache very easily. However, not all the required data can be loaded into the data cache at the time of application bootstrap. For example, personalized recommendations for each user can be different. So, for ten million users, and ten movies per user in their personalized recommendations list, there can be 100 million different movies in the list of personalized recommendations. Typically, the online movie database would not cache all 100 million movie posters across all the users to the data cache during bootstrap because:

- It will take a long time to load so much data into the data cache, slowing down the bootstrap process.
- Not all these movie posters may fit into the data cache, as the size of movie posters can be large.

So, instead of loading all 100 million movie posters across all users, the data serving nodes can cache only those movie posters that are in the list of personalized recommendations for the users connected to that node. In such cases, only a subset of data is cached, and this subset is loaded into the cache on demand. This type of on-demand loading of the data cache, triggered by an operation like user login, is called **prefetching**.

Note: In case of prefetching, the data load is not explicitly requested. It gets triggered via a different operation (like user login) to yield better performance.

In other words, prefetching is a technique that triggers the loading of specific data into the cache, which is likely to be accessed soon. In our example, there are two user-specific sections on the home page:

- Personalized Recommendations
- Visit Again

The movie lists in both sections are very specific to the user. So, the movie posters needed for these two sections can be prefetched from AWS S3 into the data cache when the user logs in, even without a web browser running on the user's computer, which makes the request to get the data.

Figure 14.3 shows the order of events that transpire at the time of prefetching, which helps us understand the benefit of prefetching:

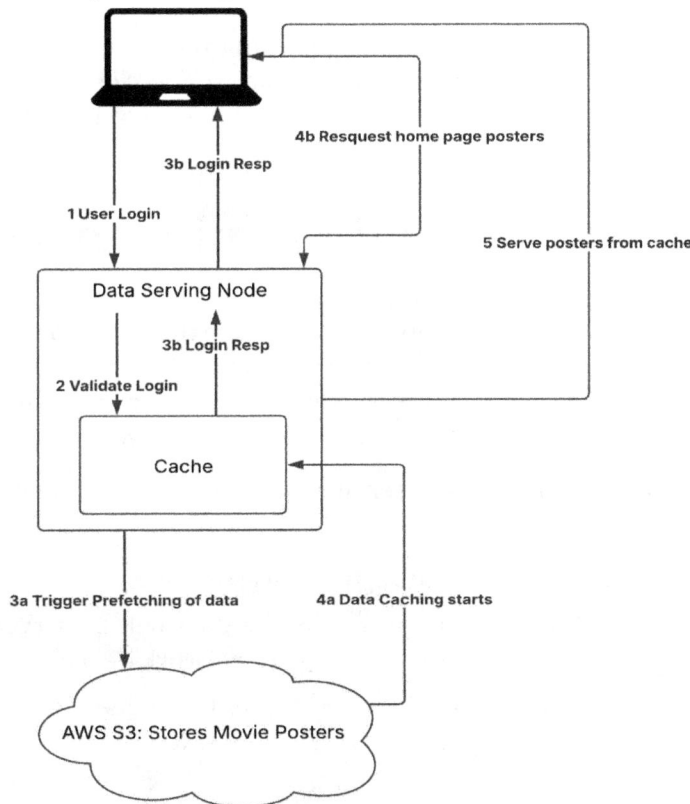

***Figure 14.3**: Benefits of prefetching*

In *Figure 14.3,* we can see the following events:

- The user sends the login request to the data serving node.
- The node performs the user validation.
- Once the validation is successful on the data serving node, two actions will be triggered simultaneously.
  - o Trigger the prefetching of user-specific data
  - o Send a response to the successful user login
- Both of the following events happen in parallel:
  - o Caching of the user data starts
  - o The web browser on the user's laptop receives the login response and requests for the movie posters to be displayed on the home page. As the caching has already started, the data caching node is likely to find the required data in the local data cache
- Data present in the cache will be served from the cache, leading to lower latency in loading the home page.

Until now, we have investigated the benefits of caching the data on the data serving node. However, the data can also be cached at other locations. The closer the data is cached, the faster it can be served. Many websites utilize data caching in web browsers to speed up data serving.

Caching on laptops and mobile device

Let us continue with our example of caching the data needed by the user's home page. After logging into the website, the user will continue to browse movies, movie reviews, and other content. During this time, the user may return to the home page multiple times. Each time the home page needs to be loaded, the web browser must load the corresponding movie posters. And the web browser will need to load these posters from data serving nodes.

To avoid fetching the data from the data serving node on *reload* of the home page, browser caching can be implemented.

Figure 14.4 depicts the benefit of data caching in the web browser, and we can see that:

- If the data is cached in the browser cache, the data will be served from there. This avoids delays in loading the home page due to network delays.
- If the data is not cached in the browser cache, the request to get the data will be forwarded to the data serving node on the server side.

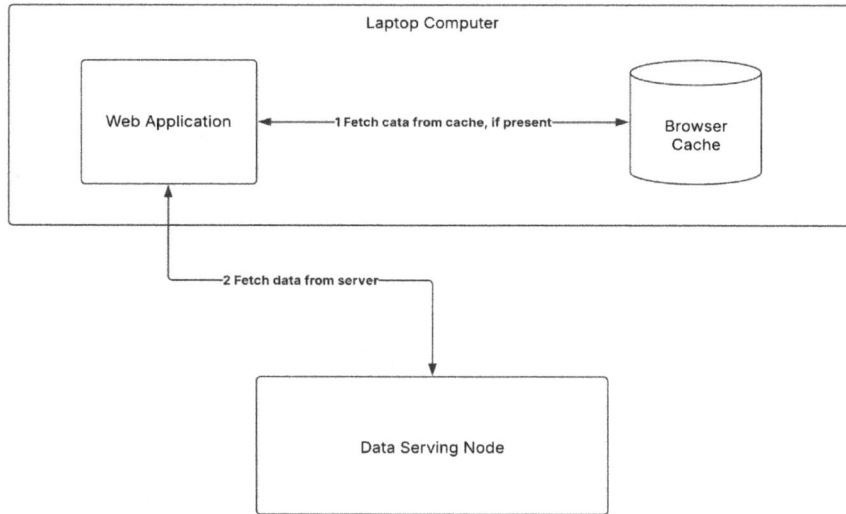

Figure 14.4: Benefits of browser cache

IndexedDB is a popular, open-source, NoSQL database used for caching images, files, etc. in web applications.

In theory, there is no conceptual difference between the local cache hosted on data-serving nodes and the web browser cache running on a user's laptop. All the concepts and solutions, such as cache population, prefetching, and staleness, are the same for both types of caches. Similarly, the quality of both caching solutions will be defined by the cache hit ratio.

Similarly, the benefits of caching in the web browser are similar to those of caching on mobile devices. The cache on mobile devices will speed up the loading of the mobile app.

Conclusion

In this chapter, we started with a new use case for an online movie database website. Such a website offers a range of modern features, including personalized recommendations, what is new, etc. Focusing on the online movie database, we identified various use cases that required low-latency data serving to ensure a high-quality user experience.

Then we looked into data caching and how data caching can be used to speed up the process of user login and loading of the personalized home page for the users. One of the most popular data caching tools is Memcached, which is a key-value data store. Memcached simplifies the implementation of local data caching by providing features such as LRU-based cache eviction and cache invalidation based on expiry time for each object. With the help of Python code, we visualized the mechanism for populating the data cache and reading data from it.

We then learned about the requirements of cache eviction and various cache eviction policies. We also explored different methods for invalidating the data cache implemented using

Memcached. Then we learned about the concept of prefetching by understanding the use case of loading user-specific documents in response to certain user actions. We also defined the quality of the cache using the cache hit ratio.

Finally, we discussed the possibility of further reducing data loading latency by moving the data closer to the consumer, i.e., on the user's device itself. We achieved this by utilizing the browser cache. Browser cache can be implemented using IndexedDB.

In the next chapter, we will cover the data engineering patterns used for searching of unstructured data like text, images, videos, etc. We will explore the tools and features used for performing full-text search. We will also understand the basic concepts of representing unstructured data in the form of vectors and searching it using vector search. We will also learn about the RAG pattern.

Questions

1. Explain the use cases that will benefit from data caching.
2. Data can be cached only in one place. True or false?
3. What are the various cache eviction policies?
4. Is there a way to evict data stored in Memcached, based on its time-to-live?
5. Is it possible to reduce the latency of data loading by storing frequently accessed data on user devices, such as laptops and mobile devices?
6. What is cache staleness? How can it impact cache quality?

Join our Discord space

Join our Discord workspace for latest updates, offers, tech happenings around the world, new releases, and sessions with the authors:

https://discord.bpbonline.com

CHAPTER 15
Data Search Patterns

Introduction

In the previous chapters, we focused on various design patterns used for searching the data based on primary and secondary keys. The queries used for this type of search make use of traditional data structures like lookup indexes, hash indexes, etc. However, the results returned by these queries are deterministic. In other words, the returned results match *exactly* with the user-specified predicates.

However, many modern-day use cases cannot be solved by searching for the exact match. The users may expect to get the results that are *like* the input provided by them, but *may not* match exactly. In this chapter, we will look further into the use cases where the user is searching for results based on a similarity match or a fuzzy match.

The data engineers typically use *full test search databases* to search for text that is *similar-to* the input text. However, in recent times, similarity search using *vector databases* has gained popularity due to the commoditization of the large language models and AI-based search solutions.

In this chapter, we will look into the full text search databases and vector databases. We will learn mechanisms to tune to the results of the full text searches and the similarity searches. Such tuning is required as the quality of the result can be dependent on the user dataset, as well as the inherently non-deterministic nature of the underlying database implementation. We will also learn about the *hybrid search*, which combines the results of full text search with the results of vector search. Finally, we will end this chapter by learning about the **retrieval-**

augmented generation (RAG) pattern used for finding the best possible match with the help of vector databases.

Structure

This chapter covers the following topics:

- Full text search
- Vector search
- Hybrid search
- retrieval-augmented generation

Objectives

By the end of this chapter, you will understand various use cases of text similarity search, fuzzy search, and hybrid search. You will learn the software tools used to execute such kinds of search queries. You will also explore the methodologies to tune the search queries to get better results.

Finally, you will understand how a modern-day AI application can use the RAG pattern to improve the quality of search results.

Full text search

Suppose that you are chatting with your friends about movies, and you recall a particular plot from a movie. You tell your friends the movie plot, and everyone likes it. Then someone asks you the name of the movie. You try to recall, but you cannot. You get frustrated and wish you had a movie website that lets you search for a movie based on its plot. A software solution based on *full text search* is designed for this type of use case. In such use cases, data is searched based on unstructured text stored along with the movie information.

A modern-day movie website can allow users to search for movies based on the text in the movie plot, movie reviews, etc. Such advanced searching techniques allows the website to return more relevant results. We will take the example of searching for movie plots using full text search databases.

Full text search databases are different than traditional structured databases, as they are specially designed for the quality of the text search.

Let us understand how a full text search database works with the help of the details mentioned here:

- A full text search database will store the list of movies along with the corresponding movie plots.

- To perform searches quickly, a data engineer should create an appropriate full text search index (or an inverted index), which maps various words in the movie plot to their corresponding movie ID.

- At the time of index creation, the database will traverse the movie plot texts for all movies. For each movie plot, it will:

  o Tokenize the text.

  o Pre-process the text by performing normalization, stop word removal, stemming, etc.

  o Create an index entry mapping the words in the movie plot to the movie ID.

- When a user wants to search for a movie based on the words in the movie plot, the user will write a search text. The user's input text also undergoes tokenization and normalization. Then the index search is performed.

- The goal of index search is to return the most relevant results, often ranked by relevance score.

Now, let us understand various terminologies and technologies related to full text search:

- **Tokenization**: It is a process of separating individual words from the full text. For example, in the sentence, *the movie starts with a police officer searching the riverbed!* This text will be converted to individual words *the, movie, starts, with, a, police, officer, searching, the, riverbed!*

- **Normalization**: It is the process of converting the words to lowercase and removing punctuation marks. So, from the above, the token *The* will get converted to *the* and the token *riverbed!* will get converted to *riverbed*.

- **Stop word removal**: It is the process of removal of specific stop words, which do not have any reasonable impact on the quality of the search results. In our example, two occurrences of *the* and one occurrence of *a* and *with* will be removed.

- **Stemming**: It is the process of converting words to their corresponding stem word. In our example, the word *starts* will get converted to *start*, the word *searching* will get converted to *search*, and so on.

There are more pre-processing steps that can be performed by the full text search databases to improve the quality of search results.

Once all the pre-processing of the text is done, an index entry will be created. In our example, words like *police, officer, riverbed*, etc., will be inserted into the inverted index, along with the reference to the corresponding movie ID.

Benefits of pre-processing

The pre-processing operations ensure the following:

- Unwanted words do not get indexed. Even if the unwanted words like *the, a,* etc., can be present in the user input, these are very common words. They will be present in almost all movie plots. Indexing and searching such words can dilute the importance of words like *police and riverbed.*

- The word *searching* gets converted to its stem word *search*. This reduces the impact due to the presence of prefixes and suffixes of the words. For example, let us say the user's input query is *the police searches riverbed*. Then the keyword in the movie plot, i.e., *searching* will not directly match the input word from the query, i.e., *searches*. However, the user query is expected to match the movie plot. So, the use of stemming helps in avoiding such false mismatches.

Full text search example

There are many popular databases that provide full text search. The open-source databases like Elastic, Apache Solr, Typesense, etc., are specially designed search engines for the purpose of full-text search. They provide a wide variety of advanced search features. We will discuss these features later in this chapter.

In this chapter, we will use an Elastic database for the coding example.

Typically, the data engineers choose one of the transactional databases, like MySQL or DynamoDB, to store the movie details. These databases serve the transactional workloads very well. However, databases like Elastic are better suited for full text search workloads. So, all the details of the movie, which can be classified as structured data like release date, name of the director, name of the producer, etc., will be stored only in the transactional database. However, fields that require full text search will be stored in both transactional and full text search databases. The movie plot is stored in the transactional database to display it on the movie details page, while the copy stored in the search database is indexed specifically for search queries.

Elastic database exposes the basic interface to create a search index, add documents to the search index, and perform full text search. In the following example, we will see how these basic interfaces can be used to write a full text search program.

So, the data engineer needs to perform the following steps to set up and use Elastic:

1. Set up an Elastic server.

2. Create a search index. The following REST command can be used to create a basic search index in Elastic:

```
curl -X PUT "localhost:9200/movie_plot_index" -H 'Content-Type:
application/json'
```

3. Add the initial set of documents to the search index. The following REST command can be used:

```
curl -X POST "localhost:9200/movie_plot_index/_doc" -H 'Content-Type:
application/json' -d '
{
  "movieID": "Movie-1",
```

```
    "plot": "Two detectives travel from New York to San Francisco in search
of a criminal."
    }'
```

4. Keep adding documents to the index whenever new documents are generated.

5. Perform an index search whenever the user wants to perform a full text search query. The following is a REST command for an example search query to search for the word **"detective"** in the movie plot:

```
curl -X POST "localhost:9200/movie_plot_index/_search" -H 'Content-Type:
application/json' -d '

{
    "query": {
      "match": {
        "plot": "detective"
      }
    }
}'
```

Figure 15.1 shows how the user application can interact with transactional as well as full text search databases, based on the user workload:

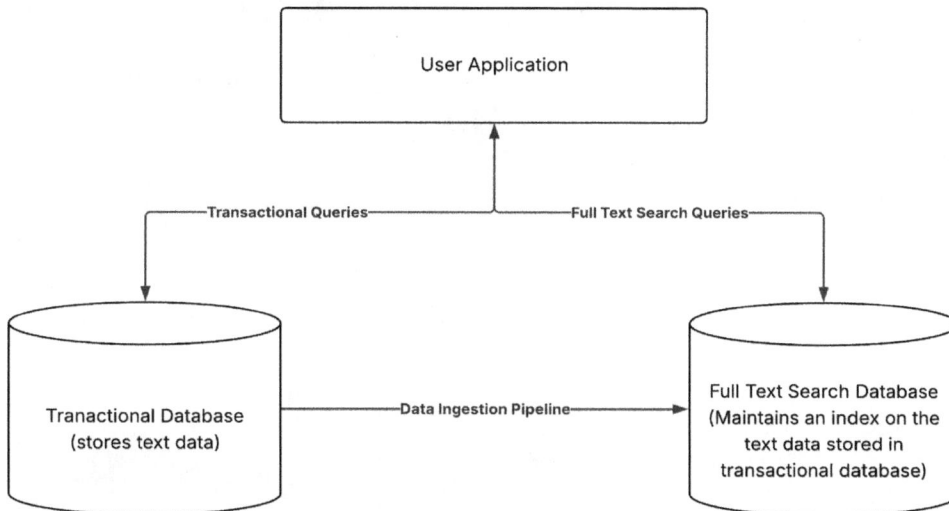

Figure 15.1: *Using a full text search database*

In the figure aforementioned, we can see that:

- The user application communicates with the transactional database for the transactional workload.

- The user application communicates with the full text search database for the full text search workload.

- A data ingestion pipeline is established between the transactional database and the full text search database. This pipeline ensures the consistency of the data between the two databases.

Advanced features of full text search

As mentioned previously, full text search performs a text search based on similarity, and the matching results need not be exact matches. So, full text search systems implement some advanced features that help users get more relevant results.

The following is the list of such features:

- **Edit distance:** It is the ability of the full text search system to ignore minor differences in input text and the data stored in the database, at the time of searching. This mechanism is useful to handle scenarios where there can be typographical errors in either the user input or the stored data. Continuing with our example, if the user wants to search for detective movies, but instead of typing **detective**, the user types *detectiv* (notice the missing *e*, at the end). In such cases, full text search databases allow users to find documents with minor mismatches.

  Using Elastic, edit distance can be specified using the **fuzziness** parameter, which can be specified at the time of query. The following query depicts the use of the **fuzziness** parameter:

```
curl -X POST "localhost:9200/movie_plot_index/_search -H 'Content-Type:
application/json' -d '
{
  "query": {
    "match": {
      "plot": {
        "query": "detectiv", // Notice missing "e" at the end
        "fuzziness": "1",
      }
    }
  }
}
```

  In the aforementioned query, the fuzziness value is 1. That means if there is a difference of one character between the input query and the stored text in the database, the document is treated as a match. So, the user will get the document with the word **detective** in the query output.

- **Synonyms**: While searching for detective movies, the user does not use the word **detective**. On the other hand, the user can use the word **police**, which is a synonym for the word **detective**. Now, conceptually, the document with reference to the word **detective** should match, even if the user's input is **police**. To handle such scenarios, full text search databases provide the ability to specify synonyms at the time of index creation.

  The following REST command can be used to specify synonyms at the time of index creation:

```
curl  -X  PUT  "localhost:9200/movie_plot_index/  -H  'Content-Type:
application/json' -d '
{
  "settings": {
    "analysis": {
      "filter": {
        "synonym_filter": {
          "type": "synonym",
          "synonyms": [
            "police, detective",
          ]
        }
      },
      "analyzer": {
        "synonym_analyzer": {
          "tokenizer": "standard",
          "filter": [
            "lowercase",
            "synonym_filter"
          ]
        }
      }
    }
  },
  "mappings": {
    "properties": {
      "plot": {
        "type": "text",
        "analyzer": "synonym_analyzer"
      }
```

```
      }
    }
  }
```

In the aforementioned code, we make use of custom analyzers with Elastic to perform a synonym search. Since the user has provided a synonym analyzer, at the time of index creation, the user query searching for **police** will receive a document with **detective** in the movie plot as the search result.

Here, we have learned that the full text search tries to find a match with the specific *words* from the input. However, the user may not need specific words. In some cases, the sentiment behind the words is more important to get the relevant results. This type of search is called **semantic search**, which is typically solved by *vector search*.

Vector search

In the previous example, we saw how users can search for movies related to *police* or *detective* by searching for the words and their synonyms in the full text search database. However, there can be too many movies with words like *police, detective*, etc. in the movie plot. This can lead to returning many results. However, what if the user wants to write a complete English language sentence, and wants to search for the movie plot that matches the semantic meaning of it?

Let us take an example movie plot, *a corrupt police officer keeps troubling innocent citizens and eventually faces legal consequences.* Now, if the user searches with a search query, *a police officer commits crimes and ends up in jail*, then we can see very little similarity in the words used in these two sentences. *A police officer* is a common phrase, but *troubling innocent citizens* and *commits crimes* not only do not use the same words, but also are not synonymous. Similarly, *faces legal consequences* is syntactically very different from *ends up in jail*, but it is semantically very similar.

In this type of search query, the ability of full text search system falls short, but vector search systems have the ability to return relevant results. So, let us deep dive into the concepts related to vector search.

Introduction to vector

A vector is a mathematical representation of (typically) an unstructured piece of data, like text, image, video, etc.

The following points help understand the basic concepts related to vectors:

- Special software tools (called **vector embedding models**) are used to convert unstructured data to its corresponding vector representation.
- A typical vector will be an array of floating-point numbers.

- All the arrays generated by a particular vector embedding model will have the same number of elements.
- The size of the array is also known as **vector dimensionality**.

Vector similarity search

The vector embedding models make use of heuristics collected across *very large sized* datasets, identify salient data points in each of the data items, and mathematically represent salient data points with their relations with each other, to form a vector. For example, text embedding models will have the ability to differentiate between positive and negative sentiment. Image embedding modes have the ability to identify features like edges and corners in an image. Geometrically, the vectors that have similar features will be close to each other. While the vectors with different features will be far from each other in the *n* dimensional vector space.

So, when a user needs to search for a text stored in the database that is similar to the user input, one just needs to find the vectors stored in the database that are closest (in distance) to the input vector. Popular ways to calculate the distance between two vectors are:

- Find the Euclidean distance between two vectors
- Find the cosine of the angle between two vectors.

The algorithm used to find the closest vectors for the input vector is called the **k-nearest-neighbors** (**KNN**) algorithm.

Vector databases and vector indexes

A vector database is a database that allows users to store and retrieve vectors in a performance-efficient manner. A typical vector database is designed specifically to optimize performing vector-specific operations (like calculating vector distances, implementing the KNN algorithm, etc.). However, it may not be fully optimized for regular transactional operations.

Vector databases allow users to create vector indexes. Vector indexes, similar to primary and secondary indexes, provide users with a fast access path to the vector data. Many times, vector indexes are optimized to find *approximate* nearest neighbors, i.e., ANN (instead of exact nearest neighbors), to speed up the query process, at the cost of a loss of precision of the returned results.

Using vector database

Similar to the full text search, vector databases are also customized for vector search use cases. They provide various vector search-specific features. But the non-vector data needs to be stored in the transactional database for transactional workloads (like fast lookups based on non-vector inputs). So, the data engineers need to configure a transactional database, a separate vector database, and a data ingestion pipeline between the transactional and vector databases.

The transactional database will store raw unstructured data (like text, images, etc.) as well as its vector embeddings. The vector embeddings can be inserted into the vector database by implementing a data ingestion pipeline between the transactional database and the vector search database. So, the vector search database will store only the vector embeddings and will allow users to search for vector embeddings with the help of a vector index. *Figure 15.2* depicts how a user application can use a vector database to serve vector queries:

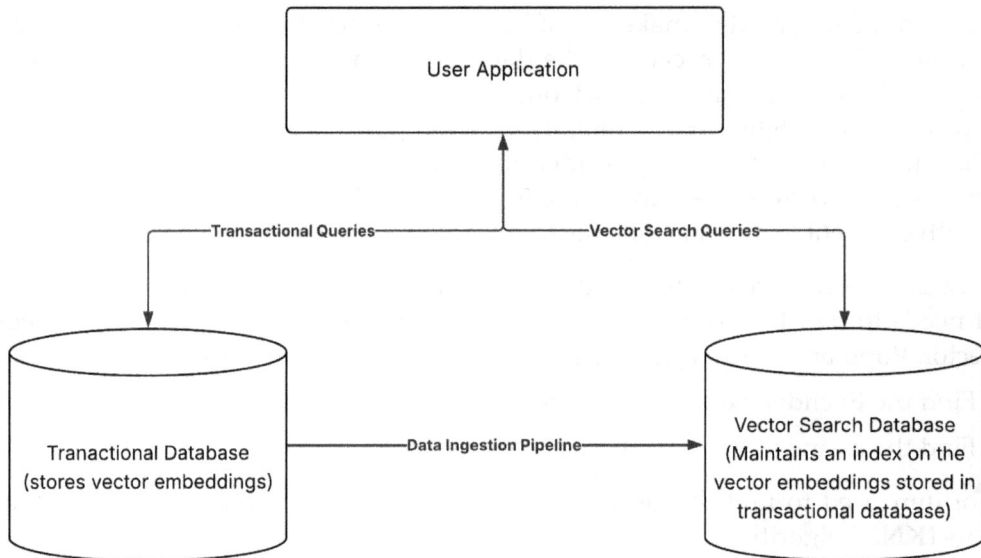

Figure 15.2: Using a vector database

Vector search example

Let us look at an example of vector search using vector databases. Continuing with our example of the movie plot, we will store all the movie details in the transactional database. The transactional database will store the vector embeddings generated from the movie plot. We will use Elastic as a vector database. There are other popular open-source vector databases like Milvus, Qdrant, PGVector, etc.

A data ingestion pipeline will be created between the transactional database and the vector database. A vector index will be created in the vector database (Elastic), and the data ingestion pipeline will ensure ingestion of the vector embeddings in the vector index.

The following REST command can be used to create a vector index using Elastic:

```
PUT /movie-plot-index
{
  "mappings": {
    "properties": {
```

```
      "title": {
        "type": "text"
      },
      "movie_plot_embedding": {
        "type": "dense_vector",
        "dims": 128,
        "index": true,
        "similarity": "cosine"
      }
    }
  }
}
```

The following REST command can be used to ingest the vector data into the vector index:

```
POST /movie-plot-index/_doc/<MovieId>
{
  "title": "Movie Title",
  "movie_plot_embedding": <array of 128 floating point numbers>
}
```

To search for the movie by plot, the following REST command can be used. In this example, the movie plot is searched by finding the **"K"** nearest neighbors of the query vector embedding using the **"knn"** operator:

```
POST /movie-plot-index/_search
{
  "knn": {
    " movie_plot_embedding ": {
      "vector": <Vector embedding for the user query>,
      "k": 10
    }
  }
}
```

Note: The user needs to pass a textual query to the vector embedding model to generate the vector embedding. This generated vector embedding can be passed as an input to the vector search operation. Also, one needs to use the same vector embedding model for generating query vectors as the one that was used at the time of storing the vector embeddings in the vector index.

Quality of vector search results

The quality of vector search depends upon the following:

- The quality of the vector embedding being used
- The number of dimensions of vectors. The more dimensions, the more information is stored in the vector
- The underlying algorithm used to find similar vectors
- Underlying data structures used to store vectors

However, there is no guarantee that vector search will always return the exact results you are looking for. This limitation is due to the following:

- Information loss during the generation of vector embeddings
- Precision loss due to the approximate nature of vector search

However, full text search does not struggle with these limitations, which means that the choice between vector search and full text search has its own trade-offs. To overcome this problem, the data engineers can implement a solution based on the hybrid search.

Hybrid search

Hybrid search is when the user wants to combine the results of full text search with the results of vector search to get more relevant results for the search query. In our example of searching for movies based on movie plots, vector search will return the list of movies having a plot semantically similar in meaning to the user query. On the other hand, the full text search will return similar results as per the keywords in the user query.

Now, in theory, there will be two different sets of documents selected to be returned during the execution of the hybrid search, one set selected by the full text search and the other set selected by the vector search. A hybrid search execution engine can combine these results to generate a single set of results. Elastic users can use the **"boost"** parameter to tune the final order of results returned to the end user. The boost parameter value, specified in the match clause, dictates the importance given to the full text search results (over vector search results).

Note: **Elastic sorts the resulting documents based on a metric called relevance score. The boost parameter helps in boosting the relevance scores for specific documents matched by the specific "match" predicate.**

Let us see the example code for hybrid search here. The following command can be used to create a hybrid search index using Elastic:

```
PUT hybrid_index
{
```

```
  "mappings": {
    "properties": {
      "plot": { "type": "text" },
      "plot_vector_embedding": {
        "type": "dense_vector",
        "dims": 384,
        "index": true,
        "similarity": "cosine"
      }
    }
  }
}
```

The following command can be used to perform a hybrid search using Elastic. In this query, the boost parameter is used in the **match** clause to dictate the importance of full text search results over vector search results:

```
POST hybrid_index/_search
{
  "size": 5,
  "query": {
    "bool": {
      "should": [
        {
          "match": {
            "plot": {
              "query": <user query text>,
              "boost": 1.5
            }
          }
        },
        {
          "knn": {
            "plot_vector_embedding": {
              "vector": <user query vector embedding>,
              "k": 10,
              "num_candidates": 100
            }
          }
```

```
        }
     ]
    }
  }
}
```

In the recent times, **large language models** (**LLMs**) have become ubiquitous, given the number of problems they can solve. As the LLMs have exhibited their power in processing texts, data engineers are more inclined towards using the text embedding models exposed by the authors of LLMs.

The quality of results returned by the LLMs depends on the relevance of the context given to them. One of the ways users can improve the LLM results is by using vector search to generate better contexts. This type of design pattern is called RAG.

Retrieval augmented generation

RAG is a data engineering design pattern where the data engineer wants to improve the outcome of an LLM. To do that, the data engineer needs to provide relevant context to the LLM. To find relevant context, the data engineers can introduce a vector database in the solution.

Let us continue with our example of an online movie database. For understanding RAG, we will take a use case of generated specific movie summaries. LLMs are good at summarizing the textual data. However, the LLMs are typically trained over a large amount of data, mostly from the large amount of available information on the internet. So, LLMs may not perform well on inputs like *summarizing the criticism received by the director of Movie-A*. For this type of LLM task, it is useful to provide specific information in the context of the LLM to get better results. The online movie database will store the user reviews of the movies, and the specific user reviews (or snippets from the user reviews) criticizing the director can be provided to the LLM as a part of the context.

Now, the challenge is to find the user reviews that criticize the director. This can be implemented using vector search, as learned earlier in this chapter. This process of searching for relevant information in the vector database to improve the LLM's results is called RAG.

RAG is a two-step process. In *step 1*, the helpful information is *retrieved* from the vector database. In *step 2*, the retrieved information is given to the LLM (along with the user query) to *generate* a better response from the LLM.

Figure 15.3 helps in visualizing the RAG pattern:

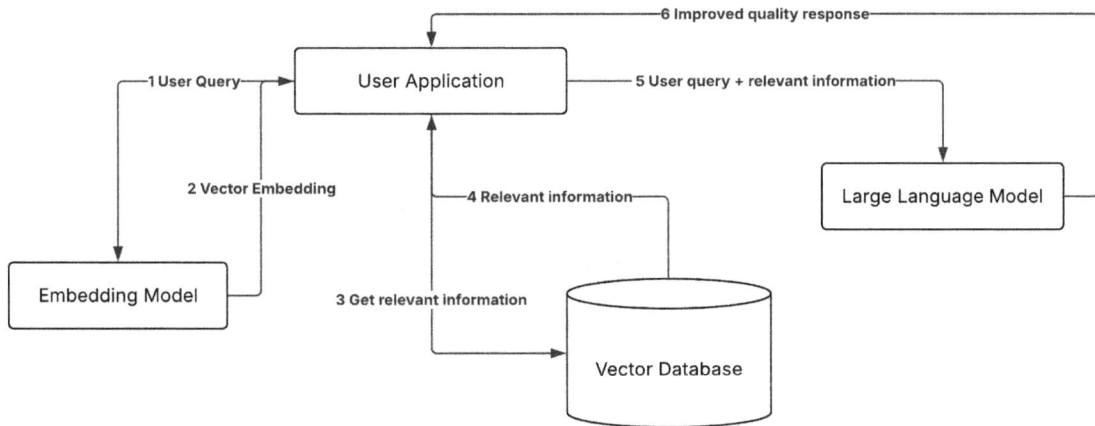

Figure 15.3: Retrieval-augmented generation

Conclusion

In this chapter, we learned various use cases that require various search techniques to find relevant data. We started with understanding the basics of full text search and learned an example of full text search using Elastic. Then we studied advanced Elasticsearch features. We then continued with understanding limitations of full text search, specifically how it cannot search for data with a similar semantic meaning to that of the user query. This paved the path towards the requirement of the vector search.

We learned the basic concepts of the vector representation of unstructured data (like text, images, etc.) along with the concepts of vector similarity search. We then learned the limitations of vector search and highlighted how the vector search and the full text search are functionally limited when performed individually. This led to the concept of hybrid search. Finally, we learned how vector search can be used for RAG applications.

In the next chapter, we will study various domain-specific design patterns. These domains include the domain of time series data and the domain of low-connectivity networks.

Questions

1. Is the full text search based on the keywords in the text data? Yes or no?

2. What is a vector? How can you determine the similarity between two given vectors?

3. Vectors can have only three dimensions. True or false?

4. How can you overcome the limitations exhibited by full text search and vector search when performed individually?

Join our Discord space

Join our Discord workspace for latest updates, offers, tech happenings around the world, new releases, and sessions with the authors:

https://discord.bpbonline.com

CHAPTER 16
Domain Specific Patterns

Introduction

In the previous chapters, we studied the examples of e-commerce websites, online movie databases, online travel aggregators, etc. These examples exhibit the most common use cases and user requirements for any commercial large-scale web application. The data engineering design patterns learned in previous chapters are universal and can be applied to a large number of domains. This is primarily true because these patterns, at the core, try to solve very common problems like: how to ingest the data efficiently, how to store the data with reduced cost, how to retrieve the data at low latencies, how to pre-process the data, etc.

However, there are some data engineering design patterns used in very specific domains of large-scale software design. In this chapter, we will focus on learning design patterns used in specific domains.

We will start with the domain of time series data, where we will learn when and how to use the time series database. After that, we will study how a typical offline application is designed for handling the data at the edge. Furthermore, we learn a few data engineering patterns related to the field of machine learning.

Structure

This chapter covers the following topics:

- Time series data
- Offline data applications
- Understanding machine learning
- Machine learning model versioning

Objectives

By the end of this chapter, we will learn some of the domain-specific design patterns focusing on domains like machine learning, time series data management, offline application design for the data at the edge, etc. These design patterns provide you with the essential tools and solutions used to solve the data engineering problems in these respective domains.

Time series data

Time series data is the set of data objects whose value changes over time. Along with the value of the data object, the timestamp associated with it is also equally important. Let us take an example of a stock value prediction application, where the data represents the change in the value of the stock, at regular time intervals (like every minute, every five minutes, etc.). A typical stock value prediction application needs to look at the changes in stock values over time to predict the future stock value. For such applications, one of the important requirements is to have the ability to store and retrieve a large amount of time series data in an efficient manner. So, time series data processing applications use specially designed databases called **time series databases**.

A set of problems that represent the use of time series data is as follows:

- **Stock market prediction**: Stock price changes across time are used to determine future stock prices.
- **Weather forecasting**: Changes in temperature, humidity, etc. are analyzed over time to predict precipitation.
- **Anomaly detection in stats generated by servers**: Sudden change in server stats across time.
- **Alert**: Like temperature or pressure from IoT devices crosses a pre-defined threshold.

As we can see in the aforementioned examples, the values of the data objects at a specific time are important to perform the required data analysis or prediction.

Some popular open-source time series databases are Timescale, Prometheus, InfluxDB, etc. Often, the time series databases support a specialized interface (other than SQL) for expressing time series concepts in a better fashion. For example, the Prometheus database allows users to use **Prometheus Query Language (PromQL)**, which supports a rich set of features used specifically for accessing time series data.

Features of the time series databases

Time series databases differ from traditional relational and NoSQL databases in a few aspects, which make them efficient for managing time series data. The following is the list of such features:

- Use of the time-optimized data store, which uses time partitioning
- Support specially designed data compression algorithms like Gorilla encoding or delta encoding
- Support time-based data retention policies
- Natively support time-based queries and functions like moving averages, rate of change, etc.

Figure 16.1 shows the time series application architecture:

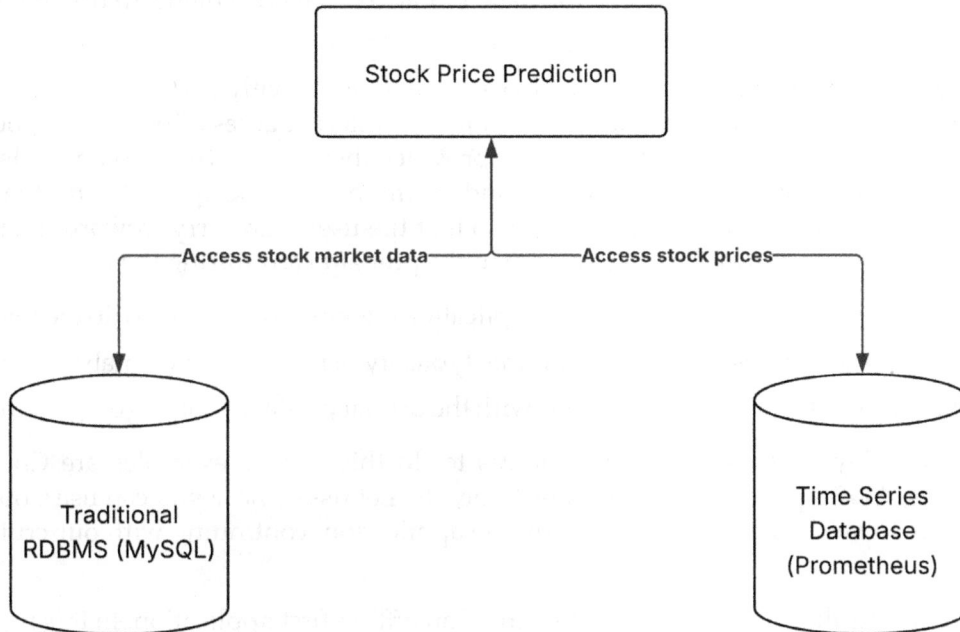

Figure 16.1: *Time series data application uses traditional RDBMS as well as a time series database*

Although time series databases provide optimal storage and access to time series data, they are not well designed for storing and retrieving regular data (like structured or semi-structured data). Let us take an example of a stock market prediction application. This application will need to store information about the following:

- Various stock markets across the globe
- Different stocks
- Time series data about the stock prices

In such cases, the data engineers will divide the data into two types, i.e., regular structured data and time series data. As shown in *Figure 16.1*, we can see that the user application will use two different databases. It will use MySQL for storing information about stocks, stock markets, companies, etc., and it will also use Prometheus (a time series database) to store stock prices at regular time intervals.

Offline data applications

All the user applications we learned until now were designed by assuming full connectivity to the data. What that means is, the data is stored somewhere in either a data center or cloud, and the user applications have full access to the data over the internet. Even in the case of a catastrophic event, the data is still accessible due to data replication. However, some applications (based on their domain) may require offline access to the data. The offline access is not only limited to offline reading of the data, but also has requirements to update the data in an offline manner.

Let us take an example of a cruise ship that provides users with value-added services on board. When the cruise ship is sailing, it does not have internet access. To ensure a good user experience, let us say that the cruise operator provides the users with pre-paid cards. Users can pre-pay the money against these cards, and the money can be spent during the cruise. When the cruise ends, the balance is retained so that the users can carry forward the balance to the next cruise. It is allowed to add balance to the prepaid card during the cruise as well.

The aforementioned use case of offline data applications requires the ability to do the following:

- Record transactions that happen offline, typically using an offline database
- Synchronize the offline transactions with the primary database after going online again

Many modern-day databases provide features to do this. A few examples are Couchbase App Services, AWS AppSync, Azure Offline Sync, etc. Let us see how you can use Couchbase App Services to tackle the use case of the offline application, continuing with our cruise ship example.

Figure 16.2 depicts the deployment architecture of an offline-first application. In this figure, we can see the following:

- As usual, the online applications will continue to communicate with the Couchbase Cloud Server.

- The offline-first applications are deployed separately, and they are connected to the Couchbase Edge Server. Edge server is a lightweight database server that provides the basic functionality required for the application. It also provides the ability to synchronize with the Couchbase server whenever needed, with the help of Couchbase App Services.

- The Couchbase App Services provide the ability to bi-directionally synchronize the data between the Couchbase Server and the Couchbase Edge Server.

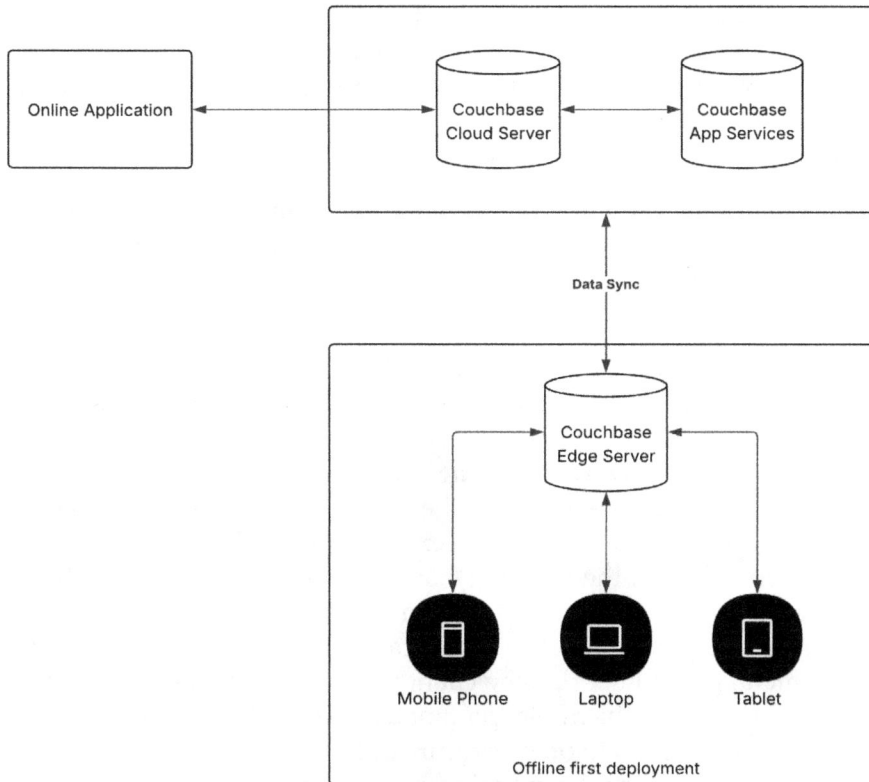

Figure 16.2: Deployment architecture of an offline-first application

The following sequence of events depicts the offline behavior of the application:

1. Before the cruise ship sails, the cruise company will issue cruise cards to the customers. These cards will have pre-loaded credit points. Customers can use the cruise cards to spend credit points on the goods and services provided on board.

2. The edge server will be synced with all the required data before the ship sails.

3. Once the ship sails, the connection with the cloud server will break. Now, when the customers spend the credit points using the cards, the edge server will get updated with the details of all the transactions.

4. Once the ship comes back to the shores, the connectivity with the cloud database will be re-established. At this time, the data from the edge server will be synced with the cloud server, so that all the transactions get reflected in the database.

5. Conflicts during the data sync need to be resolved to reach a consistency point.

Understanding machine learning

Machine learning is one of the most popular domains of the modern age. Using machine learning techniques, engineers are practically able to solve numerous problems using software that was not easily solved earlier using traditional methods. For example, in today's world, problems like fraud detection, face recognition, weather prediction, sentiment analysis, etc., are solved using machine learning techniques.

Like many other domains we studied in this book, the domain of machine learning requires data engineers and data scientists to work with a very large amount of data. This data is processed, cleansed, filtered, and fed into a mathematical entity, popularly known as **machine learning models**.

There are various machine learning techniques that use data differently from each other. For example, traditional machine learning techniques like linear regression, classification, recommendation systems, etc., require the machine learning model to be *trained* before it can be used for its actual purpose. During *training*, the model is fed with the previously known information to fine-tune its parameters. Once the training is done, the machine learning model can be used to *serve* the data. Let us take an example of predictive analytics for predicting future stock prices. In this case, the machine learning model is fed with the historical data of the stock price. Based on the historical data, the model fine-tunes its parameters to represent the pattern of changes in stock price. The historical data will also include a variety of inputs (like market sentiment, government policy changes, etc.) that dictate the stock price change. This mechanism of fine-tuning the model parameters is called **model training**. Once a model is trained properly, it can be used to predict future outcomes. Data scientists typically tune the models by varying the data fed to the model during the training phase.

Let us take an example of a fraud detection use case with the help of machine learning.

Fraud detection using machine learning

One of the most common financial frauds is committed through fraudulent credit card transactions. To detect a potentially fraudulent transaction with the help of machine learning, the machine learning model needs to learn the pattern of credit card transactions. During the training, the model is fed the historical list of legitimate as well as fraudulent transactions. The model is also told which transactions are fraudulent. Based on this information, the model tunes itself to determine if any future transaction is likely a legitimate one or not. For this kind of use case, a typical data scientist will provide the details about the credit card transaction.

Such details are as follows:

- Transaction amount
- Online vs. card swipe
- Physical location, city, state, country
- Time of the day
- Type of expense (like retail, restaurant, shopping, etc.)

There are many more details that can be provided to the model. The more details provided, the more accurately the model can predict the legitimacy. Such details provided to the model are called **machine learning features**. Managing various machine learning *features* is one of the important tasks performed by data engineers.

At any given time, multiple data science teams can evaluate the impact of using various features on the quality of prediction. These teams can use the same underlying data engineering infrastructure to save costs. If different teams are working on the same machine learning features, there is a potential for the reuse of the features. The machine learning *feature store* provides the ability to identify, store, reuse, and manage the features.

Machine learning feature store

A feature store is a repository of commonly used features, which can be computed only once but can be used many times. The feature store exposes the capability to browse the feature repository and identify features for possible reuse.

One of the popular open-source feature stores is called **Feast**. Now, let us learn how a feature store can optimize data engineering costs. Let us continue with our example of identifying potential fraudulent transactions. In our example, we will assume that a fraud detection system already exists, which uses the above-mentioned features, viz. transaction amount, online vs card swipe, physical location, time of the day, and type of expense. However, the quality of the prediction is not very good. So, the business head has asked the data science team to improve the quality of the prediction. The head of the data science department wants to try out multiple new features to see which ones help in the quality improvement. So, two different data science teams are formed. One team identifies two new features to be added to the model, viz., average transaction amount on the credit card, and total number of monthly transactions on the credit card. The second team identifies one feature as the same as the other team (i.e., average transaction amount on the credit card), and one different feature, such as the maximum transaction amount for the last three months. Now, in this example, we can see that both the data science teams want the same machine learning feature for the average transaction amount, which can be reused.

Now, let us see the benefits of having a feature store, as follows:

- With a feature store, the users will be able to search for already existing features quickly from the feature repository.

- Once found, the users can reuse the already existing features from the repository, leading to cost reduction. The cost reduction will be due to:
  - o Avoiding re-computation of the feature. For example, calculating the average transaction amount for any user requires iterating over all the transaction amounts by the user and computing the average. With feature reuse, this cost will be avoided.
  - o Avoiding the cost of storing the same feature multiple times.

- Manage feature versions. Having the versioning ability allows users to roll back to a previously known good version, in case of feature corruption. More details about versioning will be covered under the topic of model versioning.

Figure 16.3 depicts the conceptual diagram of a typical feature store:

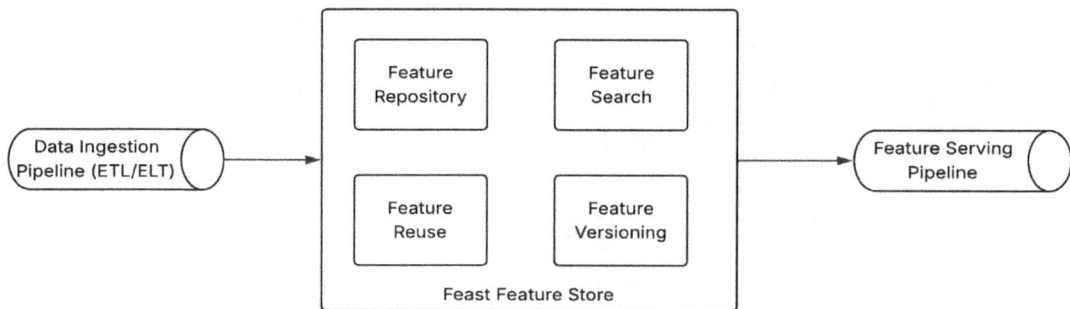

Figure 16.3: Feature store conceptual diagram

In *Figure 16.3*, we can see that the feature store exposes functionalities like feature repository, feature searching, feature reuse, and feature versioning. The feature store itself does not implement complete ELT/ETL workflows.

Machine learning model versioning

As we discussed previously in this chapter, the machine learning models keep evolving as the data scientists keep improving them regularly. This requires regular updates to the machine learning models. Before upgrading the models running in the production setup, data scientists perform a large array of tests and validation steps to ensure that the new model is an improvement over the previous one and that the new model does not regress in functionality as compared to the previous model. Such a test is performed in a lower-level environment, such as a test environment or a staging environment.

Data engineers try to ensure that the lower-level environment replicates the behavior of the production environment, but ensuring this can be costly and time-consuming. So, as a trade-off, many times, a lower-level environment may not replicate all the parameters of the production environment. This can lead to a problematic situation when a sub-optimal machine learning model gets deployed in production, due to a lack of testing or validation.

When such a scenario is identified, the typical steps taken to resolve the issue are to revert to the *last known stable state*. In most cases, reverting to the last known stable state takes much less time than fixing the problem in the new model and deploying it in production. The model versioning pattern can help in reverting to the last known stable state.

Figure 16.4 helps visualize the model versioning:

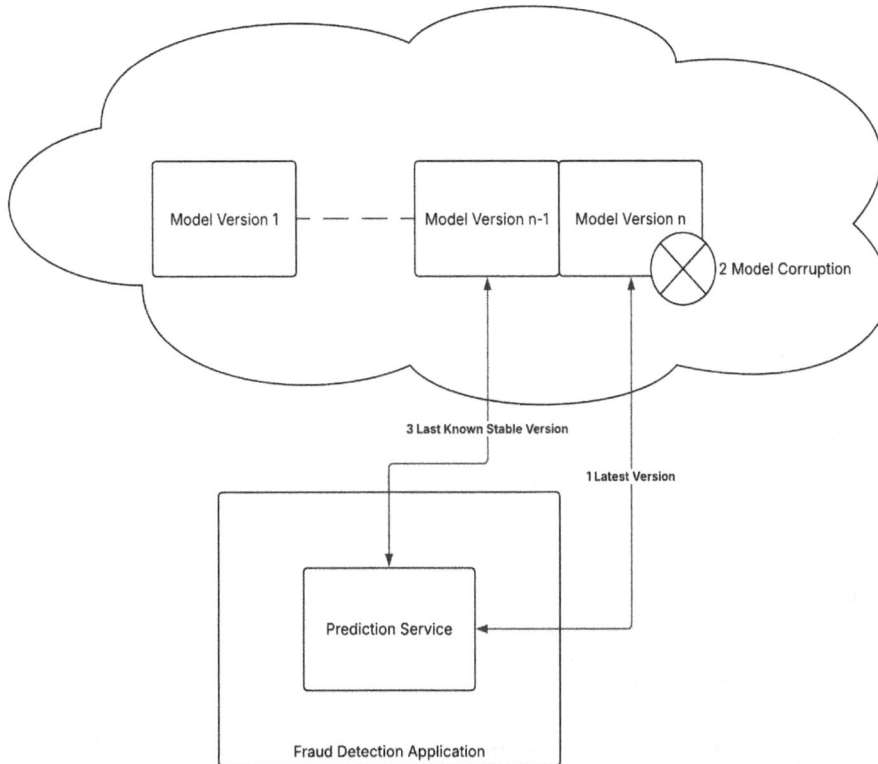

Figure 16.4: *Visualization of machine learning model versioning*

In this figure, we can see that the fraud detection application uses a prediction service to predict if a new incoming credit card transaction is fraudulent or not. To make that prediction, the prediction service needs to use a pre-trained ML model. Every time such a model gets updated, a new version of the model is created, keeping the previous one intact. Let us try to understand what happens when a model gets corrupted.

The following list explains the model corruption scenario:

- Let us assume that the prediction service has recently started using the latest version of the model, i.e., version n.

- After a day or so, the customer-facing team realizes that a lot of false-positive alerts are getting generated by the fraud detection application. The data scientists observe that the alerts are false, and the newly updated machine learning model is likely corrupted.

- Data engineers, just make the prediction service start using the old version of the model, i.e., version n-1. As the model versions are stored in the cloud (typically in an AWS S3 Blob), switching between models is typically a quick process.

This type of versioning mechanism saves a lot of time in a crisis, like model corruption.

Conclusion

In this chapter, we learned various domain-specific models. We started with understanding the domain of time series data and how time series databases help in optimizing data storage and access for time series data. Then we learned the use case of offline data access, and the offline tools like Couchbase App Services help the data engineers synchronize offline data with online data.

We then started with the domain of machine learning. We studied the basic overview of machine learning with the example of fraud detection. We learned two new data engineering patterns, viz., feature store and model versioning, to solve the machine learning specific use cases.

In the next chapter, we will explore the data security patterns, where we will learn about concepts like data encryption, access control, secure transmission of data, etc. We will focus on data security at all phases of the data lifecycle.

Questions

1. How to identify time series data?
2. What are the features of time series databases?
3. Can conflicts occur while synchronizing the data from the Couchbase Edge Server to the Couchbase Cloud database?
4. Does a feature store allow users to implement an entire ETL pipeline?
5. Without machine learning model versioning, how much downtime can a user application expect in case of model corruption?

Join our Discord space

Join our Discord workspace for latest updates, offers, tech happenings around the world, new releases, and sessions with the authors:

https://discord.bpbonline.com

CHAPTER 17
Data Security Patterns

Introduction

This chapter explores the data security patterns that are critical for any data engineer to know to build secure data engineering systems that prevent data breaches. We cover various aspects of data security patterns and see how each of those aspects is used to make a system secure. This chapter makes the user design a system leveraging the data security pattern and implement it with code. We will also show real-world examples of how data security patterns are used across industries.

Structure

The chapter covers the following topics:

- Authentication and authorization
- Encryption
- Auditing
- Design and implement secure system
- Technical stack for data security patterns
- Real-world example

Objective

By the end of this chapter, you will have an in-depth understanding of all data security patterns. You will also be able to design and build secure data systems and write code to implement the design. You will know the technical stack to use for building secure data systems. Finally, you will also understand the real-world use cases where this pattern can be used with examples from the banking domain.

Authentication and authorization

Every data engineering system needs authentication and authorization. Authentication is used to identify who the actor is using the system, and that they have access to the system, and authorization is used to check what activities the actor can perform on the system. These two aspects ensure only the users who have the appropriate privileges interact with the system.

Authentication

There are several authentication methods used in data engineering systems. In this chapter, we will look at the most common ones, which are frequently used.

The first method is basic authentication. This method is also called password-based authentication, where the authentication is done based on the user ID and password. This is the most rudimentary form of authentication and is commonly used. However, it is not very secure, and any password compromise can lead to unauthorized access to the system. To make this type of authentication more secure, **multi-factor authentication** (**MFA**) was introduced. This builds on top of basic authentication. The first step in the authentication is done via a user ID and password combination; however, there is a second step where additional credentials, like OTP or biometric authentication, are used.

The following figure showcases how basic authentication works with MFA for successful authentication, with a sequence of steps numbered:

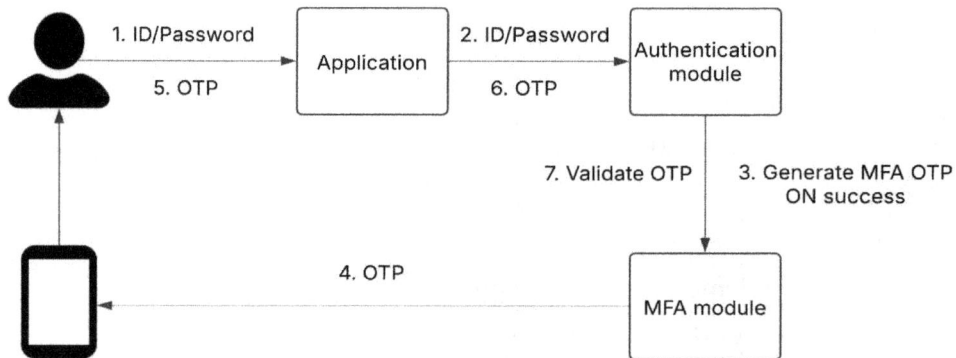

Figure 17.1: Multi-factor authentication

In modern systems, applications typically use token-based authentication. Once the user authenticates using basic auth or MFA, the system provides tokens back. This token can be used for further requests. This process ensures the minimal exposure of permanent access credentials like passwords by avoiding sending them on each and every request. The tokens are typically time-bound and expire, but there are use cases that use permanent access tokens as well. When tokens expire refresh token can be used to get new access tokens without going through the full authentication cycle again. **Java Web Tokens (JWT)** and OAuth tokens are common examples of token-based authentication.

Single sign on (SSO) is another popular method of authentication in modern web systems. This method does not require you to authenticate against multiple systems, but as the name suggests, it uses a single system to authenticate against, and the tokens provided by that authentication are then used to sign on to other systems. SSO can be implemented using any OAuth vendor available in the market, though common ones are Google SSO in social media and Okta in enterprises.

Apart from these enterprises, which have very stringent security requirements like logging into critical systems, the authentication uses a hardware device. This ensures that physical access to the device is necessary for authentication, and this password is never compromised. This is an expensive method of authentication to implement, as each user needs to have a hardware device where the password is generated on the fly, but in turn provides a very secure authentication mechanism. YubiKey, HID, and RSA are common vendors in this space.

The following figure shows how hardware-based authentication works:

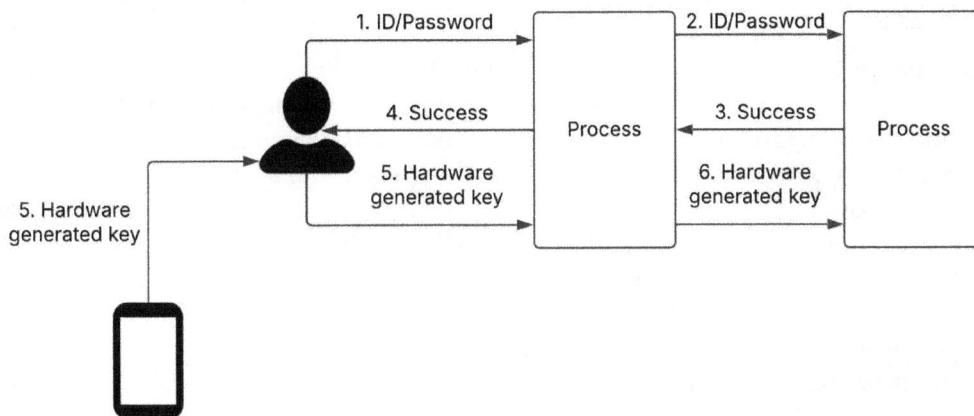

Figure 17.2: Hardware based authentication

Authorization

Authorization is the process of validating the permission levels of the user once they are authenticated against the system. Every system has different levels of access on it, varying from read-only access to superuser access, which can pretty much do everything on the system. Authorization checks the level of access a user has on the system and ensures they are only allowed to perform the operations allowed for that level of access.

To implement authorization, the system needs to have a role-based access control for users, which describes the roles in the system and the various permissions that can be given to those roles. The users are then mapped to the roles depending on the activity they perform. These roles can be permanent or temporary. Once the user-to-role mapping is done, specific permissions are granted to the roles. This allows the users who are tagged to a role to inherit those permissions from the role. It is also possible to use attributes of a user, like their organization, shift hour, etc., to provide attribute-based access control for further fine-grained control.

Encryption

In this section, we cover how data is protected by encrypting it. Encryption can be applied to data that is stored on disk or data that is moving over the network. In both cases, data needs to be protected using encryption to avoid unauthorized access to the data. Encryption ensures that even when a malicious actor gets access to the data, they are not able to use it.

Encryption at rest

Encryption at rest ensures secure storage of data that is stored for the long term as well as the short term. So, encryption at rest encompasses the encryption done when data is stored on local disks, distributed file systems, object storage, archival storage devices, or any other type of storage used.

Encryption at rest can be done at multiple levels; the storage subsystem itself has encryption technologies that encrypt the data before writing it to the physical media. An example of this is encryption support in S3 or Hadoop, which ensures that even if the application API call to the storage system provides unencrypted data, the underlying storage subsystem will encrypt the data and store it. When the data is retrieved from the storage using the APIs provided, the data is decrypted before it is handed back to the application. This type of encryption only prevents the data from being misused by untrusted actors or physical theft. Even if the storage system is compromised, the bad actors cannot leverage the data that has been stolen, as it is encrypted. However, it does not protect from misuse by trusted actors who can make a read API call to the storage system.

The following figure showcases both the encryption and decryption processes for the storage-backed encryption:

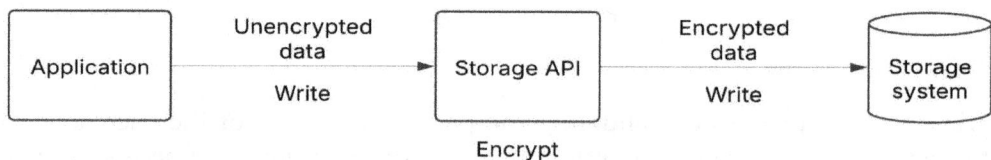

Figure 17.3: Encryption with native storage encryption

The following figure is a continuation, showcasing both the encryption and decryption processes for the storage-backed encryption:

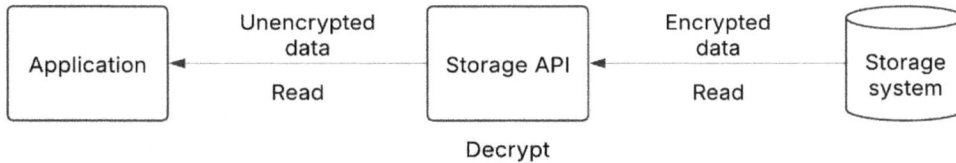

Figure 17.4: Decryption with native storage encryption

To provide a stronger encryption where even trusted actors who have access to the storage sub-system cannot compromise the data, another level of encryption called **application encryption** is commonly used. In this type of data encryption at rest, the application deals with the data and does its own encryption of data prior to making calls to the storage write API. This ensures only the application has access to the encryption keys that are used to encrypt the data. When the data is read back from the storage system, the data continues to remain encrypted until the application uses its encryption keys to decrypt the data. This way, even actors who have access to the storage system cannot misuse the data, as they do not have the decryption keys. This type of encryption is commonly used in industries where security is paramount, like defence, fintech, and insurance, and the data needs to not only be protected from threats outside the organization, but also needs to be secured from internal threats.

The following figure shows application encryption combined with storage layer encryption:

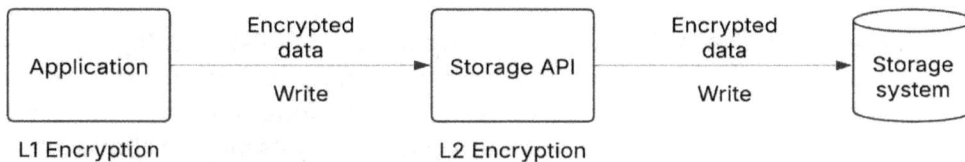

Figure 17.5: Application-based encryption

The following figure is a continuation of the application encryption combined with storage layer encryption:

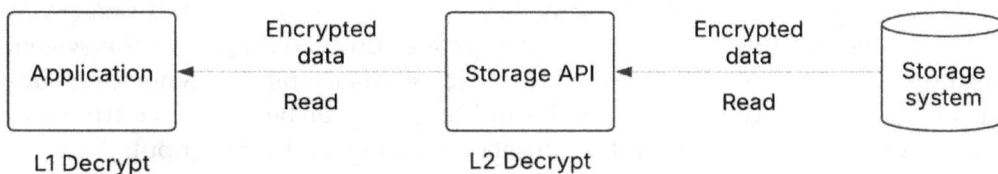

Figure 17.6: Application-based decryption

Encryption in transit

Encrypting data in transit is needed to ensure the data is not snooped on or tampered with when it is moving through the network. The most common and popular mechanism to achieve this is using the **Transport Layer Security (TLS)** protocol for communication. TLS is a protocol that uses public cryptography to secure the data in transit. TLS can be run in two modes.

TLS without certification validation

In this mode, when the client connects to the server, the client does not validate the server certificate returned. The certificate is only used for encryption and not for validating the authenticity of the host. This can lead to MITM attacks when the client and server are not running inside a trusted network. This mode of TLS is not recommended for production systems.

TLS with certificate validation

In this mode of TLS, the client validates the certificate sent by the server with a CA authority to ensure the server is authentic. This prevents MITM attacks as the client will not accept a connection with a server if the certificate does not verify the server's authenticity. Along with encryption, the certificate also proves that the server is really the host that it claims to be. In such systems, it is very critical that the server certificate is not compromised and only resides on the server system where it is supposed to be used, and also secured with appropriate permissions.

Auditing

Auditing is the process of recording every activity done on the system to ensure there is a trail of all user activity on the system for future reference and regulatory purposes. Audit logs can also be used to generate alerts when users exhibit suspicious behavior on the system. For example, in a payment processing system, contact center analysts may be allowed to view the account information of a customer to address a support case, but if they try to do a bulk view or download of account information, that can trigger an alert based on the audit rules.

One aspect that needs to be considered while designing any audit system is the cost of auditing from a performance and cost perspective. The audit functionality needs to be balanced between the security requirements of the system and the performance and cost penalty that is paid in doing the auditing. Extremely aggressive auditing can bog down the system while providing little value in making the system more secure. Also, while implementing auditing in a system, it is a good practice to evaluate if the auditing itself can be decoupled from the critical transaction path to avoid impact on the transaction latency and throughput. An example of such a design would use database transaction logs to generate the audit records instead of using the native database audit facility, which logs in the critical transaction path. The audit logs can be asynchronously read by an agent that performs the audit of user activity without impacting the database performance.

It is important to consider privacy concerns and review data retention policies when implementing audit log functionality for a data system. Audit logs should not contain sensitive

PII information, and the logging system should redact all sensitive information before writing it to the log. Though audit logs need to be retained for longer periods than system logs to meet the audit requirement, the data retention policy should purge the audit log when the data retention period is over.

Design and implement secure system

Secure by design is a critical philosophy many engineering teams are following now to design systems that consider security as a core tenet of the design and not as an afterthought. Let us take an example of a system that processes and stores financial transactions for a banking customer.

When designing a system that processes and stores financial transactions, we need to consider the following core security tenets.

Authentication

Before providing access to the system, the user trying to access the system needs to be authenticated by using one of the authentication methods discussed previously. For example, if the database being used for the application is MySQL, the following code demonstrates how to connect to MySQL using JDBC with authentication:

```java
1.  // Declare a class that implements a JDBC Connection
2.  public class MySQLJDBC {
3.      private static final String DB_CONNECT = "jdbc:mysql://ip:port/db";
4.      private static final String DB_USER = "ID";
5.      private static final String DB_PASSWORD = "PASSWORD";
6.      public static void main(String[] args) {
7.          // Call the Driver manager to connect to the database using user-id and password
8.          try (Connection conn = DriverManager.getConnection(DB_CONNECT,
9.                  DB_USER,
10.                 DB_PASSWORD);
11.
12.         } catch (SQLException e) {
13.             e.printStackTrace();
14.         }
15.     }
```

Encryption

The data should be securely stored to prevent unauthorized access, and it should also be securely transmitted between the frontend, backend, and database layers. In the authentication section example, you will notice that the connection to the database is being authenticated, but the communication between the client and server is done over an unencrypted connection. This results in the **ID** and **PASSWORD** being passed in over an insecure channel, and bad actors can exploit this to gain access to the **ID** and **PASSWORD** to the database. To prevent this, we will enhance that example to now use TLS with JDBC.

The following is the new code with TLS enabled for JDBC:

```
1.  // Declare a class that implements a JDBC Connection
2.  public class MySQLJDBC {
3.      private static final String DB_CONNECT = "jdbc:mysql://ip:port/db/ useSS
    L=true&requireSSL=true&verifyServerCertificate=true»";
4.      private static final String DB_USER = «ID";
5.      private static final String DB_PASSWORD = «PASSWORD";
6.      public static void main(String[] args) {
7.          // Call the Driver manager to connect to the database using userid
    and password
8.          try (Connection conn = DriverManager.getConnection(DB_CONNECT,
9.                      DB_USER,
10.                     DB_PASSWORD);
11.
12.         } catch (SQLException e) {
13.             e.printStackTrace();
14.         }
15.     }
```

Before running this program, MySQL needs to be enabled for TLS by creating the server-side certificate and setting it up on MySQL. Those steps are beyond the scope of this book. With these code changes, the connection is now secure, and bad actors cannot get access to plain **ID** and **PASSWORD** even if they snoop on the connection from the JDBC program to the MySQL server.

Authorization

Validate the access levels of the application or the person accessing the data via the authorization process. There may be read-only applications or users, as well as ones that can read and write data. The authorization process can check if the application is entitled to do what it intends to. The authorization checks can even be fine grained by checking if the data contains sensitive fields and prevent access to particular data fields.

Let us now look at how **role-based access control** (**RBAC**) is implemented on MySQL.

First, let us start by looking at SQL statements to create users and grant permissions to them before we validate the authorization:

```
CREATE USER 'read_user'@'localhost' IDENTIFIED BY 'password';

CREATE USER 'readwrite_user'@'localhost' IDENTIFIED BY 'password';

GRANT SELECT ON 'table-name' TO 'readonly_user'@'localhost';

GRANT SELECT, INSERT, UPDATE, DELETE ON 'table-name'  TO 'readwrite_user'@'localhost';

SHOW GRANTS FOR 'read_user'@'localhost';

SHOW GRANTS FOR 'readwrite_user'@'localhost';
```

Once the users have been created and permissions granted, let us validate authorizations. The code is as follows:

```
mysql -u read_user -ppassword

SELECT * FROM 'table-name'

INSERT INTO 'table-name' (name) VALUES ('Test');
```

The select statement aforementioned will successfully execute as the user read-user has read permission, but the insert statement will fail with authorization failure as the user read-user does not have insert permission. If the same statements were executed by connecting to the MySQL database as readwrite-user, both the select statement and the insert statement would execute, as the authorization check would pass for the readwrite-user.

Auditing

In any financial transaction processing, it is imperative to track and record all data access for future reference. This is a regulatory requirement as well in PCI and SOX compliance. Auditing in databases is typically done using the native audit capability of the database, which records information on every database read/write request. For application-side auditing, the application has to implement recording requests for audit.

In this example, auditing on a MySQL database can be enabled by installing the audit plugin for MySQL and restarting the MySQL server as follows:

```
INSTALL PLUGIN audit_log SONAME 'audit_log.so';

Update MySQL Config file

[mysqld]

audit_log_format=JSON
```

```
audit_log_file=/var/log/mysql_audit.log
audit_log_policy=ALL
sudo systemctl restart mysql
```

Technical stack for secure systems

The technical stack for building authentication systems can be as simple as password and user ID databases, to using OAuth or MFA providers. For SSO authentication, it is common to use public providers like Google SSO or private providers like Okta. Authorization is commonly built into every application directly, as the authorization concepts vary from application to application. For example, databases have role-based or fine-grained authorization mechanisms. Filesystems mostly use discretionary authorization techniques, which are also built into the system.

Encryption algorithms commonly used are asymmetric ones, like RSA, or symmetric ones like AES-256. There are open-source libraries available to implement these algorithms. For data encryption at rest, most enterprise databases and filesystems support native encryption out of the box in the system or recommend using a plugin. Similarly, auditing is also commonly available in application software. However, for databases, audit software like *Imperva* is used to avoid the burden of auditing on the database itself. These can provide auditing on critical databases while avoiding the performance burden of auditing on the database and providing the security admin direct control over auditing.

Real-world example

Let us look at a practical example of a secure data pattern in action in the payments domain. This example shows multiple concepts like authentication, authorization, and secure data transfer with application encryption.

Credit card transaction processing

Credit card transaction processing systems are one of the most secure financial data systems in the world. They leverage every data security pattern to ensure customers' personal and financial data is secure during and after the transaction. In this example, let us look at the data flow and various security measures taken during a credit card transaction on an e-commerce application.

The user flow starts with the user trying to purchase a product on the e-commerce application. The user will enter their card number and CVV, which act as the user ID and password for authenticating the card. Since this is a card-not-present transaction, which basically means the user is not physically present at the point of sale, the transaction needs further authentication, which is handled via MFA. Once the credit card number and CVV are authenticated, the user receives an OTP over their mobile number for MFA. The user enters the OTP received on the e-commerce application, and the transaction is fully authenticated at this point. The communication between the e-commerce application and the payment gateway is all done over an encrypted connection using TLS to ensure all the data in transit is encrypted, and the credit card number, CVV, or OTP passed onto the gateway via the e-commerce application cannot be snooped on.

The next step in the transaction is authorization. In the case of a credit card transaction, authorization basically means approving the transaction based on access permissions and other rules. For example, the user may have a limit on their credit card, and the transaction needs to be authorized to validate that the transaction value does not exceed their card limit. Similarly, the users may have restrictions on what geographies the card may be used in, and during authorization, these rules are validated.

Once the transaction is authorized, the payment goes through on the payment gateway, and transaction details are stored in the database. The critical fields in the transaction, like card number, location of purchase, etc., are encrypted by the application to ensure the data is not visible even to the employees of the payment network. The data is further encrypted at the storage layer using the database's native encryption to further secure the data. Once the retention period in the transactional database is complete, the transaction data is moved to the data lake for long-term storage and analysis. The data movement between these systems is also over TLS to ensure no internal threat actor snoops on the sensitive data, like card information or PII information. The data continues to be both application-encrypted and storage-encrypted on the data lake as well.

The following figure shows the end-to-end security aspects of this card transaction processing system:

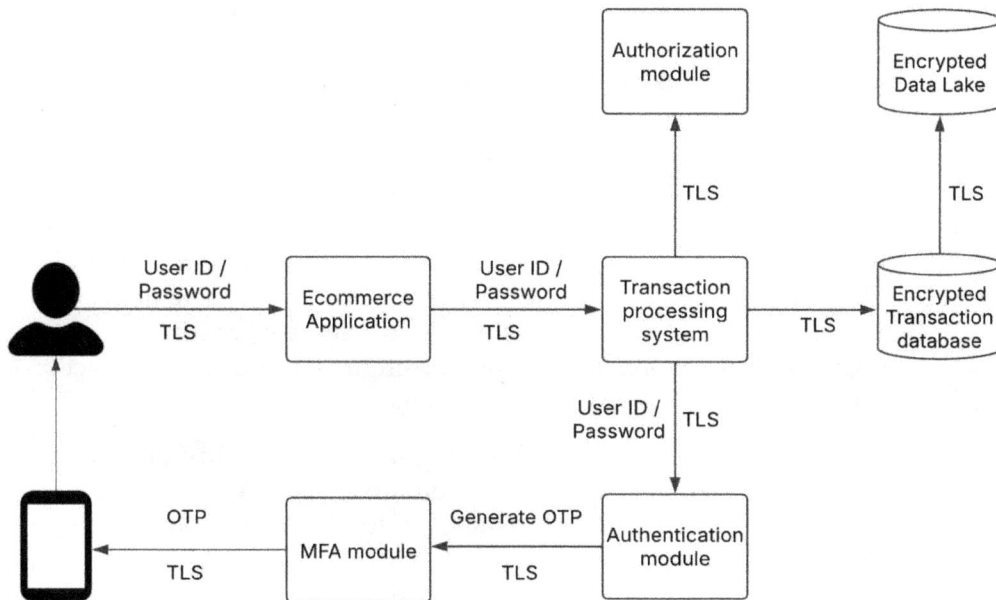

Figure 17.7: Security in card payment

The following is a flow chart representing the flow of the authentication and authorization process:

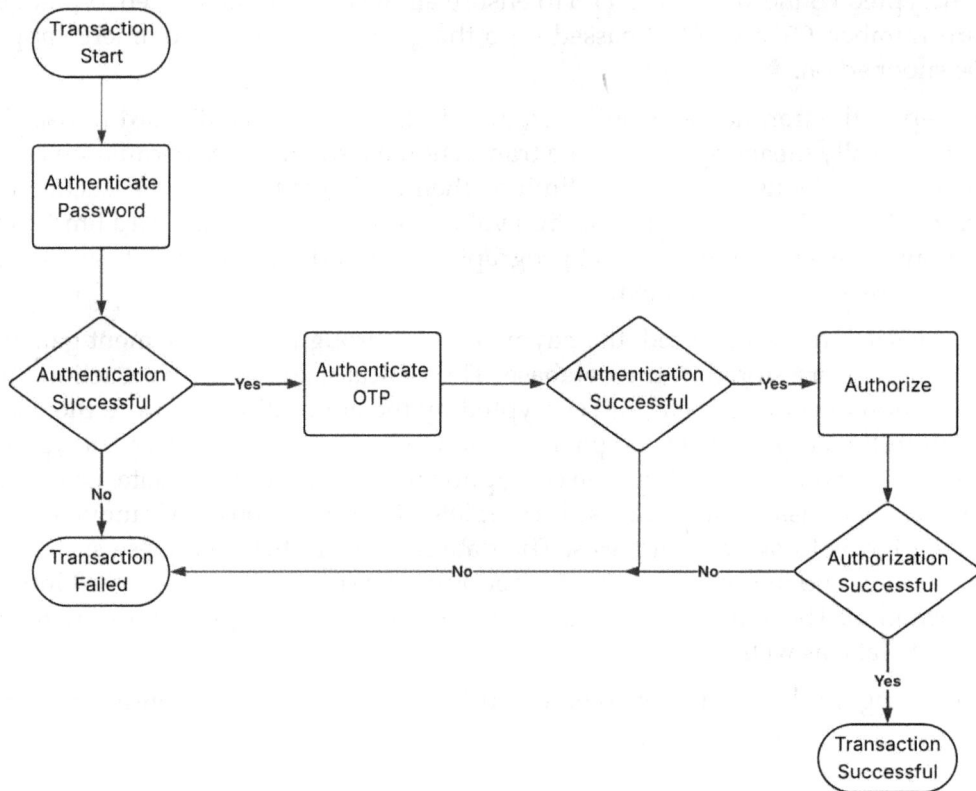

Figure 17.8: Authentication and authorization flow

Conclusion

In this chapter, we covered the key tenets of security in any data system, like authentication, authorization, encryption, and auditing. We also learnt best practices in each of these tenets. We learnt about how to include those security tenants while designing a data system and its implementation. We also covered technologies used to implement good security practices in a data system. The chapter also covered a real-world example in credit card transaction processing, which is one of the most secure data systems built.

In the next chapter, we will be covering monitoring and observability of data systems. We understand anomaly detection, data quality, and data integrity. We also cover alerting and incident management, and finally look at examples of implementing observability on a real industry use case.

Questions

1. Why is application-level encryption necessary when storage systems provide their own encryption capability?

2. What version of TLS should be used to securely transfer data?

3. What is the most secure authentication mechanism among all the authentication mechanisms covered in this chapter?

4. Why is it critical to consider security during the design phase of the project?

Join our Discord space

Join our Discord workspace for latest updates, offers, tech happenings around the world, new releases, and sessions with the authors:

https://discord.bpbonline.com

CHAPTER 18
Data Observability and Monitoring Patterns

Introduction

This chapter explores the data observability and monitoring patterns that are necessary for making any data system production-ready. We cover topics on monitoring, log collection and analysis, data quality and integrity, and finally, alerting and incident management in the chapter. This chapter will cover designing a system that has observability and monitoring built into it and demonstrate how to implement it. We will also show real-world examples of how data observability and monitoring patterns make a system production-ready.

Structure

The chapter covers the following topics:

- Metrics, log collection, and analysis
- Data quality, integrity, and anomaly detection
- Alerting and incident management
- Design and implement using observability pattern
- Technical stack for observability and monitoring patterns
- Real-world example

Objectives

By the end of this chapter, you will be able to have an in-depth understanding of how to build monitoring and observability for data systems. You will also be able to design and write code to implement the design for monitoring and observability. You will know the technical stack to use for monitoring data systems to make them production-ready. Finally, you will also understand, with a real-world use case, how monitoring and observability are added to data systems.

Metrics, log collection, and analysis

In a data engineering system, a collection of metrics and logs, and analysis of the collected data form the core of the observability of that system. Metrics and logs help both end users of the system and the site reliability and support teams to identify problems in the system and get to the root cause of the issue. Analysis of metrics and logs collected from the system can also help identify long-term improvements for the system, like sizing issues or architectural issues. Metrics can be anything from data points that measure the performance of the system to data points that reflect the quality of data. Every measurable entity that can help improve the data system can be considered a metric and then collected and processed.

Metrics

Let us first look at how metrics can be collected and leveraged to build a system that can be maintained and improved over time. Every application should collect metrics that explain the behavior of the system over a period of time. The selection of metrics to collect is very critical, as careful analysis is needed to understand how each metric will be used for investigative or improvement purposes. Several times, data engineers collect a ton of metrics from the system, but it is unclear how those metrics will be used, and this leads to a bloated metric system, long-term storage costs, and eventually the failure of the entire monitoring system. To avoid this, it is imperative that metrics are selected very carefully and with a lot of deliberation. However, once the metric is short-listed for collection, it needs to be collected reliably and stored for consumption. One of the key purposes of a metric is to provide information about the performance of the system to the end user and the support and site reliability engineers. Histograms of metrics over time can show how the system behaves under various situations and usage patterns.

The common metric collection patterns are either pull-based vs. push-based, and agent-based vs. agentless. For data systems that are long-running, like databases, application servers, messaging clusters, etc., the pull model is ideal. In this model, the metrics are periodically scraped from the long-running service and sent to the collection system. An example is database services exposing their query metrics on a Prometheus endpoint on the service, and these metrics being scraped by an exporter and sent to the Prometheus server. The push-based model of sending metrics is more suited for workflow or job-based applications. Here, there is no long-running service that can host the Prometheus endpoint, but instead, the workflow or the job can periodically push the metrics to a gateway like a Prometheus gateway.

In case of agent-based metric collection systems, there is a metric collection agent running next to the application that periodically collects the metric. This model is used where we do not wish to put undue load on the data service to publish the metrics. The agents take the burden of scraping and pushing the metrics while the service only exposes the metrics in the expected format. An example is a Datadog agent running on the system locally to the data service. The agentless model runs primarily by leveraging APIs, where the monitoring system scrapes the metrics over an endpoint and port combination. The push model of metric collection can also be considered an agentless model, as the service pushes the metrics to the metric server endpoint.

Let us look at the architecture of a metric system that leverages agents to scrape metrics from an endpoint and push to Prometheus:

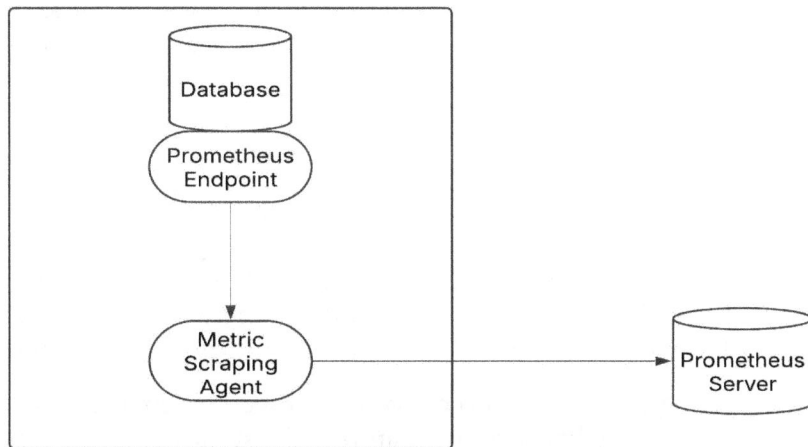

Figure 18.1: Agent-based metric collection

The following table highlights the differences between the push-based and pull-based metric collection:

Aspect	Pull-based collection	Push-based collection
Basic approach	The target system actively requests data from source systems	Source systems send data to the target as soon as it becomes available
Real-time capabilities	Less real-time due to the request-response cycle	Immediate delivery of new data
Scalability	Excellent scalability with the ability to easily add new consumers	Can become overwhelmed if the consumer falls behind the production rate
Flow control	Consumer controls the pace of data ingestion	Difficult to control flow rate; risk of overwhelming consumers

Data replay	Easy to replay missed data through re-polling	Hard to recover missed messages; only published once
Security	Requires bidirectional firewall configuration	More secure; source systems do not listen for connections
Service discovery	Requires a service discovery mechanism	Does not require service discovery
System health monitoring	Better visibility into target system health	Less visibility into the target system status
Configuration management	Centralized administration of collection intervals	Configuration distributed across source systems
Best use cases	Regular monitoring metrics, systems with variable load, batch processing scenarios	Real-time streaming data, IoT devices, and continuous data generation

Table 18.1: *Difference between the push-based and pull-based metric collection*

Log collection and analysis

Log collection is necessary for making a system serviceable. In any software system, it is unavoidable to encounter problems over long periods of operation; however, what is critical is the ability to investigate those issues and debug them quickly to resolve the problem.

To achieve this, every logging system needs to have three key components, which are log collection, log search, and visualization. An example of a stack that can support these three key capabilities is **Elastic Logstash Kibana** (**ELK**), where Logstash provides the log collection, Elastic provides the search, and Kibana provides the visualization capability.

Log collection, similar to metric collection, can be operated using a log message push or a log file pull pattern. In the log message push pattern, the data system writes the logs using APIs to a logging system. For real-time logging systems, even message queues like Apache Kafka can be used to push the logs. In case of the pull log pattern, the log entries are written to local files first, and periodically, the file is extracted from the local system to a centralized logging store. The selection of the push or pull logging pattern depends on various factors. For example, certain systems, due to their critical nature, do not allow log entries to be sent out from the system unless there is an incident investigation. In those systems, pulling log patterns works well as the log files stay on the local system until they need to be pulled for investigation.

Logging systems can be based on agent or agentless patterns, similar to metric collection. In the case of a logging system with agents, there are logging agents installed on the data system that collect and forward the logs. An example of such a system would be using Logstash or Fluentd. In the case of an agentless pattern, the log data is sent to the logger via API calls, or the logging system pulls the logs directly from remote systems. An example of such a system would be an agent writing log messages to a Kafka topic via the Kafka API.

Once logs are collected, if the logs are structured properly, they can be machine-analyzed. Hence, it is critical that structured logging is applied, and log messages are generated in standardized formats that can be parsed and processed by code. Standard formats like **Common Log Format** (**CLF**) or Syslog format are recommended, as these formats enable interoperability of logs when compared to proprietary formats. When formats like CLF are used, it is very easy to predefine the errors the system can encounter and parse the CLF log to check for these predefined errors and generate alerts when those errors occur.

Data quality, integrity, and anomaly detection

Every data engineering system is successful only when the data generated by the system is trustworthy and of high quality. If the quality of data is not good and business decisions are made based on the wrong data, it can lead to incorrect business decisions and negative outcomes for the business.

Data quality and integrity

Data quality and Integrity patterns ensure the data meets the expected business quality. The following are the common data quality and integrity patterns used in data engineering:

- **Data correctness pattern**: This pattern validates the data content to ensure its correctness with respect to business rules. For example, address validation to correct naming conventions, ensuring the state names are one of the valid state names, reference codes are one of the possible reference codes as per business rule, etc., are data correctness checks. These rules are typically defined by business teams and enforced by technology teams.

- **Data uniqueness and deduplication pattern**: This pattern is used to ensure duplicate data is not stored in the system. For example, in a banking system, it is very important to uniquely identify a customer and implement a single source of truth record for a customer. The same customer might be registered with different name variations and addresses, but the system reconciles the customer into a single entity.

- **Data referential integrity pattern**: This pattern validates that data between different systems or tables is correctly associated. For example, when a product review is entered in the system, it is important to associate it with the right product in the product catalogue. Referential integrity is used to make the association between the review system and the product catalogue.

- **Structure validation or schema validation pattern**: This pattern is used to validate that the incoming data adheres to the structure defined by the system. This pattern could be enforced at multiple layers in the application, from the API to the database design. Structure enforcement pattern is critical to ensure the schema is not deviating from what the application expects, as schema deviations can lead to application failures if the application is not able to handle the addition or removal of fields or non-deterministic behaviour if the new data gets processed incorrectly.

Anomaly detection

Anomaly detection is the process of finding deviations in the system behavior from various perspectives. The deviation could be in data quality, data speed, data structure, and many types of variations. It is important that these deviations are detected early and remediated to ensure the data quality and integrity remain consistent throughout the lifecycle of the system. Anomaly detection is a very vast area, and exploring the details of every aspect is beyond the scope of this chapter.

Let us look at a few common anomaly detection patterns:

- **Data structure and value anomaly detection pattern**: This anomaly detection pattern is used to detect changes in the schema of the data, as well as the possible values for the data fields beyond the given domain of the dataset. This type of detection over the lifecycle of the application is critical to detect if the data is still trustworthy or if there has been a drift in the data. For example, if the schema of the data starts to receive fields that are not expected from an upstream system, they may not be processed correctly or processed at all. Missing detection of such scenarios can lead to data loss or may require major reprocessing of data in the future. To prevent such situations, alerting and incident management have to be combined with anomaly detection to alert data engineers of data structure or value anomalies right away.

- **Data speed and volume anomaly detection pattern**: This pattern helps data engineers detect variation in the quantity and the velocity of data that is arriving in upstream systems. It is important to track volume and velocity because problems in the upstream system or in the pipeline may lead to a loss of records. For example, if the upstream system is sending only 50% of the daily data, then this pattern will compare the average daily data arrival rate to the current arrival rate. Any major variation will trigger an alert to data engineers to review the variation in volume and velocity of data. The variation may be genuine, for example, when a major natural disaster occurs in a city, the transactions for any business system will decline, or the variation may be due to a bug in the data pipeline, which is missing records.

Alerting and incident management

These patterns ensure the SRE teams are notified of alerts and define the process for SRE teams to handle the alerts for reliable application operations. These patterns provide guiding principles for building alerting and incident management systems, more than defining exact methodologies that vary from system to system.

Alerting

Alerting and incident management form a critical aspect of maintaining the reliability of a data engineering pipeline and ensuring appropriate SRE response to any failures or faults. Without a robust alerting and incident management system, all metrics and logging are present in the system.

Alerting patterns can be categorized into three categories:

- **Rule-based alerting**: Rule-based alerting is often used to enforce security practices on the system, where rules define access controls on a system, and any attempt to violate the access control generates an alert. It also applies to enforce business rules and alert domain owners when business rules are violated.

- **Metric-based alerting**: Metrics are collected and monitored by the observability system to generate alerts based on thresholds. Thresholds can be set for every metric collected, and alerts can be generated when the metric's threshold is breached. The thresholds can be hierarchical as well, and alerts can be tagged with informational, warning, and critical. For example, when the CPU utilization metric jumps every 5%, an information alert can be generated, when utilization crosses 70%, a warning alert can be generated, and finally, if the utilization crosses 90%, a critical alert can be generated.

- **Event-based alerting**: Event-based alerting is used to generate alerts for failure events that need immediate action from SRE. For example, when a user signs up fails for some reason, this leads to the signup event failure alert firing so that the operations team can immediately address the cause of failure. It is critical that the right events are identified for alerting, as generating too many event-based alerts causes noise in the monitoring system and can result in critical event alerts being missed in action.

Incident management

Incident management is the process of identifying, responding to, and resolving data-related issues that could impact business operations or data quality. Incident management does not apply pre-canned patterns, as handling each incident is a unique situation. Instead, incident management follows a sequence of processes to ensure a successful outcome from the incident.

The three processes primarily followed in incident management are as follows:

- **Incident mitigation**: In any data engineering system, failures are unavoidable, and incidents can occur. The most important part of incident management is incident mitigation. The goal of incident mitigation should be to reduce the end customer impact and the blast radius of the incident.

- **Incident remediation**: Incident mitigation should focus on bringing the system back to a running state, even if the system is in a degraded state. One of the key aspects of incident management is to set up a process to avoid the blame game, but instead, keep the focus on recovering the system to remediate the incident.

- **Incident retrospection**: For every incident that had customer impact, it is very important to identify the root cause of the incident. This is necessary to ensure the system can be enhanced and safeguarded against such incidents in the future. Incident retrospection, when done consistently over long periods of operation, significantly improves the reliability and availability of the system.

Whenever an incident occurs, incident mitigation is the first priority and happens first. Once the incident has been mitigated, the next step is to fix the problem that caused the incident in the incident remediation step. Finally, once the system has been updated with the fix for the incident, retrospection helps understand what went wrong and assists in building processes that can ensure similar incidents are avoided in the future.

Design and implement with observability pattern

In this section, let us understand how to implement observability for a web service that leverages a backend database. We will see how metrics can be collected and processed, and what technologies can be used to collect and process.

Let us implement a monitoring and alerting system for a web service that accepts a user input SQL statement and runs it against a MySQL database. The service will expose its query latency metrics as a Prometheus metric and generate alerts whenever the query latency is over one second. Let us start by looking at the web service first implemented using FastAPI. The service exposes a query endpoint that can be called via a REST API call with a query to be executed. The service connects to the MySQL database using the Python MySQL connector and executes the query.

The next step is to add the Prometheus metric for the query execution time and run a Prometheus server inside the service from where the metric can be read. Prometheus fetches this metric, and Grafana alerts can be set up on top of this metric.

The following is the figure representing this implementation:

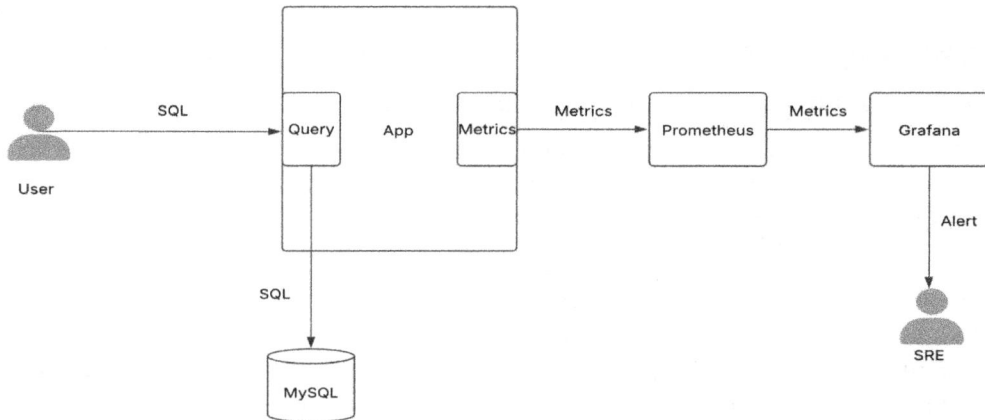

Figure 18.2: Observability with Prometheus and Grafana

The following code provides the implementation for this app:

```
from fastapi import FastAPI, HTTPException
from pydantic import BaseModel
from typing import Any, List
```

```
import mysql.connector
import time
# Prometheus metrics
from prometheus_client import start_http_server, Summary
from prometheus_client.core import CollectorRegistry
from prometheus_client import generate_latest
# Create the FastAPI application
app = FastAPI()
# Prometheus metrics
QUERY_EXECUTION_TIME = Summary('sql_query_execution_time_
seconds', 'Time spent executing SQL queries')
# Define the SQL Query input model
class SQLQuery(BaseModel):
    query: str
# Database connection details
DB_CONFIG = {
    "host": "hostname",
    "user": "username",
    "password": "password",
    "database": "database",
}
# Function to execute the SQL query
@QUERY_EXECUTION_TIME.time()  # Automatically measures execution time
def execute_query(query: str) -> List[Any]:
    QUERY_COUNTER.inc()  # Increment query counter
    try:
        connection = mysql.connector.connect(**DB_CONFIG)
        cursor = connection.cursor(dictionary=True)
        start_time = time.time()
        cursor.execute(query)
        cursor.close()
        connection.close()
        return result
    except mysql.connector.Error as err:
        QUERY_ERROR_COUNTER.inc()  # Increment error counter
        raise HTTPException(status_code=400, detail=str(err))
```

```
# Define the API endpoint for query execution
@app.post("/query")
def run_query(sql_query: SQLQuery):
    result = execute_query(sql_query.query)
    return {"result": result}
# Prometheus metrics endpoint
@app.get("/metrics")
def get_metrics():
    return generate_latest()
# Start Prometheus metrics server
start_http_server(8001)  # Prometheus metrics available at http://
localhost:8001
# To run the server, use the command:
# uvicorn app:app --reload
```

Technical stack for observability and monitoring patterns

ELK stack is the most used and popular open-source stack for building logging systems. Logstash collects and stores the logs in Elastic, enabling search on the logs. Kibana provides visualization of the log data, making it easy to debug problems. In the commercial software, Splunk and Datadog are popular due to their simplicity and usability for logging cloud-based solutions. Of late, many systems also log the application logs to cloud object storage due to their cheap storage and access costs. Custom log implementations over object storage are not uncommon, but they suffer from poor search and analysis capabilities. The logs need to be moved from object storage to other systems like *Apache Lucene* or *Solr* to provide search capability over the logs. Hence, it is crucial that data engineers evaluate their log search patterns while finalizing the log storage system.

Monitoring of metrics emitted by data systems is typically captured using Prometheus. Prometheus metrics have become the default standards for monitoring a system due to support for both pull and push and agent vs. non-agent models. Prometheus can not only be used to monitor metrics for stats, but also to monitor pipelines for anomalies in conjunction with metadata and lineage tools like *DataHub*. Among commercial off-the-shelf technologies, Datadog is popular for collecting both metrics and logs. Hyperscale cloud providers also offer a native observability system, like *AWS CloudWatch*, that is closely integrated with native services in the cloud. While from a usability perspective, Datadog or CloudWatch can provide a simpler integration for metric and log collection in the cloud, they need to be used carefully to avoid significant cost bloat due to their premium pricing compared to equivalent Prometheus or ELK-based solutions.

Anomaly detection is done in multiple ways, and rule-based anomaly detection technologies, like *IBM DataStage* and *QualityStage*, can be used. However, modern data pipelines go much beyond rules and leverage ML to build anomaly detection. Standard ML libraries like *Scikit-learn* or *TensorFlow* can be used to build ML-driven anomaly detection systems. Finally, alerting can be done using integration of monitoring with enterprise messaging systems like *Slack* or *Microsoft Teams*, or dedicated alerting platforms like *PagerDuty*. While selecting an alert notification system, it is critical to also identify alert acknowledgement and alert suppression capabilities of the alert notification system. Alert acknowledgement ensures all the stakeholders are kept in the loop on the actioning of the alert, and alert suppression is needed to make sure false alerts do not create noise in the system.

Real-world example

Let us look at a real-world example of an observability pattern in play for a credit card transaction processing system. The response times of databases in credit card processing systems are very critical, and this example shows how database latency can be monitored by putting additional load on the system.

Credit card transaction processing

Credit card transaction processing systems serve as the backbone of commerce across the world. They process hundreds of millions of transactions a day and drive billions of dollars of business. It is imperative that these systems are monitored closely, metrics collected, and alerts are generated whenever there is any impact on these systems. Let us look at how observability patterns are used in this domain.

Whenever a user does a credit card transaction, the transaction needs to be authorized. To authorize any transaction, the system needs to validate the user's PIN number, ensure that a sufficient credit limit exists, run a risk score on the transaction, etc. All these system actions are underpinned by database read and write operations. It is important to collect and monitor the database response times and generate alerts whenever the response times go above a particular pre-defined threshold. Let us further understand how this can be done using monitoring and observability patterns.

Firstly, the database response times need to be collected for monitoring. In a critical system like this, we need to ensure the metric collection does not put undue load on the database itself. To achieve that, we use the pull pattern for metric collection where the database exposes its response time metrics for each request on a Prometheus endpoint on the service. The metric is scraped from this endpoint by an agent and sent to the Prometheus server. As you can see, both metric pull and agent pattern are used together to extract metrics from the database server.

Credit card transaction processing systems have very low tolerance for variation in database response times. Once the metrics are collected, as shown above using both the metric pull and agent patterns, we need a monitoring and alerting setup for those metrics.

Let us look at the architecture of the system, as show in the following figure, where the database latency metrics are scraped and pushed to Prometheus:

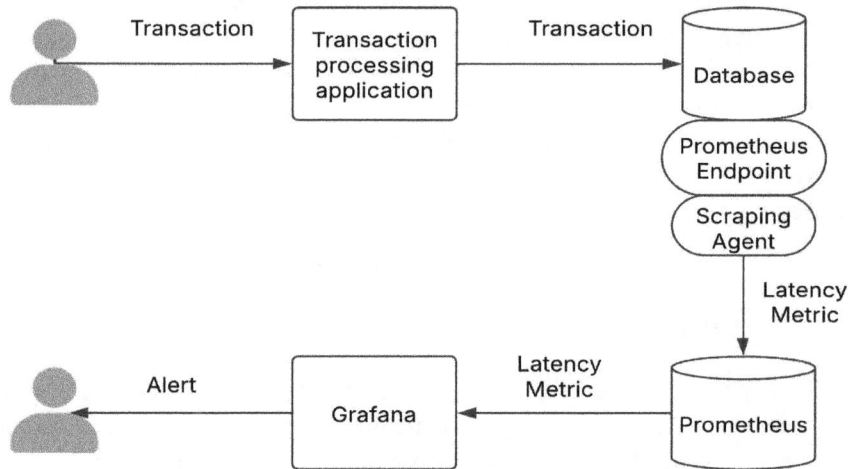

Figure 18.3: Database metrics with Prometheus

Conclusion

In this chapter, we covered the key topics of monitoring and data observability patterns. We learnt the different ways to build monitoring and logging using both push and pull patterns. We learnt about how to design observability for a data system and its implementation using open source technologies. The chapter covered technologies used to implement observability and alerting in enterprise data systems. We also covered a real-world example in observability and alerting in credit card transaction processing systems using the patterns learnt previously in the chapter.

In the next chapter, we will cover what we understand as idempotency and data deduplication. We explore techniques and patterns to achieve data idempotency and avoid duplicate data. We will also review example implementations of idempotency and data deduplication.

Questions

1. How do metric collection patterns differ for long-running application services vs. short-running workflows or jobs?

2. When should agent-based metrics or logging be preferred over agentless architecture?

3. What pattern should be used to reduce the computational burden of monitoring the service being monitored?

4. Design and implement a system that reviews Prometheus metrics and generates alerts if the metric threshold crosses a certain limit.

CHAPTER 19

Idempotency and Deduplication Patterns

Introduction

For any state-of-the-art application of modern times, ensuring data consistency and availability is paramount for day-to-day business operations. The last few decades have given users a variety of solutions in the field of distributed systems, which in turn ensure that the data is replicated, kept consistent, and can be retrieved at a reasonable speed. One of the implicit requirements in such distributed systems solutions is to ensure the idempotency of the operations performed on the data. Idempotency of an operation means its effect is seen only once. For example, an operation of recording a bank transaction should be reflected in the underlying database only once, even if the application retries the operation after a request timeout. This chapter will introduce design patterns for ensuring the idempotency of the operations.

The last decade has also seen an exponential surge in data generated by various internet applications. Often, a large amount of duplicate data gets generated or uploaded to the internet. A technique to avoid storing and transferring duplicate data is called data deduplication. In this chapter, we will learn various data deduplication design patterns used by modern-day data engineers.

Structure

This chapter covers the following topics:

- Idempotency of operations

- Understanding duplicate data
- Data deduplication

Objectives

By the end of this chapter, the reader will understand the importance of idempotent operations and methods to implement them. The reader will also learn design patterns used to ensure idempotency. Afterwards, we will learn methods to identify duplicate data and various design patterns used in data deduplication.

Idempotency of operations

Operations performed in a distributed system environment are vulnerable to failures. The failures can occur at different layers, like disk errors, network timeouts, database software errors, data replication errors, etc. If any such failure occurs, the user application can report such failure to the end user, so that the user can retry the operation. However, this can lead to a bad user experience. Let us take an example of order finalization for an e-commerce website. During order finalization, if the operation fails and the user is required to perform a manual retry, the user may choose not to finalize the order, leading to revenue loss. To fix this, application designers can implement an automatic retry mechanism to reduce the failures in user-facing workflows.

> Note: Retry mechanism helps in case of transient errors (like momentary network outages), or in the presence of self-healing systems (like databases supporting single-node automatic failover mechanisms). In case of non-transient error (like quorum failures, which is typically not supported by the databases), a simple retry may not work, and revenue loss cannot be prevented.

Even though retries can help improve the user experience, good care must be taken before implementing retries, as the operation being retried can have a side effect. Let us take an example of network timeout as described in *Figure 19.1*. We can see the order of events happening in the system:

1. The e-commerce user application decides to commit the order details and sends a request for further processing, and sends the commit request to the underlying database.

2. The database persists the order details for further processing.

3. Due to slowness in the network and/or the database layer, the user application does not get a response to the order commit request in time, and it times out.

4. The database sends the response back to the e-commerce application, but the response is never seen by the user application due to a timeout.

After this order of events, the user application does not know if the order details were committed to the underlying database:

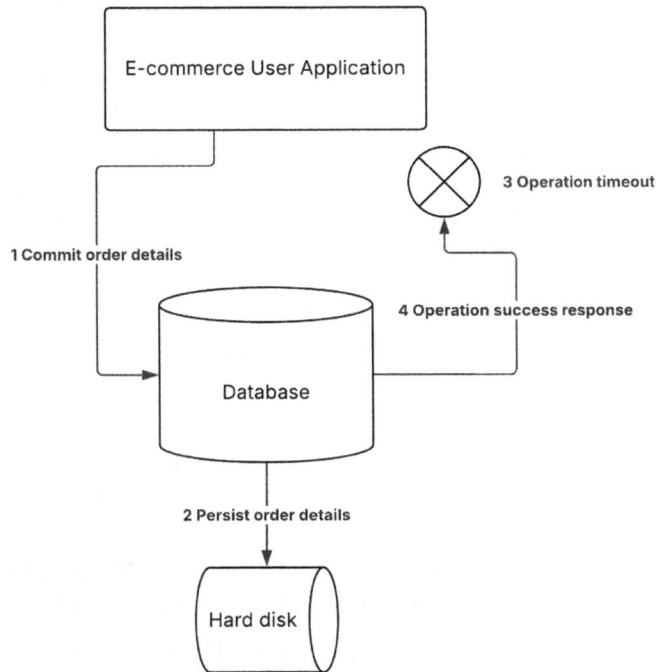

Figure 19.1: Database operation timeout

In this example, there are two intricacies of the design that need deeper understanding. These intricacies are the network timeout and the operation retry mechanism. Let us investigate these intricacies one by one to understand the problem domain better.

Importance of network timeout

In our example, we assumed that the user application has implemented a network timeout. At first glance, it seems as if the network timeout was not implemented; the user application would have received the response without any issues. Even if it is true, for our example, not implementing a network is not a good software design pattern.

The failure can occur at different places. For example, what if the network request for committing the order details gets lost before reaching the database? In such a case, without a network timeout, the e-commerce application will keep waiting for the response, which will never be received. Furthermore, it becomes difficult to let the user know whether the order was committed successfully, leading to a bad user experience. That is why user applications implement network timeouts and use other data engineering patterns, like using **universally unique identifiers (UUIDs)**, to avoid inconsistencies due to network timeouts. Later in this chapter, we will learn the use of UUIDs to avoid such inconsistencies.

Importance of operation retry

The underlying data storage systems and networking platforms are vulnerable to different types of failures. If a system failure can lead to user-facing errors, it can lead to a bad user experience. In the longer term, the users may not want to buy anything from an e-commerce website that reports a lot of errors. The simplest way of handling the errors is to retry the operation in the hope of a successful retry. However, as we discussed, the retry can have side effects based on the implementation. So, modern-day user applications implement operations in an idempotent manner, avoiding any side effects of retries.

Implementing idempotent operation

To understand the idempotency of operations, let us first consider a non-idempotent implementation of the order commit operation. This non-idempotent implementation will use the auto-increment feature of MySQL to generate the primary key. So, when the user application commits order details, a new primary key will be automatically generated for that order. As discussed in *Figure 19.1* above, if response times out, and the user application retries, the duplicate record will get stored in the database (due to the retry), but with a new primary key. After the duplicate record is stored in the database, it is not possible to know if the user wanted to order the same order twice, or if it was due to an error and a retry.

To implement the operation in an idempotent manner, the following steps can be performed:

1. Do not use auto-increment for the primary key.

2. Divide the operation into two steps. First is to allocate a new primary key, and second is to store the order details using the pre-allocated primary key.

3. Each step is performed separately and retried separately. So, the user application will keep retrying the operation to allocate a primary key until it succeeds. In the worst case, a few primary keys will remain unused due to retries, but that should not have any business impact.

4. Once a primary key is allocated successfully, that primary key will be used to commit the order details.

5. Even if the order commit is retried, it will be retried with the same primary key. So, any previously stored data will be overwritten, if any. This will ensure the idempotency of the operation.

Now, let us learn different methods to generate a primary key. For our use case, two popular mechanisms are as follows:

- **Persistent counter**: The user applications can implement a persistent counter in the underlying database to generate a unique identifier. Such an identifier can be used as a primary key.

- **UUID**: The user applications can implement a mechanism that returns unique identifiers, on demand, which can be used as a primary key.

Persistent counter implementation

The following code helps in visualizing the implementation of a persistent counter in MySQL. Here, we first create a table in MySQL with a single field, i.e., counter value. The data type of the counter value is **BIGINT**, and it is also set up for auto increment:

```
CREATE TABLE persistent_counter(
    value BIGINT AUTO_INCREMENT PRIMARY KEY
);
```

To allocate a new counter, we perform an insert operation with a **NULL** value and get the last insert ID. The operation to get the last insert ID is atomic for a specific database connection:

```
INSERT INTO persistent_counter VALUES (NULL);
SELECT LAST_INSERT_ID();
```

The last insert ID is the auto-increment ID of the last row that was inserted in the table. In this case, after inserting a **NULL**, the **LAST_INSERT_ID** will return the auto-incremented value of the column.

Note: **Previously in this chapter, we explained why using AUTO_INCREMENT in the order details table for the primary key can be problematic. However, in case of counter implementation, it is fine as there is no side effect on business operation due to a lost counter value.**

Universally unique identifier implementation

MySQL database exposes a function to generate UUIDs. The code to generate a UUID is written as follows: The function **UUID** will return a 128-bit UUID.

```
SELECT UUID()
```

Note: **Depending upon the implementation, there is a possibility that the UUID generator can generate duplicate identifiers. However, for all practical purposes, the probability of getting a duplicate value is very low. In any case, it is recommended that the engineers understand the underlying UUID implementation before using it.**

In this example implementation, we ensured idempotency by overwriting the data on the retry. Another way to ensure idempotency is to check if the data was written during the timed-out operation, before triggering another write operation. This data engineering pattern is called **test-and-set**.

Test-and-set for idempotency

The test-and-set design pattern helps in avoiding the persistence of duplicate data, as it enforces programmers to check if the data already exists before it is written to the underlying database.

The following algorithmic steps help in visualizing the test-and-set operations for the use case of committing an order:

1. Generate a unique identifier using either the persistent counter or the UUID generator. For our example, we will consider UUID.

2. Use the UUID to commit the order details to the database. This is a network call, which is vulnerable to network timeouts.

3. If *step 2* fails due to a momentary network timeout, check the database table for the entry with the UUID as the primary key. If found, treat the operation as successful.

4. If the entry with UUID as the primary key is not found in the previous step, then continue with *step 2*, using the same UUID.

Note: **In the test-and-set operation, the same UUID is being used during the retry for the same order. If a new UUID is used, it can lead to duplicate orders getting stored.**

Understanding duplicate data

A large amount of data leads to high data storage costs. Data deduplication techniques help reduce the data storage costs and other data management overheads. To understand the data deduplication techniques, we will learn the use of a large-scale data sharing website.

Let us consider a typical data-sharing website that allows users to upload and share data among different users.

The following is the list of features provided by the data sharing website:

*   Allow users to upload files to the data sharing website.
*   Users can organize the uploaded files in folders and subfolders.
*   Enable users to share files and folders with other users.

Let us take the use of User-A, who wants to share a set of photos with User-B. The User-A will identify the photos to be shared and upload them to the photo sharing website in a folder named **shared-with-B**. Let us say that this folder has three photos, viz. **photo1.jpg**, **photo2.jpg** and **photo3.jpg**. Once all three photos are uploaded to the folder, User-A shares the entire folder with User-B so that User-B can view the photos. Refer to the following figure:

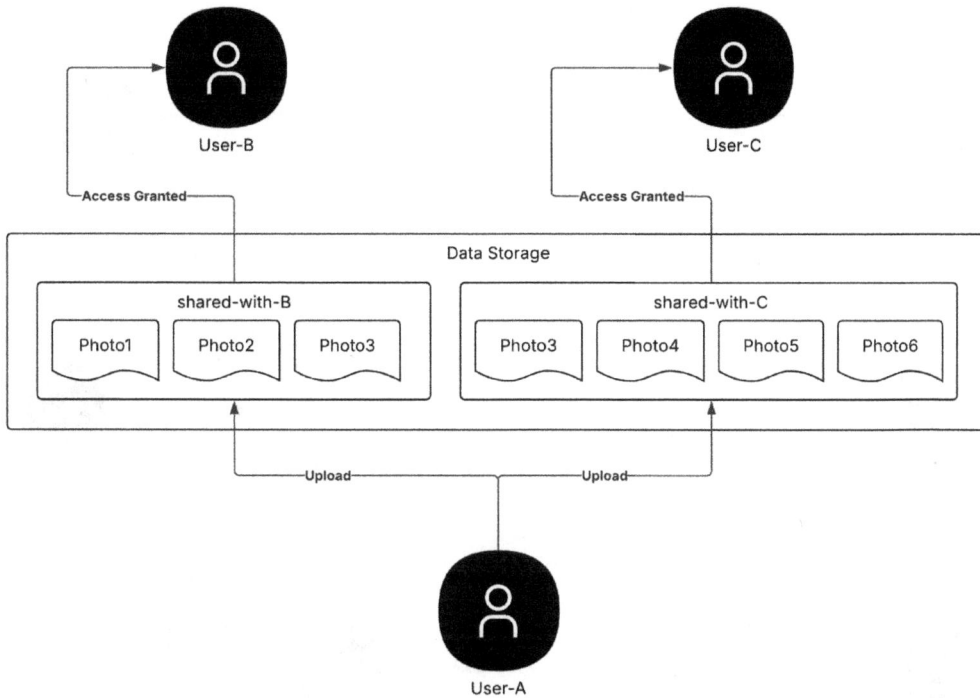

Figure 19.2: Duplicate data, scenario 1

After a few days, let us say that User-A wants to share some photos with User-C. Now, to keep things simple, User-A creates a new folder named **shared-with-C** and uploads the four photos, viz. **photo3.jpg**, **photo4.jpg**, **photo5.jpg** and **photo6.jpg**. Here we can notice that User-A has uploaded **photo3.jpg** twice, once in the folder **shared-with-B** and once in the folder **shared-with-C**. For the data sharing website, it is duplicate data. Let us call this *scenario 1* for data duplication.

Figure 19.2 helps visualize *scenario 1* for duplicate data. This type of data duplication is called **local data duplication**, as the duplicate data belongs to a single user.

Furthermore, let us say that User-B wants to share some photos with User-D. One of the photos User-B wants to share is **photo2.jpg**. So, User-B downloads the photo, creates a new folder called **photos-shared-with-D** on the data sharing website, and uploads **photo2.jpg** to the newly created folder. Here, we can observe that the **photo2.jpg** was uploaded twice, once by User-A and once by User-B, in two different folders (owned by individual users).

Let us call this *scenario 2* for data duplication, as shown in the following figure:

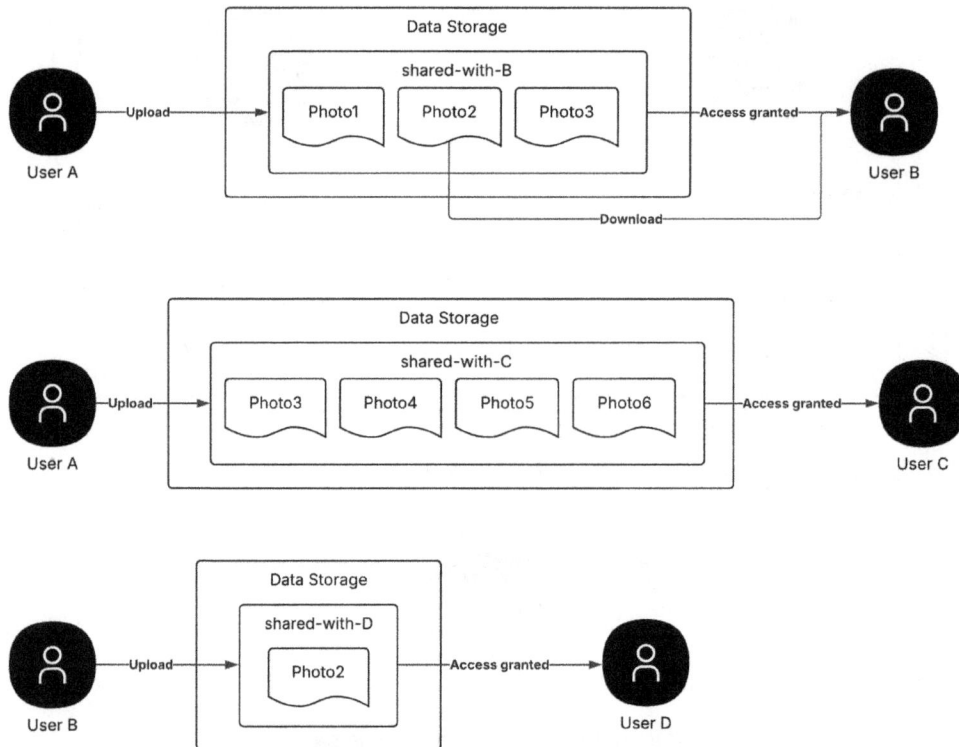

Figure 19.3: *Duplicate data, scenario 2*

Figure 19.3 helps in visualizing *scenario 2* aforementioned. This type of data duplication is called *global data duplication*, as the duplicate data belongs to more than one user.

Methods to check duplicate data

In both scenarios (i.e., *scenario 1* and *scenario 2*) aforementioned, there is a potential to exploit the data duplication. There are two popular methods to identify duplicate data:

- **Byte-by-byte comparison**: In this case, the contents of two files need to be compared, byte-by-byte, to know if the two files are duplicates.

- **Checksum comparison**: In this case, a unique signature of the contents of the two files is calculated using checksum algorithms like SHA-256, and the checksums are compared. The checksum algorithms like SHA-256 ensure negligible chances of collision (i.e., having the same checksum for two different data contents).

Comparing checksums can have reduced CPU cost as opposed to comparing the entire data, especially for large files and when a large number of files need to be compared.

Data deduplication

A typical method of performing data deduplication has the following steps:

1. Identify duplicate data objects.
2. Generate a separate unique identifier for each distinct data object.
3. Maintain the deduplication metadata for bookkeeping.

Earlier in this chapter, we discussed how to identify duplicate data objects. We have also learned the mechanisms to generate UUIDs and persistent counters, which can be used as unique identifiers for data objects. SHA-256-based signature can also be used as an identifier. Now, we will discuss the mechanism used to maintain the deduplication metadata. Before looking at the details of the metadata, we need to understand the requirements related to it.

The following is the list of requirements:

- When a new data object is being stored, check if duplicate data is already stored.
- If the duplicate data is already stored, there is no need to store it again.
- If the duplicate data is not already stored, store the data object.
- In case of deduplication, when the user's data object gets deleted, ensure no data loss.

If we look at the aforementioned requirements closely, the first three requirements are the obvious requirements for data deduplication. However, the fourth requirement to ensure the consistency of the data on deletion needs to be handled well. For that, deduplication metadata needs to be maintained. Let us continue with the file sharing example, where the same file is uploaded twice, viz. **folder1/photo.jpg** and **folder2/photo.jpg**. *Figure 19.4* helps in visualizing the data deduplication, along with the metadata needed to manage the deduplication bookkeeping:

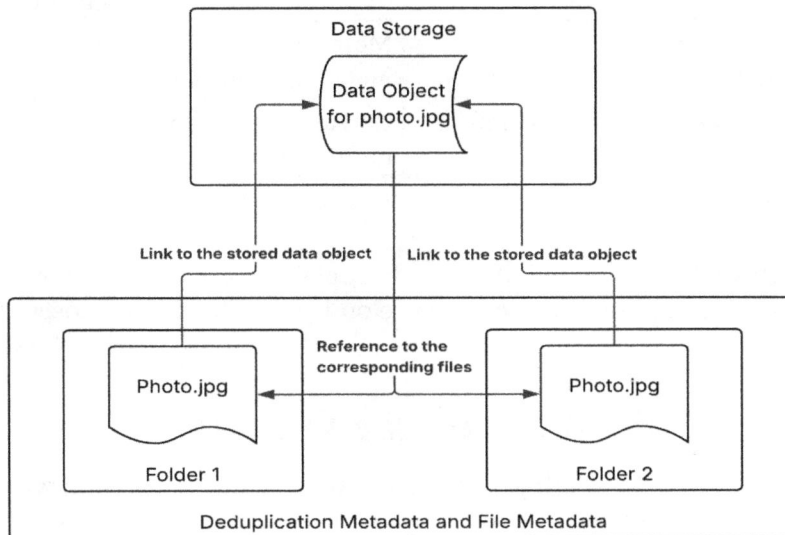

Figure 19.4: Deduplication metadata

As we can see in *Figure 19.4*, deduplication metadata needs to maintain two pieces of information:

- Link from the user's object to the actual stored object in the data store (forward link).
- A reference from the stored object to the user's data objects (reverse link).

Both forward and reverse references are required for maintaining data consistency. The forward link is useful in looking up the stored data object when the user wants to download the file. On the other hand, when the user deletes a file, the reverse link from the data object to the file gets deleted. If there are any other reverse links, then we know that the data object is still being referenced by the other files and cannot be deleted. However, when all the reverse links are deleted, then we know that there are no references to the data object, and it can be cleaned up.

Local vs. global data deduplication

Earlier in this chapter, we saw that data duplication can exist within a particular user's data, or it can span across the data belonging to multiple users. As a data engineer, one needs to decide whether to deduplicate the data across multiple users. This decision has trade-offs associated with it. *Table 19.1* helps us in understanding the trade-offs between local vs. global deduplication:

Local deduplication	Global deduplication
Local deduplication will avoid storing the duplicate data belonging to a single user.	Global deduplication will avoid storing duplicate data spanning across multiple users.
Less savings on storage space, as the duplicate data across users is not deduplicated.	More savings on storage space, as the duplicate data across users is deduplicated.
Lower overheads due to deduplication metadata management.	More overheads due to deduplication metadata management.
Corruption of the stored data objects impacts only one user.	Corruption of the stored data objects impacts multiple users.

Table 19.1: Local vs. global data deduplication

Until now, we have learned how to save the data storage cost with the help of data deduplication. Now, let us see how we can save on large data transfer costs with the help of data deduplication techniques.

Data deduplication at source vs. target

Let us continue with our file-sharing website example. Until now, we have only looked at the technique used on the server side for the purpose of data deduplication. In this case, the users will end up uploading the duplicate data to the server, and the server will perform the deduplication steps. As the data is being uploaded from the user's device to the server, for this data transfer, the user's device will be treated as a source device, and the web server will be treated as a target device. As the deduplication happens on the web server side, we call this *deduplication at the target*.

Uploading duplicate data multiple times will cost time and upload bandwidth. To avoid this, *deduplication at source* can be attempted.

The following algorithm helps in visualizing deduplication at source:

- Once the files to be uploaded are identified, the SHA-256 checksum will be calculated at the user's device.

    Note: **This consumes CPU on the user's device.**

- This SHA-256 will be sent to the server, along with file metadata like file name, file path, etc.

- The server will check if the data with the same SHA-256 has already been uploaded. If yes, the server will create the required deduplication metadata.

    Note: **Here, the duplicate data will not be transferred over the network.**

- If not, then the user's device will send the data to the server, along with the required metadata.

Until now, we have investigated the examples where deduplication was performed at the file level. However, for very large files, we can exploit the benefits of deduplication at a more granular level (i.e., block level). Let us learn more about block-level deduplication.

Block-level deduplication

Different types of files have their own data format. For example, files like Word documents, Excel sheets, PDF documents, etc., are mostly unstructured. On the other hand, files like JSON documents, images, videos, mailboxes, database files, etc., are semi-structured or structured. Empirically, semi-structured and structured files have exhibited duplication of the data within a single file, but across different blocks of the file. For such files, deduplication is performed at the block level as follows:

- When a file needs to be uploaded or transferred, it is logically divided into multiple subparts.

- For each sub-part, a separate SHA-256 checksum is calculated. The data for which SHA-256 is not found on the server will be uploaded. For the rest of the data, only metadata will be uploaded.

- On the server side, a complete file will not be stored as-is. Only blocks will be stored separately, along with the block metadata needed to reconstruct the file.

- During download, the file will be downloaded block-by-block, and the complete file will be reconstructed from the blocks, with the help of the afore-mentioned block metadata.

- If a subset of blocks from the file undergoes changes, and the file is uploaded again to a different directory, then only changed blocks will be uploaded, as unchanged blocks are already present on the server side.

The command-line tools like **rsync** help in performing block-level deduplication for file transfer.

Conclusion

In this chapter, we started with understanding the importance of idempotent operations and the business impact of the side effects of non-idempotent operations. We also learned a mechanism to convert non-idempotent operations to idempotent operations with the help of improved data modelling, use of persistent counters, use of UUIDs, and the test-and-set pattern.

Later, we learned how to identify duplicate data and the importance of data deduplication from the perspective of saving storage costs, saving data transfer costs, and saving time during data transfer. We studied local vs. global deduplication by studying their trade-offs. We also learned the method of performing deduplication at the source. Finally, we learned about block-level deduplication and its uses around that.

In the next chapter, we will learn various data orchestration patterns that ensure the smooth flow of data among various systems.

Questions

1. Instead of a persistent counter, can we use an in-memory counter to ensure idempotency? Can an in-memory counter guarantee the uniqueness of an identifier across process restarts?

2. UUIDs are always unique, true or false?

3. Does global data deduplication help in reducing the blast radius in case of data corruption?

4. What types of files benefit from block-level deduplication?

Join our Discord space

Join our Discord workspace for latest updates, offers, tech happenings around the world, new releases, and sessions with the authors:

https://discord.bpbonline.com

CHAPTER 20
Data Orchestration Patterns

Introduction

This chapter delves into the data orchestration patterns that are necessary for automating, scheduling, and managing complex data workflows, ensuring that data flows seamlessly across various systems and stages of processing. We cover topics on pipeline chaining, event-driven orchestration, fan-out/fan-in, and the use of **directed acyclic graphs** (**DAGs**) in the chapter. This chapter also explains various types of schedulers and when and how to use them. We will also show a real-world example of how a data pipeline is implemented using these data orchestration patterns.

Structure

The chapter covers the following topics:

- Pipeline chaining
- Event-driven orchestration
- Fan-in and fan-out pattern
- Directed acyclic graphs
- Design and implement using data orchestration pattern

- Technical stack for data orchestration pattern
- Real-world example

Objectives

By the end of this chapter, you will be able to orchestrate complex data pipelines by stitching together various orchestration technologies. You will also be able to design and write code to implement the orchestration data patterns. You will know the technical stack to use for orchestrating data pipelines. Finally, you will also understand with real-world use cases how pipelines are orchestrated and managed in production.

Pipeline chaining

Pipeline chaining is the concept of linking multiple data pipelines together, forming a chain. The completion of one pipeline triggers the next, thereby allowing the data engineer to orchestrate a sequence of smaller pipelines to execute a larger pipeline. This data pattern is used to simplify complex data pipelines by breaking them down into smaller individual pipelines, which can be monitored and debugged easily. This concept is similar to modularization of code in software engineering, where each module has a specific job to do and can be reused. Similarly, in pipeline chaining, the individual smaller pipelines are designed for a specific purpose and can be reused across multiple larger data pipelines. For example, a specific pipeline may be designed to read data from the source database and push it to Kafka, and another pipeline's job may just be reading data from Kafka to ingest into a data warehouse. Similarly, a separate pipeline can exist to perform data cleansing operations. All these can be stitched together to form a larger pipeline and also be reused across multiple pipelines.

Pipeline chaining makes the whole pipeline modular and easily debuggable. Individual pipelines can be developed and tested in parallel by different data engineers and can be stitched together to form a complex pipeline. Any errors in individual pipelines are simpler to investigate as these pipelines can be tested independently. One more advantage of pipeline chaining is that it makes data engineers clearly think about interfaces when developing the pipeline, as each pipeline hands over data to the next one. This ensures pipelines are well thought through from a design perspective and are made reusable. Pipeline chaining helps different data engineering teams with expertise in specific areas of a pipeline collaboratively work together to deliver a complex pipeline.

Though it is common for pipeline chaining to have pipelines run sequentially, it is not uncommon to see pipelines have branches and parallel execution paths as well. More complex orchestrators like Apache Airflow are used to develop such pipelines, where the pipeline may be more like a graph than a chain. The following figures are architecture diagrams showing the stitching of three pipelines to deliver a complex pipeline that reads data from a transactional system in real time and loads cleansed data into a data warehouse.

The first figure shows a data pipeline ingesting data from a transactional system to Kafka via change data capture:

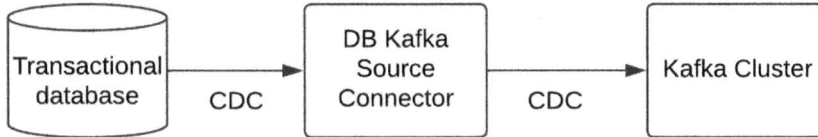

Figure 20.1: Reading source data using CDC

The second figure shows a data pipeline ingesting data from Kafka into a data cleansing program in Spark and pushing back to Kafka. The cleansing operation can be any standard data cleansing, like address sanitization, name standardization, currency conversion, etc.:

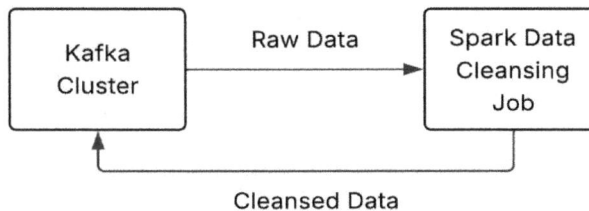

Figure 20.2: Writing cleansed data back to Kafka

The third figure shows a data pipeline reading data from Kafka and ingesting the cleansed data into the data warehouse. Writing the cleansed data back to Kafka and reading the data back using the Kafka connector for the database allows for real-time streaming of cleansed data into the data warehouse. Though the spark job could directly write the data to the data warehouse, writing it back to Kafka allows other data consumers to consume cleansed data as well:

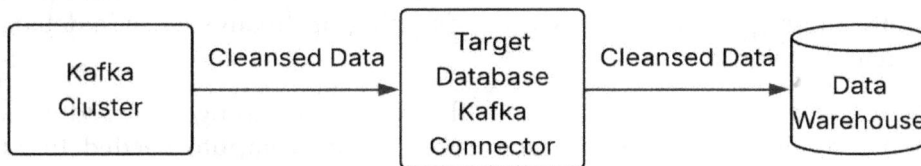

Figure 20.3: Writing cleansed data to the data warehouse

The fourth figure shows pipeline chaining, stitching all three pipelines together, forming a full ETL pipeline that extracts data in real time from a transactional system to a data warehouse. There are multiple ways to chain the pipeline together. It can be done either by setting up dependencies between these individual jobs in a workflow management platform or by leveraging event-driven architecture when the upstream pipeline triggers an event, like a trigger file uploaded, that initiates the downstream pipeline, as shown:

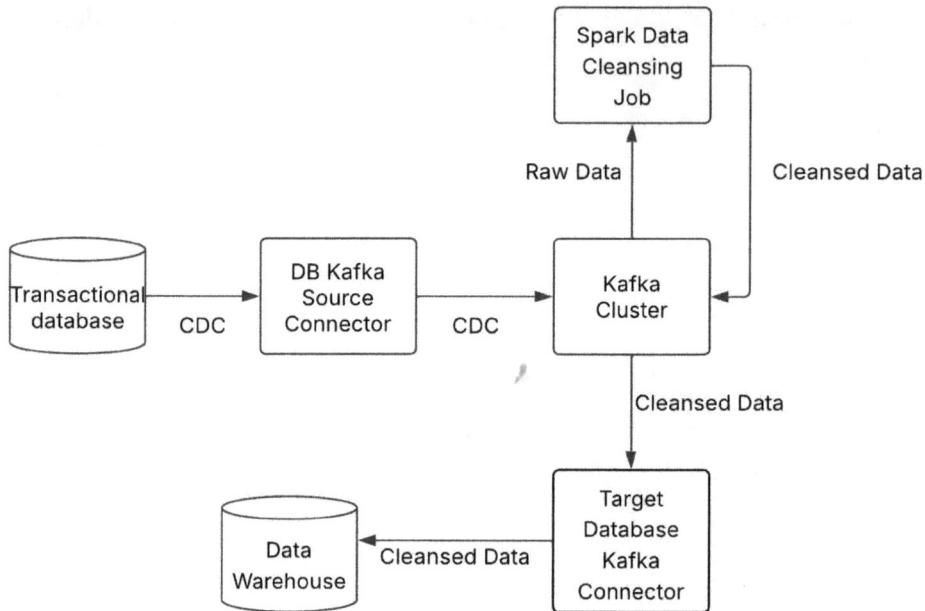

Figure 20.4: *Pipeline chain*

Event-driven orchestration

In event-driven orchestration, pipelines are triggered by events instead of schedulers. These are more suited for real-time use cases where the occurrence of an event should immediately lead to the data being processed instead of the pipeline running at a later scheduled time. The event can be of different types, like a file being placed at a pre-defined location on an S3 bucket, a Kafka message being sent from the triggering upstream system, a database record being written to the table, etc.

Event-driven systems can be combined with pipeline chaining to build sophisticated orchestration techniques for pipelines and optimize the compute needed to run a data pipeline. Event-driven systems allow pipelines in a pipeline chain to be launched only on a specific event, thus reducing the need for running the pipeline perennially, thereby reducing the compute needs of the pipeline. Leveraging modern cloud architectures like *Lambda*, further reduction in compute is possible by dynamically provisioning the pipeline compute at runtime. While event-driven pipelines allow just-in-time runs, they do make the pipeline orchestration and management difficult compared to scheduler-orchestrated pipelines and hence need to be used judiciously. The following figure is the architecture of a pipeline chain implemented using an event-driven pipeline and Lambda. First, let us look at a pipeline that uploads a file to an S3 bucket when a bunch of records are ready for processing:

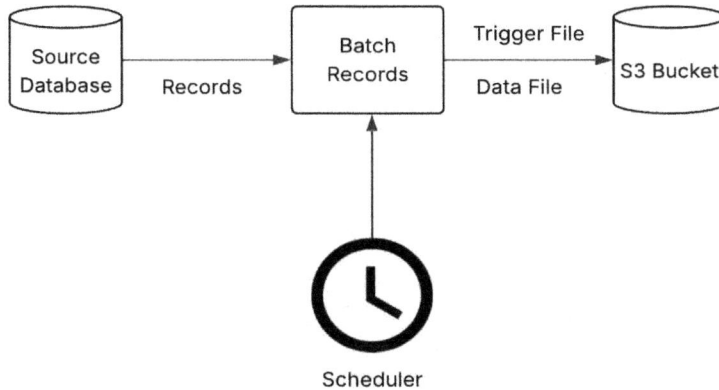

Figure 20.5: Trigger indication

The second pipeline reads from the file on the S3 bucket containing a bunch of records when the trigger file is available for further processing. The trigger file acts as the event in this pipeline chain to start the second pipeline in the chain. The following figure shows the second pipeline, which reads the data file when the trigger file is available using Spark and loads the data into the target system:

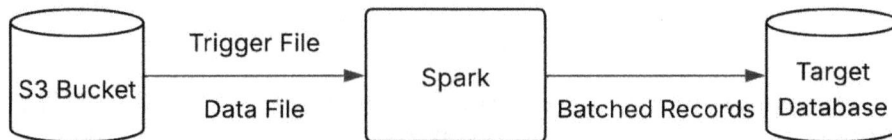

Figure 20.6: Trigger processing

Fan-in and fan-out pattern

The fan-in and fan-out pattern is used to implement parallel execution of data pipeline steps using the scatter-gather approach. It is used to scale the pipeline horizontally to make pipeline execution faster. The fan-in and fan-out pattern also helps pipelines process a large amount of data in a reasonable timeframe, leveraging scalable compute architectures.

In data processing pipelines, it is very common to encounter use cases where the data can be partitioned based on certain criteria like date, region, type, etc. Every partition can be processed independently, and the final result can be aggregated together. The fan-in and fan-out pattern can be used in such use cases where this data partitioning can be done naturally. For example, consider having to process data for a month and aggregate it for reporting. Here, the data can be partitioned by day, and multiple days of data can be processed in parallel depending on the compute available. This parallel execution is the fan-out step of the pipeline. Once the fan-out step is complete and every day's individual aggregates are available, the fan-in step can generate the monthly aggregate, leveraging the individual daily aggregates.

Let us first look at the architecture of the fan-out phase of a data pipeline that processes data from an S3 bucket every day in parallel and writes the intermediate daily aggregate back to the S3 bucket. Refer to the following figure:

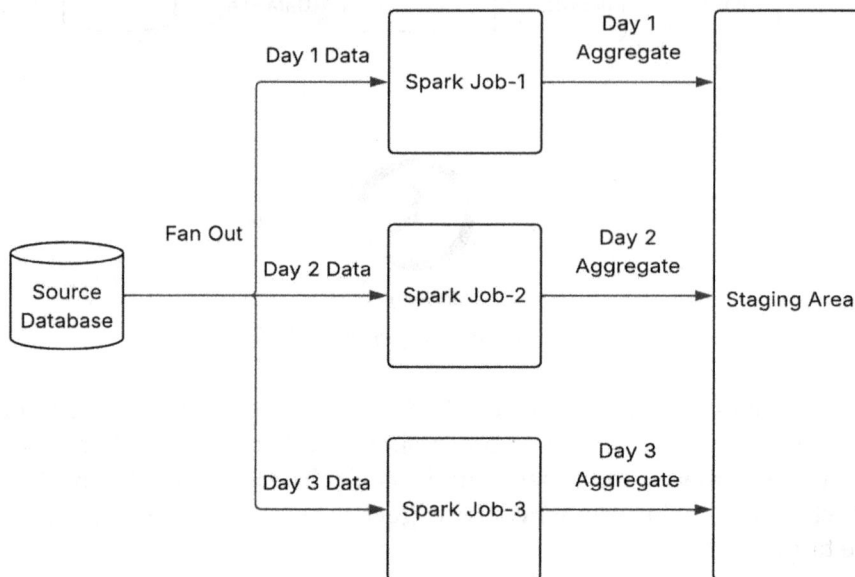

Figure 20.7: Fan-out phase

The following figure shows the fan-in phase of the data pipeline, where the daily aggregate is read from the S3 bucket and is combined to form the monthly aggregate:

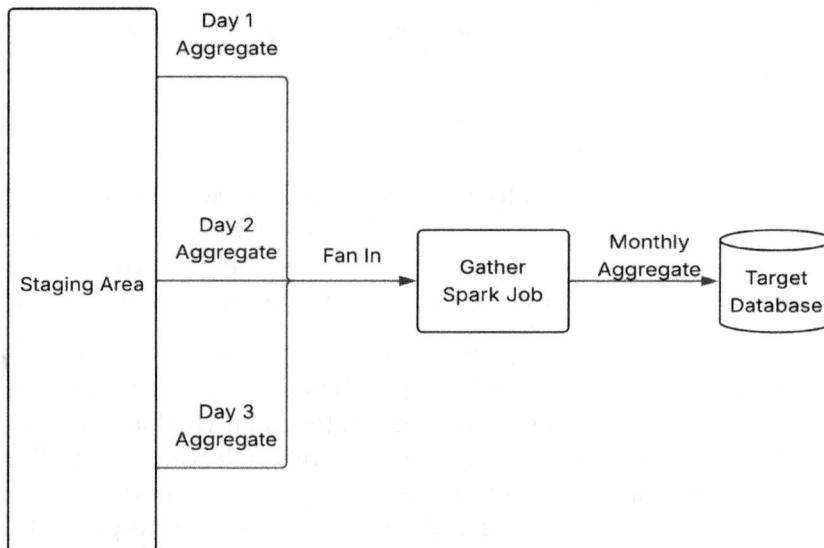

Figure 20.8: Fan-in phase

Directed acyclic graph

Directed acyclic graph (DAG) is a pipeline orchestration pattern in which tasks to be performed in the pipeline are represented by nodes, and the sequence of execution is represented by edges. Each task node is connected to other task nodes by an edge that represents the order of execution. The edges are directional and indicate the flow of control. DAGs are acyclic, and cycles are not allowed with a node connecting back to itself directly or indirectly.

The following figure shows a sample DAG for ETL:

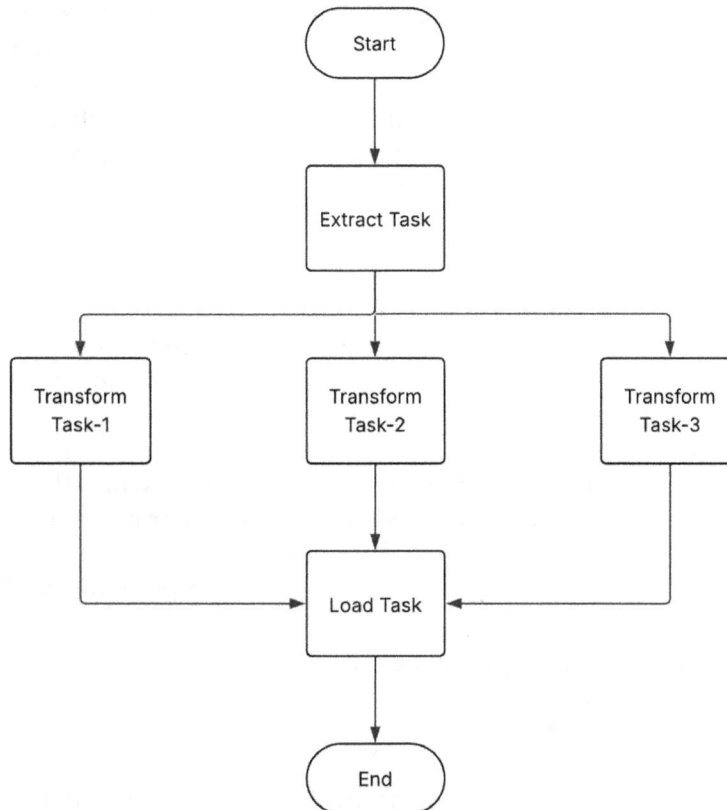

Figure 20.9: Directed acyclic graph

In *Figure 20.9*, you will see three tasks. The extract task, which runs in serial, extracting data from the source, the transform tasks are run in parallel as the data can be transformed in parallel without any dependency, and finally, the load task again runs in serial to ensure the order of rows is maintained. This DAG shows the fan-out and fan-in pattern in use, where the fan-out happens in the transform phase and the fan-in happens in the load phase. The tasks are connected by directed edges, clearly showing the sequence of execution. There is no cycle in the graph, as no task has an edge back to itself directly or indirectly.

The sample DAG representation will be as follows:

```
start >> Extract_Task
Extract_task >> [Transform_Task_1, Transform_Task_2, Transform_Task_3]
[Transform_Task_1, Transform_Task_2, Transform_Task_3] >> Load_Task
Load_Task >> end
```

Schedulers

Schedulers are used to start the data pipelines based on time or dependency completions. In the case of time-based scheduling, the scheduler runs the pipeline based on a pre-defined schedule. The schedule can be defined in many ways, like hourly, daily, weekly, monthly, or at a specific time of the day. Rudimentary schedulers like *Cron* can help schedule these fixed-schedule jobs. More sophisticated schedulers like *Control-M* or *Apache Airflow* allow you to set dependencies based on which the pipeline runs. The dependency can be of many types, for example, another pipeline completing, a file becoming available, or an upstream system sending a signal.

The selection of a scheduler is an important decision to make in any data pipeline. For running simple jobs as scripts at a pre-scheduled interval, Cron is a free, open-source scheduler that is a great choice. The learning curve to use Cron is in hours when compared to more complex schedulers like *Control-M* or *Apache Airflow*. However, Cron cannot do dependency-based scheduling, nor does it have the capability to schedule across a set of servers; in such cases, it is recommended to use enterprise schedulers like *Control-M* when the pipeline gets very complex, with multiple tasks to be performed with some in parallel and others serially, one after another, with a mixture of scheduling thrown in there, as there is a need for complex schedulers like *Apache Airflow*, which allow you to represent a pipeline as a DAG.

Design and implement using data orchestration pattern

In this section, let us implement a simple event-driven orchestration pattern using shell scripts and the Cron scheduler. The example will use two scripts, one that reads customer names from a file, converts all the names to uppercase letters, and writes the contents to another file. At the end of processing all the customer names, it writes a trigger file to a particular location. Then a Cron job, which runs every minute, runs another file that, based on the existence of the trigger file, executes a script to read the file with upper-case customer names and attaches a generated, random, unique ID to every customer.

The following figure is the architecture of this implementation of the pipeline with the sequence of execution numbered from *1* to *6*:

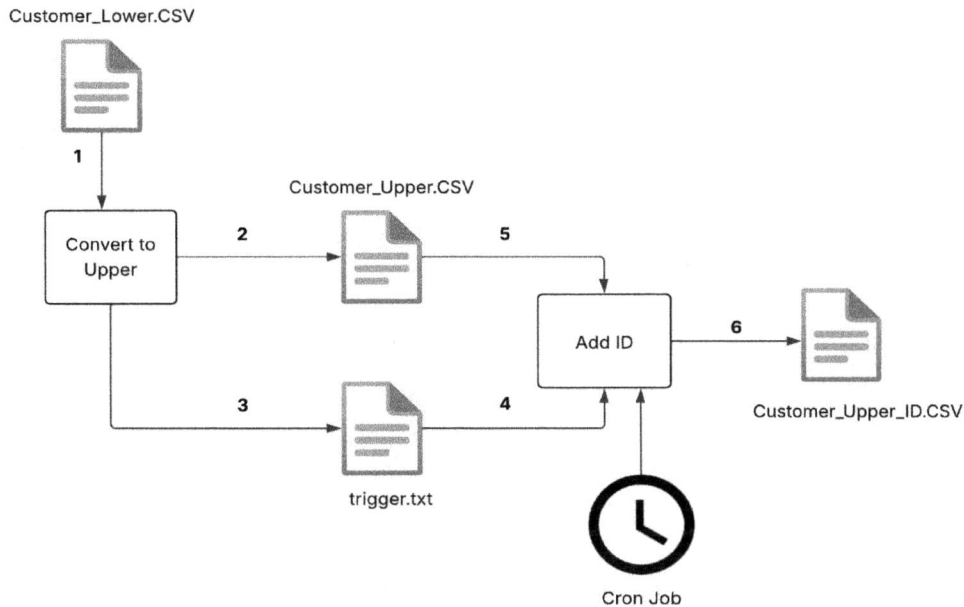

Figure 20.10: *Pipeline architecture*

Let us first look at the first script, which reads all the customer names from a file and converts them to uppercase, and writes the trigger file:

```bash
1.  #!/bin/bash
2.  # Input,output and trigger files
3.  INPUT_FILE="customer_lower.csv"
4.  OUTPUT_FILE="customer_upper.csv"
5.  TRIGGER_FILE="trigger.txt"
6.  # Check if input file exists
7.  if [[ ! -f "$INPUT_FILE" ]]; then
8.      echo "Input file $INPUT_FILE does not exist."
9.      exit 1
10. fi
11. # Clear the output file first
12. > "$OUTPUT_FILE"
13. # Read each line, convert to uppercase using 'tr', and write to output
14. while IFS= read -r line
15. do
```

```
16.   echo "$line" | tr '[:lower:]' '[:upper:]' >> "$OUTPUT_FILE"
17. done < "$INPUT_FILE"
18. echo "Conversion completed. Uppercase entries written to $OUTPUT_FILE."
19. # Write 'done' into the file
20. echo "done" > "$TRIGGER_FILE"
21. echo "Trigger file $TRIGGER_FILE created with word 'done'."
```

The second script, which reads the upper-case customer names, generates an ID for each customer, and writes it to another CSV file, is shown as follows:

```
1.  #!/bin/bash
2.  # Input files
3.  TRIGGER_FILE="trigger.txt"
4.  CUSTOMER_FILE="customer_upper.csv"
5.  OUTPUT_FILE="customer_upper_ID.csv"
6.  # Check if trigger file exists
7.  if [[ ! -f "$TRIGGER_FILE" ]]; then
8.    echo "Trigger file $TRIGGER_FILE does not exist."
9.    exit 1
10. fi
11. # Check if trigger file contains the word 'done'
12. if grep -q "^done$" "$TRIGGER_FILE"; then
13.    echo "Trigger confirmed. Proceeding to process customer file..."
14. else
15.    echo "Trigger file does not contain 'done'. Exiting."
16.    exit 1
17. fi
18. # Check if customer file exists
19. if [[ ! -f "$CUSTOMER_FILE" ]]; then
20.    echo "Customer file $CUSTOMER_FILE does not exist."
21.    exit 1
22. fi
23. # Clear output file first and add CSV header
24. echo "customer_name,customer_id" > "$OUTPUT_FILE"
```

```
25. # Process each customer and generate random ID
26. while IFS= read -r customer
27. do
28.     # Generate random ID between 1000 and 9999
29.     customer_id=$(( RANDOM % 9000 + 1000 ))
30.     # Write customer name and ID to output CSV
31.     echo "${customer},${customer_id}" >> "$OUTPUT_FILE"
32. done < "$CUSTOMER_FILE"
33. echo "Processing completed. Output written to $OUTPUT_FILE."
```

Next, we create the pipeline using the Cron job:

```
1. * * * * * /process_customers.sh >> /process_customers.log 2>&1
```

Technical stack for data orchestration patterns

Orchestration of pipelines needs two key technologies: a workflow manager and scheduler to design a complex workflow. These two technologies are used in conjunction to define the pipeline and schedule its execution.

Workflow manager is a component that allows data engineers to build a pipeline by defining tasks or jobs to execute and associating the tasks or jobs to execute in a sequenced manner. It provides the capability to not only define the pipeline steps and run it, but also to monitor the pipeline with various integrations to alerting technologies. Apache Airflow is the most popular workflow management platform today, given its capability and flexibility to design very complex pipelines. Apache Airflow also has an inbuilt scheduler, avoiding the need for an independent scheduler to run jobs at predefined schedules. However, Apache Airflow needs a steep learning curve to build complex pipelines. For simple pipelines, other tools like *Apache NiFi* or *Control-M* can be a better choice than Apache Airflow.

Schedulers play a critical role in ensuring the pipeline runs exactly when it is scheduled to run. Cron is the most popular and simplest scheduler. Since the advent of Linux, it has become the defacto scheduler for scheduling jobs on machines. It is suitable for scheduling scripts on local machines, but does not work when the schedule needs to be orchestrated across a bunch of servers. Another challenge with Cron is debugging job failures, as the Cron logs are written to Linux syslogs, which are not intuitive and difficult to debug. When scheduling is needed for jobs across multiple servers and environments, enterprise schedulers like *Autosys* or *Tidal* are preferred.

Typically, in large enterprises, workflow management and scheduling are offered as a horizontal service by a centralized data infrastructure team. It is recommended to leverage the available workflow management and scheduler offered by this team instead of each data engineering team standing up their own workflow management and scheduling service. Rarely do workflow managers or schedulers provide a differentiated advantage to a data pipeline, and data engineering teams must not invest critical effort and budgets in these services but instead focus on the core data pipeline innovations while using the workflow management and scheduling service offered by the centralized infrastructure teams. Only when the workflow management platform or scheduler offered by the centralized team does not have the features needed by a particular data pipeline should individual data engineering teams look at hosting their own workflow management or scheduler service. Given the commonality of capabilities across most enterprise workflow management and scheduler services, a missing capability in the centrally hosted workflow management or scheduler service would be a rare occurrence.

Real-world example

Let us explore a real-world example of customer onboarding that leverages orchestration patterns to trigger downstream processes when a new customer onboarding occurs. This example leverages pipeline chaining and event-driven orchestration.

Customer onboarding

Customer onboarding is a great use case to explain pipeline orchestration. We can demonstrate the use of both pipeline chaining and event-driven orchestration, leveraging this use case. In any B2C use case, customer onboarding is one of the critical pieces of the system, as a smooth onboarding experience determines the customer satisfaction score to a great extent. When a customer typically onboards, there are multiple backend flows that need to be orchestrated. For example, the accounts need to be created for the customer in various systems, there may be background checks that need to be started, if there are offers running, the customer may need to be credited with some sign-up credits, etc. All these related background tasks need to be orchestrated, as there may be dependencies between them.

Let us consider an example of a customer who needs to be provided sign-up credits only after the background check for a valid customer check passes. This needs chaining of the customer validation pipeline to run before the customer signs up for the credit pipeline. Pipeline chaining here can be done by generating the approved background check file that gets uploaded to an S3 bucket, and the sign-up credit pipeline can start processing on the availability of this file. The trigger here is the generation of the background check approval file.

The following figure shows the pipeline chaining using event-driven orchestration for a customer onboarding use case:

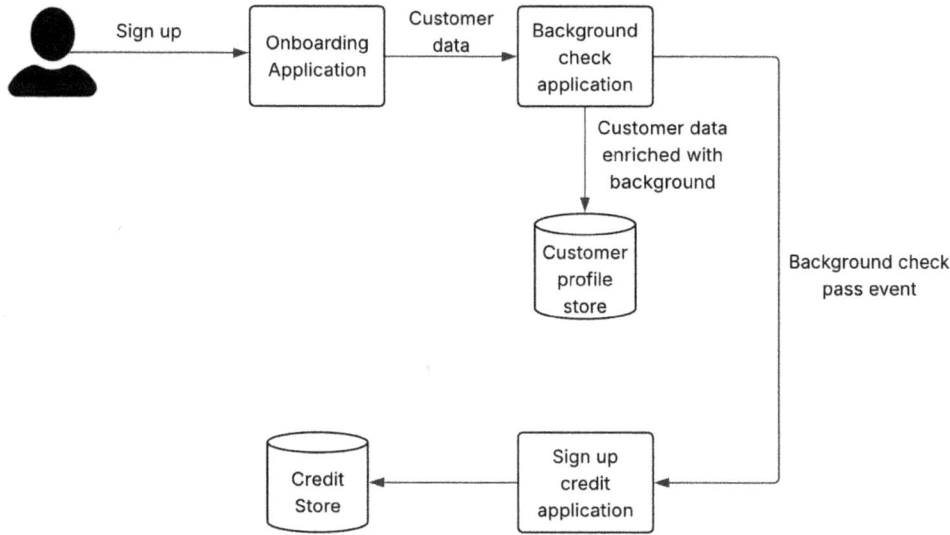

Figure 20.11: *Customer onboarding orchestration*

Conclusion

In this chapter, we covered the data orchestration patterns that help build and run pipelines. We learnt the different ways to orchestrate pipelines like pipeline chaining, event-driven, and DAGs. We learnt about orchestrating a pipeline with an example. The chapter covered technologies used to implement pipeline orchestration. We also covered a real-world example of how event-driven systems orchestration is used in customer onboarding.

In the next chapter, we will understand the various performance pitfalls data engineering systems can encounter and the techniques for overcoming them. We review data model design, query patterns, and resource allocation pitfalls. Finally, we see an industry use case from the lens of these various pitfalls and understand how to avoid them.

Questions

1. Why can DAGs not have cycles in them?
2. Which orchestration pattern should be used to scale out pipelines horizontally?
3. Design a pipeline chain for ETL combining three different pipelines.
4. Why is AWS Lambda gaining popularity for event-driven pipelines?

Join our Discord space

Join our Discord workspace for latest updates, offers, tech happenings around the world, new releases, and sessions with the authors:

https://discord.bpbonline.com

CHAPTER 21
Common Performance Pitfalls

Introduction

This chapter looks into the common performance mistakes data engineers make while designing data processing systems and data pipelines. It provides recommendations on how to avoid these common performance pitfalls and make the pipelines highly performant while not drastically increasing system cost. It covers performance pitfalls in three critical areas of data model design, query patterns, and resource allocations. We will look at a real-world example of what performance mistakes can happen while designing a data system and how to avoid them, leveraging various data patterns learnt so far in this book.

Structure

The chapter covers the following topics:

- Data model pitfalls and incorrect query patterns
- Resource misallocations
- Data skew
- Real-world examples

Objectives

By the end of this chapter, you will be able to identify common performance mistakes in data systems and pipelines. You will be able to leverage the patterns learnt in this book to fix those mistakes and build high-performing data systems and pipelines. You will understand the performance pitfalls that can be encountered in a real system and how they can be mitigated. Finally, you will have a conceptual understanding of how to tackle performance problems in data systems holistically, leveraging data engineering patterns.

Data model pitfalls and incorrect query patterns

Data model design is a very broad area, and performance mistakes can happen from multiple dimensions. This section covers the common dimensions where performance challenges occur and how to overcome those. Readers are encouraged to explore performance pitfalls in their own data pipelines once they understand the patterns in this chapter.

Incorrect data model

Data model design needs to be considered from day one of the design of a data system. It is probably one of the most critical factors in the performance of a data system. For example, consider the design of a web or mobile application that would serve millions of users like an e-commerce application. Such a system would require being able to scale the database to serve hundreds of thousands of requests per second with millisecond latency. The data model selection becomes very critical to achieve this level of performance. Historically, relational databases powered most critical applications; however, it would be a bad choice to select a relational database that struggles to scale horizontally as a backend database for this type of application. Also, most relational databases provide a strongly consistent data model, which would not be needed to serve an e-commerce product catalog, for example. Leveraging eventual consistency, NoSQL databases can provide far superior performance at a lower cost.

Another common performance pitfall in the selection of a data model is selecting a symmetric multiprocessing system over a massively parallel processing system to do analytical processing. Most databases are distributed in nature in the modern era, but how they process queries needs to be carefully understood before deciding on the type of system that needs to be selected. For example, even distributed databases run individual queries on a single node without distributing the query plan across nodes. This results in slow query processing when, instead, this could have been avoided by selecting a distributed database with Massive Parallel Processing capability that can run a single query request over multiple nodes. The following architecture figure shows the difference in query execution between Massive Parallel Processing systems and symmetric multiprocessing systems.

Let us first look at a symmetric multiprocessing database system architecture:

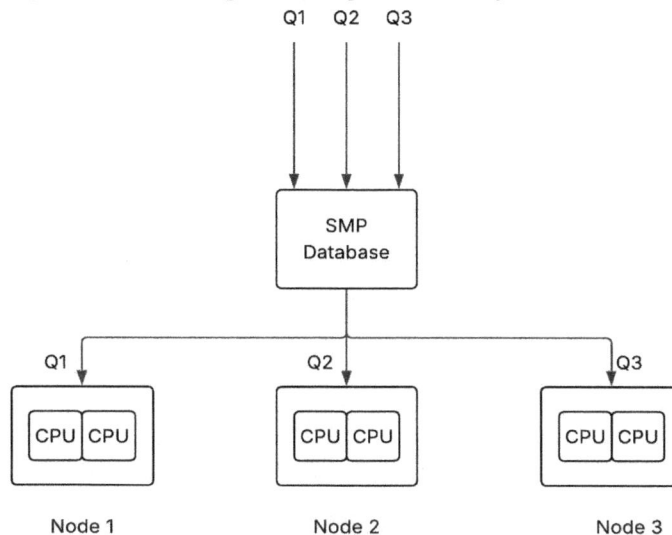

Figure 21.1: Symmetric multiprocessing

As you can see in the above architecture, every query is routed by the database to a single node for processing. The individual node may have multiple CPUs, and hence the name multiprocessing, but multiple nodes do not participate in a single query processing. This limits the scale-out potential of the query to the CPU, memory, and IO bandwidth available on a single node. Vertically scaling memory and compute on a node has physical limitations due to the largest configuration offered by server vendors. From the storage perspective, the number of disks that can be attached to a single node has a physical limitation based on the number of PCI slots available on the server board. For example, Dell PowerEdge R740xd can support a maximum of 24 NVMe drives on the server, and storage bandwidth cannot be scaled beyond these 24 NVMe drives.

Now, let us look at the architecture figure of the **Massive Parallel Processing (MPP)** architecture for databases that overcomes this challenge of vertical scaling, explained above in symmetric multiprocessing systems:

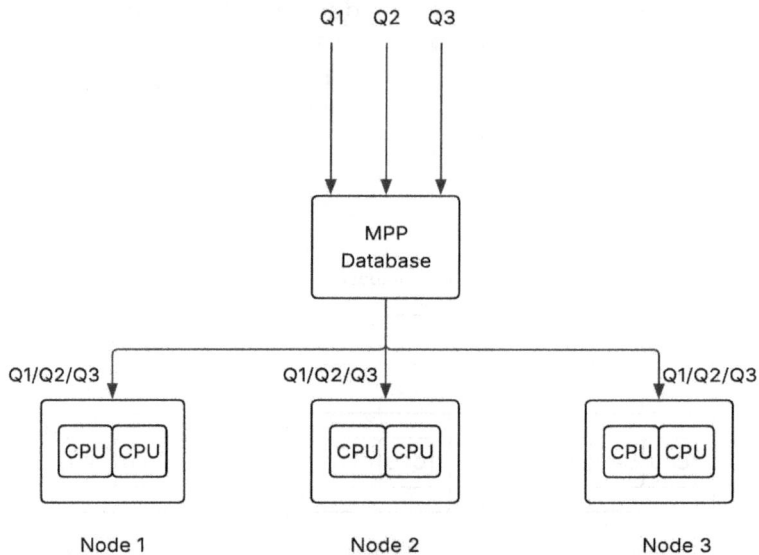

Figure 21.2: *Massive Parallel Processing*

The architecture looks similar; however, the key variation to notice is that every query is now being routed to all the nodes of the cluster in the MPP architecture. Thus, every query gets processed on all nodes of the cluster, allowing a much larger scale-out potential. The query processing time is not limited by the CPU, memory, and the IO bandwidth of a single node, but instead it is limited to the total compute available on the MPP database cluster. If the data or number of queries increases, more nodes can be added to the cluster, thereby scaling it horizontally. Horizontal scaling also makes scaling more predictable, with the latencies typically reducing by a predictable degree with the addition of every node.

Another common data model design pitfall is the normalization of data. Historically, data engineers were taught to avoid duplicating data at all costs to keep storage costs low, as storage was expensive. However, over time, the cost of storage has drastically reduced, and trading off performance for storage cost no longer makes sense. Particularly, object storages like S3 provide a large amount of storage at a very low price, allowing developers to store and retrieve data at a low cost without having to worry about scaling storage. Typically, data engineers try to enforce 4NF on schemas to fully decompose the table and avoid duplicate data; however, in modern systems backed by cheap distributed storage, it is imperative that the application of 4NF is carefully evaluated.

Missing accelerators

Most database systems today provide accelerator objects like indexes, materialized views, multi-dimensional cubes, etc., to accelerate query processing. However, it is common for data systems not to leverage these accelerators correctly to extract the best performance out of the system.

Let us first look at the pitfalls in selecting indexes that need to be created for improving application performance. It is commonly observed that index selection is done at the time of application design and build. However, over the period of the application lifecycle, the query patterns evolve, but index definitions are not kept in sync with the new query patterns. This often leads to index drift, where the index definition has drifted away from the query pattern. To avoid this pitfall, it is important that index definitions are periodically reviewed to ensure they are still relevant for the application query pattern, and new indexes are created as per the query pattern. It is also very important to drop the stale indexes in this review exercise because stale indexes not only consume storage but also consume compute and memory capacity during the data write operations, affecting the write-side performance.

Another aspect of indexes that often leads to performance pitfalls is the choice of the type of index used. Modern databases support multiple types of indexes, like primary key index, composite key index, text index, vector index, etc. It is critical to identify the correct type of index to be used, as multiple indices can be used for the same use case, with each providing a different level of performance. For example, a search pattern like brand = 'brand-name' and category match with semantic similarity can be done in two ways. The first one is by defining a vector index on category to perform the semantic match, and then filtering all the selected records by applying the brand filter, or in a much more efficient way by defining a composite index with the leading key of brand and the secondary vector key of category. The second way uses prefiltering of the vectors by applying the brand criteria, and significantly reduces the vector search space, which leads to improved query performance.

The following is an example of creating a composite index with brand and category and using a hybrid search query that can leverage pre-filtering:

```
1.  CREATE INDEX composite_index
2.  ON default(`brand`, `category` VECTOR, `docid`)
3.  PARTITION BY HASH(meta().id)
4.  WITH { "defer_build»:true, "num_partition": 4,
5.         «dimension»: 16, "description": "IVF,SQ8",
6.         «similarity»: «COSINE», «scan_nprobes»: 50};
7.  SELECT docid FROM default
8.  WHERE `brand`=»XYZ»
9.  ORDER BY APPROX_VECTOR_
    DISTANCE(category, [40, 25, 11, 0, 22, 31, 6, 8, 10, 3, 0,
    1, 30, 91, 88, 18], "COSINE", 50) LIMIT 10
```

Materialized views are another type of query accelerator which are not used often enough to improve query performance in data systems. For example, if the application has standardized reports that aggregate data over a period of time, then it is critical that materialized views are used to avoid recomputing the aggregate over and over again to serve the reports. The use of a materialized view ensures that the data for the aggregation queries is served from the precomputed view, vs. the underlying table of the view. This not only improves query performance drastically but also frees up CPU cycles on the system for performing other tasks.

Let us look at a simple example of a SALES table query that finds the total number and amount of sales of a particular product on a given day. The non-performant way to achieve this is by running the aggregation on the fly every time the query is run, and the performant way is to build a materialized view over the sales table, as shown here:

```
1.  CREATE TABLE sales (
2.      transaction_id      INT,
3.      product_id    INT,
4.      customer_id   INT,
5.      sale_date     DATE,
6.      amount        DECIMAL(10, 2)
7.  );
8.  CREATE MATERIALIZED VIEW sales_summary AS
9.  SELECT
10.     product_id,
11.     sale_date,
12.     SUM(amount) AS daily_sales,
13.     COUNT(*) AS daily_transactions
14. FROM sales
15. GROUP BY product_id, sale_date;
```

The query would look as follows, without the materialized view, where the grouping would happen on the fly:

```
1.  SELECT
2.      product_id,
3.      sale_date,
4.      SUM(amount) AS daily_sales,
5.      COUNT(*) AS daily_transactions
6.  FROM sales
7.  GROUP BY product_id, sale_date;
8.  WHERE sale_date = CURRENT_DATE
```

Once the materialized view is created, the query does not need to change, and the database system will route the aggregation request to the materialized view to fetch the data. As new data gets loaded to the sales table materialized view is refreshed with the new aggregated value so as to keep the materialized view up to date.

Note: **Given that materialized views are similar to physical tables, they need constant refreshing to keep the data in sync with the underlying table.**

The refreshes can be done manually or configured to run automatically on a change or as per schedule. Regular views do not refresh as they always query the underlying table and do not store data as a separate copy.

The examples aforementioned demonstrate how not leveraging accelerators available in database systems can seriously hamper query performance and also increase resource consumption.

Missing data relationships

Establishing data relationships in a data model is not only key for maintaining data integrity, but it is also key for performance optimizations. Access logic can leverage data relationships to optimize the access paths and improve performance. For example, databases commonly leverage a primary key relationship defined by the application to optimize distinct processing in queries. Distinct is an expensive operation to perform as it needs to either sort the final result set or use a hashing algorithm to find the distinct values in the final result before returning the data to the application. However, when the column that has the distinct clause is a primary key, it is implied that the field will not have duplicates as well, and the primary index can be used to fetch the data in sorted order.

Data relationships are also used to perform join optimizations by leveraging cardinality estimates of the relationship. Database optimizers can also eliminate certain join conditions, knowing the relationship between the primary key and the foreign key. For example, when a foreign key is joined to a primary key, the database optimizer is aware that the primary key will only yield one record for every unique value.

Data pipelines can perform appropriate data enrichment, as well as know the data relationships. These enrichments can avoid lookups or joins later in the pipeline or at query time. This preprocessing enrichment is done when preparing the data; leveraging the data relationship can improve both pipeline and data analysis performance.

Most analytical systems do not enforce data relationships like primary key and foreign key, but defining them, even when not forced, can help accelerate queries in these analytics systems.

Consider an example with two tables T1 (c11,c12,c13) and T2 (c21,c22,c23) and a primary key foreign key relationship defined between T1(c11) as PK and T2(c21) as FK. Let us look at a sample query:

```
1.  SELECT T1.c11, T2.c21
2.  from T1 join T2
3.  ON T1.c11 = T2.c21
4.  WHERE T1.c11 = 1000 and T2.c21 = 1000
```

In the aforementioned query, given the T1(c11) as PK and T2(c21) as FK relationship, the **T2.c21 = 1000** is a redundant predicate already covered by **T1.c11 = 1000**. This predicate can be eliminated and can improve query processing time.

Incorrect query patterns

Every data system has its optimized data access paths. It is important to be aware of these optimized data access paths and leverage them. For example, a NoSQL system has an optimized access path for a key-value fetch from the database. The fastest and most efficient method to access data from these systems is a key-value fetch leveraging a secondary index. But most of these NoSQL systems also offer a SQL or SQL-like query language that can be used too. However, SQL is not the most efficient access mechanism for these systems. When a general data access is needed, it is best not to fall into the pitfall of using SQL to access data from NoSQL systems, but instead, leverage the key-value access API.

Similarly, purpose-built systems like *Pinecone* or *Milvus* for vector search are good to perform semantic search; however, leveraging them to perform hybrid search by leveraging secondary indexes is an incorrect query pattern. These systems can also not perform native aggregation or join operations. These limitations can be circumvented by driving some of the aggregation and join logic to the application code, but that would lead to performance pitfalls.

Resource misallocations

Data engineering systems perform computationally heavy operations and need memory, CPU, and storage to perform their tasks. Depending on the nature of the data processing system, the amount of memory, CPU, and storage required can vary a lot. For example, certain systems may need more memory than others, while another type of system may need more CPU. Balancing the memory, CPU, and storage in the right ratio becomes critical for the optimal performance of the system.

Let us now look at a few different systems whose resource requirements vary significantly. A data pipeline that compresses or encodes data has a very high CPU requirement. Both compression and encoding are CPU-intensive operations. The memory requirements of compression and encoding are intermediate and are almost independent of storage performance. Hence, for a pipeline that compresses or encodes data, the resource allocation needs to be high CPU, medium memory, and medium to low storage throughput. Providing a fast storage system or a high amount of memory for this data pipeline would lead to the wastage of those resources.

Secondly, let us look at a database system's resource requirements and misallocations that can happen with those systems. A database system like Redis, which gets used primarily as a cache, has very high memory requirements while having medium CPU and no storage performance requirements. However, a NoSQL database like Couchbase has both high memory and storage performance requirements as it provides a durable database backed by a cache. However, if the same Couchbase database has a very high query throughput requirement on a smaller dataset, it needs a high amount of CPU as well. Finally, a relational database that is highly encrypted has a very high memory, CPU, and storage performance requirement. As you can see, even though all of these data systems fall under databases, their resource requirements are unique. Any misallocation of resources to these database systems severely degrades their performance. For example, consider a NoSQL database like Couchbase, which has not been provided enough memory, as it is considered a durable storage database. Every time a request for data is sent to the database, it needs to fetch the data from disk, which severely impacts the latency of the request. Instead, if the database is provided with enough memory and has a high resident ratio, then a good percentage of data would be cached in memory from disk and served without a scan of the secondary storage, improving the latency of the query requests.

Finally, let us look at distributed data processing systems like *Hadoop*, where the latency of serving the request is not of very high importance, but the throughput of processing a large amount of data stored on disk is critical. In such systems, allocating a lot of memory while not focusing on enough distributed storage IO throughput can lead to resource misallocation. Even if the Hadoop cluster nodes have enough CPU and memory, without enough IO bandwidth, the workers would stall on IO waits.

Data skew

Data skew is an uneven distribution of data across the nodes of a distributed system. In any distributed system, the goal is to evenly distribute the processing over all nodes to ensure almost similar processing times for the request on each of the nodes. However, data skew causes some nodes that have more data to take longer to finish when compared to other nodes in the cluster. As a result, the node with more data will be executing the request while others are idle, thus causing wastage of computing resources. This also causes out-of-resource errors on the nodes that have a high data skew because the nodes in the distributed system were sized for an even skew.

Data skew can also play havoc with database query optimizers and processing. Consider, for example, a distributed join operation. If the node that receives a large amount of data gets overwhelmed, it can overwhelm the system. This problem can be mitigated by accurate stats where the system knows the skewed partition, but even in that case, the larger partition will slow down the overall query, as it takes more time to process. For example, a group-by query would need to process the scattered subgroups by operation on every partition before doing the gather operation. The partition with the data skew would take longer to finish its grouping operation over others. The gather operator will need to wait even though all other partitions have completed, and newer queries cannot be scheduled on the other nodes, which have completed processing as well. As a result, there is wastage of computing resources on the nodes that have completed processing.

Figure 21.3 shows the problem of data skew. In this figure, Node 0 and Node 1 have the same amount of data, which is 1M records each. However, Node 3 has 5 times the data of 5M records, forming the data skew. When the query is executed on this distributed system, it completes in 10 seconds on Node 0 and Node 1 but takes 50 seconds to complete on Node 3. For the 40 seconds after completion of the query on Node 0 and Node 1, the compute is wasted on these nodes as the next query has to wait for scheduling until Node 3 completes. This problem can be solved by selecting the correct data partitioning key, which leads to even distribution of 2.33M records to each node and ensuring their individual scatter processing time is almost the same.

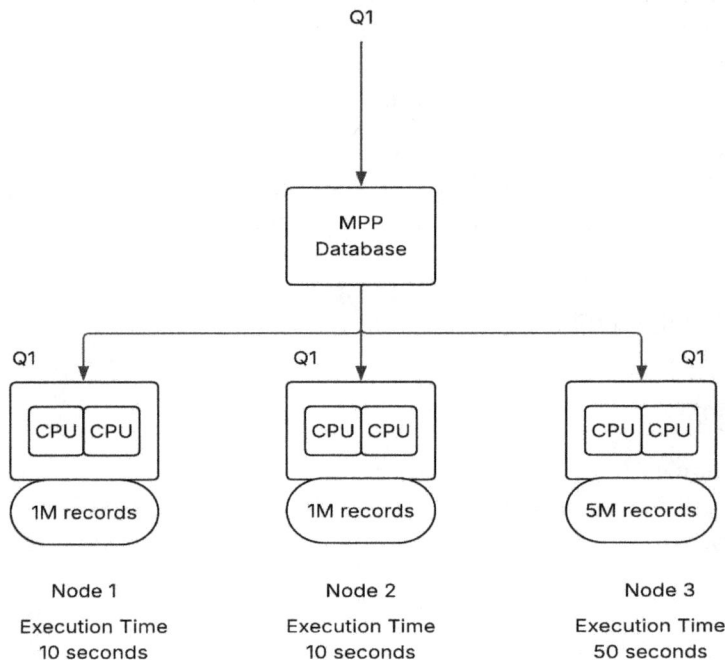

Figure 21.3: Data skew

Real-world examples

In this section, let us consider the example of building a product catalog for an e-commerce application and the common performance pitfalls data engineers encounter while building such a system. This example shows how properties of the system need to be carefully evaluated to decide on the architecture and technology to use to avoid performance pitfalls.

Any technology backing the product catalog needs to have the following properties for the application to be successful.

Low latency access

Low latency access to the product catalog is needed because when a customer browses it for shopping, the products need to be served with very little latency to provide a great shopping experience. Given that the catalog is persisted and updated mostly on an hourly or daily basis, it is tempting for developers to just use a relational database for the catalog to start with when the application is built. However, as soon as the catalog grows, the performance pitfalls of selecting a relational database for this use case start to show up. To achieve the sub-10 millisecond latency needed for most product catalogs, the relational databases need to be front-ended by a caching system like *Redis*, and data engineers end up building plumbing to keep the cache and the relational database in sync.

The following figure shows usage with an RDBMS and a cache over the RDBMS:

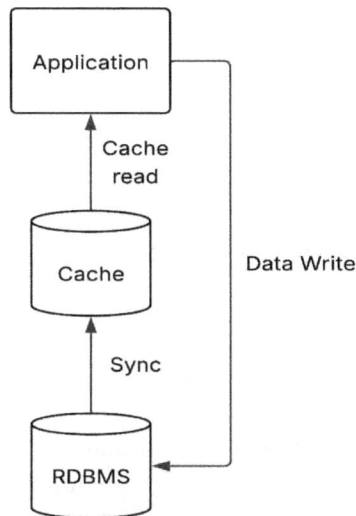

Figure 21.4: RDBMS with an external cache

Performance and operational pitfalls of integrating a cache with an RDBMS can be avoided by selecting horizontally scalable NoSQL databases like *Couchbase*, which have an integrated cache built into them. This not only provides fast access from cache while being backed by a durable storage, but also avoids the challenge of keeping cache in sync with the backend storage.

The following figure is an architecture showing a NoSQL DB with an integrated cache without the challenges of syncing data:

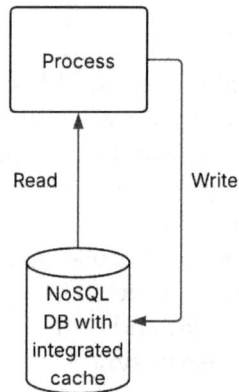

Figure 21.5: *NoSQL database with integrated cache*

Bulk writes

Catalogs can be refreshed with new products, and having the ability to bulk load new products enables the application team to be agile. Most modern database systems provide the ability to ingest data in multiple ways, one record at a time, a batch of records, or a large bulk ingest with thousands or millions of records. Both RDBMS and NoSQL databases provide the capability to perform bulk writes to the database.

The common performance pitfall in the bulk write use case is using logged data loads vs non-logged data load operations. Logged load operations are ones where database recovery log records are periodically flushed to disk to support transaction recovery. Logged load operations are significantly slower compared to non-logged load operations. However, the non-logged loads are non-recoverable, and any failure during the load operation requires a fresh full load of the data and cannot be restarted. Non-logged load operations are not recoverable as they do not write database log records as part of the transaction and ensure consistency of the table by allowing only one transaction to modify it and ensuring a checkpoint on the table before the non-logged load operation starts. Data engineers typically use logged load operations to handle the 1% of failure conditions, but that is not the most optimal approach. The common scenario is not a failed load but instead a successful load operation, and the load needs to be optimized for that scenario by using a non-logged load operation.

Most ETL tools in the market, like *DataStage* and *Informatica*, also provide a bulk load capability, which can be leveraged. However, with the advent of Apache Spark, many of the ETL pipelines are being migrated from traditional tools like DataStage and Informatica to Apache Spark-based jobs. One of the common pitfalls that happens during such migration is moving from a bulk load mechanism in the legacy ETL tool to a per-record or batch load in the Apache Spark job. This pitfall is so subtle that it is not usually identified until late into the testing cycle, where performance tests show degradation on large data load operations. There is no easy solution to this problem, given that Apache Spark does not do native integration with database loading and bulk loading tools. Until that happens, data engineers need to leverage staging-based approaches with direct use of database native bulk loading tools to get back to the same level of performance as compared to legacy tools using bulk load.

Flexible data model

Every product has its own set of properties that need to be stored and served on a search match. It is common for developers to use relational NULL semantics to try to model a flexible schema by storing NULL values for every column that does not apply to a particular product type. However, this soon turns into a nightmare due to very wide tables, as the total number of columns is the union of columns of all product types. Also, adding any new column to the table is challenging because an **ALTER TABLE** operation on a very large table needs to be executed under maintenance windows. This not only risks putting the table in rollback pending state on any failure, but also slows down how frequently the catalog can be updated. The use of NULL values to represent the breadth of products using the same schema leads to performance problems as every query needs to account for NULL checks before sending back the product detail to the application, lest the application need to handle NULL values.

The following is a relational table representation showing the product catalog:

Product ID	Name	Unit cost	MFG date	Expiry date	Ingredients	Allergy warning
1	Toy Car	1000	02-04-2025	NULL	NULL	NULL
2	Peanut Butter	200	04-05-2025	04-11-2025	Peanut, Oil, water	Can trigger a nut allergy
3	Banana	100	NULL	NULL	NULL	Can trigger an allergy

Table 21.1: Product catalog

Instead of storing these varying properties of products in a fixed schema data model, using a flexible data model like JSON overcomes all the above-mentioned pitfalls. With every JSON document storing only the field relevant to a particular product in the catalog, expensive NULL checks are not required on the query or application side. The application can directly render the JSON to the UI layer and show only the relevant properties for a product entry. There are no expensive **ALTER TABLE** statements required to add new product properties due to new catalog entries. The JSON for the new product can just contain the field relevant to it. The same product table is shown as JSON documents:

```
1. [
2.     {
3.         "Product ID": 1,
```

```
4.            "Name": "Toy car",
5.            "Unit Cost": 1000,
6.            "MFG Date": "02-04-2025"
7.        },
8.        {
9.            "Product ID": 2,
10.           "Name": "Peanut Butter",
11.           "Unit Cost": 200,
12.           "MFG Date": "04-05-2025",
13.           "Expiry Date": "04-11-2025",
14.           "Ingredients": "Peanut, Oil, water",
15.           "Allergy warning": "Can trigger nut allergy"
16.       },
17.       {
18.           "Product ID": 3,
19.           "Name": "Banana",
20.           "Unit Cost": 10,
21.           "Allergy warning": "Can trigger allergy"
22.       }
23. ]
```

Rich search capability

A rich search capability forms the core of any product catalog search in an e-commerce application. The search needs to be both text-based and semantic to identify the right products for the user. One of the common pitfalls data engineers encounter while identifying the technology for text search is leveraging the search capability within their existing database. While this may seem like a good choice to begin with by avoiding the burden of managing and operating a dedicated text search engine as soon as the catalog search requests scale, the general-purpose database text search engine starts to falter. While it is fine to use the text search capability within general-purpose databases for auxiliary search use cases, for something as core to the application as product catalog search, it is important to leverage purpose-built, high-performance text search engines like *Elastic* or *Apache Solr*.

On the other hand, semantic search is a much newer technology, and there is no clear technology leader in this space at this time. The majority of the semantic search engines are powered by technology from FAISS or similar libraries. Also, databases like *Couchbase* and *Elastic* have competitive semantic search technologies, which may blur the performance advantage provided by dedicated vector stores like *Pinecone* or *Milvus*. Overall, data engineers are better off avoiding the pitfall of leveraging text search from general-purpose databases, but can avoid creating dedicated vector stores.

Conclusion

In this chapter, we covered the common performance pitfalls data engineers encounter while designing data systems and data pipelines. We learnt about how data modelling can go wrong and lead to performance issues at a later stage. The chapter covered the resource allocation pitfalls from the CPU, memory, and storage perspectives for different types of data systems. The chapter also covered how incorrect query patterns and accelerator selection can not only lead to bad performance but also unnecessarily drain the system resources. Finally, we look at a real-world example of building a product catalog cache for e-commerce and the design pitfalls that need to be avoided while building such a system.

In the next chapter, we will understand technology and infrastructure selection for data systems in detail. We will learn about selecting data storage systems, processing frameworks, and infrastructure. We will also cover a real-world example of selecting technology and infrastructure for a tiered real-time analytical system.

Questions

1. What is the resource allocation pattern for a customer profile cache?

2. What is the use of materialized view accelerators in databases?

3. Design a data model for an e-commerce product catalog and review any data model design pitfalls that may have been introduced.

4. How do incorrect query patterns lead to query accelerator pitfalls?

Join our Discord space

Join our Discord workspace for latest updates, offers, tech happenings around the world, new releases, and sessions with the authors:

https://discord.bpbonline.com

CHAPTER 22
Technology and Infrastructure Selection

Introduction

This chapter discusses the selection of technology and infrastructure for various data use cases. It provides recommendations on databases, processing frameworks, storage solutions, and other infrastructure selection for common data platform problems. It also explores trade-offs between different technologies, such as cost, performance, scalability, and ease of management. By the end of the chapter, readers will be equipped with the knowledge to make informed decisions that best fit their data engineering needs. Even though data engineers will not be the final decision makers for many of the technology or infrastructure choices, this chapter equips them to influence decisions from database, storage, and infrastructure teams based on a deep understanding of the domain and use case. This chapter goes beyond the data engineering patterns themselves but looks at the infrastructure powering the patterns and how data engineers have a key role in that infrastructure selection.

Structure

The chapter covers the following topics:

- Data storage options
- Processing frameworks

- Infrastructure selection
- Real-world example

Objectives

By the end of this chapter, you will be able to identify the correct storage, processing framework, and infrastructure for your data engineering project. You will understand the methodology for technology evaluation in all three areas. This chapter will also equip you with the knowledge of various parameters to consider while evaluating technology for data engineering projects. Finally, you will be able to meaningfully engage with your infrastructure and software procurement teams to obtain the best technology to solve your given data engineering use case.

Data storage options

Data storage options can be divided primarily into two areas. The underlying physical storage type used and the database or distributed data storage type built on top of the physical storage subsystem. Let us look at the various database options in this section, while we look at the physical storage topic in the infrastructure selection section later in this chapter.

Every data application needs some data storage technology to power it, where the application can store and retrieve its data. The response time requirements, durability guarantees, and data models can vary from application to application, but the need for a data storage system remains paramount. Let us first look at the database technology landscape and the criteria for selection.

Database landscape and selection criteria

Databases started decades ago as simple applications that stored and retrieved data in an efficient data format in files. However, over time, they have evolved into one of the most sophisticated pieces of software on the planet, adding capabilities like durability, availability, scalability, and performance.

The most common form of databases is relational databases that store data in the form of rows and columns and expose this data to the application using a standardized interface, SQL. RDBMS provides ACID capability. Most RDBMSs scaled well vertically and delivered a good balance of read and write performance. Though initially running on proprietary hardware like *DB2* on the Mainframe, more modern RDBMS were capable of running on commodity hardware, reducing database infrastructure cost. Eventually, several open-source RDBMS were also built, like *Ingres, PostgreSQL, MySQL,* and many others, which further popularized this technology. Oracle and Microsoft built proprietary RDBMS software as well, which became widely popular. However, as data grew, only vertically growing RDBMS software became a challenge. The individual compute units could only get so much bigger, putting restrictions on the ability to scale these databases. Some databases, like *Oracle,* solved this problem by building out distributed multi-node databases like *Oracle RAC,* which leveraged complex interconnect technology like *InfiniBand*. This solved the scaling problems to a certain extent, however the cost of scaling still remained exorbitantly high.

Over time, it became clear that as applications became more web and mobile-based, the scale of data dramatically increased. Also, given the growth of consumer-facing applications, the performance and flexibility limitations of RDBMS started to show up, leading to a new set of databases called NoSQL databases becoming popular. RDBMS and NoSQL databases have co-existed for a decade now. Let us look at how to evaluate these two types of database technologies based on the use case.

Relational databases are suitable for applications where the business schema evolves slowly. Some examples of such systems are core banking, patient record management in healthcare, insurance, etc. These industries are highly regulated, and the core systems have a very slow velocity of change. Most of these systems require ACID-compliant databases and do not have elastic scalability requirements. Relational databases are well-positioned to cater to these use cases due to their simplicity of data model as well as efficient query performance.

However, applications like e-commerce catalog, customer profile stores for social media, Customer 360, AI ML feature stores, etc., have the need for a rapidly evolving, flexible schema. New attributes can be added to these applications rapidly, and each record can have different attributes. For example, in a product catalog, different types of products can have varied properties, and new properties can be added to new catalog entries very rapidly.

The following table is an example of how this application would look in relational and NoSQL systems. In a relational system, all attributes that do not apply to a record become NULL, and every time a new product that needs a new attribute needs to be added, the catalog needs an ALTER operation.

Product ID	Name	Unit cost	MFG date	Expiry date	Ingredients	Allergy warning
1	Toy Car	1000	02-04-2025	NULL	NULL	NULL
2	Peanut Butter	200	04-05-2025	04-11-2025	Peanut, Oil, water	Can trigger a nut allergy
3	Banana	100	NULL	NULL	NULL	Can trigger an allergy

Table 22.1: Product catalog relational table

However, in the NoSQL world, the catalog can be stored as a set of JSON documents with varied properties, as shown here:

```
1. [
2.     {
3.         "Product ID": 1,
```

```
4.          "Name": "Toy car",
5.          "Unit Cost": 1000,
6.          "MFG Date": "02-04-2025"
7.      },
8.      {
9.          "Product ID": 2,
10.         "Name": "Peanut Butter",
11.         "Unit Cost": 200,
12.         "MFG Date": "04-05-2025",
13.         "Expiry Date": "04-11-2025",
14.         "Ingredients": "Peanut, Oil, water",
15.         "Allergy warning": "Can trigger nut allergy"
16.     },
17.     {
18.         "Product ID": 3,
19.         "Name": "Banana",
20.         "Unit Cost": 10,
21.         "Allergy warning": "Can trigger allergy"
22.     }
23. ]
```

Apart from RDBMS and NoSQL systems, multiple purpose-built database systems have come up in the past few years to solve niche use cases. Let us look at a few of these purpose-built databases and the selection criteria for picking any of those databases. The following figure shows a world cloud of common database technologies and offerings:

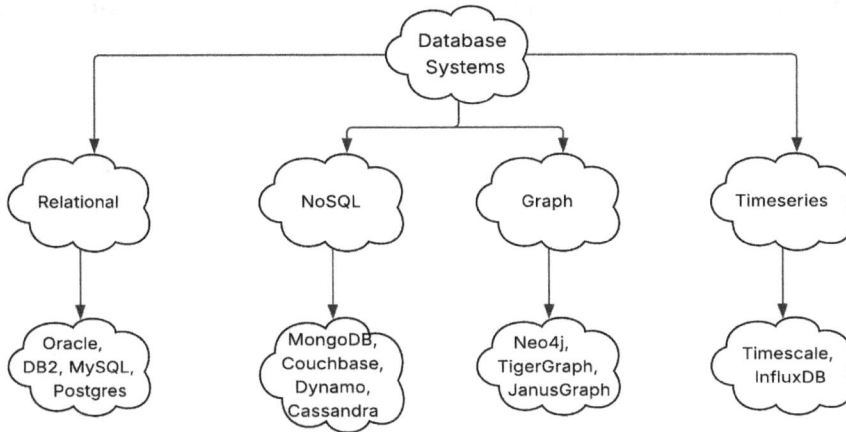

Figure 22.1: Database landscape

Many of the modern applications model the relationship between entities. These relationships could be between people or systems, or a combination of both. Let us consider a couple of examples to demonstrate such relationships. In most social media applications, there are relationships between users of the application. These relationships are typically modelled as a graph where the nodes are the users and the edges are the relationships between the users. Another use case where relationships are modelled is fraud detection. In fraud detection, not only the relationship between people but also the relationship between system entities like IP addresses and location is formed. All of these relationships can be modelled using graphs and easily traversed to identify the relationships after the graph is built. Modelling such relationships in relational databases or NoSQL databases is cumbersome and inefficient. This led to the invention of specific graph databases like *Neo4j, Tiger Graph*, and others. The following figure shows an example of a graph on social media:

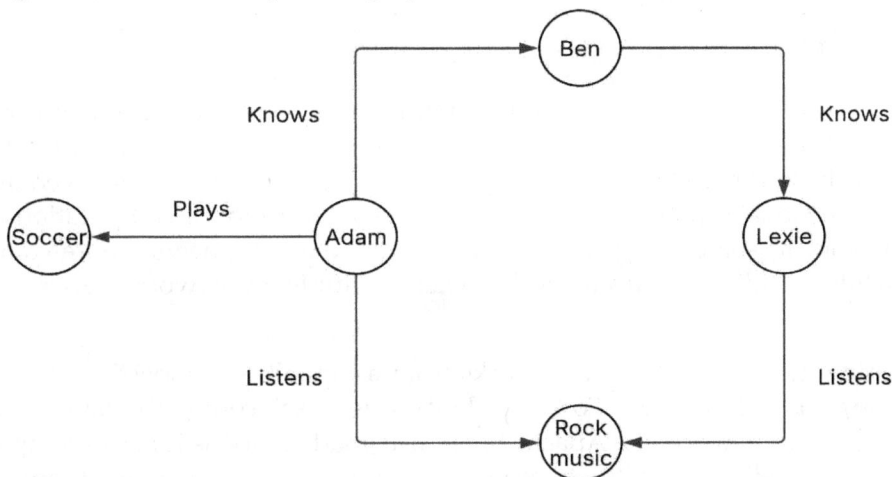

Figure 22.2: Social media graph

Let us look at how to represent this graph in Neo4j in Cypher by creating five nodes and relationships between them as edges:

1. `CREATE (a:Person {name: 'Adam'})`

2. `CREATE (b:Person {name: 'Ben'})`

3. `CREATE (c:Person {name: 'Lexie'})`

4. `CREATE (d:Hobby {name: 'Soccer'})`

5. `CREATE (e:Hobby {name: 'Rock Music'})`

6. `CREATE (a)-[:Knows ]->(b)`

7. `CREATE (b)-[:Knows]->(c)`

8. `CREATE (c)-[:Listens]->(e)`

9. `CREATE (a)-[:Listens]->(e)`

10. `CREATE (c)-[:Plays]->(d)`

The syntax `CREATE (a)-[:Knows ]->(b)` creates a relationship between node a and node b with the relationship defined as **a** knows **b**.

Another common type of data is time series, and with the advent of IoT, this type of data is being generated in large quantities today. An example of time series information is the value of a sensor in a factory continuously emitted over long periods of time, which is monitored to generate various types of alerts. As you can see, timeseries data can have a high ingestion rate as well as a fetch rate. Most general-purpose databases, both relational and NoSQL, can support time series data. However, they are neither efficient at storing time series data nor at serving it. Given the nature of time series data, specialized storage and compression techniques can be applied as the data points are measured at fixed intervals.

Processing frameworks

Data processing frameworks have gone through multiple generations of iterations, starting with SQL processing over relational data to modern frameworks like *Apache Spark*. Two aspects need to be keenly considered while selecting a processing framework for a given use case: the framework's functional capability to solve the given use case and the computational efficiency of the framework to solve the given use case. Often, data engineers ignore computational efficiency while deciding on frameworks when multiple frameworks can solve a given problem.

While exploring data processing frameworks from a capability perspective, it is effective to define the core goals of the use case. For example, if the use case's core goal is data transformation, then a processing framework like Apache Spark is a good choice as it has rich capabilities for transformation, as well as the ability to restart failed transformations from intermediate states. A database or an SQL query engine like *Trino* would be a bad choice of processing framework for only doing transformation, as they lack the restart ability of transformation jobs. However, if the goal of the use case is to perform analytics on data that is stored in S3, both Apache Spark and SQL Engine, like Trino, can be considered from a capability perspective. However, this is where data engineers need to not only consider the functional capability of each platform but also look at the computational efficiency aspect. In this example, both Spark SQL and Trino can be used to query data stored in distributed storage like S3, but Trino is computationally much more efficient in processing SQL statements when compared to Spark SQL. Though Spark is a much more powerful framework for data processing, it was not built from the ground up for SQL processing like *Trino*.

Now, let us look at frameworks for real-time data processing. It is common for data engineers to gravitate towards Apache Kafka while building any real-time system, given the historical domination of Apache Kafka in this space. However, it is important to pause and assess the use case to understand the fit for Apache Kafka or other real-time frameworks. Let us consider a use case of fraud detection in real time, where multiple transactions that occur in a window are considered to identify potential fraud. For a use case like this, the processing framework needs to be able to aggregate data over multiple events to make the fraudulent transaction decision. However, Apache Kafka provides primarily single-message transforms to work on a single transaction event. Even Kafka Streams does not provide the capability to work on a window of data. A lot of custom coding is needed with Kafka to handle multiple transactions together over a time window. Instead, a better fit for this use case would be another real-time data processing framework called Apache Flink. Flink has the capability to perform complex data processing on a stream of data when compared to Kafka. It can perform aggregations and joins across stream messages. It can operate on a sliding window of data at any given time.

Another type of use case that needs a data processing framework is performing batch data processing on a large amount of data. The data processing could be cleansing, standardization, analytical processing, aggregation, etc. Historically, these types of batch jobs were executed using frameworks like *Hadoop MapReduce* or equivalent cloud services. Though extremely reliable and scalable, the Map-Reduce jobs were not very efficient in their processing. The map-reduce paradigm required staging data often to slow storage systems like *HDFS,* and did not provide good restartability options. Often, these types of data processing jobs can be easily migrated to Apache Spark, which can execute these jobs much more efficiently. Though Apache Spark has not yet reached the operational stability of Hadoop MapReduce jobs, Spark does have the advantage of restartability, leveraging **Resilient Distributed Dataset (RDD)**.

The following are the key points to consider while deciding on process frameworks for a data engineering project:

- Latency expectation
- Data volume to be processed
- Complexity of processing
- Throughput expectation

- Cost of processing
- Integration and coexistence with the existing processing stack

Infrastructure selection

In this section, we look at the underlying physical infrastructure selection for various types of systems. Even though data engineers are not directly responsible for infrastructure, they work closely with infrastructure teams to get the correct hardware needed to run their workloads. So, it is important for them to understand the different types of infrastructure and how it can be leveraged for the various data engineering use cases.

Storage landscape and selection criteria

In the storage landscape and selection criteria, let us look at the different types of storage systems, both on the cloud and on-premises.

Object storage

Object storage provides cheap and reliable storage to store and retrieve large amounts of data. Given the standardized API, applications can interact with object storage from different vendors without application change. Though popularized originally on the cloud by AWS S3, object storage is available for on-premises use by almost every popular storage vendor in the market. Object storage originally started as cheap storage for files in the cloud, but has now become the default cloud storage platform for not only applications but also databases, data lakes, and data lake houses. With most database systems becoming storage compute separated, object storage has become the underpinning durable storage layer.

One of the challenges with object storage was the latency of data fetch, but more recently, the latency challenges are being solved by newer object storage offerings like *AWS S3 Express*, which are backed by **non-volatile memory express** (**NVMe**) drives. These provide low millisecond latency and make S3 suitable even for real-time applications now. Object storage has also evolved to provide cheap backup storage with offerings like *AWS S3 Glacier*. This provides a much cheaper storage option for data that is not retrieved often. Object storage performance also leads to greater improvement in hybrid cloud performance, accelerating its adoption.

Block storage

Block storage is used by applications where the performance of S3 is not acceptable for the use case. For example, applications like a NoSQL database require a storage backend that can provide sub-millisecond response times while also having the ability to scale the throughput and size of the storage on the fly. Block storages are built over SSD or HDD using SAN-like software-defined storage architectures.

Block storage is also well-suited for applications that need a storage backend that appears like local storage but has the ability to mount and unmount the storage from different physical servers. This ability allows applications to build high availability for systems leveraging block storage backends. When the physical server that is serving the application workload fails, the control plane for the system can just spawn a new compute instance and attach the block storage to the new instance on the fly. This ensures the storage is highly available. A common example of this type of use of block storage is database backend storage and handling database node failure by attaching the block storage to a different database node, as shown in the following figure:

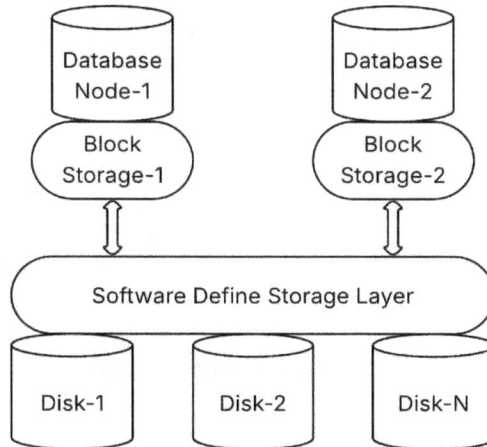

Figure 22.3: Block storage

Local storage

This is the most rudimentary form of storage that is derived from the local disks attached to the node. It is commonly used for the OS, local file system, and temporary storage on the compute node. The reliability of this type of storage is typically improved with RAID-style techniques, but if the compute node fails, the storage is inaccessible. This also provides the fastest type of storage as there is no network latency attached to the storage read/write requests; however, due to their poor availability characteristics, they are not used for critical storage like databases.

One of the common use cases for local storage in data systems, beyond being used as an OS, local file system, and temporary storage, is the use of it as a local data cache. In a storage compute separated system implemented using a durable storage like object storage, we also need a storage cache for fast data access. Every time reading the data from object storage adds significant latency to data fetch and will not meet the latency and throughput requirements of a mission-critical application like an operational database. This problem is solved by attaching a local NVMe disk to every node and having the data lazily cached to these local NVMe disks. Any failure of the node or the disk itself is a transient failure and does not result in any data loss, as the durable storage is still the object store. When the failed disk or node is brought back into the cluster, it just recaches the data from the durable object store. Every data fetch request first goes to the local NVMe disk instead of durable object storage, thereby significantly accelerating the access. The following figure represents this architecture:

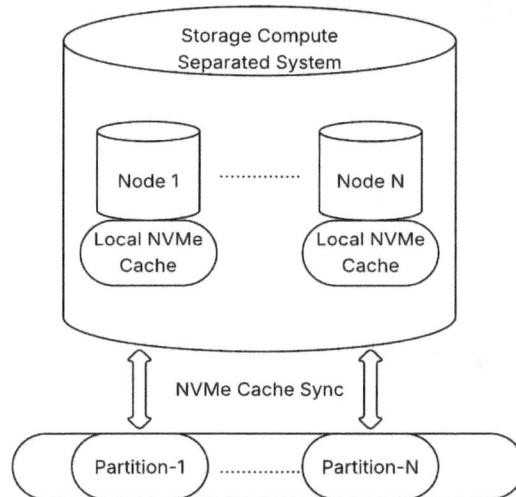

Figure 22.4: Storage compute separation

Real-world example

In this section, let us look at a real-world example of the selection of storage, processing framework, and infrastructure for a use case that consumes data from a transactional system in batches on an hourly basis and loads the data into a real-time analytical system for data analysis. The system supports three months of active data and five years of cold data, which is available for analysis at any given point in time. Most reports access only a subset of the field of given data and also query across a short time period. The data needs to be cleansed, transformed, standardized, and aggregated before loading it into the analytical system.

The solution requires deciding the three key technologies, firstly the framework for data extraction and processing from the source system, secondly the storage system needed for the target analytical system, and thirdly the infrastructure underpinning both these processing and storage sub-systems. Let us first look at the framework for data extraction and processing.

Multiple processing frameworks can be candidates for data extraction from a transactional database, starting from real-time extraction using Kafka connectors to batch-based extraction using JDBC in Apache Spark or Hadoop MapReduce jobs. Similarly, once data is extracted, the data can be cleansed, transformed, standardized, and aggregated in both Kafka and Apache Spark or Hadoop MapReduce jobs. As you can see, there are three options for both extraction and transformation for this given use case. However, it is important to examine the requirements in more detail and identify the most effective technology. As the requirement clearly states, the extraction and transformation of data in batches is acceptable; it is clear that there is no real-time data extraction and transformation needed. This allows us to eliminate Apache Kafka-based solutions, as building a real-time system adds significantly more complexity when compared to batch-based systems. Now, given the remaining two batch-based solutions of Apache Spark and Hadoop MapReduce jobs, let us look at how to select the best-fit processing framework for this use case.

Both Apache Spark and Hadoop MapReduce jobs can functionally solve the given use case of batch extraction and transformation. However, given the requirement that the batch can be extracted on an hourly basis, transformed, and loaded into the analytical system, the amount of data processed in each batch will not be very large. Also, the transformation has a requirement of cleansing, standardization, and aggregation involved, so it would be a complex transformation job. Considering both the smaller data size and complexity of the transformation job, Apache Spark is a better choice for this use case. Apache Spark jobs are much simpler to write when compared to Hadoop MapReduce, and the complexity of the transformation makes this case even stronger. The data size processed in every batch is also not very big and can be easily handled via a Spark job, and does not warrant the need for the complexity of a MapReduce job. Considering all these factors above, Apache Spark with JDBC will be the best data extraction and transformation framework for this given use case.

The following figure is a simplified selection flow chart:

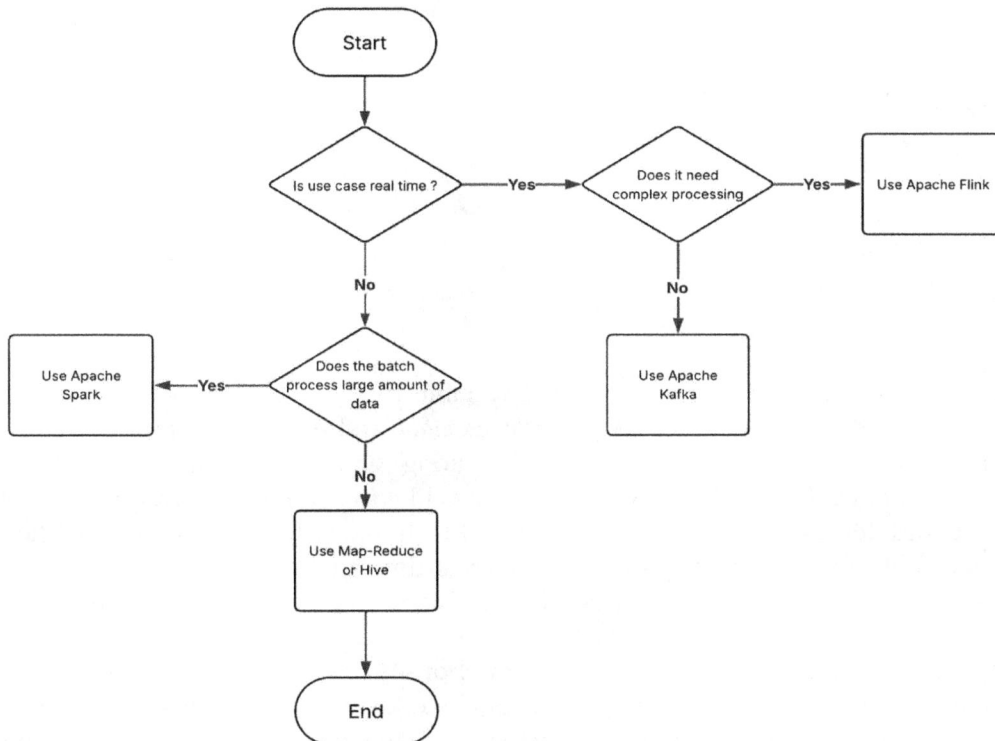

Figure 22.5: Framework selection flow chart

Next, let us look at the system to select for the analytics component. The use case clearly describes that the data is for real-time analytics, and only a subset of columns will be selected at any given time. Also, the data is being queried across a short period of time compared to the overall data stored in the system. A columnar database would be a great fit for the use case by reducing the I/O ask on the system by scanning only the fields that are selected in the query. The system can also leverage data partitioning as the query pattern only goes across a small range of dates. For example, the user may query the data across only three days while the system stores data for five years. Hence, partitioning the table across the data field will allow the system to include only those three days of data for processing and ignore the rest. Also, given that the system is a real-time analytics system, typically, the QPS of the system will be high. This is not explicitly called out in the requirement, but it is a common trait of real-time analytics systems. Now that we have analysed the use case and defined the critical assessment parameters, let us look at possible technology options.

The following syntax shows how the data can be partitioned by date to allow only the selection of the appropriate partitions at query time. The partition by clause defines how the data is stored in different partitions on disk, and the order by clause defines the sorting within the partition.

```
1.  CREATE TABLE sales_daily
2.  (
3.      order_id      UInt32,
4.      product_name    String,
5.      order_date    Date
6.  )
7.  ENGINE = MergeTree
8.  PARTITION BY order_date
9.  ORDER BY order_id;
```

There are a multitude of software systems available to solve analytical use cases, starting from traditional data warehouses like *Oracle Exadata* and *Teradata* to modern cloud data warehouses like *Snowflake* and *AWS Redshift*, along with open-source technologies like *ClickHouse* and *Pinot*. Data lakehouse query engines like *Databricks, Athena*, and *Trino* are also possible candidates. Let us look at the selection of technology for this use case by the rule of elimination. One of the critical requirements of a real-time analytics system is the capability to index data for fast query response times. The need for an index eliminates Lakehouse query engine technologies, as currently, they do not have the capability to index data at a record level. We can also eliminate traditional data warehouses from the short list because they are more suited to run complex BI queries, but struggle to keep up with thousands of short, real-time analytical queries. Considering these factors, we can narrow down to real-time analytical engines like ClickHouse to solve this use case. Next, let us look at the infrastructure selection for this system. The following figure is a word cloud that gives an overview of the technologies and offerings discussed:

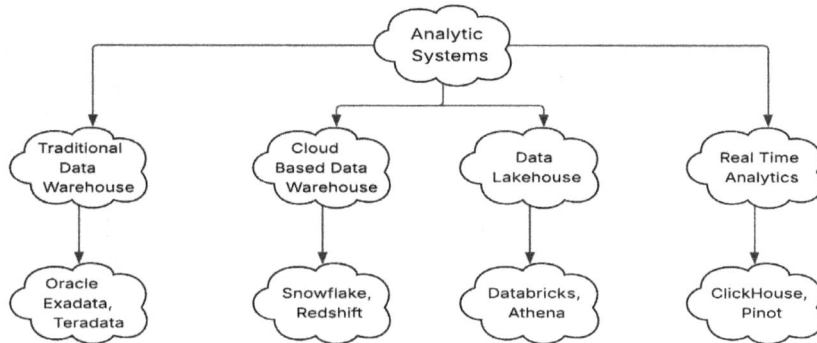

Figure 22.6: *Analytics landscape*

The infrastructure for running the data processing framework and the analytics systems is different. The data processing framework reads the data from a remote transactional system and then performs various types of data transformations on it. Reading data from remote systems requires a high-bandwidth network attached to the data processing nodes, along with enough memory and CPU being allocated to perform the data transformations. These nodes do not need a large amount of durable storage attached to them. The real-time analytics system, however, needs compute nodes that not only have enough memory and CPU to run the real-time queries but also have a local SSD attached to them. If you carefully look at the requirements, it states that three months of data is under active querying and 5 years is the data retention. This allows us to attach fast NVMe-based SSD systems to the analytics nodes enough to store three months of data and significantly accelerate the queries while still keeping the cost of the system low by storing five years' worth of data in cheap object storage. Since we picked a storage compute-separated system like ClickHouse, this storage disaggregation is possible. The following architecture figure shows a storage compute-separate system:

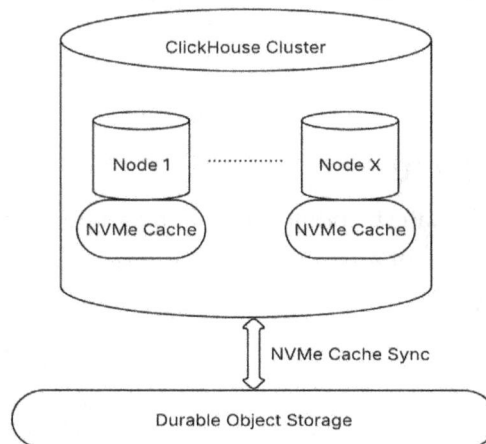

Figure 22.7: *Storage compute separation with local cache*

Conclusion

In this chapter, we covered topics around the selection of data storage, processing frameworks, and infrastructure for various use cases. We learnt about how to decide the database to use based on the application type and the use of special-purpose databases. In the processing framework section, we understand the various data processing frameworks that exist and the methodology to select the framework for a given problem. Finally, we looked at the physical infrastructure selection, which would help the reader engage more meaningfully with their infrastructure team that finally decides the hardware that powers the application. In the end, we learn how to select storage, processing framework, and infrastructure for a real-world use case.

In the next chapter, we refresh the topics previously learnt in this book and learn how to apply the learning further. We will review a quick reference guide for data engineering patterns and also learn about future reading activities for the reader.

Questions

1. What type of storage is suitable to be coupled with a data processing framework like Apache Spark?

2. Why are NoSQL databases preferred over RDBMS systems for mobile application back ends?

3. What trade-offs need to be considered while selecting NVMe storage for a database back-end?

4. When would it be better to use a distributed SQL engine like Trino to process data over Apache Spark SQL?

Join our Discord space

Join our Discord workspace for latest updates, offers, tech happenings around the world, new releases, and sessions with the authors:

https://discord.bpbonline.com

CHAPTER 23
Recap and Next Steps

Introduction

This chapter provides a recap of the data engineering patterns covered in this book. It highlights the most important patterns readers should focus on and build mastery over. It acts as a quick reference guide to readers. This book provides multiple exercises readers can do to improve their understanding of data patterns and build hands-on skills in leveraging data patterns. It provides readers with tricks and tips to stay updated on new data engineering techniques and patterns.

Structure

The chapter covers the following topics:

- Knowledge reinforcement
- Quick reference guide
- Applying learnings from this book
- Continuously upskilling
- Further readings

Objectives

By the end of this chapter, you will have refreshed most of the key data engineering patterns covered in this book. You will be aware of the resources to leverage for keeping yourself updated on data engineering. You would have learnt how to leverage the knowledge gained from this book and apply the data engineering patterns to solve complex data engineering challenges. You will have a quick reference guide to data engineering patterns to refer to while solving problems in data engineering.

Knowledge reinforcement

This section reinforces the learnings from this book by helping users recall all the patterns they have learnt in this book and a quick summary of each category of patterns.

Let us first look at the overall categorization of data engineering patterns:

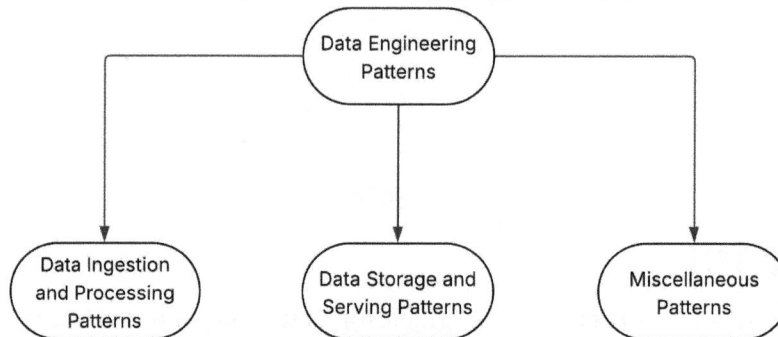

Figure 23.1: Data engineering pattern categories

Data ingestion and processing patterns help data engineers prepare the data that needs to be used to solve a data engineering use case. They are the first patterns to be used in any data engineering project, commonly as getting the data ready is the first step. Depending on the velocity of the data, the acceptable latency, the volume of data, and the processing needed, the data ingestion and processing patterns can be divided into five categories as shown in the following figure:

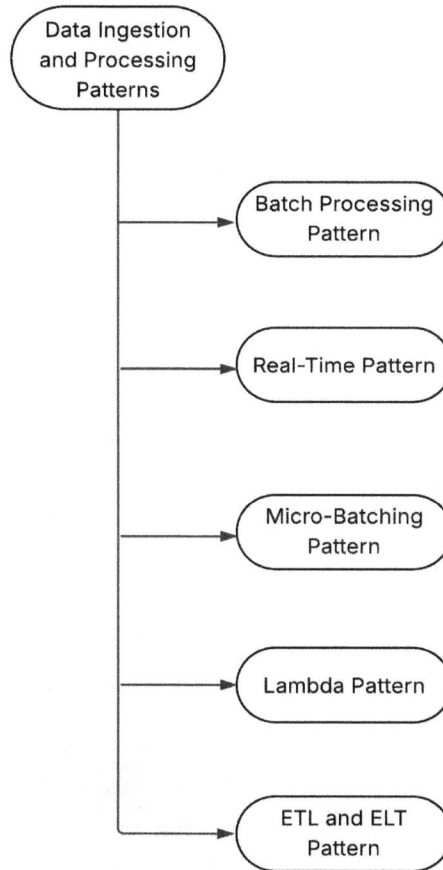

Figure 23.2: Data ingestion and processing patterns

Once the data has been processed and ingested, it needs to be stored for downstream systems to leverage. The data stored also needs to be served to applications with the appropriate latency and throughput. Data storage and serving patterns can be categorized into the categories, as shown in the following figure:

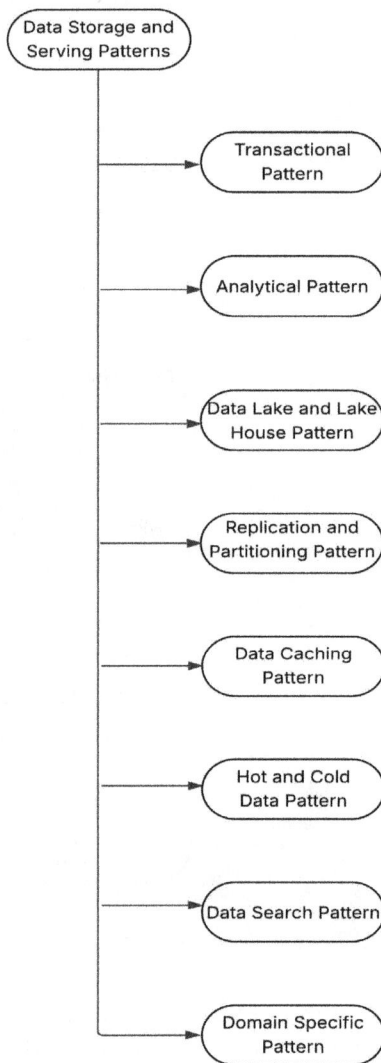

Figure 23.3: Data storage and serving patterns

Apart from these data ingestion, processing, storage, and serving patterns, there are a few patterns that are common to all types of data engineering systems. They cover fundamental aspects like security, observability, and orchestration, as shown in the following figure:

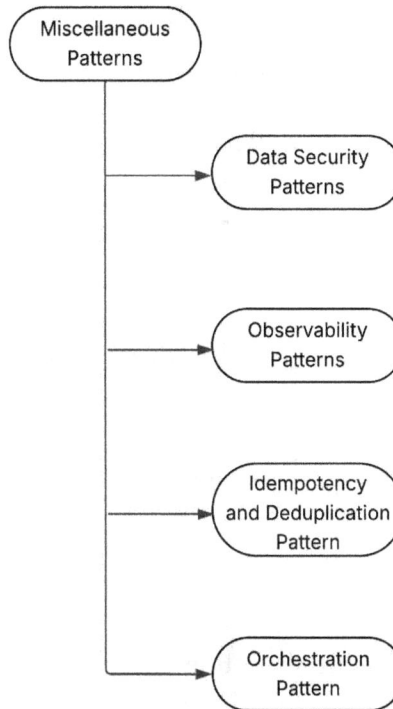

Figure 23.4: *Miscellaneous patterns*

Most complex data engineering projects would need some data engineering patterns to be leveraged from each of these categories. Seasoned data engineers are able to select the appropriate pattern combinations to use for any given business use case. Readers can leverage the next sections on how to apply learnings from this book to identify patterns to use for solving their data engineering problems.

Quick reference guide

This section provides a quick reference guide that readers can refer to when solving data engineering problems. It helps them quickly identify a subset of commonly used patterns they could potentially use and the technologies that can be explored to implement the pattern.

The batch pattern is listed in the following table:

Use case	<ul><li>Periodic data processing</li><li>Hourly, daily, monthly data loads</li><li>Process large amounts of data</li></ul>

Technologies	• Apache Spark • Hadoop MapReduce • Object storage • HDFS • Schedulers

Table 23.1: Batch pattern technologies and use cases

The real-time pattern is listed in the following table:

Use case	• Process data as it is created • Milliseconds to seconds latency • Commonly used with CDC
Technologies	• Apache Kafka • Apache Flink • Spark Structured Streaming

Table 23.2: Real-time pattern technologies and use cases

The micro-batching pattern is listed in the following table:

Use case	• Require low latency but not in milliseconds • Reduce the cost of the system compared to real-time pattern • Reducing the latency of a batch system
Technologies	• Apache Spark • Object storage • Schedulers

Table 23.3: Micro-batching pattern technologies and use cases

The Lambda pattern is listed in the following table:

Use case	• Require both batch and real-time processing • Need to combine historical data to current data • Complex to implement, choose carefully
Technologies	• Apache Spark • Apache Kafka • Apache Flink • Debezium • Object storage • Schedulers

Table 23.4: Lambda pattern technologies and use cases

The ETL and ELT pattern is listed in the following table:

Use case	• Data needs to be modified before analysis • Data needs to be pulled from various sources • Source and target systems are different
Technologies	• Apache Spark • Hadoop MapReduce • Object storage • HDFS • Schedulers

Table 23.5: ELT and ETL pattern technologies and use cases

The transactional data storage pattern is listed in the following table:

Use case	• High throughout and low latency requirements • ACID properties • Backend for mission-critical application
Technologies	• MySQL, Postgres • DB2, Oracle • MongoDB, Couchbase

Table 23.6: Transactional data storage pattern technologies and use cases

The analytical data storage pattern and data warehouse are listed in the following table:

Use case	• Complex queries over a large amount of data • Strict SLA • Historical data analysis • Querying a subset of fields for analysis
Technologies	• Snowflake, AWS Redshift • Databricks • Oracle Exadata

Table 23.7: Analytical data storage pattern technologies and use cases

The data lake, data lakehouse, and medallion pattern are listed in the following table:

Use case	• Ad-hoc data analysis • Data preparation • Historical data analysis • Long-term data storage at low cost

Technologies	• Object Storage, HDFS • Databricks • AWS Athena • Apache Spark SQL

Table 23.8: Data lake, lakehouse, and medallion pattern technologies and use cases

The data replication and partitioning pattern is listed in the following table:

Use case	• High availability • Tolerate hardware failure • Scalability
Technologies	• Distributed databases • Distributed file systems

Table 23.9: Data replication and partitioning pattern technologies and use cases

The data caching pattern is listed in the following table:

Use case	• Very low latency access in low milliseconds • Very high throughput, millions of QPS • Frequent access to the same data • Lack of need for durability
Technologies	• Redis • Couchbase

Table 23.10: Data caching pattern technologies and use cases

Applying learnings from this book

The best way to apply learning from this book is by designing data engineering systems and pipelines, leveraging the patterns that were covered previously in the book. Readers must practice identifying the applicable patterns by translating the business problems and use cases given to them into technical requirements, and then applying data engineering patterns to solve the identified technical requirements.

This chapter demonstrates with two examples the translation of business requirements into technical requirements and then identifies the data engineering patterns applicable for solving them.

The payment fraud detection is listed in the following table:

Business requirement	• Identify fraudulent transactions in flight to prevent fraud
Technical requirement	• Real-time data ingestion from transactional source system • Transform and enrich the data as it flows into the target system • Apply a machine learning model by fetching the features in real-time
Data engineering pattern	• Real-time data processing • Caching
Technology	• Apache Flink • Couchbase/Redis

Table 23.11: Payment fraud detection

The end-of-month business reporting is listed in the following table:

Business requirement	• Generate a report on all business metrics at the end of the month for compliance reporting
Technical requirement	• Batch processing and ingestion of data from various systems into a single source of truth • Enrich the data to provide all necessary business metrics • Load the data into a data warehouse or data lakehouse for reporting
Data engineering pattern	• Batch processing • Data warehouse • Data lakehouse
Technology	• Apache Spark • Snowflake • Databricks • ClickHouse

Table 23.12: Month-end business reporting

Continuously upskilling

Data engineering is a fast-evolving domain with continuous upskilling critical for engineers to stay current. Data engineering patterns evolve slowly, but technologies that support these patterns can transform rapidly. For example, real-time processing patterns have been around for a long time now, but every year we see new emerging tools and frameworks coming up that fill gaps in existing technologies. Though Apache Kafka has been a dominant technology for solving real-time use cases, its limitations in performing complex transformations led to the invention of Apache Flink. Similarly, performance limitations on Apache Kafka led to new niche offerings like *Redpanda* coming into the market with the promise of 5x lower latency than Kafka.

Data engineers can continuously upskill by following these guidelines:

- Stay current with new emerging technologies by attending conferences
- Read data engineering books to develop an in-depth understanding of new concepts
- Apply the learning by building hobby data engineering projects
- Leverage data engineering patterns to solve business problems
- Attend data engineering meetups to present and review their work

Further reading

This section covers books that users could further read to enhance their understanding of the technologies covered in data engineering patterns. Some patterns are used more often than others, and it is recommended for users to be familiar with the technologies used in those commonly occurring patterns.

Batch processing, extract, transform, load, and micro-batching patterns are some of the most commonly used data engineering patterns in the industry. In recent times, Apache Spark has become a popular technology backing all of these data patterns. Developing a deep understanding of Apache Spark helps readers better implement these patterns to solve data engineering problems. Also, readers would have understood that real-time data processing is a critical component of various data engineering systems, including the ones built using the Lambda architecture.

Data lakes and data lakehouses are enabling analysis of large amounts of data at a fraction of the cost compared to previous-generation data warehouses. Readers can gain further knowledge about implementing data lakes and data lakehouses by reading about Hadoop, object storage, and Databricks. Refer to the following:

- *Big Data and Hadoop, 2nd Edition* by Mayank Bhushan

  https://in.bpbonline.com/products/big-data-and-hadoop-2nd-edition
- *Databricks Lakehouse Platform Cookbook* by Dr. Alan L. Dennis

  https://in.bpbonline.com/products/databricks-lakehouse-platform-cookbook

Readers can gain further understanding of data caching and low-latency serving by gaining knowledge in one of the caching systems, like *Redis* or *Couchbase*. Schema-less document databases combined with caching are becoming de facto database architectures for many use cases like customer profile stores and E-commerce product catalogs. Refer to the following:

- *MongoDB for Jobseekers* by Justin Jenkins

  https://in.bpbonline.com/products/mongodb-for-jobseekers
- *Redis® Deep Dive* by Suyog Dilip Kale, Chinmay Kulkarni

  https://in.bpbonline.com/products/redis-deep-dive

Conclusion

We revisited the chapters covered in this book, and we learnt how to apply the learnings from the book. We also covered a quick reference guide that can be used by readers to quickly identify the data engineering pattern to use for a given use case. We also explored how data engineers can keep upskilling themselves, and tips and techniques that can be used for upskilling in data engineering patterns.

References

1. *Real-Time Streaming with Apache Kafka, Spark, and Storm* by Brindha Priyadarshini Jeyaraman

   https://in.bpbonline.com/products/real-time-streaming-with-apache-kafka-spark-and-storm?_pos=1&_sid=3b984bd73&_ss=r

2. *Practical Machine Learning with Spark* by Gourav Gupta, Dr. Manish Gupta, Dr. Inder Singh Gupta

   https://in.bpbonline.com/products/practical-machine-learning-with-spark?srsltid=AfmBOoqEZwf2S0hfqw1SgX-zItKdvvrMTBV_PknbeLstUIjSUsHU1Jwp

3. *Cloud Computing for Everyone* by Rohit Agarwal, Dilip K. Prasad

   https://in.bpbonline.com/collections/big-data-databases/products/cloud-computing-for-everyone

Join our Discord space

Join our Discord workspace for latest updates, offers, tech happenings around the world, new releases, and sessions with the authors:

https://discord.bpbonline.com

Index

C

D

Join our Discord space

Join our Discord workspace for latest updates, offers, tech happenings around the world, new releases, and sessions with the authors:

https://discord.bpbonline.com

www.ingramcontent.com/pod-product-compliance
Lightning Source LLC
Chambersburg PA
CBHW061800210326

41599CB00034B/6825